THE CAMBRIDGE COMPANION TO
HERMENEUTICS

Hermeneutics, the study of interpretation, is an essential and valuable branch of philosophy. Hermeneutics is also a central component of the methodology of the social sciences and the humanities, for example historiography, anthropology, art history, and literary criticism. In a sequence of accessible chapters, contributors across the human sciences explain the leading concepts and ideas of hermeneutics, the historical development of the field, the importance of hermeneutics in philosophy today, and the ways in which it can address contemporary concerns including intercultural relations, relations between subcultures within a single society, and relations across race and gender. Clearly structured and written in non-technical language, this Companion will be an important contribution to a growing field of study.

MICHAEL N. FORSTER is Professor of Philosophy at Bonn University. He has published numerous books including *Herder: Philosophical Writings* (Cambridge, 2002), *After Herder* (2010), *German Philosophy of Language: From Schlegel to Hegel and Beyond* (2011), and *Herder's Philosophy* (2018).

KRISTIN GJESDAL is Professor of Philosophy at Temple University. Her recent books include *Herder's Hermeneutics: History, Poetry, Enlightenment* (Cambridge, 2017) and *Ibsen's Hedda Gabler: Philosophical Perspectives* (2018).

OTHER VOLUMES IN THE SERIES OF CAMBRIDGE COMPANIONS

ABELARD *Edited by* JEFFREY E. BROWER *and* KEVIN GUILFOY
ADORNO *Edited by* THOMAS HUHN
ANCIENT ETHICS *Edited by* CHRISTOPHER BOBONICH
ANCIENT SCEPTICISM *Edited by* RICHARD BETT
ANSELM *Edited by* BRIAN DAVIES *and* BRIAN LEFTOW
AQUINAS *Edited by* NORMAN KRETZMANN *and* ELEONORE STUMP
ARABIC PHILOSOPHY *Edited by* PETER ADAMSON *and* RICHARD C. TAYLOR
HANNAH ARENDT *Edited by* DANA VILLA
ARISTOTLE *Edited by* JONATHAN BARNES
ARISTOTLE'S 'POLITICS' *Edited by* MARGUERITE DESLAURIERS *and* PAUL DESTRÉE
ATHEISM *Edited by* MICHAEL MARTIN
AUGUSTINE 2nd Edition *Edited by* DAVID MECONI *and* ELEONORE STUMP
BACON *Edited by* MARKKU PELTONEN
BERKELEY *Edited by* KENNETH P. WINKLER
BOETHIUS *Edited by* JOHN MARENBON
BRENTANO *Edited by* DALE JACQUETTE
CARNAP *Edited by* MICHAEL FRIEDMAN *and* RICHARD CREATH
THE COMMUNIST MANIFESTO *Edited by* TERRELL CARVER *and* JAMES FARR
CONSTANT *Edited by* HELENA ROSENBLATT
CRITICAL THEORY *Edited by* FRED RUSH
DARWIN 2nd Edition *Edited by* JONATHAN HODGE *and* GREGORY RADICK
SIMONE DE BEAUVOIR *Edited by* CLAUDIA CARD
DELEUZE *Edited by* DANIEL W. SMITH *and* HENRY SOMERS-HALL
DESCARTES *Edited by* JOHN COTTINGHAM
DESCARTES' 'MEDITATIONS' *Edited by* DAVID CUNNING
DEWEY *Edited by* MOLLY COCHRAN
DUNS SCOTUS *Edited by* THOMAS WILLIAMS
EARLY GREEK PHILOSOPHY *Edited by* A. A. LONG
EARLY MODERN PHILOSOPHY *Edited by* DONALD RUTHERFORD
EPICUREANISM *Edited by* JAMES WARREN
EXISTENTIALISM *Edited by* STEVEN CROWELL
FEMINISM IN PHILOSOPHY *Edited by* MIRANDA FRICKER *and* JENNIFER HORNSBY
FICHTE *Edited by* DAVID JAMES *and* GUENTER ZOELLER

Continued at the back of the book

The Cambridge Companion to
HERMENEUTICS

Edited by

Michael N. Forster
University of Bonn

Kristin Gjesdal
Temple University, Philadelphia

CAMBRIDGE
UNIVERSITY PRESS

University Printing House, Cambridge CB2 8BS, United Kingdom

One Liberty Plaza, 20th Floor, New York, NY 10006, USA

477 Williamstown Road, Port Melbourne, VIC 3207, Australia

314-321, 3rd Floor, Plot 3, Splendor Forum, Jasola District Centre, New Delhi - 110025, India

79 Anson Road, #06-04/06, Singapore 079906

Cambridge University Press is part of the University of Cambridge.

It furthers the University's mission by disseminating knowledge in the pursuit of education, learning and research at the highest international levels of excellence.

www.cambridge.org
Information on this title: www.cambridge.org/9781316638170
DOI: 10.1017/9781316888582

© Cambridge University Press 2019

This publication is in copyright. Subject to statutory exception and to the provisions of relevant collective licensing agreements, no reproduction of any part may take place without the written permission of Cambridge University Press.

First published 2019

A catalogue record for this publication is available from the British Library

Library of Congress Cataloging in Publication data
Names: Forster, Michael N., editor. | Gjesdal, Kristin, editor.
Title: The Cambridge companion to hermeneutics / edited by Michael N. Forster, University of Bonn, Kristin Gjesdal, Temple University, Philadelphia.
Description: New York: Cambridge University Press, 2018. |
Series: Cambridge companions | Includes bibliographical references and index.
Identifiers: LCCN 2018038870 | ISBN 9781107187603 (hardback) |
ISBN 9781316638170 (paperback)
Subjects: LCSH: Hermeneutics. Classification: LCC BD241.C3253 2018 |
DDC 121/.686–dc23
LC record available at https://lccn.loc.gov/2018038870

ISBN 978-1-107-18760-3 Hardback
ISBN 978-1-316-63817-0 Paperback

Cambridge University Press has no responsibility for the persistence or accuracy of URLs for external or third-party internet websites referred to in this publication, and does not guarantee that any content on such websites is, or will remain, accurate or appropriate.

Contents

List of Contributors		*page* vii
Acknowledgments		xi
Introduction		1
1	Hermeneutics and Theology CHRISTOPH BULTMANN	11
2	Hermeneutics and Nature DALIA NASSAR	37
3	Hermeneutics and Romanticism FRED RUSH	65
4	Hermeneutics and German Idealism PAUL REDDING	87
5	Hermeneutics and History JOHN H. ZAMMITO	110
6	Hermeneutics and Positivism FREDERICK C. BEISER	133
7	Hermeneutics: Nietzschean Approaches PAUL KATSAFANAS	158
8	Hermeneutics and Psychoanalysis SEBASTIAN GARDNER	184
9	Hermeneutics and Phenomenology BENJAMIN CROWE	211

10 Hermeneutics and Critical Theory   237
    GEORGIA WARNKE

11 Hermeneutics: Francophone Approaches   260
    MICHAEL N. FORSTER

12 Hermeneutics: Non-Western Approaches   286
    KAI MARCHAL

13 Hermeneutics and Literature   304
    JONATHAN CULLER

14 Hermeneutics and Law   326
    RALF POSCHER

15 Hermeneutics and the Human Sciences   354
    KRISTIN GJESDAL

    Bibliography   381
    Index   411

Contributors

Frederick C. Beiser is Professor of Philosophy at Syracuse University, New York. His many books on German philosophy include *The German Historicist Tradition* (2011), *The Genesis of Neo-Kantianism, 1796–1880* (2014), and *Weltschmerz: Pessimism in German Philosophy 1860–1900* (2016).

Christoph Bultmann is Professor of Biblical Studies at the Martin-Luther-Institut in the Faculty of Education at the University of Erfurt, Germany. His publications include *Die biblische Urgeschichte in der Aufklärung* (1999) and *Bibelrezeption in der Aufklärung* (2012).

Benjamin Crowe is a Lecturer in the Philosophy Department at Boston University. His publications include *Heidegger's Religious Origins* (2006) and *Heidegger's Phenomenology of Religion* (2007). He translated and edited J. G. Fichte's *Lectures on the Theory of Ethics (1812)* (2016), and is editor of *The Nineteenth Century Philosophy Reader* (2016).

Jonathan Culler is Class of 1916 Professor of English at Cornell University. His publications include *Flaubert: The Uses of Uncertainty* (1974), *Structuralist Poetics* (1975), *On Deconstruction* (1983), *The Literary in Theory* (2006), and *Theory of the Lyric* (2015).

Michael N. Forster is Alexander von Humboldt Professor, holder of the Chair in Theoretical Philosophy, and Co-director of the International Centre for Philosophy at Bonn University. His publications include eight books, numerous articles, and several edited volumes.

Sebastian Gardner is Professor of Philosophy at University College London. His writings on the philosophy of psychoanalysis include *Irrationality and the Philosophy of Psychoanalysis* (Cambridge, 1993).

Kristin Gjesdal is Professor of Philosophy at Temple University and Professorial Fellow of Philosophy at the University of Oslo. She is the author of *Gadamer and The Legacy of German Idealism* (Cambridge, 2009) and *Herder's Hermeneutics: History, Poetry, Enlightenment* (Cambridge, 2017).

Paul Katsafanas is Associate Professor of Philosophy at Boston University. He is the author of two books: *Agency and the Foundations of Ethics: Nietzschean Constitutivism* (2013) and *The Nietzschean Self: Moral Psychology, Agency, and the Unconscious* (2016).

Kai Marchal is Associate Professor in the Department of Philosophy at National Chengchi University, Taipei. He is the author of *Die Aufhebung des Politischen* (2011) and co-editor of *Carl Schmitt and Leo Strauss in the Chinese-Speaking World: Reorienting the Political* (2017).

Dalia Nassar is Senior Lecturer in Philosophy at the University of Sydney. She is the author of *The Romantic Absolute: Being and Knowing in German Romantic Philosophy, 1795–1804* (2014), editor of *The Relevance of Romanticism: Essays on German Romantic Philosophy* (2014), and co-editor of two special issues of journals on Goethe and Environmentalism (*Goethe Yearbook*) and Kant and the Empirical Sciences (*Studies in History and Philosophy of Science*).

Ralf Poscher holds the chair for Public Law and Legal Philosophy at the University of Freiburg. His recent publications include *Vagueness and Law: Philosophical and Legal Approaches*, co-edited with Geert Keil (2016).

Paul Redding is Emeritus Professor of Philosophy at the University of Sydney. Among his published books are *Hegel's Hermeneutics*

(1996), *Analytic Philosophy and the Return of Hegelian Thought* (Cambridge, 2007), *Continental Idealism: Leibniz to Nietzsche* (2009), and *Thoughts, Deeds, Words, and World: Hegel's Idealist Response to the Linguistic "Metacritical Invasion"* (2016).

Fred Rush teaches philosophy at the University of Notre Dame (USA). He is the author of *Irony and Idealism: Rereading Schlegel, Hegel, and Kierkegaard* (2016) and *On Architecture* (2009), and editor of *The Cambridge Companion to Critical Theory* (Cambridge, 2004).

Georgia Warnke is Distinguished Professor of Political Science at the University of California, Riverside and Director of its Center for Ideas and Society. Her publications include *Gadamer: Hermeneutics, Tradition and Reason* (1987) and *After Identity: Rethinking Race, Sex, and Gender* (Cambridge, 2007). She is also the editor of *Inheriting Gadamer: New Directions in Philosophical Hermeneutics* (2016).

John H. Zammito is John Antony Weir Professor of History at Rice University. His publications include *The Genesis of Kant's Critique of Judgment* (1992), *Kant, Herder, and the Birth of Anthropology* (2002), and *A Nice Derangement of Epistemes: Post-Positivism in the Study of Science from Quine to Latour* (2004).

Acknowledgments

This volume has been in preparation for some time and we have incurred many debts of thanks in the course of preparing it. We would like to thank Hilary Gaskin of Cambridge University Press for suggesting it in the first place, advising us on how best to develop it, and shepherding it through to production. We would also like to thank three anonymous reviewers for the press who gave very thoughtful and constructive feedback on the project proposal, which among other things led to the addition of several chapters. The volume was prepared for by means of a conference that we organized at Bonn University in April of 2017 at which contributors presented their contributions and received feedback from each other. In that connection we would like to thank the Alexander von Humboldt Foundation for generously funding the conference and Bonn University for hosting it. We would also like to thank several of Michael Forster's graduate student assistants at Bonn University who worked both on the conference and on the volume itself: Jaroslaw Bledowski, Eva Jeske, Jan Paffrath, Melanie Riedel, and Simon Waskow. At Temple University, we would like to thank Meryl Lumba for her editorial assistance. And of course we would also like to thank the contributors themselves for all of the hard work they put into writing their pieces and participating in the conference.

Introduction

In its original sense hermeneutics is the *theory of interpretation and understanding*. Hermeneutical questions (What is human meaning? How do we understand others? What happens in textual interpretation and how is it best done? What about understanding discourse? Art? How can we facilitate understanding between cultures and across time periods?) are at the heart of academic, aesthetic, political, legal, and religious practices. The present volume is committed to hermeneutics in this profound and original sense.

Throughout these fifteen chapters, leading scholars from philosophy, literature, history, legal studies, and theology discuss how hermeneutical issues relate to their respective areas of research. In this way, the present volume shows not only the centrality of hermeneutical questions across academic fields and divisions, but also how hermeneutical discourse benefits from interdisciplinary and non-partisan approaches. Or, put even more emphatically, it is in the spirit of this volume not only to ask what hermeneutics is and how it is best conceived, but also to demonstrate how hermeneutical thinking thrives and develops through concrete, interdisciplinary reflection.

Understood as a theory of interpretation, hermeneutics is as old as philosophy itself. Forms of hermeneutical thinking can already be found in Protagoras, Plato, Aristotle, the Stoics, and the competing critical schools of Alexandria and Pergamon, for example. The present volume, however, is concerned with hermeneutics in its modern forms. In order to grasp the importance and relevance of the modern hermeneutical tradition, it may be helpful to have a basic roadmap of its developments and of the historical and cultural contexts within which it emerged.

In its modern forms, hermeneutics is largely a German achievement. With the new impulse of the Protestant Reformation, the responsibility for interpreting the Bible was shifted from the Church to the individual. Eighteenth-century Protestant theorists such as Johann August Ernesti, Johann Salomo Semler, and Johann David Michaelis then made a number of important contributions. These included recognizing the obstacle to interpretation posed by historical and cultural distance, the importance of paying close attention to word-usage in order to discover a text's distinctive meanings, the need to take into account a broader social context, and the inadequacy of relying on divine inspiration in order to interpret the Bible. Several Protestant theorists indeed not only gave hermeneutics such a secular form but also extended its application far beyond religious texts to include writings of other sorts (e.g., literature, oral discourse), and art as well. The prime examples of this were Johann Gottfried Herder and Friedrich Schleiermacher.

Schleiermacher delivered his famous lectures on hermeneutics during the first third of the nineteenth century. And largely under his influence, the discipline then went on to play a very important role in the nineteenth century. It made a vital contribution to the flowering of such human sciences as classical scholarship, legal scholarship, historiography, scholarship of the Bible, historiography of philosophy, and (at the end of the century) cultural anthropology. It contributed essentially to an important debate about the nature and method of historiography and the human sciences that took place – especially among such thinkers as Johann Gustav Droysen and Wilhelm Dilthey – in the aftermath of the rise of the natural sciences. It became the methodological tool of the broad movement known as "historicism" that swept across the human sciences generally and philosophy in particular. Moreover, it underwent an important extension to incorporate several radical new approaches that Paul Ricoeur has helpfully dubbed "hermeneutics of suspicion": Karl Marx's critique of ideology, Friedrich Nietzsche's method of genealogy, and Sigmund Freud's psychoanalysis. While originating in a religious and philosophical context, hermeneutics, in its modern form, is thus relevant for (and has substantially gained from interactions with) a broader range of intellectual practices.

In the twentieth century, hermeneutics took on another radically new form in the ambitious philosophical theories of Martin Heidegger and Hans-Georg Gadamer. Since then, it has continued to accrue further important contributions and has shaped the work of thinkers from Jean-Paul Sartre, Paul Ricoeur, Jacques Derrida, Roland Barthes, and Tzvetan Todorov to Julia Kristeva in France, or, in the Anglophone context, from Eric Donald Hirsch and Donald Davidson to Quentin Skinner. While continental philosophers have long acknowledged the importance of hermeneutics, it is only more recently that analytic philosophers have turned to this tradition and contributed to its further development and relevance.

There are already a number of volumes available that offer histories of hermeneutics or treatments of individual hermeneutical theorists. This volume approaches the subject differently. It neither aims to give an exhaustive history of the discipline nor provides in-depth accounts of individual theorists. Instead it focuses primarily on movements, traditions, and debates. For it is often by examining these that what is at stake in the discipline comes most clearly into focus.

Christoph Bultmann, in "Hermeneutics and Theology," begins with an account of a conception of a *philologia sacra* from the seventeenth century, emphasizing that it carefully distinguished between several different aspects of interpretation. He then turns to the sharply contrasting approaches that were developed by the German Enlightenment, in particular Ernesti, Semler, Lessing, Kant, and Herder, whose tendency was to be skeptical about both the historical claims of the Bible and the idea of relying on the Holy Spirit in order to ensure its interpretation in favor of reading it as a human document. Rather like Spinoza before him, Kant insisted that truths (in particular, moral truths) are universal in character so that they can be grasped by philosophy and that the biblical narrative is strictly irrelevant to establishing them. Lessing, on his side, developed a less radical version of this position and envisaged interpretive interaction with the Bible as sometimes a means of new discoveries, not only in natural religion and morals but in principle even beyond them.

Dalia Nassar, in "Hermeneutics and Nature," argues for a relationship of mutual influence between hermeneutics and natural science in the eighteenth century. Whereas Linnaeus treated the organic phenomena he classified in an abstractive way, Buffon and Diderot sought a more holistic approach. Herder then developed this more fully. He began with a strong commitment to holism in interpretation, but then extended it to nature as well. In his early work, Herder argues that the concept of a "world" needs to be taken into account in interpretation and that a certain circularity arises as a result. Similarly, he views animals as part of a larger world and as having a specific circle within it. This, in particular, allows him to explain the specific character of human language in terms of a broad circle that human beings occupy within nature.

Fred Rush, in "Hermeneutics and Romanticism," considers the forms that hermeneutics took in German Romanticism specifically. Novalis devoted relatively little attention to hermeneutics, whereas Friedrich Schlegel saw it as important within the context of his conception of irony. Then, with Schleiermacher it became a central object of study. Schleiermacher in particular emphasizes the role of *mis*understanding in interpretation, wavering between a stronger and a weaker, more plausible version of this idea, as well as various forms of holism. Wilhelm von Humboldt continues this focus on hermeneutics, especially conceiving it in the context of his work in linguistics.

Paul Redding, in "Hermeneutics and German Idealism," considers the relationship between these two traditions at the historical point where they intersected. Hamann and Herder in their respective "Metacritiques" of Kant's *Critique of Pure Reason* both argue that reason is based on language. The Jena romantics, Schelling, and Ast then continue the hermeneutical project. Fichte makes two interventions: First, in an early essay on language, he develops a sort of idealist competitor to the Hamann-Herder approach. Then later, in his *Addresses to the German Nation* (1808), he makes a turn toward the Hamann-Herder position of emphasizing the fundamental role of language for forming national identities. Finally, Hegel, too, stands close to the hermeneutical tradition. In the *Phenomenology of Spirit* (1807) he in particular assigns to language a fundamental role, for example as an implicitly assumed medium of communication in the struggle for "recognition."

John H. Zammito, in "Hermeneutics and History," begins with observations about the current disciplinary insecurity of history, for which earlier theorists may in fact already have provided the remedy. The ground was initially prepared by Herder who in the eighteenth century articulated insights into the individuality of epochs and cultures, their organic character, and the cumulativeness of their historical development. Schleiermacher then elaborated a hermeneutics with claims to a scientific status. Another important theorist in this tradition was Wilhelm von Humboldt. The most important inheritor of all this was Droysen. His conception of history was hermeneutics-based, conceiving historiography as beginning with a pragmatic and material context, thence proceeding to psychology, and finally culminating in the "ideas" that guide historical epochs. Dilthey continued this approach. It then provoked a backlash from Windelband, who saw its historicism as threatening claims to objectivity, a worry that would persist to this day. Zammito concludes with the moral that history needs hermeneutics.

Frederick C. Beiser, in "Hermeneutics and Positivism," worries that a distorted conception of the historicist and hermeneutical traditions has led to an artificial division between analytic and continental philosophy. In championing the covering law model of explanation for history, positivists such as Carl Hempel overlooked the problem that in order to establish covering laws one would first need to establish the facts from which they generalize. In order to do this, however, the historian has to employ the different and demanding method of interpretation. In so far as the positivists consider the hermeneutical tradition at all, it is caricatured as identifying understanding as psychological re-enactment and as involving dualism – neither of which is true.

Paul Katsafanas, in "Hermeneutics: Nietzschean Approaches," focuses on the striking breadth of application that Nietzsche gives to the concept of "interpretation," his conception that all knowledge is interpretation- and value-laden, his holism, his perspectivism, his method of genealogy, and the role of interpretation in his treatment of nihilism. But Katsafanas also questions whether Nietzsche has a real hermeneutical method and accordingly questions Ricoeur's idea that he practices a "hermeneutics of suspicion." Rather, Nietzsche just seeks interpretations that are better in a methodologically unregulated way. In important respects, Nietzsche's approach has influenced figures such as Simmel and Foucault.

Sebastian Gardner, in "Hermeneutics and Psychoanalysis," argues that while Freudian psychoanalysis is famously interpretive, it does not offer a general hermeneutics and the relation between Freud's own form of interpretation and hermeneutics is an uneasy one. Gardner considers Sartre's and Wittgenstein's critiques of Freudian psychoanalysis and identifies a certain generic similarity beneath their more obvious differences. Gardner then turns to Habermas's and Ricoeur's attempts to recuperate a form of psychoanalysis for their own projects. In critiquing his acquaintance Brentano (whose position resembles Sartre's), Freud explains his theoretical justification for positing the unconscious. Gardner further emphasizes the realist character of Freud's commitment to such deeper levels of the mind. He also notes that there is a strand in Freud that sees meaning of the relevant sort as extending down into organic nature as a whole. In this way, there turns out to be an affinity between Freudian intuitions and the philosophy of nature of the early nineteenth century.

Benjamin Crowe, in "Hermeneutics and Phenomenology," considers the twentieth-century nexus of Heidegger and Gadamer. For these thinkers meaning, and therefore interpretation, is ubiquitous. Focusing on the period before *Being and Time* (1927), Crowe identifies an explicitly hermeneutical project that emphasized historicity and the critical destruction of what Heidegger saw as misguided conventional modes of interpretation, tradition, and history. Gadamer in *Truth and Method* (1960) picked up this approach and developed it further, rehabilitating "prejudice," emphasizing the mediating role of tradition, envisaging a "fusion of horizons" between interpreter and interpretee, drawing on Aristotle's concept of *phronesis* as a model for interpretation, and incorporating a critical reading of Hegel.

Georgia Warnke, in "Hermeneutics and Critical Theory," considers hermeneutics in relation to three generations of Frankfurt School philosophers. She begins with an account of Horkheimer's position during the 1930s, which aimed to excavate the hidden depths of our social practices by calling to aid a variety of empirical disciplines – and by doing so in a self-consciously situated and evaluative mode. She then turns to Habermas's and Honneth's critiques of Gadamer's hermeneutics. While accepting aspects of Gadamer's position, Habermas consistently blames Gadamer for underestimating the extent to which tradition contains systematic distortions. Habermas proposes different remedies to this problem at different stages of his career: initially drawing on forms of psychoanalysis and, later, on a theory concerning implicit claims to universality that he thinks are involved in all linguistic communication. Honneth's criticism turns on distinguishing between several different forms of the "I-thou" relationship that he sees as characteristic of Gadamer's approach to tradition: it can be objectivizing, condescending, or radically open. Honneth argues that what we need is not the second of these, but instead a sort of combination of the first and third. Finally, Warnke considers Gadamer's explicit reply to Habermas, which amounts to a claim that while tradition is inescapable, it allows room for critical correction. In light of this, Warnke also infers how Gadamer might have replied to Honneth.

Michael N. Forster, in "Hermeneutics: Francophone Approaches," discusses hermeneutics in France. He points out that one of the main pillars of the distinctive approach of German hermeneutics, its recognition of radical difference across historical periods and cultures, originally came from France. So did more specific hermeneutical applications of it in Germany, such as the recognition that the interpreter must take into account both the individuality of the culture he is concerned with and that of its particular author (originally an insight of Condillac's) and the recognition that genres are constantly changing over the course of history (originally an insight of Voltaire's). Forster then surveys twentieth-century French interpretation-theory. He argues that the core approaches of Sartre and Ricoeur are sensible but not very original, and that Derrida's approach is largely misguided. However, he suggests that Ricoeur's concept of a "hermeneutics of suspicion" is important, that Derrida's insistence that texts are often inconsistent is correct, and that Barthes, Todorov, and Kristeva all make important contributions as well.

Kai Marchal, in "Hermeneutics: Non-Western Approaches," points out that both interpretation itself and interpretation-theory have long histories in such non-Western traditions as China, Judaism, and Islam. He focuses on the Chinese case in particular. Both Mengzi (or Mencius) and Zhu Xi advocate an approach to interpretation that encourages an active involvement of the interpreter's own perspective and envisaged application (rather like Gadamer in the West). Marchal then reflects on Western hermeneutics' attitude to the non-Western Other. He notes that while eighteenth- and early nineteenth-century hermeneutics (Herder, Schleiermacher, and Schlegel) was very interested in cultural otherness, with Hegel that focus began to narrow to the Western tradition. But in the twentieth century, Heidegger and, to a lesser extent, Gadamer revived the broader interest.

Jonathan Culler, in "Hermeneutics and Literature," considers the relation between hermeneutics and literary studies. He explains the distinction between hermeneutics and poetics and makes a case for a collaboration between the two. Culler discusses older, allegorical versions of hermeneutics. He notes that eighteenth-century literary critics such as Pope and Johnson more or less ignored hermeneutics and theoretical issues concerning interpretation. He then explains the Herder-Schleiermacher version of hermeneutics and argues that it has a potential for literary studies that has not yet been realized. The remainder of Culler's treatment concerns the relation between hermeneutics and literary studies in the twentieth century. He discusses a representative debate between hermeneutically oriented scholarship and New Criticism in some detail. As examples of hermeneutical approaches to literature, Hirsch, Barthes, Ricoeur, and the "hermeneutics of suspicion" are covered as well. Culler points out that the last of these – the "hermeneutics of suspicion" – has been relatively neglected by literary theory, representing another underexploited potential. He concludes with the suggestion that what literary studies really needs is a *combination* of poetics and hermeneutics.

Ralf Poscher, in "Hermeneutics and Law," considers Gadamer's idea that law can serve as a model for general hermeneutics. He agrees with Gadamer's idea but disagrees with his specific way of entertaining it. For Poscher, the lessons come not from the sort of orientation to application that Gadamer had in mind, but instead from a series of subtle distinctions between different kinds of "interpretation" that have been developed in the context of law: The plain interpretation of laws, as of anything else, needs to be oriented to the author's (or authors') intentions. But then, there is also the *application* of an interpreted law [*Judiz*], *construction* in applying law, *discretion* in applying it, and the *significance* of law (as contrasted with its meaning). These are all importantly different processes, different forms of "interpretation," and general interpretation theory could benefit from following legal theory in distinguishing them carefully.

Finally, Kristin Gjesdal, in "Hermeneutics and the Human Sciences," turns to the relationship between hermeneutics (as a theory of interpretation) and the human sciences. In line with Dilthey's rehabilitation of Herder as a philosopher of the *Verstehenswissenschaften*, Gjesdal seeks to demonstrate that hermeneutics, in its early, Enlightenment form, springs from a methodological consciousness that spans the human and natural sciences alike. Later, Heidegger and Gadamer came to overlook the important insights of Enlightenment hermeneutics and, as a result, they misconstrued the history of pre-Heideggerian hermeneutics as expressing a false combination of aestheticism and positivist impulses. The chapter also assesses the debates, in the wake of the publication of *Truth and Method*, around the relevance of hermeneutics for the social sciences and suggests that this debate will be historically more nuanced and systematically more calibrated if the full spectrum of modern hermeneutical positions – including Herder, Schleiermacher, Dilthey, and the historicists – is taken into account.

It is our hope that these fifteen chapters, individually and as a joint contribution, will further facilitate and strengthen the interest in hermeneutics within philosophy, but, just as importantly, across the human and social sciences at large. We also hope that with its focus on topics and movements, the volume will reach a readership even beyond academia, narrowly speaking, and help to enhance the sensitivity to issues of interpretation in all its manifold forms.

1 Hermeneutics and Theology

Christoph Bultmann

In order to do justice to the issue of biblical hermeneutics, it is necessary to start with some observations on the *interpretandum*, i.e., the biblical texts. The Bible is a collection of writings in a number of distinct literary genres from almost ten centuries in antiquity. It therefore reflects a wide range of religious cultures in Israel as well as in Jewish and Christian diaspora communities throughout the ancient Roman Empire, and it displays a great variety of intellectual and scribal traditions which emerged more or less closely in relation to institutions of cultic ritual. At the same time, the Bible is a 'canonical,' an authoritative book through which a number of religious communities define their identity in terms of doctrine as well as practice. Whoever engages with the biblical texts in their original language is confronted with Hebrew – as well as, for a small number of texts, Aramaic – and Greek. While ancient Hebrew is mainly limited to the biblical texts themselves, related languages like Akkadian and Ugaritic have become accessible through archaeological discoveries in the nineteenth and twentieth centuries. The Greek language, which for Old Testament texts is the language of an ancient translation (the Septuagint), is the original language for the texts of the New Testament. In addition to the biblical texts, it is known through a substantial number of writings from ancient Greek and Hellenistic culture from many centuries so that linguistic features can be compared. Whereas the so-called Hebrew Bible or Old Testament was used as a sacred text in Judaism mainly in its original language, in Western Christianity the language of the Christian Bible, Old and New Testament, soon became Latin (the Vulgate). Thanks to the philological efforts of Jerome (c. 347–420 CE) and his followers, an almost standardized Latin version of the Bible had been achieved by about 400 CE and was eventually declared the one and only "authentic" text by the Council of Trent in 1546, ironically at a time when humanistic scholars had already started to engage with the original Greek and Hebrew texts, and reformers of the Church had produced and popularized a considerable number of vernacular translations of the Bible.

A sample text from the book of Jeremiah in the Hebrew Bible/ Old Testament may serve to illustrate what texts an interpreter of the Bible will seek to understand. The example is a prose text in Jeremiah 7.16–24 in the stylistic form of a direct divine address to the prophet himself, following on what is called Jeremiah's 'temple sermon' in Jeremiah 7.1–15. Like this "sermon," the text is normally assigned to a sixth-century scribal school which shaped the literary tradition of Jeremiah, who is himself remembered as a prophet in Jerusalem during the last decades of the Judaean kingdom prior to the conquest of the city and destruction of the temple by the Babylonians in 587 BCE (see Jer 1.1–3 and 38.28).[1]

> As for you, do not pray for this people, do not raise a cry or prayer on their behalf, and do not intercede with me, for I will not hear you.
>
> Do you not see what they are doing in the towns of Judah and in the streets of Jerusalem? The children gather wood, the fathers kindle fire, and the women knead dough, to make cakes for the queen of heaven; and they pour out drink-offerings to other gods, to provoke me to anger. Is it I whom they provoke? says the Lord. Is it not themselves, to their own hurt?
>
> Therefore thus says the Lord God: My anger and my wrath shall be poured out on this place, on human beings and animals, on the trees of the field and the fruit of the ground; it will burn and not be quenched.
>
> *(Jer 7.16–20)*

With regard to the issue of biblical hermeneutics, the most significant challenge to a reader in this sample text will be the idea of divine "anger and wrath." The perception of God as threatening destruction may move a devout reader to ask himself or herself how he or she can possibly relate to a God who is thus characterized by the authoritative text, and further questions such as what is the cause of such divine "anger" or what ways are there to escape the divine punishment may be raised.[2] The text itself offers ideas about apostasy and about (prophetic) intercession as religious ideas to be considered in this context. A reader may, of course, also prefer simply to regard the text as reflecting some episode in some religious culture in antiquity or as expressing some scribal opinion or, paradoxically, even as an invitation to empathize with the ritual activities of those who confidently worship their "queen of heaven" within a polytheistic conceptual framework. In biblical studies, a number of approaches to the canonical text have been developed, and it is not easy to achieve a consensus about what criteria should be employed in order to distinguish between plausible and implausible, convincing and unconvincing, constructive and misleading, correct and erroneous interpretations.[3]

PERSPECTIVES ON THE BIBLICAL TEXT AS A CHALLENGE FOR INTERPRETATION

In the early modern period a methodological standard of interpretation had been developed according to which at least theoretically a number of aspects had to be considered in regular exegetical practice. For the Lutheran tradition, Salomon Glassius (1593–1656), the author of an encyclopedic *Philologia Sacra*, can be chosen as a representative of scholarly erudition in the field of biblical hermeneutics.[4] Glassius emphasizes the importance of a critical consideration of the language and rhetoric of the biblical texts and a circumspect comparison of any particular text with related texts in its immediate as well as wider literary context. He also advocates the study of the historical origin of a text – what in Latin is called the *circumstantiae* – and provides a set of seven criteria which should not be neglected in the process of interpretation: Who is the author or speaker (*quis*)?

What is the place of the author and his audience (*locus*)? What is the time of the author and his audience (*tempus*)? What is the occasion or motivation for a specific utterance (*impellens*)? What are the stylistic features of the utterance (*modus*)? To these five criteria, which are predominantly driven by a historical interest, two more criteria are added which are more directly related to investigating the meaning of a text. What exactly is the view that is advocated by a specific text (*scopus*)? And can the text serve as the basis for some formal doctrinal teaching (*sedes doctrinae*)? Whereas the first five aspects of a process of interpretation point toward a "historical critical" study of the Bible, the sixth and seventh aspects call for a philosophical and theological engagement with the texts. The *scopus*, the core idea of a text, can only be defined through sustained reflection, and judgment about the doctrinal significance of any particular text can only be justified through an evaluation of alternative possibilities.

Thus, coming back to the example from the book of Jeremiah, the issue of author and place and time and occasion, i.e., the question whether the strange religious ritual relating to a "queen of heaven" had been witnessed by the prophet or was only witnessed or imagined by some later scribe, may be left for historians to discuss. However, the issue of what is the "scope" of the text and whether some particular doctrine can potentially be anchored in the text (as the "seat" of the respective doctrine) remains for philosophers and theologians to discuss. This would include the question whether it makes sense, e.g., to speak of divine "anger" and reasons for it on the side of the believers, to speak of prophetic intercession and the conditions for such a ritualistic practice, or to relate the military success of a conqueror to problems of religious devotion among those who are defeated. An analysis of the literary form of the text and a comparison of related texts will be required in any case (see, e.g., Jer 31.27–34). For a Christian reader, a doctrinal theological interest in the notion of divine "anger and wrath" will not least be motivated by the opening of Paul's letter to the Romans in the New Testament, where Paul employs the notion of divine "wrath" in order to delineate the background for his proclamation of divine mercy.

> For the wrath of God is revealed from heaven against all ungodliness and wickedness of those who by their wickedness suppress the truth. For what can be known about God is plain to them, because God has shown it to them. Ever since the creation of the world his eternal power and divine nature, invisible though they are, have been understood and seen through the things he has made. (Rom 1.18–20)

Another aspect of the *interpretandum*, i.e., the biblical texts, can again be illustrated from the sample text in the book of Jeremiah. While the polemics against apostasy in the form of worship of the "queen of heaven" and "other gods," quoted above, may be regarded as a purely internal religious controversy, in a successive polemics against religious ritual the relation between religion and ethics is addressed.

> Thus says the Lord of hosts, the God of Israel: Add your burnt-offerings to your sacrifices, and eat the flesh. For on the day that I brought your ancestors out of the land of Egypt, I did not speak to them or command them concerning burnt-offerings and sacrifices. But this command I gave them, "Obey my voice, and I will be your God, and you shall be my people; and walk only in the way that I command you, so that it may be well with you." Yet they did not obey or incline their ear, but, in the stubbornness of their evil will, they walked in their own counsels, and looked backward rather than forward. (Jer 7.21–4)

For an interpretation of this text, the two parallel or synonymous expressions "to obey God's voice" and "to walk in the way that God commands" would deserve greater attention than the historicizing rhetoric concerning some foundational exodus from Egypt in the time of the "ancestors" or of a conditional covenant between God and those "ancestors."⁵ The distinctive diction in which the scribe here refers to divine commandments may be compared, for example, with the notions of justice and solidarity and protection of human life in an exhortation in the immediate context (Jer 7.5–7). The text can again be juxtaposed with a section in Paul's letter to the Romans where Paul admonishes his audience:

> Do not be conformed to this world, but be transformed by the renewing of your minds, so that you may discern what is the will of God – what is good and acceptable and perfect. (Rom 12.2)

As these examples may demonstrate, biblical hermeneutics is concerned with a wide range of texts which support religious attitudes as much as they are critical of religious attitudes, texts which offer different representations of God and challenge the imagination, texts which refer to history as well as to philosophy, be it by addressing the issue of knowledge of God through the works of the creation, be it by addressing the issue of what is morally right and therefore corresponds to the will of God. For a meaningful debate about the legacy of biblical hermeneutics it is important to be aware of the many dimensions of the *interpretandum*, i.e., the biblical texts.

BIBLICAL DISCOURSE AND ITS PLACE IN HISTORY

It is not easy to escape oversimplification when trying to outline the basic structures of the use of the Bible in pre-Enlightenment theology. Throughout the history of Jewish and Christian theology, a strand of fruitful interrelationship between theology and philosophy can be observed, and some biblical books, such as Job or Ecclesiastes, and also many biblical Psalms and a number of prophetic sayings (e.g., Jer 8.4–7) could be studied more or less independently of the biblical narrative framework. However, the most obvious and most significant transformation of the perspective on the biblical texts which characterizes an Enlightenment approach to the Bible is the rejection, or at least the decline in acceptance, of the overarching biblical narrative. (1) The traditional assumption that the Bible offered an account of history from the beginning of the world (in Latin: *ab orbe condito*) through the history of the people of Israel and its ancestors to the rise and early flowering of the Christian Church came to be contrasted with the concept of a "natural history" of humankind, including a "natural history of religion." The emergence of the biblical tradition had to be assigned a place within this new conceptualization of history. (2) For Christian readers of the Bible, a problem arose in that the traditional assumption which said that the biblical history of Israel referred to Christ in a prophetic as well as a typological sense came to be contrasted with the concept of a more narrow limitation of the meaning of the individual Old Testament texts in their original settings within the religious culture of ancient Israel during the time of the First (until 587 BCE) and Second Temple (until 70 CE). What used to be developed as "allegorical readings" was no longer accepted even if certain forms of allegory were continued in the shape of applicative readings. (3) Biblical miracles which had been used for 'demonstrating' the truth of the Bible came to be ascribed to a mythological imagination which a reader may only appreciate as such. (4) The religious significance of biblical history and biblical revelation could be questioned altogether while greater emphasis was put on reason and an assumedly rational "natural religion." A short treatise *On the Proof of the Spirit and of Power* of 1777 by the German literary critic Gotthold Ephraim Lessing (1729–1781), for example, deserves mention at this point since the author addresses the epistemological status of historical traditions and declares:[6]

> If no historical truth can be demonstrated, then nothing can be demonstrated *by means* of historical truths. That is, *contingent truths of history can never become the proof of necessary truths of reason*.

This line of critical reflection is continued by the German philosopher Immanuel Kant (1724–1804), not least in a treatise *The*

Conflict of the Faculties of 1798, where he contrasts what he calls a "historical faith" with a truly significant "religious faith":[7]

> But the Scriptures contain more than what is itself required for eternal life; part of their content is a matter of historical belief, and while this can indeed be useful to religious faith as its mere sensible vehicle (for certain people and certain eras), it is not an essential part of religious faith.

One step in this direction had already been taken by Hugo Grotius (1583–1645), who had drawn a distinction between "prophetic" books of the Bible which, as he put it, had been written under an immediate divine inspiration (in Latin: *afflatus divinus*), and "historical" books which had been written by their authors on a pious impulse (in Latin: *pius motus*).[8] Thus a strong tension arose between scholarly ideas about a religious and scribal culture in Israel in antiquity and the doctrine of a divine inspiration of the biblical books.

It is at this point that due regard must be paid to what is normally considered the beginning of a "historical-critical" study of the Bible. Relying on a conceptually sharp distinction between what a particular word can mean and what it cannot mean, and how a particular word can be used and how it cannot be used, scholars condemned any forms of biblical interpretation which did not build on philological foundations as fictitious, misleading, and irresponsible.[9] To take again an example from the German academic tradition and ecclesiastical context, the renowned classical scholar Johann August Ernesti (1707–1781) transferred his expertise in the study of Greek and Roman authors into the field of New Testament exegesis and insisted on the precedence of philological competence over doctrinal declarations and pietist persuasions. In an influential textbook on hermeneutics and biblical commentary, the "instructions for an interpreter of the New Testament" of 1761, Ernesti claims:[10]

> Since all that has been explained equally applies to divine and human books, it is clear that the meaning of words in the sacred

books can be sought and discovered in no other way, as far as human effort is involved, than is usually and necessarily done with regard to human books, and under no circumstances must fanatical enthusiasts be obeyed who, while holding the study of letters and doctrine in contempt, refer everything to the divine power of the Holy Ghost: although there is no doubt that pious readers longing for divine truth are supported by the Spirit of God in investigating the meaning of Scripture, notably in those points which genuinely refer to faith and morals.

While Ernesti acknowledges that the use of language and the character of a discourse depend on conditions such as time, structure of society, political constitution, religion and school tradition, his view of the biblical writers is still constrained by the framework of an oversacralization of the biblical text and the resulting apologetics concerning differences and tensions within as well as between the individual writings. A contemporary of his, Johann Salomo Semler (1725–1791), tried to shed new light on the historical conditions which informed the reception and production of texts in early Christianity by subjecting the development of the canonical collection of the biblical writings to critical scrutiny. The traditional "place (*locus*)/time (*tempus*)/occasion (*impellens*)"-argument developed into a more rigorous historical-critical evaluation of the religious as well as intellectual culture at the time of the biblical authors.[11] However, the aim is not to abandon the concept of the Bible as the "Word of God," but to identify the significant religious ideas as a message for sustaining the faith of a believer – and in this sense as the "word of God" – within the biblical texts in all their diversity.[12] In his own particular way of understanding religion as a "human" concern, Johann Gottfried Herder (1744–1803) summarized these developments in an appeal to read the Bible "in a human way":[13]

> The Bible must be read in a human way, for it is a book written by human beings for human beings; its language is human; it has

been written and preserved by human means; finally, the mind whereby the Bible can be understood, every interpretative tool which elucidates it, and all the ends and uses to which it is to be applied are human.

Relying on the work of Robert Lowth (1710–1787) on biblical poetry and the sublime, Herder encouraged students of the Bible to pay particular attention to the religious "spirit" of Hebrew poetry as well as the representation of Jesus as teacher in the New Testament gospels.

PHILOSOPHY AND THE PLURALITY OF RELIGIOUS TEACHINGS

Beyond the challenge to do justice to the principles of philology and historiography, the Enlightenment perspective on the biblical texts is built on a philosophical foundation. Human reason, as understood in Enlightenment philosophy, aims at universal truths. Whatever is being communicated through a contingent historical tradition only cannot, therefore, by itself satisfy the standard of rationality. As far as religion is regarded as an issue in philosophy at all, religion can only be acknowledged as universal – or, in the terminology of the time, "natural" – religion and must be grounded on universal foundations. For Kant as for many philosophers before him, especially the so-called deists, this universal or "natural" religion is directly connected with a universalist ethics. Philosophy of religion is secondary to moral philosophy.[14] In Kant's definition, religion must be understood as "the sum of all our duties regarded as divine commands (and, on the subject's part, the maxim of fulfilling them as such)." Kant explains further:[15]

> As far as its matter, i.e. object, is concerned, religion does not differ in any point from morality, for it is concerned with duties as such. Its distinction from morality is a merely formal one: that reason in its legislation uses the Idea of God, which is derived from morality itself, to give morality influence on man's will

to fulfill all his duties. This is why there is only one religion. Although there are indeed different varieties of belief in divine revelation and its statutory teachings, which cannot spring from reason – that is, different forms in which the divine will is represented sensibly so as to give it influence on our minds – there are not different religions.

With this definition of "religion," Kant proves himself heir to the philosophical concept of "natural law" which had been extended into a concept of "natural religion." According to this concept, the world, as it originated in God's creation, has been endowed with a moral order, i.e., a "natural law" which can be discovered by human reason and is enshrined in the human conscience. As Grotius had famously declared, the "natural law" cannot be altered even by God in a divine revelation ("the Law of Nature is so unalterable, that God himself cannot change it").[16] The individual believer who accepts this religious dimension of a universalist ethics holds a truly "religious faith" ("Religionsglaube") – and what else does he or she need?! What else could sacred scriptures tell him or her?!

In order to do justice to the empirical reality of traditional religions and distinctive religious communities with their respective teachings, Kant suggests a distinction between this "religious faith" ("Religionsglaube") and an "ecclesiastical faith" ("Kirchenglaube") which is shaped by the doctrines, rituals, and institutional structures of a particular religious tradition. An "ecclesiastical faith" is based on some historically contingent revelation, transmitted through authoritative texts, and therefore comprises a certain amount of "historical belief" ("Geschichtsglaube") or "belief in scriptural teachings" ("Schriftglaube").

Kant's view implies a programmatic acceptance of the plurality of ecclesiastical institutions and doctrines. In this respect he continues a tradition which can be found, for example, in a popular treatise in verse by Alexander Pope (1688–1744), who states in his *Essay on Man* of 1733:[17]

> For modes of faith let graceless zealots fight;
> His can't be wrong whose life is in the right: [...]
> All must be false that thwart this one great end,
> And all of God, that bless mankind or mend.

As far as biblical hermeneutics is concerned, the critical philosophical understanding of the diversity of modes of faith or of the limited significance of any ecclesiastical faith means a transposition of the traditional and highly contested question of the clarity of scripture onto a new level. The disagreement in theology about countless doctrinal points which all of them are understood to be firmly grounded in biblical proof-texts (in Latin: the respective *sedes doctrinae*) made it only too obvious for a philosophical observer that there is no hermeneutical path toward establishing a full consensus about the interpretation of any biblical text whatsoever. The controversy between the followers of Martin Luther and those of Jean Calvin about the correct doctrine of the eucharist could serve as an example of an interpretative conundrum. If this issue is not considered an element of religious faith, but just of an ecclesiastical faith, it no longer calls for an either-or type of decision but allows for a pluralisation of ecclesiastical communities. This stance also implies that exclusive theological claims about the relevance of the correct doctrine for salvation are dismissed. Confessionalist convictions are set into perspective by an emphasis on the practical side of the life of a believer.

In his *The Conflict of the Faculties* Kant stages a kind of dialogue between a philosopher and a theologian. It reads like a rejection of elaborate theological assertions when he writes:[18]

> With regard to scriptural teachings that we can know only by revelation, faith is not in itself *meritorious*, and lack of such faith, and even doubt opposed to it, in itself involves no *guilt*.

Persecution for reasons of accepting or rejecting particular ecclesiastical doctrines which are claimed to be authentically scriptural doctrines thus becomes inconceivable. In terms of biblical hermeneutics, it is left to the individual believer to determine what understanding should be derived from biblical texts which do not directly refer to the essential religious faith.

PHILOSOPHY AND BIBLICAL HERMENEUTICS

The biblical historical narrative as well as the biblical mythological imagination may generate more or less inspiring examples of scriptural interpretation for particular communities of believers. However, there are two concerns for philosophers to address: (1) ecclesiastical teachings soon turn into a moral issue if they are imposed on a believer in such a way that this believer's sincerity (*Aufrichtigkeit*) is violated, and (2) if such teachings are regarded as "superior to morally good works" and therefore undermine the religious faith. If we assume that in a dialogue the theologian put the question to the philosopher of what scriptural, revelational doctrines in ecclesiastical faith are in view, the answer would be that believers will be deluded about religious faith if the idea of divine forgiveness of sins, and in Christian doctrine especially the idea of Christ's atonement for human sins, is proclaimed in such a way that it does not corroborate the moral energy of religious faith. Kant draws up the following hermeneutical rule:[19]

> if certain texts seem to regard faith in revealed doctrine as [...] superior to morally good works, we must interpret them as referring only to moral faith, which improves and elevates the soul by reason [...]

Surprising as this hermeneutical directive may sound, it is not original since a theologian would be familiar with the concept of a guiding "analogy of faith" (derived from Rom 12.6) and some overarching general message of the Bible (in Latin: *unicus scopus*, according to seventeenth-century textbooks on hermeneutics). In Christian theology, this message would have been the message of salvation through faith in Christ, i.e., a more or less exclusive emphasis on divine mercy, forgiveness, atonement, satisfaction, and reconciliation. However, theologians would also be aware of a tension between this emphasis and the challenge to translate faith into charity, i.e., acts of practical piety. Paul, for example, in his letters to early Christian communities in Galatia in Asia Minor coins the expression of "faith working through love" (Gal 5.6). In his first letter to the Christians in Corinth, he summarizes his exaltation of "love" or "charity" in a statement: "And now faith, hope, and love abide, these three; and the greatest of these is love" (1 Cor 13.13).

Kant seems to be designing a hermeneutical rule which would drive the interpreter openly to manipulate the text which he or she is studying. When he states that "the only thing which matters in religion is *deeds*" and claims that "this final aim and, accordingly, a meaning appropriate to it, must be attributed to every biblical dogma,"[20] the theological interpreter is challenged by the philosopher to enforce a coherent message on all biblical texts. Problematic as this may sound, there is an obvious rationale behind this rule: any religious doctrine would to some extent inform the believer about how to conduct his or her life, and from a moral point of view neither neglecting moral duties nor violating moral standards can be plausible options, so that some affirmation of moral duties must follow from religious sentiments in their conceivable diversity (e.g., admiration of the universe and miracles in it, self-dedication to Christ as savior, celebrating religious worship and festivals, imagining a storyline in a historical vein, feeling close to angelic beings, translating divine blessings into the human world, etc.).

The Enlightenment contribution to biblical hermeneutics can thus far be summarized by the concluding statement in Kant's *The Conflict of the Faculties* where he makes two points, first:[21]

> It is in this way, according to the principle of the morality which revelation has in view, that we must interpret the Scriptures *insofar as they have to do with religion* [i.e. other aspects are abandoned to ecclesiastical faith] –

Kant emphasizes this first point by considering the alternative of a form of scriptural interpretation in the field of religious faith that does not strengthen morality:

> – otherwise our interpretations are either empty of practical content or even obstacles to the good.

The second point is that Kant claims such an interpretation in the sphere of religious faith to be the only possible "authentic" interpretation, i.e., the only possible interpretation which makes an act of religious communication a successful act of communication for the human addressee:[22]

> Only a moral interpretation [...] is really an *authentic* one – that is, one given by the God within us; for since we cannot understand anyone unless he speaks to us through our own understanding and reason, it is only by concepts of *our* reason, insofar as they are pure moral concepts and hence infallible, that we can recognize the divinity of a teaching promulgated to us.

Although the philosopher does not depend on a cooperation with the theologian and does not rely on any references to the Bible in order to arrive at a philosophical understanding of religion, the philosopher is still interested in seeing whether what is essential to religion can also be detected in the biblical writings. This is the Enlightenment challenge to biblical hermeneutics. Kant calls this essential part of religion the "canon" of religion. This canon, he claims, is also there in the Bible which otherwise functions as an "organon" of religion. The Bible may even be considered to be a "supernatural revelation" as long as it serves as a "vehicle" (or "organon") of religion and "promotes moral precepts of religion."[23] It can be mentioned at this point that Grotius referred to the Ten Commandments (Ex 20.2–17; Deut. 5.6–21; see also Rom 13.9) in order to point out that "natural law" and the corresponding religion were also anchored in Israel's sacred texts.[24]

A problem with Kant's view is that he does not offer an analysis of the edifying narratives and doctrines and beliefs of ecclesiastical faith. He does not have to do this, since this task can properly be assigned to the theologians. However, the impression is created that Kant considers all those scriptural traditions as insignificant. On the side of theology, opposition to Kant has therefore in general been more dominant – including Friedrich Schleiermacher (1768–1834) in his *On Religion: Speeches to its Cultured Despisers* of 1799 – than engagement with his concept of religious faith and morality.[25]

The legacy of the biblical hermeneutics of the Enlightenment must be seen in the challenge to offer a rich account of religious attitudes which are expressed in the biblical writings, while at the same time relating them to a *scopus* which is informed by the universal moral law.

Kant's understanding of religious faith and his claim that this faith as the canon of religion can also be discovered in the biblical writings themselves can be seen as a re-assertion of the philosophical view which Baruch Spinoza (1632–1677) had developed in his *Theological-Political Treatise* of 1670.[26] What matters for Spinoza is the divine law in so far as it stands for eternal truths, and Spinoza like Kant relies on the relevant concept of natural law. There may be some change of emphasis when Kant puts the idea of morality and practical reason at the center of his concept, while Spinoza is in a strikingly energetic manner orientated toward the notion of love of God. However, for both these philosophers, the underlying idea of a natural light as the source of human understanding has the same function. At the same time, Spinoza seems to honor the biblical idea in Deut. 6.4–5, i.e., the opening of the *Shema' Israel*, where religious faith as love of God is the subject of an exhortation:

> you shall love the Lord your God with all your heart, and with all your soul, and with all your might.

Spinoza then provides a list of biblical texts from the book of Jeremiah, chapters 9 and 22, from the book of Exodus, chapter 34, and from the First Letter of John, chapter 4, as biblical sources to support his claim that:[27]

> the only knowledge of Himself God requires of men, via the prophets, is knowledge of His divine justice and love, that is, those attributes of God that men may emulate by a sound rationale of life.

The side of religion which Kant calls "ecclesiastical faith" is also clearly distinguished from "religion" by Spinoza. In his discussion of the divine law in chapter 4 of his *Treatise*, Spinoza writes:[28]

> If we now consider the character of the natural divine law, as we have just explained it, we shall see: (1) that it is universal or common to all men, for we have deduced it from universal human nature, and (2) that it does not require belief in any kind of historical narrative [...] Belief in a historical narrative, however reliable it may be, can give us no knowledge of God nor consequently love of God either. For love of God arises from knowledge of him; and knowledge of him has to be drawn from universal notions which are certain in themselves and well-known, and so it is by no means the case that belief in a historical narrative is a necessary requirement for us to reach our highest goal.

Spinoza concludes his argument with the statement:[29]

> Thus the Bible fully endorses the natural light of reason and the natural divine law.

In other words, Spinoza, like Kant, identifies what he regards as the essence of religion, Kant's "canon" of religion, as one component of the scriptural tradition itself and in this sense emphatically directs biblical hermeneutics toward the respective texts. In his discussion of the issue, he refers directly to the "wise" king Solomon and several of the pronouncements ascribed to this more or less legendary king in the biblical book of Proverbs, and to Paul's letter to the Romans, especially the statement in Rom 1.20 which has been quoted above as an example of the biblical *interpretandum*.

REDUCTIONIST HERMENEUTICS?

With regard to Spinoza as well as Kant it is easy to polemicize against what is often called a reductionist and deficient concept of biblical hermeneutics. To their opponents, these philosophers simply seem to conflate, if not even equate, religion with morality, thereby defining guidelines of hermeneutics which would not allow justice to be done to biblical texts, neither as historical nor as religious texts. Although neither Spinoza nor Kant advocates anything like a trivial understanding of religion, it may be worth expanding the debate and looking at Lessing as one representative Enlightenment author who is seriously concerned with the relation between natural religion and the Christian religion or, as he puts it, with a revelation which does in fact "reveal" something that goes beyond the comprehension of reason.[30] Lessing devoted a treatise with the slightly ironic title *Axioms* to the issue of hermeneutics and religious persuasions.

In the first of his axioms Lessing draws a distinction between the Bible as a textual unit and the "religion" which it contains:[31]

> The Bible obviously contains more than what pertains to religion.

According to this axiom, the starting-point for biblical hermeneutics cannot be the unity of the sacred text, but only the quest for religion. Using a mercantile idiom, Lessing speaks of the "gross" and the "net" of the Bible, thus undermining an influential current in traditional Lutheran orthodoxy, which he accuses of "bibliolatry." In his artful reply to an apologetic admission on the side of doctrinal theology that a differentiation between "what pertains essentially to religion" and "what pertains to the elucidation and confirmation of the central principles which actually constitute the essence of religion" could be allowed, Lessing asks:[32]

> But what if [the *gross*] were also to include completely unnecessary *packaging*? – What if there were a good deal of

material in the Bible which simply does not serve to elucidate or confirm even the least significant religious principle?

[...] the proposition "The Bible contains more than what pertains to religion" is true without qualification. Its proper use can also be infinitely more advantageous to religion than its misuse can be harmful.

However, in terms of biblical hermeneutics the most interesting question is how to decide which are the texts that communicate "what pertains to religion." Employing the terminology of revelation, Lessing asks:[33]

Would [...] no revealed truths whatsoever be distinguishable from human additions? For does a revealed truth have no internal distinguishing marks at all? Has its direct divine origin left no trace in and upon it other than that historical truth which it shares with so many absurdities?

The interesting hermeneutical problem of such "internal marks" can also be approached from the other side: what impact does historical certainty have on the status of any religious doctrine? This aporetical question brings Lessing to introduce the concept of the "inner truth" of religious doctrines:[34]

Let us take it as given that the books of the Bible furnish proof of all the facts on which the Christian doctrines are in part based; books can furnish proof of facts, and why should these books not do so? It is enough that not all of the Christian doctrines are based on facts. The rest are based, as already conceded, on their inner truth; and how can the inner truth of any proposition depend on the authority of the book in which it is put forward?

With this turn of his polemics against the Lutheran dogmatist, Lessing arrives at a point where the hermeneutical issue can be identified more clearly: in what way can the inner truth of a religious doctrine be recognized in a reader's encounter with scripture? In studying biblical texts, Lessing claims, the inner truth must become the "test" of "hermeneutic truth." How does the reader become aware of such inner truth? Lessing rejects a hypothetical model according to which a reader would have an understanding of the inner truth at hand prior to his or her encounter with a biblical text. For a debate about the relation between natural religion and the Christian religion such a model of understanding could not be helpful since the Christian message cannot be given prior to a full involvement in an act of communication of this message. Lessing therefore dismisses the assumption that the reader would know "beforehand" about the inner truth:[35]

> *Beforehand*? Why beforehand? Whoever does the one [i.e. explain the biblical text], also does the other [i.e. show a conception of the inner truth]. If someone explains to me the inner truth of a revealed proposition (I say explains, not *seeks* to explain), he surely proves quite adequately that he has a correct conception of this inner truth himself.

This statement must be regarded as the pivot of the debate about axioms in Lessing's hermeneutical treatise. The idea is that the reader, if he or she achieves an explanation of the inner truth of some religious teaching, becomes himself or herself aware, in the very process, of this inner truth at some level of individual insight or experience which can, however, be communicated to another person. Unfortunately, Lessing does not offer any examples at this point. One probably has to assume that such an act of explanation fails if a reader is prevented by some other convictions – which would possibly even be the teachings of a philosophical natural religion – from achieving an explanation.

In this sense three aspects are relevant for an explanation or evaluation of religious "doctrines" which are qualified as such by their inner truth. Lessing in his rhetoric contrasts the biblical scholar and the honest layman and speaks of doctrines which have been "extracted" from the Bible and which a believer, he claims,[36]

> does not regard [...] as true because they were extracted from the Bible, but because he realises that they are more worthy of

God and more beneficial to the human race than the doctrines of any other religion – and because he *feels* that these Christian doctrines give him comfort.

The first two of these three aspects ("worthy of God," "beneficial to the human race") are related to natural religion: while the existence and attributes of God are conceptualized at a philosophical level, Lessing opens up a space for other ideas which would not contradict the divine attributes in natural religion, but go beyond them, and while the moral law belongs to the essence of natural religion and would again not be jeopardized, he opens up a space for even "more beneficial" ideas – and obviously not "more beneficial" for some sectarian community only, but within the same dimension of universality as the moral law.[37] The third aspect – referring to religious consolation – allows a criterion of *feeling* to enter the hermeneutical process, and Lessing advocates the individuality of the believer who experiences some sort of immediacy in the encounter with a religious idea and is also able to express this experience in *explaining* a relevant scriptural text.[38]

Is Lessing's view of biblical hermeneutics as developed in his *Axioms* a part of theology or only a part of Enlightenment thought? Does he shield from criticism an experience in the engagement with biblical texts which Kant ignores? The legacy of Enlightenment biblical hermeneutics would certainly include the emphasis on natural religion and a universalist ethics. However, a slight irritation remains about components of the biblical (or indeed any other scriptural) religious tradition which might not be fully absorbed into the concept of natural religion, and Lessing represents a voice that has not abandoned a theological engagement with the biblical texts with a view toward such components. "Intercession" may be one such idea to be encountered in the biblical *interpretandum*. It is clear that a theological reception of these components – whether or not one calls them elements of an "ecclesiastical faith" – must not violate the moral boundaries of religion. However, believers in the wide plurality of religious communities are invited to search for them and to respond to them in their subjective and individual attempts at carving pious selves.

NOTES

1 All biblical quotations are from the New Revised Standard Version (1989/1995). For introductory commentary on the texts see, e.g., John Barton and John Muddiman (eds.), *The Oxford Bible Commentary* (Oxford: Oxford University Press, 2001). In the New Testament, 1 Pet 4.1–3 with its polemics against idolatry or Eph 1.15–19 with its concept of prayer may be compared.

2 In the early modern history of biblical interpretation, Spinoza discussed the anthropomorphic representation of God as "jealous" or "angry" with reference to Deut. 4.24. See Baruch (Benedict de) Spinoza, *Theological-Political Treatise*, ed. J. Israel, trans. M. Silverthorne and J. Israel (Cambridge: Cambridge University Press, 2007), 100–1, 183; *Tractatus Theologico-Politicus* (Latin and German), ed. G. Gawlick and F. Niewöhner (Darmstadt: Wissenschaftliche Buchgesellschaft, 1979), 236–8, 438.

3 For a highly polemical review of "approaches" to the Bible in modern biblical studies see Stephen D. Moore and Yvonne Sherwood, *The Invention of the Biblical Scholar: A Critical Manifesto* (Minneapolis: Fortress Press, 2011). A survey of "lines of approach" is offered in John Barton (ed.), *The Cambridge Companion to Biblical Interpretation* (Cambridge: Cambridge University Press, 1998).

4 Salomon Glassius, *Philologia Sacra* (Leipzig: J. F. Gleditschius, 1743), 493–506; the following paragraph builds on a treatise "De scripturae sensu eruendo" ("On Investigating the Meaning of Scripture"). The first edition of Glassius's book was published in 1623–1636. The treatise is also mentioned in Christoph Bultmann, "Historical-Critical Inquiry," in *The Hebrew Bible: A Critical Companion*, ed. J. Barton (Princeton: Princeton University Press, 2016), 431–54; on Glassius see Christoph Bultmann and Lutz Danneberg (eds.), *Hebraistik–Hermeneutik–Homiletik. Die "Philologia Sacra" im frühneuzeitlichen Bibelstudium* (Berlin: de Gruyter, 2011).

5 It should be noticed that in the biblical tradition the age of the "ancestors" remains more or less historically unspecific; the first name

of an Egyptian pharaoh occurs at 1 Kings 14.25 (Shishak/Shoshenk, about 945–924 BCE).

6 Gotthold Ephraim Lessing, *Philosophical and Theological Writings*, trans. and ed. H. B. Nisbet (Cambridge: Cambridge University Press, 2005), 83–8, esp. 85; see also Hugh Barr Nisbet, *Gotthold Ephraim Lessing: His Life, Works, and Thought* (Oxford: Oxford University Press, 2008), 537–70.

7 Immanuel Kant, *Religion and Rational Theology*, trans. and ed. A. W. Wood and G. di Giovanni (Cambridge: Cambridge University Press, 1996), 233–327, esp. 263.

8 Bultmann, "Historical-Critical Inquiry," 439–40.

9 For a careful discussion of the "literal" and the "mystical" ("allegorical," "typological") sense of the Bible see Glassius, *Philologia Sacra*, 347–492. The pattern of reception of Old Testament texts in the writings of the New Testament proved a major obstacle for a critical perception of "biblical" authors as authors within the religious culture of their time who would have written texts just at the "literal" level.

10 Johann August Ernesti, *Institutio Interpretis Novi Testamenti* (Leipzig: Weidmann, 1761), 11 (own trans.); *Elements of Interpretation*, trans. and ed. M. Stuart (Andover: Flagg and Gould, 1822), 15; *Principles of Biblical Interpretation*, trans. C. H. Terrot (Edinburgh: Thomas Clark, 1832/1833), 30–1. The book was republished in several editions until 1809, and there are two English translations (with supplements) by Moses Stuart (1822) and Charles H. Terrot (1832/1833). On Ernesti see Constantin Plaul, "Johann August Ernesti. Institutio Interpretis Novi Testamenti (1761)," in *Handbuch der Bibelhermeneutiken. Von Origenes bis zur Gegenwart*, ed. O. Wischmeyer (Berlin: de Gruyter, 2016), 651–62 [=*HdbB*]; John Sandys-Wunsch, "Early Old Testament Critics on the Continent," in *Hebrew Bible/Old Testament: The History of its Interpretation. Vol. 2: From the Renaissance to the Enlightenment*, ed. M. Sæbø (Göttingen: Vandenhoeck & Ruprecht, 2008), 976–80 [=*HBOT*]; William Baird, *History of New Testament Research. Vol. 1: From Deism to Tübingen* (Minneapolis: Fortress Press, 1992), 108–15; Werner Georg Kümmel, *Das Neue Testament. Geschichte der Erforschung seiner Probleme* (Freiburg: Alber, 1958), 67–70; on Moses Stuart see the entry in Donald K. McKim (ed.), *Dictionary of Major Biblical Interpreters* (Downers Grove: InterVarsity Press, 2007), 952–6.

11 Johann Salomo Semler, *Abhandlung von freier Untersuchung des Canon* (Halle: C. H. Hemmerde, 1771), 1–113; Semler's insistence on the historically contingent character of the biblical writings is often impregnated with an unwarranted anti-Jewish tone. On Semler see Marianne Schröter, *Aufklärung durch Historisierung. Johann Salomo Semlers Hermeneutik des Christentums* (Berlin: de Gruyter, 2012), esp. 100–21; also 'Johann Salomo Semler. Vorbereitung zur theologischen Hermeneutik (1760)' in *HdbB*, 729–42; 'Johann Salomo Semler. Neuer Versuch die gemeinnü(t)zige Auslegung und Anwendung des Neuen Testaments zu befördern (1786)' in *HdbB*, 743–54; Henning Graf Reventlow, *History of Biblical Interpretation. Vol. 4: From the Enlightenment to the Twentieth Century* (Atlanta: Society of Biblical Literature, 2010), 175–90; John H. Hayes, "Historical Criticism of the Old Testament Canon" in *HBOT* 2: 995–1005; Baird, *History of New Testament Research*, 117–27; Kümmel, *Das Neue Testament*, 73–81.

12 Thus in his dedicatory letter of his "*Abhandlung*" of 1771, Semler refers to ideas of "moral advancement" (*Besserung*) and "consolation" (*Beruhigung*), relying on the theologian Johann Joachim Spalding (1714–1804). See also David Sorkin, *The Religious Enlightenment: Protestants, Jews, and Catholics from London to Vienna* (Princeton: Princeton University Press, 2008), 113–63, for a study of Semler's academic teacher Siegmund Jacob Baumgarten. On an alternative view, Enlightenment biblical hermeneutics is considered to have been a transformation of the Bible from a religious resource into a "cultural" Bible; see, e.g., Jonathan Sheehan, *The Enlightenment Bible: Translation, Scholarship, Culture* (Princeton: Princeton University Press, 2005).

13 Johann Gottfried Herder, *Against Pure Reason: Writings on Religion, Language, and History*, trans. and ed. M. Bunge (Minneapolis: Fortress Press, 1993), 218 (from: *Briefe, das Studium der Theologie betreffend*, 1780–1781, letter 1). On Herder see Christoph Bultmann, "Herder's Biblical Studies," in *A Companion to the Works of Johann Gottfried Herder*, ed. H. Adler and W. Koepke (Rochester: Camden House, 2009), 233–46; Markus Buntfuss et al., "Theologie," in *Herder Handbuch*, ed. S. Greif, M. Heinz, and H. Clairmont (Paderborn: Wilhelm Fink, 2016), 319–85, esp. 351–8.

14 On Enlightenment debates about religion and ethics see Peter Byrne, *Natural Religion and the Nature of Religion: The Legacy of Deism* (London: Routledge, 1989); *The Moral Interpretation of Religion* (Edinburgh: Edinburgh University Press, 1998); *Kant on God* (Aldershot: Ashgate, 2007).
15 Kant, *Religion and Rational Theology*, 262.
16 Hugo Grotius, *The Rights of War and Peace*, ed. R. Tuck (Indianapolis: Liberty Fund, 2005), I: 155 (bk. 1, ch. 1, sect. 10.5).
17 Alexander Pope, *The Major Works*, ed. P. Rogers (Oxford: Oxford University Press, 2006), 270–309, quote 298. In the edition of 1743, two lines with an allusion to 1 Cor 13.13 were added: "In faith and hope the world will disagree, / but all mankind's concern is charity"; see Alexander Pope, *An Essay on Man*, ed. M. Mack (London: Routledge, 2002), 125.
18 Kant, *Religion and Rational Theology*, 267.
19 Kant, *Religion and Rational Theology*, 267.
20 Kant, *Religion and Rational Theology*, 267.
21 Kant, *Religion and Rational Theology*, 271.
22 Kant, *Religion and Rational Theology*, 271–2.
23 Kant, *Religion and Rational Theology*, 262, 269.
24 Grotius, *The Rights of War and Peace*, II. 1032 (bk. 2, ch. 20, sect. 14.1).
25 Friedrich Schleiermacher, *On Religion: Speeches to its Cultured Despisers*, trans. and ed. R. Crouter (Cambridge: Cambridge University Press, 1988); see also the relevant chapters in Jacqueline Mariña (ed.), *The Cambridge Companion to Friedrich Schleiermacher* (Cambridge: Cambridge University Press, 2005).
26 Spinoza, *Theological-Political Treatise*; *Tractatus Theologico-Politicus*. On Spinoza see Steven Nadler, *Spinoza: A Life* (Cambridge: Cambridge University Press, 1999); also "The Bible Hermeneutics of Baruch de Spinoza," in *HBOT* 2: 827–36.
27 Spinoza, *Theological-Political Treatise*, 176; *Tractatus Theologico-Politicus*, 420/422.
28 Spinoza, *Theological-Political Treatise*, 61; *Tractatus Theologico-Politicus*, 140/142.
29 Spinoza, *Theological-Political Treatise*, 67; *Tractatus Theologico-Politicus*, 158.

30 Lessing, *Philosophical and Theological Writings*, 66 ("Counter-propositions of the editor," 1777).
31 Lessing, *Philosophical and Theological Writings*, 120–47, quote 123 ("Axioms," 1778).
32 Lessing, *Philosophical and Theological Writings*, 124.
33 Lessing, *Philosophical and Theological Writings*, 125–6.
34 Lessing, *Philosophical and Theological Writings*, 132.
35 Lessing, *Philosophical and Theological Writings*, 139.
36 Lessing, *Philosophical and Theological Writings*, 143.
37 It should be mentioned at this point that while the treatise *Axioms* is focused on a controversy with a Lutheran church official, Lessing reflects on the plurality of scriptural religions (esp. Judaism, Christianity, Islam) in his "philosophical drama" *Nathan the Wise* of 1779.
38 Friedrich Schleiermacher, *Hermeneutik*, ed. H. Kimmerle (Heidelberg: C. Winter, 1959), 55, may still be seen to continue this line of thinking which Lessing advocates in his *Axioms* when he states, in his lecture notes on hermeneutics from the 1810s, with regard to the sacredness of the books of sacred scripture: "You can only know that they are sacred once you have understood them" ("Dass sie heilig sind, weiss man nur dadurch, dass man sie verstanden hat"). For Schleiermacher's extensive elaboration of the aspect of the potential and dynamics of language, on the one hand, and the (religious) personality of the human author of any biblical text, on the other, see his lectures on hermeneutics from the 1810s and 1820s, in *On Religion: Speeches to its Cultured Despisers* (1998); *Hermeneutik* (1959).

2 Hermeneutics and Nature

Dalia Nassar

Over the last few years, historians of science have turned their attention to the ways in which the study of history, human languages and cultures influenced the development of various natural-scientific disciplines.[1] Two claims have emerged from this research: the first is a critique of previous histories of science, which anachronistically applied the late nineteenth-century division of the *Naturwissenschaften* and the *Geisteswissenschaften* onto earlier centuries, and thereby overlooked the mutual influence the two fields exerted on one another.[2] The second is that it was primarily the methodological practices and insights of the humanistic disciplines that influenced certain natural-scientific fields.[3]

Although this work has been largely focused on Renaissance and Early Modern scientific practices,[4] recent scholarship on the eighteenth century has become increasingly attuned to the need to investigate the role of the natural sciences in the development of key fields of the humanities.[5] This is most evident in studies on the rise of historicism, which have (at least) noted the role that natural history played in the development of the historical study of human cultures.[6] The same does not hold for research into the emergence of modern hermeneutics, arguably the human science par excellence.[7] This might be due to the fact that most studies of hermeneutics focus on (or begin with) the nineteenth century, and thus largely assume Dilthey's distinction between the human and the natural sciences.[8] Alternately, or additionally, it might have to do with the fact that one of the most influential voices in twentieth-century hermeneutics, Gadamer, criticizes the natural sciences for overlooking their situatedness, and in so doing overlooks the possibility that pre-positivist (i.e., eighteenth century) natural science may have influenced the emergence of hermeneutics.[9]

Whatever the reason, it is perhaps telling that research focusing on the eighteenth century, in contrast to more general work on hermeneutics, has recognized the role of the natural sciences in the emergence of the study of interpretation.[10] However, these studies, along with the work on historicism, have interpreted the relationship as uni-directional: the natural sciences influenced the rise of historicism and hermeneutics. But is it possible that the influence was bi-directional – that hermeneutics was not only influenced by natural history but that it also influenced certain aspects of the study of nature, leading to new insights and discoveries? Could the study of nature in the late eighteenth century have involved hermeneutic methods and insights that ultimately transformed the ways in which we approach and represent the natural world?

To answer this question, I will consider the relationship between hermeneutics and natural science in the eighteenth century, focusing on three figures, Buffon, Diderot, and Herder. Though Kant has been recognized as developing something like a hermeneutics of nature in the *Critique of the Power of Judgment* (1790) – through reflective judging and the idea of life[11] – these thinkers developed the notion of an interpretation of nature well before Kant (such that many of Kant's key claims are already present in their work), and they were able to integrate the hermeneutic method into their study of nature more coherently than Kant ever did or was able to do.[12] After all, unlike Buffon, Diderot, and Herder, Kant remained wedded to the idea of science as founded on mathematics,[13] such that he could not agree with the "liberalization" of science that took place in the mid-eighteenth century, which led to the introduction of new modes of knowledge into scientific research.[14] My claim then is that the emergence of a hermeneutics of nature must be understood in light of this liberalization of science, heralded by Buffon, designated by Diderot, and carried out most comprehensively by Herder. As I will argue, it was Herder's new methodology – developed for the interpretation of historical texts and authors – that furnished the most concrete response to a key problem facing both Buffon and Diderot and that offered significant insights that resulted in the development of a new, dynamic natural history and geography.[15]

THE EIGHTEENTH-CENTURY LANDSCAPE

In 1735 Linnaeus placed the human being in the class "quadruped" and created the anthropomorphic order, which included monkeys, lizards, and sloths. The reasoning for this was that they all shared the same arrangement of teeth. Buffon, among others, considered this to be both arbitrary and far too narrow a way by which to draw classifications. Linnaeus's classification, he argues in the *Histoire naturelle* (1749–1804), is based on "a metaphysical error." He writes:

> it is easy to see that the great fault in all of this is a metaphysical error ... in wanting to judge a whole by only one of its parts: a very obvious error, and one that is surprisingly found everywhere; for almost all of the classifiers have employed only one part, such as teeth, claws, or talons, to classify animals, and leaves or flowers to categorize plants, instead of using all of the parts, looking for the differences and similarities in the entire individual thing.[16]

By confusedly taking the part for the whole, by narrowly focusing on one aspect of an animal's or plant's structure without taking account of the "entire individual thing," Linnaeus's system imposed abstract categories onto nature, which had little or nothing to do with nature itself. Thus Buffon contends, "that way of knowing is not a science, it is only a convention, an arbitrary language."[17]

In light of his critique of abstraction and convention, Buffon introduced the distinction between "physical" and "abstract" truth. One kind of abstract truth, he argued, is mathematical truth, insofar as it is an invention of the human mind. Physical truths, by contrast, are real; they exist in the natural world and are the proper object of human inquiry.[18]

Buffon's emphasis on real or physical truths led him to a new, historicized conception of species and of nature more generally. In the place of Linnaeus's arbitrary classifications, Buffon argued that natural history must be concerned with "real" relations, which can only be discerned through historical insight. Thus, he writes,

> [natural] history must follow description, and must solely center around the relations which natural things have among themselves and with us: the history of an animal must not be the history of the individual, but that of the whole species; it must treat their generation ... the number of their young, the care of their parents ... their place of habitation, their food ... and finally the services they can render us.[19]

In other words, in order to overcome the abstract systems of taxonomy, it is necessary to reconceive natural history: natural history must consider a species in relation to its context, and, most importantly, regard it not as a static (eternal) entity, but as the continuation of a group of individuals (in time) through reproduction.[20] In one stroke, Buffon offered a new definition of species, historicized nature, and redefined natural history.

In the *Histoire naturelle* Buffon identified a difficulty with his approach, one that has to do with the difference between the way in which our intellect operates and the way in which nature operates. Our intellect proceeds linearly, taking only single steps in one direction. Nature, by contrast, "does not take a single step except to go in all directions; in marching forward, she extends to the sides and above."[21] With this apparent incongruity between the mind and nature, the question arises as to how it is possible to glean any unity in nature's infinite multiplicity. Lacking a priori theoretical foundations, it is not evident how natural history can capture nature's diversity in a coherent or meaningful way.

It was precisely this question that Diderot posed in his *Pensées sur l'interprétation de la Nature* (1753/1754[22]). Like Buffon, Diderot was deeply critical of the mathematical and a priorist methodologies of his predecessors, writing that "the domain of mathematicians is a world purely of the intellect, where what are taken for absolute truths cease entirely to be so when applied to the world we live in."[23] Nonetheless, Diderot notes that lacking mathematical or a priori foundations, it appears impossible to achieve unity in natural history, such that "[e]ven if experimental science continued to work for century after century, the materials which it accumulated would eventually have become too great to fit into any system, and the inventory of them would still be far from complete."[24]

For Buffon and Diderot the solution to this dilemma is found in analogy and comparative analysis.[25] Thus Buffon writes in the *Histoire naturelle*:

> This goal is the most important one ... to combine observations, to generalize about facts, to tie them together by the force of analogy [*par la force de l'analogie*], and to try to arrive at this high degree of knowledge where we can judge that particular effects depend on more general effects, where we can compare nature with herself in her great operations, and from where we can finally open up the paths that will permit us to perfect the different parts of physics.[26]

Natural history requires analogy because it is only through comparing various structures that we can begin to discern similarities and recognize differences between species. Thus in his account of anatomy, Buffon notes that it was not until anatomists began to compare human and animal bodies that any knowledge was achieved. For, he explains, "What real knowledge can be derived from a single object? Is not every science founded on the comparison of similar and different objects, of their analogous or opposite properties, and of all their relative qualities? Absolute knowledge, if it has an existence, exceeds the powers of man: we can only judge by the relations of things."[27]

By discerning similarities and differences, analogy provides a means by which to grasp continuity in nature – real relations – that are not based on just one structural similarity, or an a priori taxonomy. Such an analogically based account of nature differs, however, from a systematic account founded on mathematical construction or axiomatic demonstration. For one, it necessarily remains open to being corrected – analogical inference may be wrong. Furthermore, it cannot establish certainty – analogical inference achieves probability only.[28]

The road to the "interpretation of nature," as Diderot put it, was opened. The use of analogy implied that the study of nature could not yield certain, eternal knowledge, but it also implied that natural history was not and cannot be the mere accumulation of disconnected facts. Rather, natural history must involve observation guided by a literary tool – analogy – in order to discern similarity and difference. In other words, the way to resolve Diderot's problem was to invoke a literary device in order to "interpret" nature. The natural scientist, as John Zammito has noted, became more than an *observateur* of nature (Bacon); she was now an *interprète* of nature.[29] In the *Pensées*, however, Diderot did not provide a detailed account of the methodology of the interpretation of nature. Though Buffon provided insights into overcoming this difficulty, he too did not furnish a comprehensive methodology. It was Herder who, through his *new methodology* of hermeneutics, provided the first comprehensive "interpretation of nature."

HERDER AND BUFFON

Herder was familiar with Buffon, and makes ample reference to him throughout his writings.[30] He was, furthermore, sympathetic to many of Buffon's ideas: Buffon's critique of apriorism and mathematical-universalist accounts of nature; his claim that human history must be considered part of natural history; and his critique of abstraction in science. However, Herder's attitude toward Buffon was, as John Zammito notes, mixed.[31] Herder worries that Buffon was not able to achieve his aims, because he remained tied to the prejudices of his age. For although Buffon sought to develop a concrete, holistic account of the natural world – an account that is not focused on one aspect of an organism's structure – his tendency was to analyze and distinguish, rather than synthesize and unify.

In his study of Thomas Abbt, Herder distinguishes Buffon as the anti-systematic thinker who is needed to combat the likes of Linnaeus in the study of the human spirit. Thus, he writes, "when our systematic philosophers become *Linnaeus* in the study of the mind, classifying according to their own principles [*eigensinnig*], then an unsystematic mind, like *Buffon*, must be placed alongside them ... in order to analyze the individuals" (FHA 2, 572).[32]

While this statement appears sympathetic, it also harbors Herder's worry about Buffon, namely Buffon's apparent tendency to dissect and analyze without finding a way by which to synthesize. This worry is clearly expressed in Herder's 1772 prize essay on the origin of language, where he places Buffon alongside Condillac and Bonnet, and criticizes all three for their failure to unify what they have dissected. Herder writes: "All dissections of sensation in the case of *Buffon's, Condillac's,* and *Bonnet's* sensing human being are abstractions; the philosopher has to neglect one thread of sensation in pursuing the other, but in nature all these threads are a single web!" (HPW 107).[33] Although Herder is here specifically concerned with their respective accounts of human psychology and physiology, his critique obtains for what he sees as a general tendency in Buffon's approach. Though Buffon *intends* to offer a holistic account of the natural world, his efforts are not fully realized. This can be seen in Buffon's account of "climate," and in Herder's transformation of this (somewhat superficial) conception into a key methodological tool for natural history (and ultimately geography).

Buffon introduces the notion of climate, alongside nourishment, in order to account for differences among animal species and among humans.[34] By climate, Buffon implies primarily temperature but also geography.[35] Speaking of horses, he remarks that "studs kept in dry light soils produce active, nimble, and vigorous horses, with nervous limbs and strong hoofs; while those kept in moist ground, and in too rich pasturage, have generally large heavy heads, gross bodies, thick legs, bad hoofs, and broad feet. It is easy to perceive," Buffon concludes, "that these differences proceed from the varieties in climate and food."[36]

Climate and nourishment are thus regarded as the ultimate causes of differences within species. This is evident, for instance, in Buffon's claim that variation in human skin color is due to, on the one hand, the climatic zone a human inhabits, and, on the other, the influence of food.[37] In contrast to Buffon's two categories, Herder contends that "it is much more the case that a large storehouse of other forces, both disadvantageous and advantageous, are connected to us" (FHA 6, 265). Though Herder does not specifically point to Buffon here, this statement resounds with his earlier critique of Buffon's tendency to dissect. The claim is that Buffon – despite his efforts – was unable to follow nature's many directions, along a non-linear path, and find unity therein. In his emphasis on just two categories, Buffon remains one-sided in his analysis; he does not account for the complexity and multi-directionality of nature's (many) "forces."[38]

In contrast to Buffon's climate and nourishment, Herder develops the notion of a "world" or a "circle," which aims to recognize and encompass multiple essential aspects of a natural (and cultural) environment, the relations between these aspects, the ways in which these aspects reflect and are reflected in individuals and species, and most importantly, the ways in which these various aspects form an integrated unity. Working with analogies, Herder, like Buffon, aims to discern similarities among the multiplicity of natural phenomena. However, through the notion of a world, Herder extends his use of analogy beyond a one-to-one comparison (i.e., comparing the structure of one species or variety to another in light of a specific natural phenomenon, such as heat). For, as we shall see, the idea of a world implies a multiplicity of factors – a "chaos of causes and effects" (FHA 6, 266) – and their co-determination. Herder invokes the notion of a world in order to follow nature's many paths and discern unity in the multiplicity. How does Herder arrive at this idea of a world, and how does he apply it to resolve Buffon's and Diderot's dilemma? I will begin with the first question, and argue that although Herder introduces the notion of a world in the prize essay on language, it was in his preceding writings on the interpretation of historical individuals and texts that he developed the idea.

HERDER'S HERMENEUTICS

Herder's hermeneutics, like Buffon's methodology, is critical of a priori theories of interpretation. In their place Herder develops a theory of interpretation that employs a bottom-up approach that seeks to grasp the particularity of a culture, and understand it from within (FHA 1, 97). As he puts it in *This Too a Philosophy of History* (1774), "every nation has its own center of well-being with itself, just as every globe has it center of gravity" and the task of the interpreter is to grasp precisely this center (FHA 4, 39). The question thus is: how is an interpreter to grasp the "center" of a culture long gone, or discern the "center" of a text or work of art? What, in other words, are the methods that the historian or interpreter must invoke in order to achieve this kind of knowledge?

Well before his writings on the philosophy of history, Herder had begun to consider these questions in relation to biography and the interpretation of works of art. In the essay on Thomas Abbt, Herder's concern is with how he – as the biographer of Abbt – is to approach his subject in the right way. For Herder the right way involves recognizing both Abbt's individuality *and* his indebtedness to his time and culture. As Herder puts it, "most of all it is necessary to distill [*abzieht*] what belongs to *the author's time* or to the *past world*, and what he leaves over for *the world of posterity*. He bears the chains of his age, to which he offers his book as a gift; he stands in his century like a tree in the realm of earth into which it has driven its roots, from which it draws nourishing juices, with which it covers its originating members" (FHA 2, 579; HPW 172, translation modified). The natural imagery serves to elaborate Herder's point: an author, like a tree, is not born isolated; rather, both are dependent on the surroundings, the climate and the geography, into which they are born. They become what they are only in relation to this larger context. The aim of the interpreter (like the natural historian) must therefore be to discern *the individuality* or *distinctness* of an author (of a species) *within* her culture (within the natural environment), and not beyond or above it. Thus, Herder continues, whoever wishes to rob the author of the "birthmarks of his time," risks "taking from him the traits of his individuality [*Eigenheiten*]" (FHA 2, 579; HPW 172). An author neither exists nor can be understood outside of her or his cultural framework; it is this framework that enables the author to write, to become an author. The framework, then, is not something artificially imposed, nor is it a hindrance to understanding; rather, it must be taken into account in order to discern the author's distinctive contribution or individuality.

This means that the interpreter must, first, avoid any a priori generalizations about the author or the work: given that the author is born in a specific time and place, one cannot make any presumptions about her work or aims without first investigating the particularities into which she is born. The interpreter must, however, also avoid sinking into particularities and failing to find a "center," a meaningful and coherent unity in light of which the author's work is to be interpreted. Thus, just like the historian of nature, so the interpreter must avoid both abstraction and the mere accumulation of data; the interpreter must find a way to grasp the particular and find significance, coherence *therein*. This means, importantly, that the interpreter's aim is not to regard the author as a mere reflection of the mores of her time and place; rather, by seeking to discern the author's individuality within her context, the interpreter's aim is to discern how the author is a participant in and a contributor to her context. As such, Herder's conception of unity (context) is not of an undifferentiated or homogenous whole, but of an internally differentiated one, composed of the individual contributions of its various members, whose contributions are themselves dependent on this unity, this context. There is, in other words, a reciprocity at work here, such that neither the whole nor the parts can exist without the other.

In the essay on Abbt, Herder explains that the means by which to achieve the goal of interpretation is by explaining "one in terms of the other [eins aus dem andern erkläret]," i.e., by seeing how the context is reflected in the individual author's work, and how the individual author's work adds to, or challenges aspects of, this context (FHA 2, 575; HPW 171). It is only by seeing one (the author) through the other (her age) that their similarities and differences come to light.[39] In this way, Herder extends analogical reflection, beyond a one-on-one comparison, to encompass the world that the author inhabits and which inhabits the author (the relation, as we have seen, is reciprocal). This extension is demonstrated in Herder's own hermeneutic practice, and can be seen, for instance, in his essay on Shakespeare (1773; draft 1771).

In the essay, Herder challenges French views of theater, which take Aristotle's understanding of tragedy as foundational for aesthetic judgment, in order to demonstrate their mistaken interpretation of Shakespeare. The trouble with the French approach, Herder notes, is that it fails to recognize that the world out of which Greek tragedy emerged fundamentally differs from Shakespeare's world. "In Greece," Herder contends, "the drama developed in a way that it could not in the north. In Greece it was what it can never be in the north. In the north it is not and cannot be what it was in Greece" (FHA 2, 499; SWA 292).[40] After all, he continues, "as everything in the world changes, so Nature, the true creator of Greek drama, was bound to change also. *The Greek worldview, manners, the state of the republics, the tradition of the heroic age, religion,* even *music, expression,* and *the degrees of illusion* changed" (FHA 2, 503; SWA 294). Thus, to judge Shakespeare according to the rules of Greek drama is not only problematic, but also absurd. A work of art is, like a writer, of its time, such that its appropriateness, its "genius," can only be measured and determined in relation to its time.

Herder begins his interpretation of Shakespeare by noting general differences between ancient Greek drama and Shakespeare's, differences that are fundamentally connected to their respective worldviews. In ancient Greece there was an overarching sense of unity of time and place, as well as a sense of simplicity among the Greek people and their polity. One can say that the Greeks lacked a modern sense of history and of cultural differences. This was, Herder contends, reflected in their dramatic works (most, though not all, of Greek drama occurred in one place, for instance). By contrast, Shakespeare's world is one composed of "a rich variety of different estates, ways of life, convictions, peoples and idioms – any nostalgia for the simplicity of former times would have been in vain" (FHA 2, 508; SWA 298). For this reason his works do not occur in one place, but move from one location to the next, and involve people from a variety of backgrounds. It is also for this reason, Herder continues, that for Shakespeare plot no longer held the meaning the Greeks had bestowed upon it (i.e., a single action), but came to mean "event" or "great occurrence." Ultimately, in Shakespeare's works we witness transitions and movements that are simply not present in Greek drama, and this is a reflection of the world that Shakespeare inhabits.

Furthermore, Herder notes that ancient Greek drama was a public institution *and* a religious event, while Shakespearean drama did not have religious motivations (FHA 2, 516; SWA 304; see also SW 16, 101).[41] This means that the *aim* of a Greek drama differed from that of a Shakespearean drama, and it is only in light of this difference of aim that either can be properly appreciated and understood. Shakespeare's tragedies, for instance, include comedy – a fact that challenges the distinction between tragedy and comedy that has been upheld since Aristotle (FHA 2, 525). However, given that the aims of Shakespeare's drama differ from those of Greek tragedy, there is no reason to abide by the Aristotelian understanding of tragedy in order to judge Shakespeare's work.

A further important difference between Greek tragedy and Shakespearean drama is the origin of their dramatic form, the source from which they drew their inspiration. While the Greeks drew on the dithyramb, mimed dance and the chorus (FHA 2, 500; SWA 292; see also SW 16, 100), Shakespeare drew on history (FHA 2, 508; SWA 298; see also FHA 2, 525; see also SW 16, 101). For this reason, Shakespeare's plays are themselves a presentation of history. Thus, Herder writes, "in Othello," we have before us a *"living history of the genesis, development, eruption, and sad end to the passion of this noble and unfortunate man!"* (FHA 2, 511; SWA 300). The Greek tragedian was, by contrast, no historian, and his genius did not lie in his ability to draw on historical events. For this reason, Herder argues that the origin or inspiration of a work of art must be taken into account when we judge its value. In other words, genius must be measured differently – Shakespeare's genius is a different kind than the one exhibited by the Greek tragedian.[42]

What then is the genius of Shakespeare? According to Herder, it is not unlike the genius of a historian. For it has to do with Shakespeare's ability to assemble the various characters, estates, and ways of life into a meaningful whole. Shakespeare "embraces a hundred scenes of a world event in his arms, orders them with a gaze, and breathes into them the one soul that suffuses and animates everything," Herder writes, echoing not only the aim of the historian but also that of the natural historian (FHA 2, 511; SWA 300). As Buffon put it in the *Premier Discours*, "one can say that the love and study of nature presuppose in the spirit of the investigator two qualities that are opposed: the grand view of an ardent genius, who embraces everything in one glance [*embrasse tout d'un coup d'oeil*], and the detailed attention of a laborious instinct that does not attach itself to any one point."[43] Shakespeare's genius lies in this two-fold ability, of noting every detail and ordering them with one glance.

While contemporaries may have been similarly inspired by the emerging historical consciousness and the increasingly differentiated world they inhabited, Shakespeare was able to *present* this multivalent world on stage in a *coherent* way. Thus despite the highly differentiated set of characters, locations, and events, Shakespeare's dramas display a unity, and it is in this that Shakespeare's genius lies. Herder thus locates Shakespeare's genius *in relation to* his time and place. Shakespeare's distinctiveness is not sought in either an a priori criterion (for instance, one that accords with Aristotle's account of tragedy), nor is it sought in a merely particularizing account of Shakespeare, i.e., in a character sketch or vignette, that fails to place Shakespeare in his time, and thus fails to see where his genius lies. The first approach (the approach assumed by the French) moves from the universal or a priori to the particular. In so doing, it overlooks or denies the particularity of the particular. The second approach, by contrast, focuses entirely on the particular, and thus fails to rise above the particular. Though the two approaches seem opposed, they share one important commonality: neither is able to mediate between the universal and the particular – neither is able to "embrace a hundred scenes" and "order them with a gaze."[44]

Herder's wording is telling here; as with Buffon, the emphasis is on both multiplicity and unity, on a hundred scenes and one gaze [mit dem Blick]. The implication is that the interpreter of a work of literature must proceed by reading each part after the other, i.e., linearly. The work, however, extends in many directions: each of its parts is in dialogue not only with the part that preceded it or the one that comes after it, but also with the opening as well as with the closing acts, for instance; the same holds for the characters, whose relations are not limited to those characters with whom they appear, etc. Thus although the reader proceeds sequentially, the meaning of the work, and the significance of each scene, cannot be grasped simply through a sequential reading. At the end of the reading, the interpreter realizes what unifies the various parts (which is not simply their sequential ordering), and must go back and consider every scene, every act, and every character's words, in light of this unity. The reader must, in other words, re-present the parts, which are apprehended sequentially, non-sequentially, i.e., as partaking in and contributing to a multi-directional and meaningful whole. The reader must therefore find in the sequence a non-sequential unity, a unity that is not determined by the way in which we apprehend the work (or nature), but that nonetheless determines each part of the sequence. Of course, the work of interpretation is never completed. The reader must continue to move back and forth between the parts, and revisit her interpretation in light of a deeper understanding of the connections between the various parts, and of the ways in which they portray the whole from a different angle.

This hermeneutic circle, which Herder develops in his essays on literary and artistic interpretation, is, I believe, the basis for his parallel notion of a "circle" or a "world" that he introduces in his essay on language in order to explicate differences between animals, and between animals and humans, and that he goes on to invoke in the *Ideen* in order to explicate the relations between species, and between species and their natural environment.

HERDER'S NOTION OF A CIRCLE OR WORLD

Herder's notions of a circle or a world may have been inspired by Buffon's notion of "climate."[45] In contrast to climate, however, Herder's understanding of a circle takes account not only of temperature and geography, but also of the ways in which an animal (or a human) reflects and is reflected in its (his or her) world. A circle, for Herder, is not simply an external cause that effects the development of a species, but an inhabited world, which must be understood *in relation to* its inhabitants and vice versa. Every essential aspect of a world must be taken into account, because through understanding this world, we understand its inhabitants, and through understanding its inhabitants, we understand it. Herder's "world," like the world of an author, does not simply affect its inhabitants (i.e., the author), but is also influenced by them. Put differently, a world does not have a solely uni-directional impact, but is a complex reality that reflects its inhabitants as much as it is reflected in them.

As noted, Herder first articulated his notion of a "circle" or a "world" in his essay on the origin of language and thus in response to the question posed by the Berlin Academy. Herder's aim in the essay was to develop a naturalistic account of the origin of language that resolved the difficulties faced by the naturalist positions of Condillac and Rousseau. It was Rousseau who first articulated these difficulties. In his *Discourse on the Origin of Inequality*, he noted that while human languages are artificial, and involve a certain amount of arbitrariness and convention, natural (i.e., animal) language does not.[46] Yet, if human language emerged from natural language, then, Rousseau surmised, it is necessary to explain this transition, this jump from the one to the other. Lacking any such explanation, it was not evident how a naturalistic account could be sustained.[47] Herder responds to this difficulty by following a different path than the one taken by Rousseau.

Rather than conjecturing an imagined past (as Rousseau had done), Herder begins by observing and describing what is before him,[48] with the aim of answering the question: what is it like to be human, and what might it be like to be animal? The first striking characteristic of the human being, he notes, is the fact that the human is "far inferior to the animals in strength and sureness of instinct, indeed ... he ... lacks what in the case of so many animal species we call innate abilities for and drives to art [*Kunsttriebe*]" (FHA 1, 711; HPW 77–8). Animals, by contrast, are born with specific strengths and capacities, which reflect and are reflected in their natural environment. There is an intimate reciprocity between the animal and its context, such that its abilities map onto what Herder calls the animal's "circle [*Kreis*]." He writes: "*Each animal has its circle* to which it belongs from birth, into which it immediately enters, in which it remains all its life and in which it dies." This circle corresponds to the animal's inborn capacities: "the sharper the animals' senses are, and the more marvelous the products of their art, then the smaller their circle is, the more limited in kind the product of their art" (FHA 1, 712; HPW 78). There is an inverse proportion between the animal's capacities (its "drives and arts") and its circle: the larger the circle, the less defined, the less focused and distinct the capacities; the smaller the circle, the more defined and focused the capacities. This is evident in the case of bees, for instance, whose circle is the beehive; within the beehive, their "drives and arts" are a display of precision and efficiency. Once the bees exit the beehive, however, their distinctive and focused capacities, which are perfectly suited for the beehive, place them in a precarious position. Their capacities, so attuned to the beehive, are inversely unfit for the non-beehive environment. The same, Herder notes, obtains for other insects, such as the spider, whose "world" is its web, and whose capacities are perfectly attuned to this world – but hardly beyond it.

When considering those beings whose "circle" is much wider, the opposite appears to be the case. In contrast to bees and spiders, animals that roam, for instance, are far less focused, their capacities are not as clearly determined for or by their very specific context. This leads to a general decrease in the power and efficiency of their senses in relation to their surroundings. As Herder puts it, "on the other hand, 'the more numerous the functions and the destiny of the animals are, the more dispersed their attention is over several objects, the less constant their manner of life is, in short, the larger and more diverse their sphere is, then the more we see their sensuousness distribute itself and weaken'" (FHA 1, 712; HPW 78). This dispersion of attention and weakening of the senses is most clear, Herder continues, in the case of the human, who lacks a circle or specific context altogether. The human being does not live in any one environment, but can inhabit a multitude of geographic contexts, and this is connected to the fact that human capacities are far less focused and not at all shaped or molded by needs that are specifically relevant to a particular context, or a particular function. Thus Herder goes on, "The human being has no such uniform and narrow sphere where only a single sort of work awaits him; a world of occupations and destinies surrounds him." For this reason, "His senses and organization are not sharpened for a single thing; he has senses for everything and hence naturally for each particular thing weaker and duller senses" (FHA 1, 713; HPW 79).

The difference between humans and animals, then, has to do with the human lack of a specific circle, and with what that entails in terms of innate capacities. In contrast to animals, humans lack "direction," which means that the human being has *"no drive to art, no skill for art* – and, one thing which is more especially relevant here, *no animal language."* In other words, the human being, in contrast to animals, is not born with innate capacities that fit its environmental needs; the human being, one can say, suffers from a poverty of innate skills, one of which is animal language. Thus while animals certainly have language, as Herder notes, their language is something with which they are born; it is an instinct. By contrast, humans lack innate skills, including animal language. This is the real difference, according to Herder, between humans and animals, and it is the reason why human language differs from animal language. The former is not instinctual; it must be acquired, or as Herder puts it "invented" (FHA 1, 722; HPW 87).

By focusing on context, and seeing the animal and the human in relation to its context, Herder is able to maintain a naturalistic account of language, that is, an account that does not rely on divine origins, without, however, succumbing to the difficulties faced by Condillac's and Rousseau's positions. By invoking the notion of a circle or a world, and seeking to understand the individual animal in relation to its world, to its lived environment, Herder is doing nothing less than "explaining the one through the other," i.e., seeing how the context is reflected in the individual animal and, in turn, how the individual animal contributes to its context. By moving back and forth between the animal and its circle, Herder discerns an indelible unity and reciprocity between the two, and, in this way, begins to recognize important differences between various animals and between humans and animals. These differences are not based on an a priori account, or a general perspective, nor are they based on the mere accumulation of data. Rather, the differences emerge through hermeneutic work, through seeing the parts in their relation to the whole and, in turn, seeing how the whole is manifest in the parts. By relying on this methodology, Herder does not need to offer a conjectural history of humanity, nor does he need to account for a "jump" from natural to artificial language. Rather, Herder's methodology allows him to focus on what is before him, and locate meaning – an indelible unity or reciprocity – in and through what he sees.

While Herder's introduction of the notion of a world provides a solution to the question concerning the origin of language, its significance goes beyond the 1772 essay. Herder invokes the notion of a world in the *Ideen*, where he seeks to develop a natural history of humanity, which commences with a natural history of non-human nature. In seeking to understand the structure of birds, for instance, he does not focus on one aspect of its structure, nor does he get lost in its various aspects. Instead, he focuses on the relation between the structure of the bird and its environment, its world. "The bird flies in the air," such that "every divergence of its form from the build of land animals can be explicated through its element." By contrast, "The fish swims in water; its feet and hands are grown into fin and tail: it has only little articulation of its members" (FHA 6, 75–6).

Just as in the language essay, so here Herder sees an integral connection between the animal and its environment. The relation is, importantly, not merely superficial. Herder's point is that the animal's *very structure*, its build [*Bau*], is in dialogue with its environment, such that this structure both serves its environmental needs and is served by its environment (FHA 6, 73). Furthermore, for Herder, recognizing the ways in which the bird is in dialogue with its context, and comparing it to fish and terrestrial animals, is an important means by which to discern how the bird both differs from and reiterates the structure of other animals. In other words, by grasping the bird in its environment, and comparing the relation between its structure and environment to that of the fish and other animals, one begins to understand not only the bird's relation to its environment, but also the bird's relation to other animals, and thereby discern both their differences and similarities, and thus glean a continuity in nature that does not imply identity.

CONCLUSION: HERDER'S HERMENEUTICS OF NATURE AND ITS IMPACT

Herder has been credited with providing a more "dynamic" view of nature, a view that ultimately led to the foundation of geography as a discipline in the nineteenth century.[49] Such a dynamic perspective implies, above all, a relation of reciprocal determination between the natural world and its inhabitants. While this perspective was most comprehensively carried out by Alexander von Humboldt, my claim is that Herder's notion of a world – developed through his hermeneutic theory and practice – played an essential role in the development of dynamic natural history. It is thus not surprising to recognize a fundamental affinity between Herder and Humboldt's aims.[50] What distinguishes Herder and Humboldt from their predecessors is their disinterest in classification, and by contrast, their interest in grasping a "world," an inhabited reality that is reflected in the very structure of its inhabitants. This enabled both of them to move beyond superficial descriptions of climatic influence to the view that the natural world is an effecting and effected reality, transforming and transformed by its inhabitants. Or, to conclude with Humboldt's own words:

> I was passionately devoted to botany, and certain parts of zoology, and I flattered myself that our investigations might add some new species to those which have been already described; but preferring the connection of facts which have been long observed to the knowledge of insulated facts, although they were new, the discovery of an unknown genus seemed to me far less interesting than the observation of the geographical relations of the vegetable world, or the migration of social plants, and the limit of the

height which their different tribes attain on the flanks of the Cordilleras.[51]

NOTES

1 This is evident, for instance, in the recent special issue of the history of science journal *Isis* which focuses on the influence of the humanities on the development of the natural sciences. Rens Bod and Julia Kursell, eds., "The History of Humanities and the History of Science," *Isis* 106 (2015): 337–40.
2 In their article on the history of science and the history of philology, Lorraine Daston and Glenn W. Most disagree with "current ways of conceptualizing the history of science and the history of the humanities," which "have imposed anachronistic divisions among the great regions of knowledge and thereby obscured commonalities that are deeper, broader, and more enduring than this or that case study about specific instances of interaction, influence or borrowing would suggest." Lorraine Daston and Glenn W. Most, "History of Science and History of Philologies," *Isis* 106 (2015): 381–2.
3 As Daston and Most put it: "philological practices of grammatical analysis, collation and comparison of texts, glosses and commentaries, indices and tabulations, and perhaps most significant of all, detection and correction of all manner of inconsistencies in form and substance, were (and in some cases, still are) the foundation for many scientific practices, especially in medicine and natural history." Daston and Most, "History of Science," 384.
4 Brian Ogilvie, for instance, argues that the work of comparing texts in the Renaissance influenced the work of comparing flora and fauna and developing taxonomies. Brian Ogilvie, *The Science of Describing: Natural History in Renaissance Europe* (Chicago: University of Chicago Press, 2006). Similar research has been undertaken to demonstrate the significance of note-taking practices in philology and the emergence of "field work" in natural history in the Early Modern Period. See Ann Blair, "The Rise of Note-taking in Early Modern Europe," *Intellectual History Review* 20 (2010): 303–16.
5 Not all eighteenth-century scholarship on this topic is recent, though the majority is. Two exceptions are Peter Reill's 1992 article on historical

thought in Germany and Great Britain, which offers a large brush-strokes account of the development of natural history, arguing that it must be understood in relation to the development of historical thought more generally. Peter Hanns Reill, "Buffon and Historical Thought in Germany and Great Britain," in *Buffon 88*, ed. Jean Gayon (Paris: Vrin, 1992). Hans-Dieter Irmscher's 1984 article on Herder's philosophy of history notes Herder's use of biological metaphors to describe historical phenomena, but does not consider whether Herder's methodology reflected insights gained from natural history. Hans-Dietrich Irmscher, "Grundfragen der Geschichtsphilosophie Herders bis 1774," in *Bückeburger Gespräche über Johann Gottfried Herder 1983*, ed. Brigitte Poschman (Rinteln: Bösendahl, 1984).

6 This recent work strongly contrasts with earlier approaches to historicism. See for instance, Friedrich Meinecke, *Historism: The Rise of a New Historical Outlook*, trans. J. E. Anderson (London: Routledge & Kegan Paul, 1972 [1936]). Though in his 1992 article Peter Reill (see n. 5 above) emphasizes the mutual influence of the natural and the human sciences, his earlier book on historicism does not. Peter Hanns Reill, *The German Enlightenment and the Rise of Historicism* (Berkeley: University of California Press, 1975). For more recent work which at least acknowledges the role of the natural sciences in the development of historicism, see Frederick Beiser, *The German Historicist Tradition* (Oxford: Oxford University Press, 2011), 6–10 and John Zammito, "Philosophy of History: The German Tradition from Herder to Marx," in *The Cambridge History of Philosophy in the Nineteenth Century (1790–1870)*, ed. Allen W. Wood and Songsuk Susan Hahn (Cambridge: Cambridge University Press, 2012). Beiser's changing perspective on the relation between historicism and natural science epitomizes these changing attitudes. While in a 2007 article he argues that there is a difference in kind between the methods of the historical and natural sciences, in his 2011 book on historicism, he notes that now he "reject[s] this distinction." The reasons are twofold. First, very few historicists regarded the methods of history as distinct from those of the natural sciences. And second, Beiser claims, "historicism *grew out of* a naturalistic program in the Eighteenth Century," namely the attempt to create a "science of man" by applying Newtonian laws and methods to history (Beiser, *The German Historicist Tradition*, 3, note 5, and 6).

7 Though one can argue that historicism and hermeneutics are very closely associated, maybe even identifiable (as Gadamer claims), I follow Beiser who distinguishes the two because many historicists were not hermeneutic thinkers, and many hermeneutic thinkers did not aim to formulate a general theory of history (Schleiermacher, for instance). Beiser, *The German Historicist Tradition*, 10. Furthermore, studies of historicism have generally not focused on the hermeneutic tradition, leading to this lacuna.

8 See for instance Thomas M. Seebohm, *Hermeneutics: Method and Methodology* (Dodrecht: Kluwer, 2004).

9 Gadamer is generally uninterested in examining scientific practices, and more interested in philosophizing about science more generally. Furthermore, his account of the emergence of hermeneutics is largely one-sided, identifying, for instance, romantic hermeneutics with the "aesthetic attitude," which Gadamer rejects in favor of his own version of universal hermeneutics. Gadamer's unreliable history of hermeneutics should thus not serve as a guide to its historical development. See Kristin Gjesdal, *Gadamer and the Legacy of German Idealism* (Cambridge: Cambridge University Press, 2009). For an account of positivist and post-positivist science, see John Zammito, *A Nice Derangement of Epistemes: Post-Positivism in the Study of Science from Quine to Latour* (Chicago: University of Chicago Press, 2004).

10 Michael Forster's chapter on Herder's philosophy of language, which also considers Herder's hermeneutics, is a case in point. Forster notes that for Herder there are deep and intrinsic methodological similarities between the interpretation of historical texts and scientific research. Forster's chapter does not, however, consider the ways in which Herder employs or develops scientific methodology in light of his hermeneutics, or the extent to which Herder's scientific knowledge (and his sources) may have influenced his hermeneutics. Rather, Forster simply emphasizes a methodological parallelism between the two. Michael N. Forster, *After Herder: Philosophy of Language in the German Tradition* (Oxford: Oxford University Press, 2010), 45–50 and 140–1.

11 See Rudolf Makkreel, *Imagination and Interpretation in Kant: The Hermeneutic Import of the Critique of Judgment* (Chicago: University of Chicago Press, 1990). Though Makkreel is mostly interested in

the first part of the *Critique of the Power of Judgment*, he does claim that Kant's notion of teleological judgment is part and parcel of the larger hermeneutic/interpretive work developed earlier in the book, making note, for instance, of the fact that for Kant the idea of life has a descriptive as opposed to explanatory role, which is what makes Kant's method – *pace* Makkreel – hermeneutic. See esp. 99–103.

12 On the reasons for Kant's rejection of the use of reflective judgment in science, and how he differs in this regard from Herder, see my "Understanding as Explanation: The Significance of Herder and Goethe's Science of Describing," in *Herder: Philosophy and Anthropology*, ed. Anik Waldow and Nigel de Souza (Oxford: Oxford University Press, 2017), 106–24.

13 What Kant designates as "proper science," in contrast to "improper science." For an account of this distinction, see my "Analogy, Natural History, and the Philosophy of Nature: Kant, Herder and the Problem of Empirical Science," *Journal of the Philosophy of History* 9 (2015): 240–57, esp. 251–3.

14 On the "liberalization" of the sciences, see John Zammito, *Kant, Herder and the Birth of Anthropology* (Chicago: University of Chicago Press, 2002), 222–3. Zammito is following Sergio Moravia, who argues that it was through this liberalization that anthropology emerged as a distinctive field. Sergio Moravia, "The Enlightenment and the Sciences of Man," *History of Science* 18 (1980): 247–68. Stephen Gaukroger's account of the "collapse" of seventeenth-century mechanical-mathematical philosophy demonstrates the reasons for this opening up of science, and the ways in which various thinkers responded to this opening up (above all, through the proliferation of new scientific disciplines and objects of study). Stephen Gaukroger, *The Collapse of Mechanism and the Rise of Sensibility: Science and the Shaping of Modernity 1680–1760* (Oxford: Oxford University Press, 2012).

15 Though modern hermeneutics is often identified with Schleiermacher, Herder is now recognized as a leader in hermeneutic thought and a major influence on Schleiermacher's hermeneutics and Romantic hermeneutics more generally. On Herder's influence on Schleiermacher, see Forster, *After Herder*. On his influence on the Romantics, see Michael N. Forster, *German Philosophy of Language: From Schlegel to Hegel and Beyond* (Oxford: Oxford University Press, 2011). According

to Forster, it is impossible to imagine Romantic hermeneutics (including Schleiermacher's) without Herder.
16 Georges-Louis Leclerc, Comte de Buffon, *Histoire naturelle, générale et particulière* (36 vols.) (Paris: L'Imprimerie royale, 1749–1778), vol. 1 (1749), 20. All references to the *Histoire naturelle* will be abbreviated (*HN*), followed by a volume number, date and page.
17 Buffon, *HN* 1 (1749), 16.
18 For an account of Buffon's distinction between "real" and "abstract" truths, see Philip Sloan, "Buffon, German Biology and the Historical Interpretation of Biological Species," *The British Journal for the History of Science* 12 (1979): 109–53.
19 Buffon, *HN* 1 (1749), 30.
20 See Philip Sloan, "The Buffon-Linnaeus Controversy," *Isis* 67:3 (1976): 356–75; here: 370.
21 Buffon, *HN* 14 (1766), 22–3. Quoted in Jacques Roger, *Buffon: A Life in Natural History* (Ithaca, NY: Cornell University Press, 1997), 293.
22 An earlier version of the *Pensées* was published in late 1753 under the title *De l'interprétation de la Nature*; however, the book as it is known today was published in early 1754 under the new title.
23 Denis Diderot, *Pensées sur l'interprétation de la Nature* (Paris, 1754), 6, paragraph II; *Thoughts on the Interpretation of Nature and Other Philosophical Works*, trans. Lorna Sandler (Manchester: Clinamen Press, 1999), 35.
24 Diderot, *Pensées* 18–19, paragraph IV; *Thoughts*, 37–8.
25 Diderot and Buffon also emphasized the role of the imagination in grasping whole objects. See Jessica Riskin, *Science in the Age of Sensibility: The Sentimental Empiricists of the French Enlightenment* (Chicago: University of Chicago Press, 2002), 98, 210–11. On the importance and widespread use of analogy in eighteenth-century life science, see Peter Hanns Reill, *Vitalizing Nature in the Enlightenment* (Berkeley and Los Angeles: University of California Press, 2005).
26 Buffon, *HN* 1 (1749), 50–1.
27 Buffon, *HN* 7 (1758), 22.
28 Buffon famously claimed in the *Histoire naturelle* that "a series of like facts or, if you wish, a frequent repetition and an uninterrupted succession of the same events, make up the essence of physical truth: what one calls physical truth is thus no more than a probability,

but a probability so great that it equals certainty." Buffon, *HN* 1 (1749), 55.

29 Zammito, *Kant, Herder and the Birth of Anthropology*, 229.

30 See Eugen Sauter, *Herder und Buffon* (Rixheim: F. Sutter & Cie, 1910), 6–11. Sauter's account of the relationship is, however, missing the first reference Herder makes to Buffon, namely in his 1768 essay on Thomas Abbt (Sauter claims that the first mention is from the 1769 *Journal meiner Reise*). Furthermore, Sauter maintains that it was through Hamann that Herder became familiar with Buffon. While this may be true, given the popularity of the *Histoire naturelle* and its German translation (by Abraham Gotthelf Kästner in 1760), Herder may have come to Buffon through other sources.

31 Zammito, *Kant, Herder and the Birth of Anthropology*, 332.

32 FHA = Johann Gottfried Herder, *Werke in zehn Bänden*, ed. U. Gaier et al. (Frankfurt am Main: Deutscher Klassiker Verlag, 1985–1998).

33 HPW = *Herder: Philosophical Writings*, ed. and trans. Michael N. Forster (Cambridge: Cambridge University Press, 2002).

34 On the influence of food and climate on the degeneration of species, see Philip Sloan, "The Idea of Racial Degeneracy in Buffon's *Histoire naturelle*," *Studies in Eighteenth-Century Culture* 3 (1973): 293–321. Thanks to Jennifer Mensch for directing me to this article.

35 According to Jacques Roger, Buffon's notion of "climate" changed over the years, such that by 1775, it denoted temperature alone. Roger, *Buffon*, 415.

36 Buffon, *HN* 4 (1753), 215.

37 Roger, *Buffon*, 178; Sloan, "Racial Degeneracy," 307–9.

38 A similar point has been made by Chenxi Tang, who argues that Herder's view of nature as "a dynamic system of forces" strongly contrasts with "a static surface lending itself to schematic description in the manner of Bergman, Buffon, and other descriptive geographers." Chenxi Tang, *The Geographic Imagination of Modernity: Geography, Literature and Philosophy in German Romanticism* (Stanford: Stanford University Press, 2008), 108.

39 Herder employs the same methodology in speaking about the natural world in *Ideen zur Philosophie der Geschichte der Menschheit*. Thus he writes that in order to understand connections between species and varieties, the natural historian must "explain the one through the other [*Ein Exemplar das andre erkläre*]" (FHA 6, 73).

40 SWA = Herder, *Selected Writings on Aesthetics*, ed. and trans. G. Moore (Princeton: Princeton University Press, 2006).
41 SW = *Johann Gottfried Herder Sämtliche Werke*, ed. B. Suphan et al. (Berlin: Weidmann, 1882–1909).
42 For a more comprehensive account of the main differences between ancient Greek and Shakespearean tragedy according to Herder, see Forster, *After Herder*, 172. See also Herder's critique of Winckelmann's assessment of ancient Egyptian and ancient Greek sculpture. According to Herder, Winckelmann's account fails to recognize a fundamental difference in the aims (and thereby in the genre) of Greek and Egyptian sculpture, precisely because it is divorced from the culture in which the respective sculptures emerged. As Forster notes, Winckelmann does not only fail in his interpretation of these works, but also in his valuation of them. Forster, *After Herder*, 173–5.
43 Buffon, *HN* 1 (1749), 4.
44 For a detailed account of how Herder's hermeneutics mediates between these two (insufficient) approaches, see Kristin Gjesdal, *Herder's Hermeneutics: History, Poetry, Enlightenment* (Cambridge: Cambridge University Press, 2017).
45 See Sauter, *Herder und Buffon*, 22–3.
46 As Avi Lifschitz notes, Rousseau identified three main challenges with the naturalistic account, including the problem of how convention can be achieved without consent, which requires speech. See Avi Lifschitz, *Language and Enlightenment: The Berlin Debates of the Eighteenth Century* (Oxford: Oxford University Press, 2012), esp. 78–80.
47 As Lifschitz recounts, "Rousseau's exasperation at the difficulties posed by the human invention of language became a focal point for conservative authors, from Beauzée to de Maistre," and ultimately led to Süßmilch's argument for the divine origin of human language. Lifschitz, *Language and Enlightenment*, 79; see also 83–7.
48 His intention is made explicit when he states that, unlike previous philosophers who have sought but failed to offer a causal explanation of various human and animal capacities, his aim will be to offer "observations [*Bemerkungen*]" which can at least "throw much light on the doctrine of the human soul" (FHA 1, 712; HPW 78).
49 On the emergence of "dynamic" natural history and its influence on modern geography, see Tang, *The Geographic Imagination of Modernity*, ch. 1. Tang maintains that Herder was the first to contribute

to the dynamization of natural history (108). Eugen Sauter similarly claims that Herder played an important role in the emergence of modern geography, above all through influencing the geographer Carl Ritter. Sauter, *Herder und Buffon*, 88.

50 Otto Heller, one of Humboldt's first biographers, describes the relation between Herder and Humboldt in the following way: "What Herder had enthusiastically attempted in the 'Outlines of a philosophy of the history of mankind,' Humboldt wants to do scientifically in 'Kosmos': to connect the development of the culture of the human race to its native soil." Quoted in Nicolaas A. Rupke, *Alexander von Humboldt: A Metabiography* (Chicago: University of Chicago Press, 2008), 71. Hanno Beck, another Humboldt biographer, contends that the title of Humboldt's *Ideen zu einer Physiognomik der Gewächse* (1806) comes from Herder's *Ideen*. Hanno Beck, "Kommentar," to *Ideen zu einer Physiognomik der Gewächse* by Alexander von Humboldt (Darmstadt: Wissenschaftliche Buchgesellschaft, 1989), 287–328. Annette Graczyk also claims that Humboldt's notion of a "general physical geography of plants" originates in Herder's statement, in the *Ideen*, that his goal is to develop a "general botanical geography of human history." Annette Graczyk, *Das literarische Tableau zwischen Kunst und Wissenschaft* (Munich: Wilhelm Fink, 2004), 290–1.

51 Alexander von Humboldt and Aimé Bonpland, *Personal Narrative of Travels to the Equinoctial Regions of America, During the Years 1799–1804*, vol. 1, trans. and ed. Thomasina Ross (London: Bohn, 1852), x.

3 Hermeneutics and Romanticism

Fred Rush

It is possible to divide the history of hermeneutics, broadly construed, into three main periods. In the first, "hermeneutics" refers to a loosely gathered set of practices inculcated and deployed to aid in the human understanding of texts or utterances taken to be of divine or near-divine origin. The main spur to developing such practices – practices that would not be needed, say, in understanding one's neighbor's injunction to keep one's ram tethered – is that human understanding may be systematically and radically deficient in its everyday use when confronted with divine utterance. In such a case, special training would be needed to decode texts, to glean esoteric from exoteric content. The dissemination of the results of such hermeneutics too might be restricted to an enclave of adepts; perhaps each act of interpretation would be *sui generis*, strictly unrepeatable, and only understood by the present select.[1] A second epoch in the history of hermeneutics begins, in Europe, in the eighteenth century and crests in German-speaking lands in the early- to middle-nineteenth century.[2] Here a concern to pivot cutting-edge biblical scholarship toward Protestantism conjoins with nascent social science and historiography. The religious component involves developing a more tightly structured discipline of reading sacred texts that answers to the idea that proper Christian devotion requires objective understanding by each for each of the relevant text. A serious reader of the Gospels will employ principles of interpretation that ensure that an audience is privy to the writer's intents from the writer's point of view. Matthew, Mark, Luke, and John step forward as authors in such an event, and one's account of what is communicated adjusts itself in terms of interpretative principles that take into account their varying styles and points of views. One is thereby entering into the mentality of the text as such and, where the text is historically or culturally distant from one's own point of reference, these conditions of its expression and making must be discounted for as well. On the social scientific side, anthropology, political theory, history, etc. were all greatly interested in their status as "sciences" correctly so-called, both because they posed for themselves questions of the systematicity and individuation of their domains and because they were concerned to secure scientific credentials in a way that preserved the autonomy of such disciplines from the rapidly advancing natural sciences. Hermeneutics for those reasons becomes concerned explicitly with *methodological* questions, and not merely with *method*, and it is with this self-consciousness that hermeneutics comes into being as a systematic discipline. In its third period, which extends from the early twentieth century to the present, hermeneutics increases in scope, graduating from a special science to an account of human self-constitution: the main figures here are Dilthey, Heidegger, and Gadamer.

This chapter discusses the emergence of the modern discipline of hermeneutics in the second period sketched above, concentrating on German romanticism, as found primarily in the work of Friedrich Schlegel. There are a number of challenges – one might even call them hermeneutic challenges – in gaining clean purchase on the phenomenon of the emergence of modern hermeneutics through romanticism. One difficulty stands out and is worth marking at the outset. One of the primary aspects of the emergence of hermeneutics from romanticism is an increased attention to the ways historical consciousness informs interpretation. The enlargement of hermeneutics from a textual discipline to a general account of human experience that begins in romanticism takes place against this background concern. Gadamer has exercised a retrospective formative power over the reception of the hermeneutics of German romanticism. Unfortunately, an appreciation on its own terms of romantic hermeneutics is possible only if one rolls back Gadamer's interpretation of it.[3] There are several ways of characterizing Gadamer's gambit, the most illuminating of which sees in him an acolyte of Heidegger. The broadening of hermeneutics into a general theory of experience, according to which the primary value of interpretive understanding resides in the self-transformation of the interpreting agent (and not the understanding of another), is an application of Heideggerian phenomenology to the problem of historical self-constitution. One might even go so far as to say that Gadamer undertakes to draft a methodology governing the planned but never-written second part of *Sein und Zeit*. In any case, the romantic conception of hermeneutics does not sacrifice objectivity in this manner.

STARTING OVER

The early German romantics were a loosely affiliated group of thinkers whose activities centered on the university city of Jena in the last half-decade of the eighteenth century. The central figures included the brothers August and Friedrich Schlegel and Friedrich Hardenberg, who wrote under the pseudonym "Novalis." The novelist and translator Ludwig Tieck and theologian Friedrich Schleiermacher were important satellite figures. Jena was a hub of philosophical and literary activity because Fichte had taken a chair at the university dedicated to "Critical Philosophy" just vacated by its inaugural holder K. L. Reinhold. Reinhold's early writings served to popularize Kant's philosophy, but his philosophical importance lay in his attempt to ground Kantian philosophy of mind in a unitary principle. Fichte continued this work in ways that depart from Reinhold, but one thing that he inherited from his predecessor was a tripartite dialectical basic schema for the grounding principle. Schelling, also an important presence in Jena at the time and a romantic of sorts, extrapolated this schema diachronically, such that dialectic develops in a series of necessary, interlocking steps of conceptual discovery and failure. This idea was to have immense impact, in turn, on the young Hegel, who lived in Jena from 1801 until 1807. Hegel probably attended Schlegel's lectures in 1800–1801, but for all his time in Jena he was remarkably distant from the romantics and their ideas. It also bears mentioning that Goethe had taken a hand in Jena, helping Schiller's installation there as a history professor.

It is fair to say that Friedrich Schlegel and Novalis comprised the center of the group. Both were educated in law, but were serious autodidacts in philosophy and history. Novalis only lived to the age of twenty-eight, dying of tuberculosis in 1801. Although there are intriguing aspects to Novalis's views on the cognitive and moral status of historical understanding, hermeneutics was not his main concern. Schlegel quickly became a leading literary theorist and a foundational figure in historical linguistics, whose early philosophical writings contain much of interest in hermeneutics. And, of course, Schleiermacher, based primarily in Berlin, is a mainstay in the history of the discipline. Wilhelm von Humboldt lived in Jena from 1794 until 1797 and grew close to Schlegel. When one looks to the romantic roots of hermeneutics, emphasis naturally falls on Schlegel, Schleiermacher, and Humboldt.

It almost goes without saying that Kant's thought dominates the philosophical scene in Germany in the 1790s. The minutiae of Kant's views in metaphysics, epistemology, and moral philosophy did not set the terms of argument; it was, rather, his general intellectual outlook. Specifically, Kant promised liberation from conceptions of epistemic and moral authority explicitly derived from Christian theological sources. The prime motor of this liberation was a radical conception of self-authorizing pure reason, with two main aspects: (1) that knowledge claims are constrained by the provision of a priori capacities of reception and conception and (2) that moral agency is defined by a universal yet self-legislated law. The specific form in which Kant delivered this package of ideas was almost immediately challenged as inadequate; although there were some Kantians "of the letter," the most powerful minds took themselves to be Kantians "in spirit." What this meant in practice is that, beginning already in the 1790s, there were several systematically framed designs to place Kant's revolution on a better footing. There were many issues on the table, but two stand out for special mention: first, that Kant had unwittingly introduced a subtle and challenging new form of self-skepticism, especially in matters of moral philosophy and, second, that Kant had radically downplayed the philosophical importance of linguistic experience. Schlegel addresses both concerns in concert.

The Jena romantics received Kant's philosophy via Fichte. Novalis especially was concerned to work out a form of transcendental philosophy that radicalized Fichte's notion of what constitutes proper philosophical grounding. Novalis argued that a rigorous understanding of the structure of consciousness required one to posit a pre-predicative, completely unitary source for what on the level of consciousness were basic, diverse elements of experience (e.g., divisions between subject and object of any sort, distinction between receptive and productive forms of intellection, between conative and cognitive elements in experience, etc.). This ground he called, as was the style of the time, "the absolute."[4] Any attempt to represent such a ground must fail, since representation requires duality of its component terms. Moreover, appeal to immediate knowledge that could reclaim the "knowledge" discursively is specious. Accordingly, at best the source could be indirectly "indicated" (*angedeutet*). By "indirect" Novalis had in mind forms of conceptual circumvention "in pretense" that reveal the impossibility of such representation within the representing act. The goal is to have as full a representation of non-representability as possible without self-undermining. In particular, the *experience* of so representing is crucial. An example of such a procedure is what Novalis calls "romanticization" (*Romantisierung*), in which one defamiliarizes what is familiar and, conversely, familiarizes what is unfamiliar.[5] To defamiliarize something is to think of it as an object to which radically different possible predicates are attached. To familiarize the unfamiliar is to take an item of experience that stretches the application of given predicates, i.e., that borders on the fantastic, and import it into standard modes of thought. Novalis holds that the two aspects of the procedure serve to indicate for any given thought that it only partially accords with the singular unity of the thing being thought. This indicates the absolute, not as some transcendent and everlasting source of meaning (Novalis is only mistakenly categorized as a Platonist), but rather as an ever-receding and merely projected genealogical origin of meaning.

For his part, Schlegel had little interest in the project of providing a transposition of Fichtean categories into romantic form. Schlegel took his initial orientation, rather, from his study of classical languages and literatures. Schlegel is one of the first in a line of philosophers whose Kantianism is greatly tempered by ancient Greek thought, and this is highly relevant to his development of hermeneutics. Schlegel had planned to translate Plato's dialogues into German with his friend Schleiermacher and, although Schlegel ended up not being active in that project (over and above lending his name to it), understanding texts in their own terms at great historical and cultural distance was central to his conception of understanding *tout court*. Schlegel accordingly incorporates a broad understanding of the role of interpretation in his general response to the problem of post-Kantian philosophical orientation. The main vehicle for this increase in scope is his account of philosophical irony.

The first thing to mark about Schlegel's conception of irony is that it is dialectical. Schlegel deploys slightly different vocabularies to talk about the elements in an ironic orientation toward a given object (e.g., a statement) but it is possible to abstract a common structure. Irony is a mental activity in which: (A) there is an element of identification with the truth, falsity, or pragmatic force of the statement; (B) there is a countervailing element of distancing from that truth, falsity, or pragmatics; and (C) the relation between (A) and (B) is one of equipoise.[6] The principal idea is that the optimal form of address with respect to one's relation to one's own subjectivity is to at one and the same time both feel the pull of a statement under its given specification and treat it under that specification as only partially given – as capable of other, perhaps even radically other, specification. This undercuts the univocity of the statement – its claim-like force, if you will. This accommodates best one's subjectivity because one is a subject only as one stands in relation to overall meaning – an absolute that cannot be experienced but only posited, its provision for finite, human experience modeled indirectly. It is crucial not to let this idea lapse into the innocuous. It borders on the obvious to say that humans might not exhaust possible meaning, just as it would be foolish to deny that any knowledge is provisional, as more may be found out. Such platitudes are not what Schlegel wishes to drive home by deploying ironizing protocols. The idea, rather, is that it is *part* of any claim, part of the action of staking claim, to be fundamentally tentative (i.e., not just tentative because there might be more determinate options on the horizon, not tentative in an "armchair" sense of there always being "out there" as yet unactualized relevant possibilities). To be fundamentally tentative is to carry with one as an agent that it is in the nature of agency itself to embed in any fixed stance with regard to the world or oneself the partiality of the claim. In other words, to say that no claim is fixed forever is to go only halfway, if that. The more telling formulation is that tentativeness is the way or form of claiming or believing.

There is much that could be asked about the scope of such claims, issues I leave aside here.[7] What is important to see at this juncture is that "irony" palpably is not an explanatory concept or procedure; it has no predictive force. Rather, it is an interpretative category; it aims at maximizing understanding of oneself and of others. The contention that irony intensifies intersubjectivity might strike one as implausible. But Schlegel is marking that ironic interchange brings with it the prospect of interpreting one another endlessly. This is so because the indeterminacy that irony introduces with respect to a statement can always be supplemented by other (ironic) statements.

Although Schlegel does not use the term "hermeneutic" to describe his view that interpretation is the primary mode of human understanding, interpretation is the mainstay of irony's semantic and pragmatic force, a force that is not limited to the self-understandings of isolated subjects.

SCHLEGEL AND THE HERMENEUTIC IMPULSE

Novalis and Schlegel invented a term to describe their collaborative work: *Symphilosophie*.[8] They did not mean for such co-authorship to seamlessly meld two voices into one; rather, the outcome of such collaboration was a system of what Schlegel called "fragments."[9] Single fragments were the responsibility of single authors, but in their ensemble fragments played off of one another in a kaleidoscopic, yet unified way. By "unified" Schlegel would not have meant "reduced to a common denominator or root"; rather, the form of unity is a dynamic "identity in difference," where fragments are juxtaposed so that they interact without threat of assimilation.[10] Schlegel analogizes this conception of a fragment in many ways – the one most familiar to philosophers is to Leibniz's conception of a world comprised of monads[11] – but the important point is that a fragment is: (1) an object of ironizing, crafted specifically to that purpose, (2) that is, therefore, a product of interpretation made for reinterpretation, (3) which interpretation and reinterpretation constitutes as well *Symphilosophie*, (4) and, thus, intersubjectivity, and, therefore, (5) sociality.[12] Such sociality consists in overlapping cells of interpretation; the issue of comprehensibility (sometimes Schlegel puts it in the negative, i.e., incomprehensibility (*Unverständlichkeit*)) is always in play.[13] Any shared meaning is but a special case of the more explicit challenges that attend understanding remote cultures or historical forms of life. They are all expressions of the absolute – that is, of the total range of possible human meanings. Schlegel's thoughts on interpretation are, typical of the romantics, not set out in a treatise. They are rather set out in their enactment, in what some philosophers of the period called an "exhibition" (*Darstellung*). There are three main collections of fragments from Jena romanticism that perform this task: the *Athenaeum Fragments*, the *Lyceum Fragments*, and the *Ideas*. Also relevant are the essays *Goethe's Wilhelm Meister* (1798) and *On Incomprehensibility* (1800), as well as Schlegel's writings in linguistics and philology.

The importance of interpretation for Schlegel must be understood in connection with three other aspects of his theoretical work: the operation of imagination, the significance of historical consciousness, and the nature of language and its relation to thought. For Schlegel, interpretation must take care not to assimilate the meaning of its object in terms of the prejudices of the interpreter.[14] *Interpretantia* involve exercises of imagination to understand *interpretanda* in their own terms. In such exercises, one is precisely not supposed to project oneself as the interpreter into the interpretative field. Put otherwise, the interpreter is not fated to have to discount interpretation in terms of effects that the interpreter has in forming what is understood in her own terms. Of course, there is a process of correcting interpretation that does involve such adjustments; however, there is no irremediable, objectivity-spoiling subjective interpretive "screen." When romantics like Schlegel speak of the infinity of interpretation they mean to highlight that any *interpretandum* can always provide more meaning, not that the *interpretans* is inherently suspect. Further, empathy has no role in Schlegel's hermeneutics; however, immanent interaction with the object is a desideratum for him – it is an ideal that may not be reached without remainder but to which one holds oneself, always at the ready to go one step further. Interpretation is highly interactive as well. In the case of the exchange of ideas, understanding is reciprocal interpretation on the above model – i.e., both participants attempting to understand each other, adjusting one's interpretative "stream" in real time and taking care to attempt to put oneself in the other's place, which place is not only changeable but is so relative to the other's attempt to understand one. The fragmentary nature of understanding contains a continuous requirement of nested interpretations. This need not converge on a single, mutually agreeable understanding. It is rather like dancing, adjusting one's step to one's partner's, where the aim is not to end up in a preordained, static place but rather to have a satisfying dance. Put otherwise, Schlegel advocates an open-ended dialogic process of coming-to-understand, not a process closed around a single principle or around the revolution of a complete series of possible understandings.

Schlegel holds that thought depends upon and is bounded by language;[15] moreover, he belongs to that strain of German linguistic philosophy for which more "indeterminate" modes of language, e.g., poetry, are basic and, in some sense, "better."[16] Being indeterminate in the way it is – i.e., expressive of a plurality of meaning that can never be exhausted – poetry is a more adequate vehicle for modeling the absolute. Schlegel is one of the founding figures of historical linguistics – in addition to excellent Greek and Latin, he acquired classical Persian and Sanskrit – and his interests in language, and more particularly in the language-thought relation are always historically indexed. Schlegel appreciated the power of history to mold human practices on its own and, therefore, did not suppose that a universal grammar undergirds diverse linguistic practices. To take stock: any thought is linguistically bounded and, since languages are historical entities, historically bounded as well. Since interpretation is a linguistic category, it is also so bounded. This means that the interpreter of a text or utterance will have to reconstruct immanently the social-historical context for the linguistic meaning governing the text and, in turn, tender judgments about the individuality of the text relative to that structure. Uncovering the particular, perhaps even signature, ways in which the text exploits the possibilities that the linguistic structure as a whole affords is a core interpretive task.

It may seem that Schlegel's account of irony enshrines final authority concerning the meaning of an utterance or text in its author, but that is not so. *Symphilosophie* does not support this Cartesian result; indeed, its conception of subjectivity is self-consciously fluid. This comes out vividly in its attitude toward theories of agency that define the limits or substance of action in terms of rules or laws. No rule can specify one's subjectivity for one, even a purportedly self-given one. I *am* a continual process of *becoming* according to the Jena romantics, so a rule is precisely what fails to capture my subjectivity. There is always a possibility of misunderstanding oneself on this picture, given the mercurial nature of the self, which can provide no stable point of self-critical superiority even under the best of conditions. Accordingly, it is possible that an interpreter understands better what she has interpreted than does its author. In like vein, Schlegel holds that interpretation must attempt to penetrate the surface of works in order to probe their latent, unconscious meanings.[17] "Unconscious" here has two senses. Because the content is latent, it is not content of which the author was explicitly aware at the time of composition. But it may also be the case that the content is one that the author could not acknowledge even when confronted with it. The thought that immediately suggests itself is that the meaning is unconscious in the first sense because it is so in the second, but it would be going too far to say that Schlegel is in possession of a *theory* of the unconscious. That said, the idea of unconscious meanings is extraordinarily important for him and is of a piece with his emphasis on poetry as primordial speech. This idea that texts worth interpreting are lambent with artifacts of buried meaning is of signal importance for later hermeneutics.

As we saw, interpretation, for Schlegel, is an infinite process. The claim that interpretation is infinite joins another aspect of Schlegel's thought, also previously mentioned, that is present in his linguistic writings: the idea that the meanings of single terms or sentences are dependent on whole meaning-structures, that is, are holistic. "Holism" of course is not a univocal category – there are many views on the structure and force of wholes upon their parts. The first thing to mark about Schlegel's view is that the part-whole relation is configured in terms of his account of fragments. Any whole will be a fragment itself with fragment-parts; consequently, the constitutive force of the whole with regard to the parts (and vice versa) will be radically non-standard even within the annals of holism. Any relative determination of a part in terms of its whole is also relative to that whole's being relative with regard to the absolute (and with regard to any greater whole, for that matter). This is just to say that holism and infinite interpretability are mutually limiting in Schlegel. This dyad interacts with an important component of Schlegel's linguistic theory: that grammatical features of a language, as well as its lexis, are aspects of developing meaning that the linguist must treat historically. The sum of this now tripartite schema is that ongoing, deep interpretation of works often unearths meanings dependent on the interaction of parts and wholes, in a fashion similar to the way a language is meaningful, i.e., not just as an accumulation of constituent meanings (words, phrases, sentences) or as a whole, but in the reciprocation of the parts and whole – in their structural interrelation. In other words, primary meaning involves the ways in which parts and wholes interact. Similar thoughts guide Schlegel's account of the importance of genres (and their mixing).

Last, even under holistic constraints aimed at deep meaning, what one may come up with – and what one has to be on the lookout for – is the possibility that the text harbors as yet digested or undigested pockets of incomprehensibility. Indeed, Schlegel's views on irony and the absolute foreordain some incomprehensibility, since all texts must reach for what they cannot adequately represent or express *in toto*. Explicitly ironic texts are more philosophical in that they mark incomprehensibility pointedly; they goad the interpreter into marking this as well. Put another way, pressing a work to reveal what Schlegel calls its "confusion" (*Verwechslung*) is a point of entry into its hermeneutic density, since this is likely to be a fundamental form of meaning of the work – at base, works will be most expressive of the friction between the absolute and emergent meaning.[18] Incomprehensibility is by no means a sign of semantic or stylistic deficiency; to the contrary, it is a form of meaning, and a basic one at that.

SCHLEIERMACHER AND HERMENEUTICS AS HERMENEUTICS

Schlegel's views in hermeneutics are not set forth as a disciplinary methodology. Schleiermacher is the first of the romantics to offer a theory of interpretation discernable as such, although he never published a work devoted to its study. He did lecture on the topic, however, several times over a period of a quarter-century during his professorate in Berlin. Several transcripts of these lectures survive, which form the basis for what we know of his views on hermeneutics.

Schleiermacher was trained as a Lutheran theologian and pastor and was taken by the difficulty of understanding canonical texts in ancient languages. But, unlike some of his predecessors in theology-driven hermeneutics, Schleiermacher was concerned to extend the discipline of hermeneutics to understanding *any* linguistic object at *any* time of its making. When Schleiermacher says that it is the task of hermeneutics to be "universal," this is primarily what he means. That said, Schleiermacher's paradigm case is how one understands a linguistic object at extreme remove, where shared intelligibility is difficult to establish and maintain. Schleiermacher holds that the apparent seamless ease of (most) everyday linguistic understanding masks difficulties of precise comprehension, difficulties that are exacerbated in the domain of historically and linguistically remote texts.[19] There is scholarly dispute concerning how strongly misunderstanding conditions understanding for Schleiermacher. German philosophy after Kant, from early idealism through Schopenhauer and neo-Kantians (*vixere!*) attempted to improve on what it took to be Kant's best thoughts by reincorporating empiricism. Schleiermacher is no exception to this trend, as is also the case with precursor figures like Herder and Schlegel. There are transcendental a priori aspects to Schleiermacher's work in dialectics and ethics, however, and they are present as well in his hermeneutic theory. If one takes it that this aspect is controlling, one might also ascribe to Schleiermacher the view that there is with every interpretative act a superadded subjective filter that renders the object in the subject's terms. Moreover, this masking of the object is very difficult to detect and perhaps impossible to extract. Misunderstanding becomes a constitutive and ineliminable element of understanding. This adds grist to Gadamer's mill. At times Schleiermacher appears open to a less stringent idea: that interpretative interactions are difficult, that misunderstanding must be accounted as a standing danger, but one that can in principle be overcome. There is ample textual evidence for the strong thesis on misunderstanding. The main evidence for the weaker thesis is conceptual, i.e., that Schleiermacher never draws the conclusion that there is a disabling incommensurability problem inherent in hermeneutics, a conclusion that would almost be self-recommending if he were to have embraced the stronger thesis. On the weaker thesis, which is closer to Schlegel's views, interpretation is never completed – there can never be a final meaning given to a text or utterance. But that is significantly different from saying that at each step of the way there is infiltration of *interpretantia* into *interpretanda*.

Schleiermacher distinguishes two main dimensions of interpretation, both of which must be investigated in order for an interpretation to be proper. The first is what he terms "linguistic." Here the interpreter infers from the use of words to the linguistic conventions that govern them, thereby establishing the semantic content of the text. The second dimension is what Schleiermacher calls "psychological." It has to do with establishing the author's intention in deploying the particular idiom present in the text. Investigating these two dimensions requires situating the text in the broader historical-linguistic environment in which it is written, thereby establishing the range of possible meanings of terms and text. Attention to the author's psychology charts against that general background of possible meaning the specificity of the actual meaning of the text. Only by means of psychological interpretation, Schleiermacher reasons, is one able to track non-semantic elements like force and pragmatics. Issues of style reside here as well. We saw these ideas already present in Schlegel, but developed less systematically. Schleiermacher also deploys a contrast between what he terms "comparative" and "divinatory" (*divinatorisch*) interpretative methods. The first method is relatively straightforward; comparative interpretation pertains for the most part to linguistic matters and consists in inferences of the sort mentioned above, i.e., from word-uses to rules in terms of which those uses can have meaning. Put in more modern terms, it is a form of abduction. The nature of divinatory interpretation is considerably murkier. It operates primarily along the psychological dimension noted above, i.e., it involves interpreting the specific authorial intent of the text. On the traditional scholarly understanding of the term "divinatory," this sort of interpretation involves empathic projection, not reasoning.[20] Nowadays, it is agreed among the best commentators that this incorrectly assimilates Schleiermacher either in terms of the debates in Berlin with J. F. Fries (where the idea of *Ahndung* is key) or anachronistically forward in terms of Dilthey (where divination is interpreted as a form of *Einfühlung*). Here is what Schleiermacher says on this count: "[t]he divinatory is the [mode of understanding *(Verstehensweise)*] that seeks, as it were [*gleichsam*], to immediately seize the individual by transforming oneself into the other."[21] The qualifying *gleichsam* should be marked. Schleiermacher later glosses this process as "making an educated guess" (*erraten*). On what basis? This is where the early German romantic idea of *Symphilosophie* does further duty. What Schleiermacher has in mind is deep interpretative engagement – through the target context – to the point that one can imagine that context from the point of view of a participant in it. This would only establish projective "co-habitation" with the author; one would not be precisely in her shoes.

Schleiermacher views interpretative activity as being holistic. In fact, he has a robust version of holism that operates along several dimensions at once: metaphysical, epistemic, and semantic. It has seemed especially remarkable to commentators that Schleiermacher endorses the view that words cannot be truly polysemic, i.e., that all meanings of a sign or term have a common semantic root, which root is still active in meaning.[22] Schlegel is also attracted to the idea. As odd as the idea may seem, it is possible to give it context in a topic already broached in this chapter. If one holds that the further back one traces the etymology of a term one has a more focal, poetic meaning of terms (perhaps even *Cratylus*-like mimesis of their referents), and if one thought that these etymologies were still covertly operative in the present meanings of terms, one might take the lesson that term-meaning must be unitary. In any event, one important result of Schleiermacher's holism is a particularly clear manifestation of what has come to be known as the "hermeneutic circle." To understand any bit of text is to understand it in its total context, context that goes well beyond single texts, texts collectively of that author, of that school, indeed, beyond texts in their local social-historical condition. But, of course, understanding those conditions is only possible by understanding their elements. This is not bothersome for Schleiermacher. Understanding is provisional, and the circle is but an artifact of being situated as an interpreter. It is advisable to read a text openly, a step-by-step process that establishes as much context for meaning as one is able going forward with the hope that once greater context is reached one can retrospectively adjust the details in terms of the added context (thereby generating a new, better context, and so on).

WILHELM VON HUMBOLDT AND "FIELD ROMANTICISM"

Humboldt was a polymath with an insatiable appetite for diverse realms of knowledge and experience. He was nearly incomparable in sheer intellectual *élan* for the time; only Goethe, Herder, and Humboldt's younger brother Alexander might claim more. He made contributions of the first-order to political theory, philosophy of language, and comparative linguistics, and his thoughts on hermeneutics are laced throughout these works. What perhaps sets Humboldt apart from other German romantics is that he conducted empirical research that stands to support what might otherwise remain mere speculation. This is true especially with regard to the interaction of his philosophy of language and comparative linguistics. More than even for Schlegel, philosophy of language becomes a matter of "first philosophy" for Humboldt, and it repays effort to pinpoint the philosophical kernel of this connection of it to linguistics and then transfer the results to elucidate his hermeneutics.

Humboldt was an extraordinary linguist. Not only did he develop in-depth knowledge of close to twenty languages upon which he could draw, he compiled (with the help of his brother's travels and funds) what was for the time the most extensive library in world languages. Unlike other romantics, Humboldt's linguistic interests and knowledge extended well beyond Indo-European cases; he had informed views about North and South American indigenous languages (a small number of the total, but by no means inconsequential) and South Pacific languages.[23] His work on Basque, which insisted against all rival accounts that the language was an isolate, still stands up today. His later work on the Javanese-Balinese language Kawi argued compellingly that it could not be easily assimilated to Sanskrit, a view still current. So positively impressive is Humboldt's learning and impact on the empirical side of comparative linguistics that its roots in a more recognizably philosophical approach to language and its role in cognition can be lost.

Humboldt had made an intensive study of Kant prior to his arrival in Jena, but the two most important figures for him are surely Herder and Fichte. From Herder, and perhaps from Schlegel and Schleiermacher as well, Humboldt takes the idea of "reflection" (*das Reflectiren*); the operative synonyms in Herder are *Besonnenheit* and *Besinnung*.[24] Herder's terms are difficult to translate; typically, they are rendered in English simply as "reflection" or "awareness." The verb from which both terms are taken is "besinnen," which in everyday German (both now and in Herder's time) means "to reflect upon" or "to recollect." The noun "Besinnung" ordinarily figures in stock phrases about losing or regaining consciousness. It is a bit less cognitive in flavor than the more prevalent philosophical term "Bewusstsein." The past participle "besonnen," which forms the stem of the more abstract (because less gerund-like) noun "Besonnenheit" has a more evaluative meaning: "moderate," "thoughtful," or perhaps best, "mindful." It is the word Schleiermacher chose to render σωφροσύνη in his translations of *Protagoras* and *Charmides*.

One must distinguish two dimensions of the meaning of these terms while also keeping in mind that the dimensions are not ultimately discrete. Along the first, the terms denote the primary mental process distinguishing human from non-human animals. Herder, Schleiermacher, and Humboldt abjure a merely additive view of human mental capacities, according to which humans have the subdiscursive capacities of non-human animals *plus* reflective capacities. Rather, human capacities are bundled in a specifically human way; they have no strict "modularity." This interpenetrating of capacities pertains to even the most primordial form of awareness. But, even granting this is so (or, especially given that it is so), it is very important not to recast simple awareness in *too* cognitive a way. *Besinnung* is the process by which humans first are aware of discrete bits of experience; it is the capacity for focal attention.[25] As such, it is the basic mode of reception, but it is crucial to emphasize that it is not, for that, passive. It is the capacity to punctuate the flow of experience in order to have specific experiences and is possible due to the human capacity to differentiate itself as a subject of experience from the experience to which it is subject. The vernacular and emphasis in the way Humboldt makes the point betrays his heavy involvement in Kant's third *Critique* and in Fichte, perhaps especially his substitution of *Reflexion* for *Besonnenheit*.[26] Such a power gleans pattern in an otherwise coarse, seamless run of experience, without however fixing it under a limited set of forms. By discerning units of experience *Besinnung* imparts sense (i.e., *be-sinnt*) to sensation. Subjects form themselves as subjects by forming experience. Synthesis of manifolds of intuition in apprehension according to rules is possible to the extent that the synthesis has a formal point of departure in the agent of synthesis that is in principle distributed across the combined units of experience.

The second dimension to *Besonnenheit* mentioned above pertains to an even more explicitly Fichtean heritage (although the idea is in Herder too): this sort of awareness is attuned to the vocation of freedom, both practical and theoretical. *Besonnenheit* is primordial human *doing*, and this is where the range of meanings having to do with composure and self-moderation take hold. Human attention is geared to taking the measure of experience; once units of experience are in play, there is proleptic comparison of them. By measuring unit against unit, one can experience a continuity of units. Unlike the seamless continuity of animal sensation, this continuity is made. Language comes in at just this conceptual point. Kant marked a potential problem for his theory of cognition: considered in themselves intuitions were strictly particular and concepts entirely general; given this, how can they combine in judgment? His answer was the Schematism chapter in the first *Critique*, where the imagination in its productive aspect is deemed able to mentally inscribe the universal in the particular and the particular in the universal. Humboldt faces a similar quandary. Reflection delivers comparative awareness of units of experience, which units anticipate reflective requirements that they be capable of comparison. But in virtue of what do sensuous experience and reflection overlap such that they constitute a unified structure? His answer – one might even say his recasting of Kantian schematism – is: in virtue of being embedded in language. Language at one and the same time is sensuous (i.e., is phonetic) and pertains to thought (i.e., is syntactic/semantic).[27] Where there is thought, there is language, even if that thought is internal to an agent. This may seem odd; how is it that thinking to oneself is talking to oneself complete with sound? Humboldt is willing to live with developing a quite abstract notion of the phoneme in order to accommodate this.[28] (It is here that emphasizing *be-sinnen*, by playing at detaching the inseparable prefix, pays dividends, given the role that the concept *Sinn* plays in philosophy of language.)

Accordingly, thought is dependent on language and restricted to its terms. Humboldt's account of the dependency of thought on language has immediate impact on his theory of interpretation. His empirical work in comparative linguistics points to extraordinary diversity in languages. Coupled with the view just considered, that language in its lexis and syntax determines thought, one may draw the conclusion that thought differs substantially both synchronically and diachronically, and with it culture.[29] This brings with it Schlegel's and Schleiermacher's concerns with misunderstanding in interpretation and holism. When such difference is in place, the project of understanding the meaning of a language – or, now, a culture – becomes a matter of on-the-go "field" reconstruction. To be sure, Humboldt does not think there is a "measurement problem" here, as do twentieth-century anthropologists like Evans-Pritchard and Geertz, i.e., problems of discounting influence of one's "home scheme" on the "target scheme." Nor is his holism so severe and self-sealing that he finds problems of mutual intelligibility insuperable. Still, understanding is a matter of explicit reconstitution of meaning as situated in the overall context of the culture.

A final point: Chomsky's *Cartesian Linguistics* presents a concise history of the notion of universal grammar, beginning in Descartes and Port Royal and ending with Humboldt.[30] That Humboldt held that there is universal grammar may disappoint (and may be surprising, given what we have set out above concerning his views on the plurality of culture), but it is doubtless a feature of his thought, diverging strongly from Schlegel. It is probable that the seed for the idea lies in the account of linguistic apprehension – reflection – canvassed above. That is, Humboldt's appeal to universal grammar may stem from the very desire to model Kantian materials (forms of intuition, categories) linguistically. In any event, while universality on this level will yield some interpretive constancy on its own, such a grammar would so underdetermine particular syntax and semantics (not to mention, phonetics) that less mundane forms of interpretation will still have much work to do.

NOTES

1 I am not suggesting that something more recognizably philosophical concerning interpretation cannot be gleaned from, say, ancient and medieval accounts of allegory. In focusing on more ritually bound

contexts here, I mean to underline the social privilege allotted to special categories of readers.
2. The first modern use of the term "hermeneutics," to my knowledge, is due to J. K. Dannhauer. See *Idea boni interpretis et malitiosi calumniatoris* (Strasbourg: Glaser, 1630). Philosophically speaking, it figures first in German rationalism, e.g., in both Wolff and Baumgarten.
3. See Kristin Gjesdal, *Gadamer and the Legacy of German Idealism* (New York: Cambridge University Press, 2009) for a point-by-point dismantling of Gadamer's interpretation of German idealism and romanticism; see also Manfred Frank, "Einleitung," F. D. E. Schleiermacher, *Hermeneutik und Kritik*, ed. M. Frank (Frankfurt am Main: Suhrkamp, 1977), 47. The best conspectus of Gadamer's thought is still Georgia Warnke, *Gadamer: Hermeneutics, Tradition and Reason* (Stanford: Stanford University Press, 1987).
4. *Novalis Schriften*, ed. P. Kluckhorn and R. Samuel (Stuttgart: Kohlhammer, 1960ff.), 2: 413 [=*NS*].
5. *NS* 2: 384.
6. *Kritische Friedrich Schlegel Ausgabe*, ed. E. Behler, J.-J. Anstett, and H. Eichner (Paderborn: Schöningh, 1964ff.), 2: 131, 149, 153, 172–3; 18: 538–47, 628 [=*KFSA*]. Cf. 2: 150.
7. For a consideration of this and allied issues, see Fred Rush, *Irony and Idealism* (Oxford: Oxford University Press, 2016), 48–58.
8. *KFSA* 2: 161, 164.
9. *KFSA* 2: 176, 197, 209; *KFSA* 18: 305; *KFSA* 24: 51.
10. *KFSA* 2: 173, 178; *KFSA* 18: 100.
11. *KFSA* 18: 42; cf. *KFSA* 2: 273–4.
12. See Wittgenstein's idea of a family resemblance or Benjamin's of a constellation. For an outstanding treatment of the degree of overlap between Wittgenstein and Benjamin, see Alexander Stern, *Fallen Language: Benjamin and Wittgenstein on the Aesthetics of Meaning* (Cambridge, MA: Harvard University Press, forthcoming).
13. *KFSA* 2: 363–71.
14. This is one of the key differences from Gadamer, for whom "prejudice" (*Vorurteil*) is a basic concept.
15. *KFSA* 6: 14. I adopt here Michael Forster's succinct formulation, which he glosses as: "one can only think if one has a language, and one can only think what one can express linguistically."

After Herder: Philosophy of Language in the German Tradition (Oxford: Oxford University Press, 2010), 16.
16 Herder suggests the same in his essays *Shakespeare, On the Origin of Language, On the Effect of Poetic Art on the Ethics of Peoples in Ancient and Modern Times*, and in the collection *Folk Songs*.
17 *KFSA* 18: 63.
18 *KFSA* 18: 227.
19 F. D. E. Schleiermacher, *Hermeneutik und Kritik*, ed. M. Frank (Frankfurt am Main: Suhrkamp, 1977), 92 [=*HK*].
20 See, for instance, that of Rudolf Otto, *Das Heilige*, 35th edn. (Munich: Beck, 1963), 173–82.
21 *HK* 169.
22 *HK* 105–10.
23 If one allows that Goethe is proto-romantic, he would qualify as an exception as well. See Katharina Mommsen, *Goethe und die arabische Welt* (Frankfurt am Main: Insel, 1988).
24 Wilhelm von Humboldt, *Gesammelte Schriften*, ed. Königlich Preussische Akademie der Wissenschaften (Berlin: de Gruyter 1968), VII: 581 [=*WHGS*]. In the *Abhandlung*, Herder uses both terms and there is some scholarly dispute concerning their synonymy. *Besonnenheit* may be read to be a more general term for Herder, referring to the complete complement of specifically human powers of awareness. *Besinnung*, on the other hand, is the specifically human activity of making sense through awareness, what Michael Forster translates as "taking awareness." J. G. von Herder, *Philosophical Writings*, ed. and trans. M. Forster (Cambridge: Cambridge University Press, 2002), 82 n.33. Kierkegaard deploys a cognate of the verb *besinnen* (*besindelse*). Heidegger's preferred use is related to these, but it will not surprise that it has aspects all its own.
25 *WHGS* VII: 581–2.
26 The notes in question, which editors entitle "Über Denken und Sprechen" (1795/1796), are written in response to Fichte's entry in the debate on the origin of language, "Von der Sprachfähigkeit und dem Ursprung der Sprache" (1795).
27 *WHGS* VII: 582–3.
28 *WHGS* VII: 94–6.
29 See *WHGS* VII: 22–32.
30 Noam Chomsky, *Cartesian Linguistics* (New York: Harper & Row, 1966).

4 Hermeneutics and German Idealism

Paul Redding

The hermeneutic and idealist traditions developed in close proximity in Germany from around the end of the eighteenth century, and while often in polemical opposition to each other, relations between them might be likened to those found between factions within some particularly fractious family. Sometimes hostilities cannot be contained in any way and the family becomes one in name only and all communication and interaction lost. But sometimes compromises are made. Relations can remain civil, and even productive, if certain topics are avoided.

The particular "family" in question here, I take to have its patriarch in the figure of Immanuel Kant as the initiator of a distinctly modern project – that of bringing philosophical thought back to bear on the world – that is, back to *this world* in which we act out our lives together, a project he conceived as involving a "critique" of the "pure reason" that can seem to be directed at some *beyond*. And in *this* sense we might, borrowing a term from J. G. Hamann, describe both hermeneuticists and idealists as having conceived of their own particular projects as "metacritiques" of Kant's, intending to free Kant's critiques from remnants of the other-worldly metaphysical tradition – that "purism" of reason – that still clung to Kant's attempt to escape it. While at the most general level each faction would accuse the other of falling short of the goal of applying genuine thought to the world, there would nevertheless be local agreements, alliances, and borrowings that rule out any simple list of differentiating factors neatly dividing the two traditions. One key focus for this chapter will concern differing stances taken to the relation of *thought* to the form of that communicative medium mediating the life of a community – its language.

In the following sections I start with the metacritiques with which Hamann and his successor J. G. Herder extended the idea of Kant's "critique" of transcendent metaphysics to Kant's own "critical philosophy," and then examine some of the responses coming from Kant and his idealist followers, especially those of Fichte and Hegel.

THE EARLY HERMENEUTICAL METACRITIQUE OF KANT'S CRITIQUE OF METAPHYSICS

In 1784, Johann Georg Hamann (1730–1788), a key figure in the so-called *Sturm und Drang* period of German culture of the late eighteenth century, fired the first shot in what would become a drawn-out dispute in German philosophy extending into the present. In *Metacritique of the Purism of Reason*,[1] a short article first circulated among friends only three years after the publication of the first edition of Kant's *Critique of Pure Reason*,[2] Hamann gave expression to ideas that would inform later hermeneutic thought: on the one hand they would suggest a language-based critique of the type of philosophical *rationalism* exemplified in Kant's critical project, on the other they would promote a range of more *empirically* based humanistic disciplines sensitive to the particularities of the cultures and languages within which human life is made determinate. While the originality of the role of Hamann here has been challenged,[3] for our purpose of understanding the hermeneutic thinkers' critique of idealism, as well as the responses of the idealists to this critique, Hamann's short text is a convenient place to start.

Hamann is probably most well-known via Isaiah Berlin's characterization as an initiator of a reactionary "counter-enlightenment" of the late eighteenth century.[4] Berlin's view has had its critics, some even portraying Hamann as a "radical enlightener" devoted to combatting the anti-liberal dimensions of the picture of "reason" promoted by other more mainstream "enlighteners" of the time.[5] Most agree, however, that Hamann's challenge to Enlightenment thought, here represented by the figure of Kant, was tightly bound up to his critical attitude to the Enlightenment's valorization of abstract reason over tradition, and philosophy over religion and literature, and that central to these critiques were his beliefs about the relation between thought and language.

Kant's *Critique of Pure Reason* had *itself*, of course, been directed against a certain rationalist conception of a "pure reason" that pursued a super-sensuous knowledge of things "in themselves," and with his "metacritique" Hamann meant to suggest that Kant's "critique" was insufficiently critical according to its own lights. It required its own *higher-level* critique. Thus Hamann delineates three dimensions of Kant's own *"Purismus"* – three lines of the *purification* of thought resulting in the empty abstractions of metaphysics. First is the attempt to make reason "independent of all inheritance, tradition, and any faith in them," next is its alleged "independence from experience and its everyday induction," and third is its purported independence from *language*, "the only, first, and last organon and criterion of reason, with no credentials but tradition and usage."[6] In *Prolegomena to Any Future Metaphysics*, Kant had toyed with the analogy of the architectonic of reason as akin to the grammar of a language,[7] and Hamann takes this analogy literally. In a twist that clearly paralleled Kant's idea of reason's own self-deception by the "transcendental illusion," Hamann had added that while being the *foundation* of reason, language was also "the centrepoint of reason's misunderstanding of itself."[8] Thus in his linguistic analogue of the transcendental illusion Hamann alludes to the type of empty metaphysics which "abuses the word-signs and figures of speech of our empirical knowledge by treating them as nothing but hieroglyphs and types of ideal relations. Through this learned troublemaking it works the honest decency of language into such a meaningless, rutting, unstable, indefinite something = X that nothing is left but a windy sough, a magic shadow play."[9]

Any chances of Hamann developing the ideas sketched and circulated in his *Metakritik* were cut short by his death in 1788, but the original piece was eventually published in 1800, a short time after the publication of another similarly titled *Metakritik* of Kant,

Understanding and Experience: A Metacritique of the Critique of Pure Reason, authored by Hamann's long-term friend and protégé Johann Gottfried von Herder (1744–1803).[10] Herder, a student of Kant in the 1760s, who carried the influence of his teacher's "pre-critical" thought and who was to play a key role in the emergence of the modern humanistic disciplines of cultural history and anthropology,[11] had not been sympathetic to the change that had given rise to Kant's more rationalistic critical project. Moreover, he had published in 1772 a work, *Treatise on the Origin of Language*, appealing to language as a precursor of thought in ways broadly similar to that alluded to later by Hamann.[12]

Herder continued the major thrust of Hamann's critique of Kant's transcendentalism. The human mind "thinks with words," thinking being simply "inner speaking."[13] Echoing Hamann, Herder describes language as the "criterion of reason, of every genuine science, as well as of the understanding."[14] In the central parts of the work Herder purports to give his language-based alternative account of Kant's transcendental aesthetic and transcendental logic with the implication that this architectonic of thought becomes radically historicized. It had been the invention of signs that are divorced from experiential sources of meaning that had produced the vacuous a priori systems of traditional metaphysics, but rather than attempt a "critique of pure reason," reason needs to "turn to the origin of its endowment ... and ask the question 'How did you come to yourself and to your concepts: how have you expressed these and employed, linked, and unified these; how is it that you attribute to them universal, necessary certainty?'" That is, metaphysics becomes a *"philosophy of human language."*[15]

In fact, Herder's *Metacritique* of 1799 had appeared toward the end of a series of increasingly acrimonious exchanges with Kant following Kant's negative review of a work that would become important in the growth of later hermeneutic historiography: the first installment of Herder's *Ideas on the Philosophy of the History of Mankind* of 1784.[16] Kant had condemned Herder's approach to history as an exercise in the type of dogmatic metaphysics which the *Critique of Pure Reason* had, Kant thought, put to rest. In particular he was critical of Herder's *explanations* of the development of human reason in terms of the interactions among *natural forces* that were regarded as continuous with those shaping the biological world. Here he was particularly critical of the idea that human progress from a state like that of other animals to one of rationality and freedom could be understood as the result of factors *external* to human reason, a theme developed in his later review of Part Two of Herder's *Ideas*.

When it appeared, Herder's full-frontal attack on Kant in the *Metacritique* provoked a vigorous and at times vicious counterattack by Kant's followers, especially by those Jena- and Berlin-based idealist and romantic thinkers who, under the influence of Reinhold and Fichte, saw themselves as followers of the spirit if not the letter of Kant's critical philosophy. It had been in the context of this reaction to Herder that Hamann's original sketch came to be published by a supporter of Kant in an effort to discredit Herder with the charge of plagiarism. But the war between Kant and Herder had introduced tensions within the allegiances of the Jena romantics themselves, many of whom had been very sympathetic to Herder's ideas.

Leaving aside questions of justification, what the response of the idealist camp signaled in particular was how central, by the late 1790s, the theme of the relation of thought to language had become for *them*. Thus the various romantic projects of the likes of the Schlegel brothers, Friedrich von Hardenberg (Novalis), Friedrich von Schleiermacher, and others had attempted to integrate a linguistic dimension into the idealist project. The background for such an engagement with language had been the effective collapse in the early part of the decade of *the first* phase of post-Kantian thought: Karl Leonhard Reinhold's attempt to ground Kant's philosophy *psychologically* in a representational theory of consciousness.

The fate of the Reinholdian phase of German idealism is well-known. Reinhold's work had attracted the rebuke of a Humean skeptic, G. E. Schulze, writing under the name of *Aenesidemus*, this criticism in turn provoking a long reply by J. G. Fichte (1762–1814),[17] which effectively initiated the next phase of post-Kantian idealism that would be centered around Fichte's *Wissenschaftslehre* project of 1894–1895.[18] For Fichte and his followers, Schulze's criticisms of Reinhold had brought out irresolvable problems inherent in Reinhold's idea of the "representational" character of consciousness, and it is not surprising that the post-Kantians, and especially the Jena romantics, would focus on the necessity of language for thought. Jena romanticism would effectively collapse at the end of the decade, but the Berlin-based Schleiermacher would go on to create an explicitly "hermeneutic" framework for the interpretation of texts, while Wilhelm von Humboldt would construct a distinctly Kantian theory of language that, in contrast to those of Hamann and Herder, would focus on its purportedly universal features.[19] In the 1800s, the idea of thought's need for linguistic form to be *determinate* would appear in Hegel's work as he continued on at Jena, although this was clearly an idea with which he would struggle in the attempt to integrate language into the systematic form taken by his idealism. Schelling, who in the late 1790s had developed his own version of the Fichtean program, had also engaged centrally with the issue of the embodiment of thought in language and other material symbolic systems, that would influence the hermeneutic thought of the philologist and Plato scholar, Georg Anton Friedrich Ast, the first to formulate the idea of the "hermeneutic circle."[20] However, of the idealists, it was Fichte himself who had first broached the issue of the relation of thought to language in the most direct way in an essay in 1795 that could be thought of as extending Kant's critique of Herder's "externalist" conception of the development of human rationality onto Herder's own turf – language.

POST-KANTIAN IDEALISM RESPONDS: FICHTE ON LANGUAGE

In *On the Linguistic Capacity and the Origin of Language*, Fichte describes language, somewhat conventionally, as the "*expression of our thoughts* by means of *arbitrary signs*"²¹ – an idea that seemingly could have been expressed by Locke or even Aristotle, in which the representational capacities of *language* seem to depend unilaterally on those of *thought*. However, Fichte's account departs from any mentalistic view when he refuses to treat language as the "arbitrary" signification of the mind's *natural* signs. He thus criticizes Locke's idea of a pictorial image as a *natural* representation because of the resemblance involved. For Fichte, a drawing of a fish, for example, is to be regarded as just as arbitrary as the word "fish": "whether signs have any natural resemblance to what is significant is totally irrelevant."²² One might think that this would lead to an *entirely* conventionalist account of language that could in turn be sympathetic to the determining role of a cultural "tradition," but this too would be subject to Kant's critique of the idea of any origin of language outside of reason.

Methodologically, Fichte's approach to the question of the *genesis* of language has parallels to Kant's response to Herder in his 1786, *Conjectures on the Beginnings of Human History*, although here Fichte's particular opponent is the *Populärphilosoph*, Ernst Platner: "One must not resort to hypothesis, to an arbitrary list of the particular circumstances under which something like a language *could have* arisen." Instead, "one must deduce the *necessity* of this invention from the nature of human reason; one must demonstrate that and how language must have been invented."²³

It is difficult to interpret Fichte's "just-so story" concerning the origin and growth of language that follows as living up to an account of how language "must have been invented." Fichte's story in fact starts with an account of natural signs understood in terms of causal connection – the roar of the lion coming to be taken by humans as a sign of the lion's presence. But Fichte is not interested in the roar as it comes from the lion, but rather as an *imitated roar* coming from humans who use it to warn others of the lion's presence. Such imitations can be compounded, as when an imitated *roar* is followed by an imitated *snore* that signals that the lion is sleeping, for example.²⁴ Such compounding produces strings of sounds with a degree of syntactic differentiation, in particular, that between subject and predicate. Here, the degree of grammatical *mediation* is taken as directly proportional to that of the *detachment* of individual sounds from their originally particularistic purchase on the world. With the "roar–snore" compound a type of "hieroglyphic" proto-language had come to exist, and the task was now to show how a type of teleological boot-strapping could lead from this proto-language into a "purely audible language" in which the mode of signification has become *fully* conventional.

Fichte's idea is that the conventionality of the sign relation implies its maintenance by a type of collective act of *the will*,[25] and so the iconicity of hieroglyphic language – what Locke had taken to constitute a natural sign – is eventually overcome in favor of the medium of the free expression of human thought in such a way that anything *non-voluntary* concerning the choice of the sign itself has been eliminated.

At the heart of this teleological account is thus an idea central to Fichte's *Wissenschaftslehre* – the conception of the human subject as an essentially *self-positing* "I=I," ideally free from external determination. Such a conception has the human being seeking "to subjugate the power of nature" in an effort to free itself from determination by what is given in experience as the *not-self*.[26] The approach here is clearly rationalist: one *subjugates* this external power, gains a power *over* the external world, when one integrates one's judgments about it into a logically coherent structure centered on the self-identical, self-positing "I=I" – Fichte's version of Kant's transcendental unity of apperception.

The hermeneutic thinker will surely here see Fichte's account of the *origin* of a rational human language out of the *Ur-Sprache* as question-begging. In this account it becomes evident that what is needed for rational language is not only a linguistic analogue for general *empirical* concepts but also genuinely "universal" ones taken to apply to "supersensibles" – concepts such as that of an enduring "substrate" underlying the perceivable changes of substances, or one adequate to the representation of the subject *doing* the representing – the "I." Here Fichte seems simply to revert to the traditional thesis of the *inessentiality* of language for thought. The concept of something supersensible, he notes, "must have been present before a signification for it could have been sought."[27] It is therefore far from clear that Fichte could easily accommodate the type of critique leveled against Kant by Hamann and Herder. Nevertheless, when Herder's "metacritical" critique of idealism appeared in 1799, the official response of the idealist camp was to come from a Fichtean intent on developing something like a linguistified version of Fichte's *Wissenschaftslehre*: August Ferdinand Bernhardi (1769–1820), who has been described as the "last and perhaps most brilliant representative of Kant's 'critical' philosophy within linguistics of the Berlin Late-Enlightenment."[28]

In a savage review of Herder's *Metacritique*, published in the Schlegel brothers' *Athenaeum*,[29] Bernhardi took on Herder on the very terrain of language itself, attacking him for his lack of a scientific understanding of language and for his ignorance of the developments in critical philosophy since Kant's *Critique of Pure Reason*. Bernhardi had already published a work on Fichte's language essay, and in the year following the Herder-review would publish the first volume of a work, *Sprachlehre* [Grammar], in which he attempted to join Fichte's linguistic thoughts to the central ideas of the *Wissenschaftslehre* in a more successful way than Fichte himself had achieved.[30]

In the 1784–1785 *Wissenschaftslehre*, Fichte had rejected any *external* account of reason by describing a *circle* "in which any finite understanding is locked," a circle that exists when "the faculty of representation exists *for* the faculty of representation and *through* the faculty of representation."[31] Construed in a psychologistic way, this would appear to be prone to the same problems affecting Reinhold's "principle of consciousness," but in his *Foundations of Natural Right* of 1796,[32] Fichte had discussed a subject's "recognition" of another's intention in that other's *act*, implicitly offering an *intersubjective* reading of such a circle. Bernhardi could thus construe Fichte's "circle," *Kreis*, explicitly as a *communicative* circle in which the active speaker, the passive interlocutor, and the presented state of affairs being talked about all found their distinct forms of representation.[33] With this, Bernhardi comes close to the idea of the "hermeneutic circle" later developed by Ast and Schleiermacher.

One important modification of Fichte's theory added by Bernhardi was the development of the idea of a "second language." In his review of Herder, Bernhardi had noted Herder's idea that the first objects of linguistic presentation were objects of sensible nature, "where the spheres of the singular signs [*einzelnen Zeichen*] are given as completely determined by conformity with the sensible impression,"[34] but such a restricted "semantics" is far from adequate to Kant's architectonic of reason. Thus in his *Sprachlehre* Bernhardi added the idea of a *second language* developing *out of* the first, a language whose "domain [*Gebiet*] is produced and enlarged by the self-activity of spirit itself" [*von der Selbsttätigkeit des Geistes selbst*]. It is this expanded circle that is the place of what he calls "*free* presentation," that contrasts with the "bound presentation" of the "first language."[35] This, of course, was a version of Herder's own ideas of how the coining of new languages could result in the *empty* vocabularies of rationalist metaphysics, but for Bernhardi there was no reason why *only* this negative consequence should be drawn. The idea of *working on* the "first language" in this way was further developed by Fichte.

In 1807, after the German states had been occupied by Napoleon's army, Fichte returned to the theme of language and its relation to a self-governing people in a series of public lectures, *Addresses to the German Nation*.[36] Here he took up the issue of the conditions that allowed a language that originally spoke only of sensuous things to develop the resources for thought about supersensible "spiritual" things – effectively what Bernhardi had discussed as the creation of *second language*. Fichte draws on and extends his earlier speculative account of language, but here with a more definite assertion of the primacy of language: since "it is very much men who are formed by language, rather than language being formed by men," Fichte asks his addressees to "join [him] in a consideration of the essence of language in general [*Wesen der Sprache überhaupt*]."[37]

What had distinguished the Germans from other European tribes, he suggests, was that they had continued to speak their original language without interruption, and in doing so had cultivated [*fortbildeten*] it.[38] In this process, particular words originally used for sensuous objects will be treated as resources for talking about supersensibles by a type of metaphorical extension – as, for example, when the ancient Greeks had employed the metaphor of *vision* for the conception of "ideas."[39] Fichte suggests that somehow such associations between the sensible and supersensible meanings contribute to the capacity to *use* such abstract vocabulary, and contrasts this natural growth of language to a situation in which an invaded people has imposed upon it the language of their invaders. Under such conditions, imported foreign words used to talk about spiritual matters will be bereft of those organic ties to the everyday life of the community, and thereby will become empty and dead abstractions.

With this idea of the meaninglessness of abstractions cut off from *linguistic life*, Fichte adopts some of the earlier linguistic critique of "empty" metaphysics found in Hamann and Herder, a critique that would also be found in the mid-twentieth century in certain strands of "ordinary language philosophy." But while with these lectures Fichte is often seen to be veering in the direction of a type of linguistic nationalism associated with Hamann and Herder, a careful reading reveals certain *cosmopolitan* themes in this work as well. The "universalising" dimension to the idealists' critique of the hermeneutic thinkers had not been completely submerged. An attempt to integrate both particularistic and universalistic dimensions here can be found in the work of G. W. F. Hegel (1770–1831).

THE EARLY HEGEL: AN ATTEMPT AT A HERMENEUTICAL FORM OF IDEALISM?

A prominent feature of Hegel's social thought was his use of the notion of *objektiver Geist* [objective spirit] to suggest the dependence of an individual's style of thinking on the historically and culturally specific form of life to which he or she belonged – an idea showing similarities to Fichte's position in *Addresses to the German Nation* and ultimately traceable back to Herder. It was a notion that was to become central to Dilthey's turn-of-the-twentieth-century contrast between the hermeneutic *Geisteswissenschaften* – the sciences of spirit – and the *Naturwissenschaften*, the natural sciences.[40] Thus, drawing on the early Hegel, Dilthey was to use the contrast of spirit to nature to provide a distinct epistemological frame for the *Geisteswissenschaften*, attempting thereby to isolate those "good" parts of the early Hegel from the "bad" systematic metaphysician from the Berlin period. Such a partitioning of Hegel's oeuvre continued to be employed into the second half of the twentieth century. Thus Habermas, for example, was to use Hegel's idea of "recognitively" mediated intersubjectivity to extract ideas closer to the hermeneutic tradition from Hegel's metaphysics,[41] as Gadamer was to draw on Hegel in his otherwise Heideggerian attempt to establish a distinctly hermeneutic conception of philosophy.[42]

Dilthey had appealed to Hegel's writings while at Jena, a period in which Hegel had closely aligned his approach with that of Schelling, who was pursuing his own somewhat "hermeneutic" approach to idealism focused on the role of linguistic and other forms of symbolism.[43] In his *Phenomenology of Spirit* of 1807,[44] Hegel was effectively to break with Schelling, and while some exclude this text from those Jena texts that *best* represent a type of language-based "hermeneutic" dimension, a sensitive reading of it can still find a rich source of ideas concerning the structuring effects of language on "spirit." Because Schelling's work of this period was effectively to take him *away* from the philosophical stance of idealism, we will restrict our attention here to Hegel's approach to language and understanding. A focus on his attitude toward the *Fichtean* notion of recognition will be a useful place to start.

Fichte had introduced the recognition theme in *Foundations of Natural Right* to "deduce" the social existence of humans within relations of mutual recognition as a necessary condition of their self-conception as beings with *rights*. When we look to Hegel's treatment of recognition in chapter 4 of the *Phenomenology*, I suggest that what we find there is not, as is often assumed, Hegel's own theory of recognition, but his *critical* appropriation of *Fichte's* account of the role of recognition in "self-consciousness."[45] And as the problems inherent in Fichte's conception of recognition were bound up with similar problems in his account of the relation of language to thought, Hegel's critical appropriation of Fichte's concept of recognition was to have consequences for the understanding of his conception of the thought–language relation, although this would only become explicit later in that work.

That Hegel has Fichte's self-positing "I=I" in his sights from the very start of chapter 4 is made clear by his use of this very formula. Here Hegel starts with the question of the nature of the "object" capable of satisfying some (self-conscious) *desire* [*Begierde*]. Nothing less than another self-consciousness, it would seem, could be an adequate vehicle within which one might recognize oneself *as* a self-consciousness.[46] Fichte had postulated that one subject, being driven by the need to free itself from the subjugation of nature, could recognize this rational drive in the actions of another such being, and this, of course, suggests that the latter could also so recognize the former. In short, each subject would recognize the other as an instantiation of the ideal self-positing "I=I" that resists external determination by nature.

Hegel brings out the contradictions in this scenario, as each subject could only recognize such an attitude as expressed in the *empirically observable* actions of the other, and here the problems of Fichte's Kantian starting point emerge. Kant's transcendental idealism posits an unbridgeable divide between a transcendentally located subject and the contents of the empirical world *given to* this subject. For Fichte's finite subject, any other subject must thus be empirically presented *as* a piece of nature to be simply overcome in its struggle for freedom.

The master–slave scenario that results from the struggle in Hegel's parable shows how the slave, in accepting the status of the natural objectivity of *non*-humanness in relation to the master's subjectivity, inadvertently stumbles on the *actual* path to a freedom that cannot be reached from the master's starting point. The ultimate triumph of the working slave over the master is thus more refutation of Fichte's idea of subjectivity than anticipation of Marx's idea of the proletariat as universal class. The master–slave scenario exemplifies the same Kantian based problems that are seen to affect Fichte's sketch of hermeneutics in the language essay. There he had stated that the capacity to recognize the purposiveness of another's action in response to one's own actions would lead to attempts to *communicate* one's intentions to another for the purpose of preventing and correcting their misunderstandings of the meanings otherwise expressed in the original actions: "How easy it is for me to misunderstand the well-intentioned act of another and respond with ingratitude. But the better I come to comprehend his intention, the more I will want to correct my mistake and, to this end, be better informed about his thoughts in the future ... Thus arises the task of *inventing fixed signs by which we can communicate our thoughts to others.*"[47] But for Hegel, the embodiment of intentions in empirical language cannot be *secondary* to their existence in thought. Thoughts expressed in language need the articulation achievable there *to be* thoughts.

This move toward an essentially Hamannian–Herderian linguistic thesis is clearly stated in the section "Spirit," where Hegel describes language as the *Dasein* – the determinate external existence – of Spirit, in a passage clearly aimed at Fichte's "I=I."

> Here again we see *language* as the existence of spirit [*die **Sprache** als das Dasein des Geistes*]. Language is self-consciousness existing *for others*, self-consciousness which *as such* is immediately *present*, and as *this* self-consciousness is universal. It is the self that separates itself from itself which as pure "I"="I" becomes objective to itself, which in this objectivity equally preserves itself as *this* self, just as it coalesces directly with other

selves and is *their* self-consciousness. It perceives itself just as it is perceived by others, and the perceiving is just *existence which has become a self*.[48]

The Fichtean struggle *for* recognition, the recognition of having one's will regarded as authoritative, had been resolved when one of the antagonists accepted the role of being an effectively *will-less* instrument *of* the other's will, but from Hegel's perspective, there is already a contradiction at the heart of this arrangement. The slave had accepted the role of will-less instrument of another, but paradoxically, this has to be seen *as* an act of *will*, as the slave had made a choice, trading freedom for being absolved from the immediate threat of death. Hence to be a slave is, in a contradictory manner, to continually *will* the state of *will-lessness*.

With this simple pattern of social life in place as a crude model of actual social relationships, we might ask after some of the minimum requirements for the master–slave relation to function. At the very least, it might be said, this institution would require the capacity for the master to convey the contents of his will to his slave – this community will surely have to be a *linguistically* mediated one, a consequence of Hegel's later explicit characterization of language as the "Dasein" of spirit. Looking at the roles of master and slave from a communicative point of view, we might think of these roles as differentiated by the type of speech act that each can employ. Most simply, only the master can utter imperatives. Only the master can *perform the speech act* whose consequence is that the one to whom it is directed *thereby* acts in a certain way, the way *specified* by the content expressed in the sentence. But the slave's understanding here gives the lie to his overt "objectivity." In needing to understand and act on the will of the *master*, the slave shows himself to be implicitly capable of the master's intentions. From a hermeneutic point of view, the master–slave institution will indeed be self-contradictory and, for Hegel, will be replaced in history by a more symmetrical one.

PUZZLES OF THE LATER HEGEL: METAPHYSICS OR HERMENEUTICAL CRITIQUE OF METAPHYSICS?

If the *Phenomenology of Spirit* brings Hegel's Jena period to a close, then it also seems to end any efforts to incorporate a hermeneutic dimension into idealism. Hegel's post-Jena philosophy is effectively that of his *system*, which falls into three component parts: the "science" of logic, and the "philosophies" of nature and spirit. While the separation of the *latter* two disciplines might give the hermeneutic thinker hope, given the clear distinction that is set up between the spheres of "Natur" and "Geist," *both* presuppose and are meant to be structured by the results found in his *Science of Logic*.[49] This work presents itself as tracing the self-unfolding of the pure "thought determinations." It will, therefore, from a hermeneutic perspective, appear to base the rest of his philosophical system on what Hamann called a "magic shadow play."

While the traditional "metaphysical" reading of Hegel finds no place in his mature philosophy for anything like a hermeneutic *metacritique* of Kant's *critique* of metaphysics, this traditional reading has nevertheless been contested by a variety of readers of Hegel since the mid-twentieth century. One of the earliest was John N. Findlay who, identifying certain parallels between Hegel and the later Wittgenstein, described Hegel's philosophy as "one of the most anti-metaphysical of philosophical systems, one that remains most within the pale of ordinary experience."[50] More recently, the Kantian "critical" dimensions of Hegel's critique of Kant's own residual metaphysics,[51] as well as the *hermeneutic* aspects of Hegel's critique of Kant,[52] have been stressed, contesting the traditional reading of Hegel. More specifically, signs of this hermeneutic dimension can be found in a preface written for a second edition of the *Science of Logic* in 1831, the year of Hegel's death and almost two decades after the work's initial publication. There Hegel notes that "the received material, the known thought-forms, must be regarded as an extremely important model or template [*Vorlage*], *even a necessary condition*,"⁵³ for the project of unpacking the logical structure of thought undertaken there. By this *"Vorlage,"* Hegel seems to mean what has been handed down to us in the logical texts of our philosophical tradition. Qua "logician," then, Hegel might be read as addressing the actual history of one form of those "cultivations" of natural language to which Fichte had alluded in his *Addresses to the German Nation* and that are understood as ultimately rooted in the language of the everyday life of the nation.

It is significant that Hegel follows these methodological remarks by what probably amount to his most explicit comments on the relation of *language* to thought to be found in his works, comments which seem to give expression to something close to the Herderian point of view. Forms of thought, he goes on, "are first set out and stored in human *language*," which penetrates "everything the human being has interiorized ... everything that in some way or other has become for him a representation."⁵⁴ Logic may be "natural to the human being," but languages, he says, differ to the degree that they provide logical expressions within which "thought determinations" can be expressed. Here Hegel counters any Humboldtian linguistic universalism, and points to the particular importance of *the German language*, with its developed provision of substantives and verbs.

A similar engagement with hermeneutic issues in Hegel's later writings is a lengthy review written in 1828 of the publication of Hamann's *Schriften* which Hegel uses as a context within which to say something about Hamann's original linguistic *metacritique* launched against Kant.⁵⁵ Indeed, Hegel's review itself can be read as a simultaneously hermeneutic and philosophical engagement with Hamann's writings.

Hegel devotes around three and a half pages to Hamann's "curious" but "clever" *Metacritique*, listing Hamann's central theses, and concludes his discussion with a summing up of his "concrete principle" which states that it is the nature of words that they "belong, as visible and audible, to *sensibility* and intuition, but also, according to the *spirit* of their employment and meaning, to *understanding* and to *concepts*, and are thus both pure and empirical intuitions and pure and empirical concepts."[56] Hegel presents Hamann's linguistic principles as analogous to Kant's transcendental idealism, and using one of Hamann's metaphors that goes back to an ancient Stoic saying on the nature of thinking, describes him as having made only a "balled fist" and having left it to the reader to "unclench" it into an "open hand" – that is, to reveal the properly *conceptual* connections in the text – indirectly suggesting that this is what *he himself* had undertaken in his own *Science of Logic*.[57] Even the late Hegel, it would seem, might not have been the type of abstract metaphysician that the hermeneutic thinkers had condemned.

In the foregoing we have focused on writings of a particular time and place, those "twenty five years of philosophy" in Germany,[58] that came to have a profound effect on modern European thought and culture. The dynamic between these two modes of thinking observed there, however, might be considered to have continued to operate well beyond that historical context, although perhaps not under these particular names, and to have contributed to the shape of philosophy and the humanities up to the present.[59]

NOTES

1. J. G. Hamann, "Metakritik über den Purismus der reinen Vernunft" in *Schriften zur Sprache*, ed. Josef Simon (Frankfurt am Main: Klostermann, 1976); English translation, "Metacritique of the Purism of Reason" in *Writings on Philosophy and Language*, ed. and trans. Kenneth Haynes (Cambridge: Cambridge University Press, 2007), 205–18.
2. Immanuel Kant, *Critique of Pure Reason*, ed. and trans. Paul Guyer and Allen W. Wood (Cambridge: Cambridge University Press, 1998).
3. See especially Michael N. Forster, *After Herder: Philosophy of Language in the German Tradition* (Oxford: Oxford University Press, 2010), ch. 2.
4. Isaiah Berlin, *The Magus of the North: J.G. Hamann and the Origins of Modern Irrationalism* (New York: Farrar Straus & Giroux, 1994).

5 See for example, Oswald Bayer, *A Contemporary in Dissent: Johann Georg Hamann as a Radical Enlightener*, trans. Roy A. Harrisfield and Marc C. Mattes (Grand Rapids: Eerdmans Publishing Company, 2012).
6 Hamann, "Metacritique," 208. While Hamann's metacritique is sometimes described as advocating the dependency of *reason* on *language*, this is expressed by saying that for him an individual's activity of reasoning is somehow dependent on the capacities making up his or her ability to speak the *particular* language that he or she speaks. He was thus a linguistic *particularist*, antagonistic to any ideas about "universal language" popular in the seventeenth century, and that some of Kant's followers would embrace.
7 Immanuel Kant, *Prolegomena to Any Future Metaphysics*, ed. and trans. Gary Hatfield, revised edn. (Cambridge: Cambridge University Press, 2004), 74.
8 Hamann, "Metacritique," 211. Hamann continues: "Not only is the entire faculty of thought founded on language ... but language is also the centrepoint of reason's misunderstanding of itself ... Sounds and letters are therefore pure forms *a priori* ... they are the true aesthetic elements of all human knowledge and reason."
9 Hamann, "Metacritique," 210.
10 Johann Gottfried von Herder, *Eine Metakritik zur Kritik der reinen Vernunft*, in *Werke in zehn Bänden*, vol. 8, ed. Günter Arnold, Martin Bollacher et al. (Frankfurt: Deutscher Klassiker Verlag, 1985–), 303–640, parts translated as "Selections from *A Metacritique of the Critique of Pure Reason*," in Jere Paul Surber (ed.), *Metacritique: The Linguistic Assault on German Idealism* (Amherst: Humanity Books, 2001), 89–130.
11 See especially, John H. Zammito, *Kant, Herder and the Birth of Anthropology* (Chicago: University of Chicago Press, 2002), and Forster, *After Herder*, ch. 6.
12 Johann Gottfried von Herder, "Abhandlung über den Ursprung der Sprache," *Werke in zehn Bänden*, Band 1. English translation, "Treatise on the Origin of Language," in Johann Gottfried von Herder, *Philosophical Writings*, ed. and trans. Michael N. Forster (Cambridge: Cambridge University Press, 2002), 65–164. Speculation over the origin of language had been started by Abbé de Condillac's "Essay on the Origin of Human Knowledge" in 1746 and had intensified over the second half of the eighteenth century.

13 Herder, "Selections," 95.
14 Herder, "Selections," 128.
15 Herder, "Selections," 90.
16 Herder, "Ideen zur Philosophie der Geschichte der Menschheit," in *Werke in zehn Bänden*, Band 6; English translation, *Ideas on the Philosophy of History of Man*, trans. T. Churchill (London: Johnson, 1800). Kant's two reviews can be found in Immanuel Kant, *Political Writings*, ed. H. Reiss, trans. H. B. Nisbet, second enlarged edn. (Cambridge: Cambridge University Press, 1991).
17 J. G. Fichte, "Aenesidemus, oder über die Fundamente der von dem Hrn. Prof. Reinhold in Jena gelieferten Elementar-Philosophie," *Gesamtausgabe der Bayerischen Akademie der Wissenschaften*, ed. Reinhard Lauth, Hans Jacob, and Hans Gliwitsky (Stuttgart: Friedrich Frommann, 1964–), vol. I,2. A partial translation can be found in J. G. Fichte, "Review of Aenesidemus," in *Between Kant and Hegel: Texts in the Development of Post-Kantian Idealism*, ed. George di Giovanni and H. S. Harris (Albany: SUNY Press, 1985), 105–35.
18 J. G. Fichte, "*Grundlage der gesammten Wissenschaftslehre als Handschrift für seine Zuhörer*," *Gesamtausgabe*, Band I,2. English translation as *Foundations of the Entire Science of Knowledge* in *The Science of Knowledge*, ed. and trans. Peter Heath and John Lachs (Cambridge: Cambridge University Press, 1982).
19 See in particular, Michael N. Forster, *German Philosophy of Language: From Schlegel to Hegel and Beyond* (Oxford: Oxford University Press, 2011), chs. 3 and 4.
20 Friedrich Ast, *Grundlinien der Grammatik, Hermeneutik und Kritik* (Landshut: Jos. Thomann, Buchdrucker und Buchhändler, 1808).
21 J. G. Fichte, "*Von der Sprachfähigkeit und dem Ursprung der Sprache*," *Gesamtausgabe*, Band I,3. English translation as "On the Linguistic Capacity and the Origin of Language," in *Language and German Idealism: Fichte's Linguistic Philosophy*, ed. Jere Paul Surber (New York: Humanity Books, 1996), 120.
22 Fichte, "On the Linguistic Capacity," 120.
23 Fichte, "On the Linguistic Capacity," 119, emphasis added.
24 Fichte, "On the Linguistic Capacity," 134–5.
25 Fichte, "On the Linguistic Capacity," 126–7.
26 Fichte, "On the Linguistic Capacity," 121.

27 Fichte, "On the Linguistic Capacity," 131–2.
28 Joachim Gessinger, "August Ferdinand Bernhardi," in *History and Historiography of Linguistics: Volume 2: 18th–20th Century*, ed. Hans Josef Niederehe and Konrad Koerner (Amsterdam: John Benjamins, 1990), 562. Jere Surber points to the role of Bernhardi, as well as translating his review of Herder and fragments of *Sprachlehre* in Surber, *Metacritique*. While the role of Berhardi in accounts of the development of post-Kantian idealism and romanticism had been long ignored, the importance of his philosophy of language has been underlined by Angela Esterhammer in *The Romantic Performative: Language and Action in British and German Romanticism* (Stanford: Stanford University Press, 2002), ch. 2, and Brigitte Nerlich and David D. Clarke, *Language, Action and Context: The Early History of Pragmatics in Europe and America, 1780–1930* (Amsterdam: John Benjamins, 1996), ch. 2.
29 August Ferdinand Bernhardi, "Verstand und Erfahrung. Eine Metakritik zur Kritik der reinen Vernunft von G. G. Herder," in *Die Athenaeum: Einer Zeitschrift von August Wilhelm Schlegel und Friedrich Schlegel*, Band 3, 266–281. English translation as "Review of Herder's Metacritique," in Surber, *Metacritique*, 138–56.
30 August Ferdinand Bernhardi, *Sprachlehre* (Berlin: Heinrich Frölich, 1801), partial translation as "Theory of Language," in Surber, *Metacritique*, 157–70.
31 Fichte, *Science of Knowledge*, 143.
32 J. G. Fichte, "Grundlage des Naturrechts," *Gesamtausgabe*, vols. 1, 3 & 4. English Translation as *Foundations of Natural Right*, ed. Frederick Neuhouser (Cambridge: Cambridge University Press, 2000).
33 Bernhardi, *Sprachlehre*, 101.
34 Bernhardi, "Review of Herder," 141.
35 Bernhardi, *Sprachlehre*, 101–2.
36 J. G. Fichte, "Reden an die Deutsche Nation," in *Gesamtausgabe*, Band I.10. English translation, *Addresses to the German Nation*, trans., intro., and notes by Isaac Nakhimovsky, Béla Kapossy, and Keith Tribe (Indianapolis: Hackett Publishing Company, 2013).
37 Fichte, *Addresses*, 45.
38 Fichte, *Addresses*, 47. The theme of the "Bildung" – education, formation, or cultivation – of the nation is central to Fichte's *Addresses*.

39 Fichte, *Addresses*, 48.
40 See, for example, Wilhelm Dilthey, "The Construction of the Historical World in the Human Studies," in *Selected Writings*, ed. and trans. H. P. Rickman (Cambridge: Cambridge University Press, 1976), 168–263.
41 Jürgen Habermas, "Arbeit und Interaktion. Bemerkungen zu Hegels Jenenser Philosophie des Geistes," in *Natur und Geschichte. Karl Löwith zum 70. Geburtstag*, ed. H. Braun and M. Riedel (Stuttgart: Kohlhammer, 1967), translated as "Labor and Interaction: Remarks on Hegel's Jena *Philosophy of Mind*," in *Theory and Practice*, trans. John Viertel (Boston: Beacon Press, 1974), 142–69.
42 Hans-Georg Gadamer, *Wahrheit und Methode: Gründzuge der philosophischen Hermeneutik* (Tübingen: Mohr Siebeck, 1960), translated as *Truth and Method*, trans. William Glen-Doepel, Donald G. Marshall, and Joel Weinsheimer (London: Bloomsbury, 2013).
43 Daniel Whistler, *Schelling's Theory of Symbolic Language: Forming the System of Identity* (Oxford: Oxford University Press, 2013).
44 G. W. F. Hegel, "Phänomenologie des Geistes," in *Werke in zwanig Bänden*, ed. Eva Moldenhauer and Karl Markus Michel (Frankfurt am Main: Suhrkamp Verlag, 1970), vol. 3, translated as *Phenomenology of Spirit*, by A. V. Miller (Oxford: Oxford University Press, 1977).
45 See, for example, Paul Redding, "The Independence and Dependence of Self-Consciousness: The Dialectic of Lord and Bondsman in Hegel's Phenomenology of Spirit," in *The New Cambridge Companion to Hegel and Nineteenth Century Philosophy*, ed. F. Beiser (Cambridge: Cambridge University Press, 2008), 94–110.
46 Hegel, *Phenomenology of Spirit*, § 175.
47 Fichte, "On the Linguistic Capacity," 124, emphasis added.
48 Hegel, *Phenomenology of Spirit*, § 652.
49 G. W. F. Hegel, *Wissenschaft der Logik*, in *Werke in zwanzig Bänden*, vols. 5 and 6; English translation as *Science of Logic*, ed. and trans. G. di Giovanni (Cambridge: Cambridge University Press, 2010).
50 J. N. Findlay, *Hegel: A Re-Examination* (London: Allen & Unwin, 1958), 348.
51 Robert B. Pippin, *Hegel's Idealism: The Satisfactions of Self-Consciousness* (Cambridge: Cambridge University Press, 1989).
52 Paul Redding, *Hegel's Hermeneutics* (Ithaca, NY: Cornell University Press, 1996).

53 Hegel, *Science of Logic*, 12.
54 Hegel, *Science of Logic*, 12.
55 G. W. F. Hegel, "Hamanns Schriften," in *Werke in zwanzig Bänden*, vol. 11, translated as "The Writings of Hamann," in *Hegel on Hamann*, trans. Lisa Marie Anderson (Evanston: Northwestern University Press, 2008).
56 Hegel, "The Writings of Hamann," 38.
57 I have explored this further in *Thoughts, Deeds, Words, and World: Hegel's Idealist Response to the Linguistic "Metacritical Invasion"* (Aurora: Noesis Press, 2016), 65–73.
58 Eckart Förster, *The Twenty-Five Years of Philosophy: A Systematic Reconstruction*, trans. Brady Bowman (Cambridge, MA: Harvard University Press, 2012).
59 I am grateful to both Michael Forster and Kristin Gjesdal for very helpful feedback on an earlier draft of this chapter.

5 Hermeneutics and History

John H. Zammito

"Historians feel more insecure about the scientific status of their discipline than the practitioners of any other field of scholarly research," Frank Ankersmit has alleged. That is the goal for this chapter, which explores the disciplinary self-constitution of history and the role of hermeneutics in that disciplinary constitution. We have just gone through a period of peculiarly high anxiety for professional historians. Peter Novick's *That Noble Dream* (1988) offered a drastic characterization of this crisis: "As a broad community of discourse, as a community of scholars united by common aims, common standards, and common purposes, the discipline of history had ceased to exist." Ankersmit concurs: "history has irreparably lost what made it into a discipline." Raymond Martin acknowledges, "we still do not know how historians do, or should, decide among competing historical interpretations."[1]

The gallingly frequent allegation has been that historians appear constitutionally incapable of theoretical self-scrutiny.[2] They have reveled in their craftwork, their "archive-fetishism," their insistence upon the sufficiency of source-criticism in the crudest embrace of empiricism. As much as they have celebrated their autonomy from other disciplines – and especially from philosophy or social theory – they have also insisted that they practice "science" of a sort – though, as Ankersmit pointed out in the passage above, they are also anxiously aware that it is hard to make out history to be "science" at all. But we must be extremely careful about what "science" means, here. We have to shake off two formidable but unreasonable senses of "science": first, the ancient but lingering sense of *scientia* or *episteme*, the ideal of necessary and universal knowledge, which captivated the Western philosophical imagination until well into the modern period; and, second, the notion of science propagated in the positivist age from Comte (and Kant) through (neo-Kantianism and) logical positivism. The work of the last fifty years has demolished the unified theory of "science" which logical positivism/empiricism *projected* upon actual natural-scientific practices and with which it *presumed* to discredit the very idea of historical science. Willard van Orman Quine raised some trenchant philosophical objections already in the early 1950s, and after Thomas Kuhn's *Structure of Scientific Revolutions* (1962), the whole "received view" of science came unraveled. No unified theory of science – and *a fortiori* not the positivist one – stands. In its place we have a far more disunified, situated, and contingent theory of empirical inquiry that does not begin by consigning historical inquiry to essential inferiority, as was the case with positivism.[3]

My argument is that, from the outset, disciplinary history has had a very hard time with philosophy and its projections of "proper science." A consideration of the last two centuries shows repeated instances of philosophy coming forward to serve as conceptual warden for history, usually without invitation. Richard Evans makes the essential point: "very few historians have possessed the necessary expertise to discuss the theory of history at a level that a trained philosopher would consider acceptable," and, consequently, "some have indeed argued that the nature of historical explanation is best left to philosophers." Yet, as I once put it and still believe, "Historians qua historians are not philosophers, and it does not serve them well either to turn into philosophers or to despair of their projects for not being philosophy."[4] But that does not mean the discipline may wallow in theoretical naivety.

As history established itself as a discipline in Germany between the late eighteenth and the mid-nineteenth century, it struggled explicitly to justify itself as a "scientific" practice.[5] It achieved "paradigmatic" form in the mid-nineteenth century, with Leopold von Ranke and his school. The impact of Ranke's historical seminar, of his philological method, and of his emphasis on archival research, stamped the balance of historical practice irrevocably.[6] This was above all the case with the reception of two of his most famous phrases: the claim that the task of history was "to show how it really happened [*zeigen, wie es eigentlich gewesen*]" and the desire to "erase myself and just let the things speak for themselves."[7] Almost every major German historian of the nineteenth century passed through Ranke's seminar. He taught it until 1871, creating a professional cadre of historians who revered him as the "father of scientific history." Yet they perpetuated only a partial legacy of his complex practice and theory. The historical profession came to think that archival access and source criticism resolved all problems of historical interpretation. Routinization (and complacency) of disciplinary history has also characterized the American reception of Ranke and "scientific" history, as canonized with the establishment of the American Historical Association.[8] Indeed, for many professional historians, Ranke could even appear, quite falsely, to be a "positivist."

As Wilhelm Dilthey already realized, the discipline of history has need of an alternative tradition of discourse upon which to found its theoretical integrity. He sought it above all in the hermeneutical tradition he identified with Friedrich Schleiermacher. But he also recognized Johann Gottfried Herder as a founding figure.[9] Strikingly, neither Schleiermacher nor Herder were members of the academic guild of historians. Nor were two other figures who proved central to Dilthey's reconstruction: Wilhelm von Humboldt and G. W. F. Hegel. Above all, in contrast to Ranke, yet another figure has emerged as crucial in contemporary reinterpretation of the disciplinary constitution of history: Johann Gustav Droysen.[10] Though his *Historik* was largely overlooked in the time of Ranke's preeminence, Droysen proved the foremost German theoretician of historical method in the nineteenth century.[11] He has become the object of intense study recently, in line with efforts theoretically to ground current disciplinary practice. Thus, Jörn Rüsen has called Droysen "the greatest theorist of history in the German language," and Ernst Rothacker has labeled Droysen's *Historik* the "most influential document on the logic of the science of history."[12]

I propose to reconstruct Droysen's hermeneutical legacy for disciplinary history, in explicit displacement of the conventional concentration on Ranke. Indeed, I will suggest that he is more important for us today than even Dilthey, whose concern to establish a disciplinary tradition just served as my point of departure. Moreover, and ironically, while Dilthey privileged Schleiermacher as the founder of the hermeneutical method that would shape history, Michael Forster has urged that much about historical hermeneutics really needs to be traced to one of Schleiermacher's own sources, Johann Gottfried Herder.[13] The path of Droysen's own intellectual formation confirms this reorientation of historical reconstruction. Droysen fashioned his theory looking back not only to his mentor August Boeckh – and, only indirectly through him, to Schleiermacher – but also, and crucially, to Humboldt and Hegel and Herder behind them. This is the course of disciplinary constitution that Jörn Rüsen has recently reconstructed as a theoretically sophisticated legacy for contemporary history, and that I here intend to retrieve and affirm.

THE EMERGENCE OF DISCIPLINARY HISTORY AND THE ROLE OF HERDER

When history was only a discourse and not yet a discipline, already Aristotle notoriously disparaged it, not only vis-à-vis philosophy but even vis-à-vis poetry, for its failure to achieve the vantage of the universal. From Aristotle in antiquity to Christian Wolff and Immanuel Kant in eighteenth-century Germany, historical knowledge (*cognitio historica*), as merely particular, contingent, and conjectural, was deemed drastically inferior to *philosophical knowledge* from first, universal principles.[14] The disciplinary construction of history in the late eighteenth century aimed to justify the scientific status of history. But how was it possible, as Frederick Beiser puts it aptly, "to vindicate the scientific status of history in the face of Kant, the Enlightenment and the rationalist legacy?"[15] Instead of embracing the tradition of *scientia,* historians sought to establish disciplinary warrant via an accentuation of empirical research methodology, of "source-criticism."

Disciplinary history arose in late eighteenth-century Germany by drawing upon the methodological insights of three other, more established disciplines: first, classical philology, especially Johann Joachim Winckelmann's recovery of Greek sculpture and Christian Gottlob Heyne's archaeological concept of the *Totalhabitus;* second, biblical criticism, especially the historicization of the Bible from Richard Simon and Spinoza to Johann David Michaelis; and, finally, developmental linguistics, the recognition of language "families" and genealogical theories of their relation, significantly influenced by Leibniz. The new historical methodology found its most powerful articulation in the writings of the Göttingen professor Johann Christoph Gatterer during the 1760s. In 1767, in the inaugural volume of *Allgemeine historische Bibliothek,* published by the new Royal Institute for History at Göttingen, Gatterer articulated the ideal of "pragmatic history" that, as Peter Hanns Reill has established, became commonplace among the new professional historians at the Royal Institute.[16]

From a distance Herder followed this emergent historical discourse closely in the 1760s.[17] His first methodological reflections on the field date to 1767 or 1768, when he composed a letter to Gatterer for publication in the *Allgemeine historische Bibliothek.* He never sent it but it remains a very clear and imposing statement of his theory of history. It stressed the perspectival nature of human understanding: "every human eye has its own angle of vision: every one makes a projection of the object before him after his own fashion." Two observers might, everything being equal, offer pretty much the same *description* of an event, but their *judgments* about it would be far from uniform, but instead "each after the situation of his mind and after the preferred paths of his spirit of reflection."[18] In a parallel essay, he drew disciplinary implications: "Every philosopher sees things from his own point of view. How depressing to have to demonstrate that historical knowledge does not bring shame upon a philosopher."[19]

The crucial innovation in Herder's hermeneutics was to recognize the recalcitrance of the subject, not simply of the object, in interpretation. He was both aware of the fixity of the historian as subject and intensely committed to the possibility of transcending this fixity:

> to liberate oneself from this innate and enculturated idiosyncrasy, to develop distance from the irregularities of a too singular situation and ultimately to be able to relish, without [the intervention of] national, temporal and personal taste, the beautiful as it presents itself in all times and all peoples and all arts and all forms of taste [...] to taste it purely and to be sensitive to it. Happy he who can so relish![20]

Herder asserted that history must take as its object epochs, peoples, or cultures as individualities to be judged according to principles of their own articulation, not some abstract and external standard imposed from the historian's own time. "Let each moment speak for itself, and explicate itself, where possible, in its location, without our dragging in an explanation from a favorite region."[21] In *Yet Another Philosophy of History* Herder put it in its most memorable form: "every nation has its own center of well-being within itself, just as every globe has its center of gravity."[22] To embrace the idea of individual forms as the proper object of historical inquiry meant for Herder recognizing that a nation "will create its drama out of its own history, the spirit of its age, customs, views, language, national attitudes, traditions, and pastimes."[23] This indwelling spirit informed every artifact of that individual people, so that it could be read out of all forms of its practice – from folkways to political constitutions, from musical forms to business contracts. But the highest and most revealing form in which that spirit would be articulated would be literature and especially poetry.

For Herder, the uniqueness of an author was always a function of his historical situatedness. This methodological insight was clearly articulated in his 1767 essay on Thomas Abbt. "*That* commentator of an author is for me the greatest who does not *transfigure* him according to the taste of the current century but who explains him in terms of all the nuances of his own time, and thereupon elaborates." He explained more concretely what this meant:

> It is most essential that one draw from an author what belonged to *his time* or *the world preceding him*, and what he leaves behind to *posterity*. He carries the chains of his epoch, to whom he presents his book: he stands in his century, as a tree in the terrain in which it is rooted, from which it draws its sap [...] The more he makes himself of service to his own world, the more he must accommodate himself to it, and he must penetrate into its ways of thinking, in order to shape them. In the measure that he is formed according to that taste – and the first form never allows itself totally to be revised – every great writer *must* carry in him the birthmarks of his time.

Herder concluded emphatically: "That *interpreter* [*Erklärer*] is the man for me who marks the boundaries of the background, the times and the posterity of an author: what the first offered him, what the second helped or hindered, what the third carried further."[24]

It was just this approach that distinguished Herder's 1773 essay on Shakespeare, one of the landmarks of historical hermeneutics.[25] He had a quite "presentist" goal in approaching Shakespeare: to "explain him, feel him as he is, use him, and – if possible – make him alive for us in Germany." Registering historical distance was the essential first step in interpretation. "Great heavens, how far we are from Greece! History, tradition, customs, religion, the spirit of the time, of the nation, of emotion, or language – how far from Greece!" "In Greece drama developed in a way in which it could not develop in the north [...] Therefore in the north it is not and cannot be what it was in Greece." Thus, "if Sophocles represented and taught and moved and educated Greeks, Shakespeare taught and moved and educated northern men!" It was Shakespeare's project to "create a dramatic oeuvre out of this raw material as naturally, impressively, and originally as the Greeks did from theirs." Thus, Herder concluded, what each great artistic genius does is to demonstrate *situated* "authenticity, truth, and historical creativity." This insight opened the horizon for Herder's interpretation of Shakespeare: "I am closer to Shakespeare than to the Greek." And that was the lesson for the historical interpreter to take up: "How much it could contribute to our reading of history, our philosophy of the human soul, our drama!"

The most decisive idea behind Herder's conceptualization of historical interpretation was *organicism*, the idea that works of human purpose had a structure analogous to that of living organisms, in which the various parts were coordinated within a whole through which alone their particular nature and function became comprehensible. Herder helped establish in German the terms for a distinctive and as it were living "spirit" unique to a people, a nation, an epoch: *Volksgeist, nationaler Geist, Zeitgeist*. The analogy to organism, especially to plant life, could be carried further to encompass the idea of a process of development, and to conceive growth, maturity and decline of forms of human action. Combining organicism with this idea of development ("epigenesis"), Herder could then recognize higher order cumulation in history. Accordingly, historical theorists starting with Wilhelm Dilthey deemed Herder a progenitor of their practice. Indeed, the classic formulations of Friedrich Meinecke and Rudolf Stadelmann turned Herder into the "father of historicism," credited with pioneering the stress on individuality, development, and the "historical sense" of *Einfühlung* (or *Verstehen*).[26]

SCHLEIERMACHER AND BOECKH

It was Wilhelm Dilthey, with his classic essay of 1900 and through his celebrated biography, who established Friedrich Schleiermacher at the fountainhead of systematic hermeneutics. Schleiermacher's endeavor to transform hermeneutics from a vehicle for special inquiries, like biblical exegesis or legal studies, into a "general" theory of understanding claimed a philosophical rigor which would promote hermeneutics into a "science." The question whether hermeneutics is a philosophical position or a science has not only haunted interpretation generally thereafter, but has had a special thorniness for disciplinary history. Schleiermacher, on Dilthey's classical construal, took hermeneutics to be "essentially a theory of textual interpretation." He did not generalize it to historical inquiry as such. With his discrimination of linguistic ("grammatical") from psychological ("technical") components in general hermeneutics, Schleiermacher argued that an adequate interpretation would begin with the role of language in structuring an utterance but would need in addition to grasp the intention of the utterer. He construed the first consideration as "comparative" analysis of words and sentences in terms of language as an indispensable frame, and the second as a "divinatory" psychological endeavor to "re-experience" the mental process of the text's author. Starting with Dilthey and finding its classical formulation in Hans-Georg Gadamer, the claim developed that Schleiermacher's ideas shifted, over the course of his lectures from 1805 to 1833, more and more to the psychological ("divining" authorial intention) and away from the linguistic-critical, resulting in a "bad metaphysics" enabling Gadamer to assert the "questionableness [*Fragwürdigkeit*] of Romantic hermeneutics." But this interpretation has been debunked with the recovery of a more extensive corpus of Schleiermacher's writings and lectures on hermeneutics, which demonstrate that he preserved both components of his theory throughout his teaching. Moreover, the "divinatory" idea needs to be read carefully in this context. Schleiermacher wrote: "the divinatory [method] is that in which one transforms oneself into the other person in order to grasp his individuality directly." That sense of empathy has aroused objections from many quarters, but Michael Forster's assessment seems to draw a just balance on the matter: "Schleiermacher's considered conception of 'divination' does in fact turn out to be a (perfectly secular) process of guesswork, conjecture, or hypothesis, based on close scrutiny of the available evidence, but also going well beyond it." That, Forster correctly points out, is in the nature of empirical hypothesizing even in the natural sciences. It has nothing to do with a dubiously mystical "re-living," even as it remains imaginative and conjectural. Interpretative reconstruction is always a risky business. If transparent understanding attended all communication there would be no need for hermeneutics, just as if nature's operations were transparently comprehensible there would be no need for scientific inquiry. Philosophy's residual absolutism (the ideal of "scientia") has to be deflated, and the notion of empirical science brought back to contingent and fallible investigation. Schleiermacher was not altogether innocent of the ambition to *scientia* in his vision for hermeneutics, and the tradition has suffered in consequence.[27]

The crucial elaboration of hermeneutics for history was from text to context, a methodology for reconstructing actions, events, epochs, and peoples, not simply literary or documentary texts. It was Herder before Schleiermacher and August Boeckh after him who undertook to extend the organismic and developmental approach of textual hermeneutics to events, epochs, and peoples. Droysen, not Ranke, appears to us now to have been the crucial harvester of these impulses for the discipline of history.

THE UNASSIMILATED RANKE

Ranke could only partially order the practice of the discipline, and the residual would remain unruly. His actual monographs everywhere evince intervention of his personal tastes and faiths – religious, political, and aesthetic – however much he wished to efface his presence as author. Without research, certainly, Ranke believed there could be no "science," but without intuition or imagination there could be no synthesis. Thus historical practice was for him always as much art as science. Ranke believed it was the concatenation of individual events – their textured, integral individuality, but also their immersion in synchronic and diachronic patterns of order – that elicited a sense for totality in history – or, indeed, behind it, in the will of God – that needed to be imaginatively constructed and affirmed. He asserted "our task is to present the characteristic, the essential in the individual, and the coherence, the connection in the whole."[28] Historical insight was a combination of an intuitive attunement (*Anschauung*) to individualities in history – persons, peoples, institutions, or states – and intense research (*Forschung*) into their connections. As Beiser sums the matter in three succinct points, Ranke believed that history had an inescapably artistic component; he believed that metaphysics (and theology) formed a necessary backdrop to historical insight; and he had no interest in formulating general laws.[29] Yet very little of this personal vision of historical practice got institutionalized in the emergent discipline. Ranke's artistic skills in narration, like his historical knack for imaginative synthesis, remained his individual talent. They did not transmit to his "school."

HUMBOLDT

Iggers claims that "Ranke developed the most systematic and coherent exposition of historicist principles in nineteenth-century historiography."[30] In fact, that is not true. Wilhelm von Humboldt before him and Johann Gustav Droysen after him were far more systematic and penetrating in their conception of historical method. Humboldt delivered a landmark address, "The Task of the Historian," to the Prussian Academy of Sciences in Berlin in 1821 that, as Peter Hanns Reill has noted, was "probably the most important short article on historical understanding and writing composed in the nineteenth century." Humboldt emphasized the creative role of the historical interpreter, drawing the latter closer to the artist than to the philosopher, but at the same time arguing that the historian was different from the artist in harnessing imagination to evidence. The historian's task was to undertake a rigorous examination of the amassed source materials but also to synthesize them into a meaningful order which they did not possess in their fragmentary particularity. This synthesis was no artificial imposition but a discernment of an immanent principle of order: Humboldt insisted that the historian was capable of discriminating coherence in history. He believed there were "truly acting forces" informing historical actuality and that it was the task of the historian to penetrate to them. "The creative forces of world history [...] the ideas [...] are not being projected into history, but are the essence of history itself. For every force, living or dead, acts according to the laws of its nature, and all occurrences are inseparably linked."[31]

As Lorraine Daston and Peter Galison have demonstrated, there was a dramatically different sense of scientific objectivity operative in the eighteenth and early nineteenth centuries, one which drew scientific insight and artistic imagination into a far more intimate connection.[32] Humboldt belongs in that historical moment of the conceptualization of scientific objectivity. "An event [...] is only partially visible in the world of the senses; the rest has to be added by intuition, inference, and guesswork." That properly affirms the inevitably tentative practice of actual human construal of the unknown ("science in the making").[33] Interpretation is creative intervention for the sake of coherence. Strikingly, Humboldt's program has far more in common with that of Herder, though he found the latter little to his taste, than with Ranke's official program. Similarly, there is much in Humboldt that parallels another figure he disliked, G. W. F. Hegel, who had yet to offer his lectures on the philosophy of history when Humboldt presented his address.

DROYSEN

In the opening chapters of his *History of Civilization in England*, the prominent English historian H. T. Buckle proclaimed a positivist mission for history.[34] The established historical profession in Germany received this as a hostile challenge. In the long and defensive review essay he composed in response to Buckle, Johann

Gustav Droysen spoke on behalf of his entire profession in Germany in disavowing Buckle's program as the only means toward "The Elevation of History to the Rank of Science [*Die Erhebung der Geschichte zum Rang einer Wissenschaft*]," as he tellingly titled his essay. It was indeed Droysen's ambition to establish history as a science in its own right, an autonomous discipline.[35] But we must ascertain what Droysen meant by "science." Certainly, his emphasis was on empirical research: "the essence of historical method is to understand by means of research [*forschend verstehen*]." But that meant, for Droysen, to practice a *hermeneutical* inquiry, to follow a "morphological" method of individuation in comparative-developmental context.[36]

Droysen's formative experience came in his student years at the University of Berlin from 1826 onward. He was familiar with Humboldt's famous address of 1821, and he revered Humboldt as "the Bacon of the historical sciences."[37] His dissertation director and most important teacher was August Boeckh, who applied the hermeneutical methods he had himself learned from Schleiermacher to the broader problems of classical philology.[38] It is noteworthy that in this period when he studied with Boeckh, Droysen only attended Ranke's seminar one time but, in contrast, attended *six* courses with Hegel.[39] Droysen never identified with the Ranke school, adopting a decidedly revisionist stance toward Ranke and his followers, whose self-presentation as a "critical school" of history he found naive and inept.[40] In striving to set the discipline of history on more secure epistemological and methodological footing, he devoted himself to systematic theory, which he termed *Historik*, starting in 1857. He would continue to elaborate his approach through the balance of his career, but he found little response among his colleagues, who were complacently pursuing archival source-criticism and narrative reportage along the lines propounded in Ranke's institutionally decisive *Historisches Seminar*.

The key to methodological self-consciousness, for Droysen, was the awareness that historical practice proved always simultaneously *presentist* as much as *historicist*. That is, the historian was always driven by the interests arising out of his or her immediate context, and it was these interests that conjured the concrete problem that the historian would set out to investigate. Nonetheless, this investigation had constraints: it was crucial not simply to *read into* but to *learn from* the historically remote object of inquiry, to attend it in its own voice. This was the historicist dimension of Droysen's hermeneutics. Thus, in *Historik*, Droysen proposed that the historian needed to extend the *textual* hermeneutics Schleiermacher had theorized into a hermeneutics of *events*. The part-whole dialectic at the core of textual hermeneutics needed to be elaborated into a "circle" of individualities and totalities involving actors, events, epochs, and peoples. The methodological mandate of source-criticism remained for Droysen always a means, not an end. It was not sufficient to find and assess sources; the crucial task of the historian was to interpret, to offer a coherent account. This was always a creative act: making as much as finding. Always the object needed to be construed in the fundamental context of dynamics and change, of individuality and development. Thus, Droysen distinguished "Methodik" from "Systematik," analysis from synthesis. *Forschend verstehen*, in his view, needed to be grasped in terms of sequential stages of conceptualization. It always began from a problem focus, a conjecture or concern grounded in the interests of the historian's present. That then entailed a research design, whereby the relevant "facts" could be conceived and pursued. Once these "sources" were gathered, *critique* ("source-criticism") needed to assess their adequacy and warrant. But this was not the end of the process, as the "critical school" had pretended. Instead, the main work of the historian remained: interpretation [*Verstehen*], the discernment of coherent significance.

    The practice of interpretation had, for Droysen, four dimensions. First came the "pragmatic" construction of a causal account of the course of events, which would situate and make comprehensible the "ethical world" of that moment. Droysen explicitly took the term from Hegel to encompass the historical field of investigation: institutions, values, practices, and traditions. To contextualize this "pragmatic" dimension, the historian needed to supplement it with attentiveness to "material conditions" – the physical and structural setting in which the course of events took place. This enabled the "psychological" dimension: the account of individual identity and agency in the historical process. Finally, at the most synthetic level, the historian had to conceive of "ideas," the larger currents driving the "ethical world" toward actualization. Clearly, these four dimensions of interpretation resonated with Aristotle's four senses of causality. But they also took up and embraced the ideas that Droysen had soaked up from Hegel and Humboldt, from Boeckh and Schleiermacher and Herder.

Gradually, this question of interpretation led Droysen to add a third major component to his *Historik*, what he termed "Topik," the problem of historical *writing*. The issues of presentation, of communication, demanded more articulation in historical theory. This has become a major concern in more recent theoretical discussions, and this is one of the reasons for Droysen's emergence as a major antecedent. In historical writing all the questions of expression and persuasion come to the fore; all the epistemological issues associated with the "hermeneutical circle" achieve their maximal intensity. The position of Droysen, here, proves extremely valuable, for he stressed that knowledge of the past is not given but created by the historian. Coherence is made, not found, but it is made of *actualities*, not inventions. Narrative exposition, hermeneutical interpretation, involved elements of both art and empirical inquiry. That was the sense of "science," of "objectivity," that Droysen could affirm for the discipline. It consisted in "intersubjective standards and methods."[41] But Droysen believed these sufficed for disciplinary integrity.

DILTHEY

By the second half of the nineteenth century, the establishment of the various humanistic disciplines in the German university had succeeded eminently and become the envy of the Western world.

However, a new sense of *epistemological* quandary arose, associated with the hegemonic claim of positivism to an ostensibly unitary "scientific method" exemplified by the natural sciences. The humanistic disciplines might well be established and professional, but now the issue was: could they really be regarded as "scientific?"[42]

Wilhelm Dilthey saw himself confronted with the positivist philosophy of science and its hegemonic claims concerning the studies of man. Notably, he was by disciplinary training a philosopher, but his interests and achievements in the practice of intellectual and cultural history establish him as one of the great masters of hermeneutical-historical practice, as well. It was, in the end, as an epistemologist of history that he established his crucial presence in his epoch. His goal was, in explicit emulation of Immanuel Kant, to undertake a "critique of historical reason."[43] He was an avid student of Friedrich Schleiermacher and perceived clearly the centrality of hermeneutical methods for the pursuit of humanistic inquiry. Even more than Schleiermacher, Dilthey focused upon the distinctiveness of psychology, of *lived experience* (*Erlebnis*). He insisted that general laws along the lines pursued by the natural sciences could never capture what was unique and essential about that experience, namely, the perspective of the first person, an actor's own beliefs and values. Thus appropriate inquiries into experience could only be interpretive, always recognizing individuality and its holistic fusion of cognition, volition, and feeling. In stressing, as the unique project of historical hermeneutics, the constitution of individual agency, its external expressions, and the intersubjective communities which both situated and embodied them, Dilthey provoked the attacks of professional, "rigorous" philosophers. They chastised him for lack of epistemological and especially normative "objectivity" in historical knowledge.

Dilthey was a philosopher who cared about the practices of history. The neo-Kantian Wilhelm Windelband was a historian of philosophy primarily concerned to uphold the integrity of philosophy. That entailed keeping history in its place: "For Windelband, to historicize reason is to relativize reason, to undermine the universal and necessary validity of its fundamental principle." In just this measure, neo-Kantianism seized upon the disciplinary concerns of history. Windelband's pioneering essay of 1883, "Kritische oder genetische Methode?" appeared in the same year as Dilthey's *Einleitung in die Geisteswissenschaften*, and was intended as a direct challenge to it. For Windelband "validity stands above the realm of history [...] [I]f historicism were true, there would be no point or value to philosophy at all," hence it was indispensable to vindicate the standpoint of universal reason. But that meant simply that the neo-Kantians repudiated the fundamental insight that history pursued. What Windelband began, his student Heinrich Rickert carried through systematically: the assertion of disciplinary hegemony of philosophy over history via the question of epistemological foundations.[44] That occasioned the famous "crisis of historicism" that haunted the historical discipline over much of the twentieth century. In the writings of a key set of authors of the 1920s – Ernst Troeltsch, Friedrich Meinecke, Karl Mannheim, and Karl Heussi – that phrase became canonized as a *topos* of anxiety which has carried forward to our own day.[45]

CONCLUDING REMARKS

The prospect for history as a discipline is to embrace hermeneutics in its empirical inquiry without getting taken in by inappropriate notions of "science" or philosophy even in the hermeneutical tradition. The hermeneutical historicist seeks to *give an account*. This is a cognitive undertaking, not a mystical one; it involves not *reliving* (*à la* Collingwood) but *understanding*, which is, after all, the root meaning of *Verstehen*. That is not to deny imagination in the process, but it *is* to insist that this is imagination harnessed to interpretation, not unleashed to fantasy. The hermeneutical historian will refer to texts, to artifacts, to archaeological remains, to the *presence* of sources construed as evidence of the past. Concretely, historical practice cannot dispense with empirical evidence, and thus some form of reference to actuality, however problematic in the absence of the past. Even less can it dispense with some claim to coherence, to meaningful organization, which can be the subject of discriminating appraisal.

Objectivity is always the achievement of a community of inquiry, never of an isolated interpreter. To be sure, it is the very individuality of perspective of the inquirer that inspires and informs the account which is proposed to the community. Creativity and risk form the indispensably "subjective" element in the disciplinary pragmatics of history. The point is, however, that when the practicing historian offers a construction to the discipline, it is offered *not* as a subjective artifice but as a venture to construe an ostensibly common object, to be appraised by common standards of validity. Veridicality and coherence are indispensable to the practice of history, even though the standards of appraisal are disciplinary, not absolute. Historical representations articulate *something which ought to be intersubjectively discriminable* via available evidence, though not directly observable. I am arguing for the robustness of hermeneutical historicism as empirical inquiry. To be sure, a great deal remains underdetermined, but that, as Quine has taught us, represents the condition of all empirical understanding.[46] If we dispense with the positivist delusion of what science must be, and understand hermeneutical endeavor as a contingent and fallible pursuit of intersubjective discernment, we can restore theoretical confidence to historical practice.

NOTES

1 Frank Ankersmit, *Historical Representation* (Stanford: Stanford University Press, 2001), citing 250 and 152. Peter Novick, *That Noble Dream: The "Objectivity Question" and the American Historical Profession* (Cambridge: Cambridge University Press, 1988), 628. Raymond Martin, "Objectivity and Meaning in Historical Studies," *History and Theory* 32 (1993): 25–50, cited from 29.
2 See my "Are We Being Theoretical Yet?," *Journal of Modern History* 65 (1993): 783–814.

3 Thomas Kuhn, *Structure of Scientific Revolutions*, 2nd edn. (Chicago: University of Chicago Press, 1970 [1962]); see Zammito, *A Nice Derangement of Epistemes: Post-Positivism in the Study of Science From Quine to Latour* (Chicago: University of Chicago Press, 2004); Peter Galison and David Stump, eds., *The Disunity of Science: Boundaries, Contexts, and Power* (Stanford: Stanford University Press, 1996).
4 Richard Evans, *In Defence of History* (London: Granta Books, 1997), 8–9; Zammito, "Are We Being Theoretical Yet?," 812.
5 Horst Walter Blanke and Jörn Rüsen, eds., *Von der Aufklärung zum Historismus: Zum Strukturwandel des historischen Denkens* (Paderborn: Schöningh, 1984); Friedrich Jäger and Jörn Rüsen, *Geschichte des Historismus: Eine Einführung* (Munich: Beck, 1992); Otto Oexle and Jörn Rüsen, eds., *Historismus in den Kulturwissenschaften* (Cologne: Böhlau, 1996).
6 See Georg Iggers, *The German Conception of History: The National Tradition of Historical Thought from Herder to the Present* (Hanover, NH: Wesleyan University Press, 1968); Georg Iggers and James Powell, eds., *Leopold von Ranke and the Shaping of the Historical Discipline* (Syracuse: Syracuse University Press, 1990).
7 The first of Ranke's phrases is from the preface to his first book of 1824 (reprinted in Ranke, *Sämtliche Werke*, vol. 33/34 [Leipzig, 1874], vii); the second is from his *Englische Geschichte* (1860), vol. 2 (*Sämtliche Werke*, vol. 15 [Leipzig, 1877], 103).
8 Iggers writes of "the type of unreflective, professional history-writing which marked not only American historiography at the end of the century, but had already manifested itself in many German historical and legal studies" (Iggers, *The German Conception of History*, 64). See Dorothy Ross, "On the Misunderstanding of Ranke and the Origins of the Historical Profession in America," in *Leopold von Ranke and the Shaping of the Historical Discipline*, 154–69, and see also Novick, *That Noble Dream*.
9 Wilhelm Dilthey, "The Rise of Hermeneutics," *New Literary History* 3 (1972), 229–44; Dilthey, "Der Aufbau der geschichtlichen Welt in den Geisteswissenschaften," in *Gesammelte Schriften*, vol. 7 (Göttingen: Vandenhoeck & Ruprecht, 1968), 95.
10 On Droysen, see Jörn Rüsen, *Begriffene Geschichte: Genesis und Begründung der Geschichtstheorie J. G. Droysens*

(Paderborn: Schöningh, 1969); Hayden White, "*Historik* by Johann Gustav Droysen," *History and Theory* 19 (1980): 73–93; Arthur Alfaix Assis, *What Is History For? Johann Gustav Droysen and the Functions of Historiography* (New York and Oxford: Berghahn, 2014).

11 Droysen, *Historik*, historical-critical edition by Peter Leyh (4 vols.; Stuttgart/Bad Cannstatt: Frommann-Holzboog, 1977).

12 Rüsen, "Droysen heute – Plädoyer zum Bedenken verlorener Themen der Historik," in *Droysen-Vorlesungen*, ed. Lutz Niethammer (Jena: Philosophical Faculty, Historical Institute, University of Jena, 2005), 177–200; Rothacker, "J. G. Droysens Historik," *Historische Zeitschrift* 161 (1940): 84–92, citing 90.

13 Michael N. Forster, *After Herder: Philosophy of Language in the German Tradition* (Oxford: Oxford University Press, 2010), 323, 334, 362, 392, 409ff. The view that Schleiermacher drew heavily on Herder pervades the secondary literature, from Dilthey to Joachim Wach, *Grundzüge einer Geschichte der hermeneutischen Theorie im 19. Jahrhundert* (3 vols.; 1926–1933; reprint: Hildesheim: Olms, 1966), to Klaus Weimar, *Historische Einleitung zur literaturwissenschaftlichen Hermeneutik* (Tübingen: Mohr, 1975). See especially Harald Schnur, *Schleiermachers Hermeneutik und ihre Vorgeschichte im 18. Jahrhundert* (Stuttgart: Metzler, 1994), 8–16.

14 See Arno Seifert, *Cognitio historica: Die Geschichte als Namengeberin der frühneuzeitlichen Empirie* (Berlin: Duncker & Humblot, 1976).

15 Frederick Beiser, *The German Historicist Tradition* (Oxford: Oxford University Press, 2011), 15.

16 Johann Gatterer, "Vom historischen Plan und dem darauf sich gründenden Zusammenhang der Erzählungen," *Allgemeine historische Bibliothek* I (1767): 80–1. See Peter Hanns Reill, *The German Enlightenment and the Rise of Historicism* (Berkeley: University of California Press, 1975); *Aufklärung und Geschichte: Studien zur deutschen Geschichtswissenschaft im 18. Jahrhundert*, ed. Hans Erich Bödeker, Georg Iggers, Jonathan Knudsen and Peter Reill (Göttingen: Vandenhoeck & Ruprecht, 1986); *Theoretiker der deutschen Aufklärungshistorie*, ed. Horst Walter Blanke and Dirk Fleischer (2 vols.; Stuttgart, Bad Cannstatt: Frommann-Holzboog, 1990).

17 Herder began referring to Gatterer's works in *Fragmente* I (Johann Gottfried Herder, *Werke in zehn Bänden*, Frankfurt: Deutscher

Klassiker Verlag [henceforth DKV], vol. 1:625), which noted Gatterer's *Abriß einer Universalgeschichte*. Herder regarded Gatterer as the main theorist of the "art of history," noting especially the essay "Vom historischen Plan," from the *Allgemeine historische Bibliothek*.

18 Herder, "An den Herrn Direktor der Historischen Gesellschaft in Göttingen" (1768), in Herder, *Ausgewählte Werke in Einzelausgaben: Schriften zur Literatur, 2/1: Kritische Wälder*, ed. Regine Otto (Berlin and Weimar, 1990), 684–91, citing 685.

19 Herder, "Über Christian Wolffs Schriften," in Herder, *Sämtliche Werke*, ed. B. Suphan (Berlin: Weidmann, 1882–1909), vol. 32, 158 (henceforth Suphan).

20 Herder, *Viertes Kritische Wäldchen*, DKV:2:287.

21 Herder, *Zerstreute Blätter* (1792), cited in Herder, *On World History*, ed. Hans Adler and Ernst Menze (Armonk: M. E. Sharpe, 1997), 65.

22 Herder, *Auch eine Philosophie der Geschichte* (Suphan: 5:509).

23 Herder, "Shakespeare," in *Eighteenth Century German Criticism*, ed. Timothy Chamberlain (New York: Continuum, 1992), 143–63, citing 150.

24 Herder, "Über Thomas Abbts Schriften," DKV: 2:576–80.

25 Herder, "Shakespeare," 143–63.

26 Dilthey, *Der Aufbau der geschichtlichen Welt in den Geisteswissenschaften*, 95; Friedrich Meinecke, *Historism: The Rise of a New Historical Outlook* (London: Routledge & Kegan Paul, 1972 [1936]); Rudolf Stadelmann, *Der historische Sinn bei Herder* (Halle: Niemeyer, 1928).

27 Dilthey, "The Rise of Hermeneutics" (1900), and "Das hermeneutische System Schleiermachers in der Auseinandersetzung mit der älteren protestantischen Hermeneutik," in *Gesammelte Schriften*, vol. 14: 2.2 (Stuttgart: Teubner, Vandenhoeck und Ruprecht, 1966), 595–787. Scheiermacher, *Hermeneutics and Criticism*, ed. and trans. Andrew Bowie (Cambridge: Cambridge University Press, 1998) and *Hermeneutics: The Handwritten Manuscripts*, ed. Heinz Zimmerle, trans. James Duke and Jack Forstman (Missoula: Scholars Press for the American Academy of Religion, 1977); Hans-Georg Gadamer, *Truth and Method* (New York: Continuum, 2002); Forster, *After Herder*, citing 379.

28 Ranke, *The Theory and Practice of History*, ed. G. Iggers and K. von Moltke (Indianapolis: Bobbs-Merrill, 1973), 13.

29 Beiser, *The German Historicist Tradition*, 255.
30 Iggers, *The German Conception of History*, 70.
31 Wilhelm von Humboldt, "On the Historian's Task," *History and Theory* 6 (1967): 57–71. See Peter Hanns Reill, "Science and the Construction of the Cultural Sciences in Late Enlightenment Germany: The Case of Wilhelm von Humboldt," *History and Theory* 33 (1994): 345–66, citing 356.
32 Lorraine Daston and Peter Galison, *Objectivity* (New York: Zone, 2007), 55–115.
33 Humboldt, "On the Historian's Task," 57. See Bruno Latour, *Science in Action* (Cambridge, MA: Harvard University Press, 1987); Joseph Rouse, *Engaging Science: How to Understand Its Practices Philosophically* (Ithaca, NY and London: Cornell University Press, 1996); Joseph Rouse, *How Scientific Practices Matter: Reclaiming Philosophical Naturalism* (Chicago and London: University of Chicago Press, 2002).
34 Henry Thomas Buckle, *History of Civilization in England* (London: Parker, 1857), which Beiser characterizes as "something of a positivist manifesto" (*German Historicist Tradition*, 312).
35 J. G. Droysen, "Die Erhebung der Geschichte zum Rang einer Wissenschaft," *Historische Zeitschrift* 9 (1863): 1–22; reprinted in *Outline of the Principles of History* (Boston: Ginn, 1893), 61–89.
36 Droysen, *Outline*, 12; Droysen, *Historik*, I:20.
37 Droysen, *Outline*, 7; Droysen, *Historik*, I:419.
38 August Boeckh, *On Interpretation and Criticism* (Norman: University of Oklahoma Press, 1968).
39 On Droysen and Hegel see: Irene Kohlstrunk, *Logik und Historie in Droysens Geschichtstheorie: Eine Analyse von Genese und Konstruktionsprinzipien seiner "Historik"* (Wiesbaden: Steiner, 1980); Christoph Johannes Bauer, *"Das Geheimnis aller Bewegung ist Zweck" – Geschichtsphilosophie bei Hegel und Droysen* (Hamburg: Meiner, 2001).
40 Droysen wrote: "the essence of history has been recognized [by that school] as consisting in method, and this characterized as a 'criticism of the sources,' as a setting forth of the 'pure fact.'" But, Droysen queried: "Does criticism of the sources lead to anything more than the reproduction of views once held? Does it lead to the 'pure fact'?" (*Outline*, 4, 6).

41 Droysen, *Historik*, I:230–1.
42 Daston and Galison write of a substantial shift in the conception of objectivity in the later nineteenth century, driven by the experimental and exact sciences (*Objectivity*, 115–90).
43 Dilthey coined the phrase in *Aufbau der geschichtlichen Welt*, 191–2. See Hajo Holborn, "Wilhelm Dilthey and the Critique of Historical Reason," *Journal of the History of Ideas* 11 (1953): 93–116; Rudolf Makkreel, *Dilthey: Philosopher of the Human Studies* (Princeton University Press, 1975); and Michael Ermarth, *Wilhelm Dilthey: The Critique of Historical Reason* (Chicago: University of Chicago Press, 1978).
44 Wilhelm Windelband, "Kritische oder genetische Methode?" (1883; reprinted in Windelband, *Präludien: Aufsätze und Reden zur Philosophie und ihrer Geschichte*, vol. 2: 99–135 (Tübingen: Mohr, 1924); Beiser, *The German Historicist Tradition*, 366, 377.
45 Ernst Troeltsch, *Der Historismus und seine Probleme* (Tübingen: Mohr, 1922); Karl Mannheim, "Historismus," *Archiv für Sozialwissenschaft und Sozialpolitik* 52 (1924): 1–60; Karl Heussi, *Die Krisis des Historismus* (Tübingen: Mohr, 1932); Meinecke, *Historism*.
46 Quine's most explicit articulation of the underdetermination thesis came in "On Empirically Equivalent Systems of the World," *Erkenntnis* 9 (1975): 313–28.

6 Hermeneutics and Positivism
Frederick C. Beiser

A TALE OF WOEFUL NEGLECT

It has to be said that one of the worst obstacles to the study of philosophy nowadays is the still persistent and prevalent distinction between "analytic" and "continental" philosophy. This distinction is silly and bogus, to be sure, but it continues to exist, and to exert its damaging effects, if only because some people still believe in it, and if only because many people once believed in it for so long. It seems to me that the harm created by the distinction is obvious: it has erected artificial barriers that have prevented philosophers from talking to one another. It is as if there were little point in a dialogue between analytic and continental philosophers because they not only apply different methods but also address different problems. Of course, there are now promising signs that this old distinction is breaking down: some analytic philosophers are interested in Hegel and Heidegger; some German and French philosophers are now "doing" analytic philosophy. But these areas of cross-fertilization are, I fear, somewhat limited, and largely confined to epistemology. There are other areas of philosophy where the old barriers still exist and continue to have their harmful effect. One of these areas, and one of the worst affected, is the philosophy of history. The purpose of my chapter is to explain why this is so, i.e., why the philosophy of history has languished from the distinction between "analytic" and "continental" philosophy. Before I do this, let me sketch a little bit of the historical background.

Beginning in the 1950s, there was a sharp rise of interest in the philosophy of history among analytic philosophers in the Anglophone world. This new interest, which chiefly grew out of the work of

Popper and Collingwood, produced some first-rate discussions about the logic of historical enquiry. In their quality and quantity these discussions were, I believe, comparable to those that took place in Germany at the end of the nineteenth century and at the beginning of the twentieth. It is a striking feature of the analytic discussions, however, that they almost completely ignore the German historicist tradition. It is as if Humboldt, Ranke, Droysen, Dilthey, Windelband, Rickert, Troeltsch, Simmel, and even Weber, never existed. Seldom, if ever, did these analytic philosophers – W. H. Walsh, Patrick Gardiner, William Dray, Rex Martin, Isaiah Berlin, Arthur Danto – mention the work of the German historicist tradition before them. Rather than carrying forward past conversations, these analytic philosophers were content to start new ones. It is as if they were creating a completely new discipline from scratch.

Let me illustrate this tale of woeful neglect by an important, though now forgotten, book. In 1951 W. H. Walsh published his *Philosophy of History: An Introduction*, which went through several editions and many printings.[1] Though only an introduction, Walsh's book was important because it marks the beginning of the new interest in the philosophy of history in the post-war years. For decades it was the introduction to the subject in the Anglophone world. It is noteworthy, therefore, that Walsh felt the need to begin his book with an apology for his subject. It is a lamentable fact, he writes, that an author on the philosophy of history has to justify the very existence of his subject (9). Walsh raises the question why the philosophy of history has been so neglected in Britain, and comes to the remarkable conclusion that it has to do with "the predominant characteristics of the British mind and temper" (10). This temper is one of "caution and critical acumen," which has made the British skeptical of the speculative philosophy of history pursued by the Germans. Modest and skeptical, a British gentleman keeps his reserve before the flights of speculative fancy found in the works of the likes of Herder, Hegel, or Spengler. The way Walsh justifies his subject before these wary British gentleman is by distinguishing between two kinds of philosophy of history. There is the *speculative* philosophy of history, which is concerned with history understood as "the totality of past human actions"; and then there is the *critical* philosophy of history, which deals with the logic of historical enquiry (14). However much cautious British chaps might dislike the first kind of philosophy of history, Walsh wagers, they are likely to find something more to their taste in the second kind. In making this argument Walsh writes as if the philosophy of history in the critical or epistemological sense were a new preoccupation, an interest more characteristic of, and appropriate to, the cautious British mind than the philosophy of history in the speculative sense, which was more characteristic of, and appropriate to, extravagant and fuzzy headed Germans. It is noteworthy that Walsh completely ignores the fact that the philosophy of history, *in precisely his critical and epistemological sense,* had been for generations one of the major concerns of German philosophy. Though they were Germans, Ranke, Droysen, Windelband, Rickert, Dilthey, Burckhardt, Simmel, and Weber were as skeptical of the philosophy of history in the speculative sense as the most scrupulous British gentleman. Of course, mentioning this fact would have completely spoiled Walsh's strategy: he would never interest a British public, which had just fought a second war against the Germans, in the philosophy of history if he had mentioned that it had been a preoccupation of their recent enemy. Alas, the ultimate source of Walsh's neglect was not British temper, not even British provinciality, but the tragic aftermath of war.

However tragic and understandable, there has been a steep price to pay in philosophical terms for the neglect of the historicist tradition. The main cost has been the sterility and futility of much recent philosophical debate, more specifically, the long dispute about historical explanation. It is fair to say that, since the 1950s, analytic philosophical discussion about history has largely revolved around this dispute. Since the publication in 1942 of Carl Hempel's classical article "The Function of General Laws in History,"[2] analytic philosophers have devoted most of their attention to the issue whether "covering laws" – i.e., universal laws of cause and effect – are the sole form of scientific explanation in history. There has been a debate between positivists, who defend the thesis that covering laws are the *sole* form of explanation, and their "idealist" opponents, who hold that there is another form of explanation in history that is irreducible to covering laws. This alternative form of explanation usually turns out to be some version of Collingwood's theory of re-enactment, according to which the explanation of the past involves reliving or re-enacting the experiences of the past in the spectator. This debate, which lasted for decades, has now ended in something of a *cul-de-sac*, a stand-off, where neither side has been able to claim victory. The positivists have not surrendered their covering law thesis, though they have had to admit that it scarcely reflects the actual practice of historians, and that most generalizations in history are very limited in scope, such that, quite unlike natural laws, they are applicable to only a particular time and place. The idealists, for their part, still cannot accept the covering law thesis, though they have to concede that merely re-living or re-enacting the past hardly amounts to an explanation of it. The ultimate result of this stalemate is that the discipline has become moribund. At the very least the field has none of the impetus and enthusiasm that it had during the 1950s and 1960s. It is a telling sign of impending *rigor mortis* that the many anthologies from those years have been long out of print. Nothing new has taken their place.

A quick post-mortem suggests that one of the chief causes of death has been excessive sterility and insularity arising from a neglect to take into account opposing perspectives, first and foremost that of the historicist tradition, especially hermeneutics, i.e., the methods of criticism and interpretation developed by Boeckh, Schleiermacher, Droysen, and Dilthey. Neglecting this alternative tradition has greatly narrowed the debate about historical method; it has meant that analytic philosophers have not heard a significant voice in opposition against the positivist program. The historicist tradition developed techniques of criticism and interpretation that are integral to history, and that cannot be easily explained according to the covering law model. If analytic philosophers had taken account of the historicist tradition, they would have more quickly seen problems in the positivist program, and they would have broadened the scope of their investigation to cover other forms of historical enquiry. Had they recognized that there are other goals and methods of historical enquiry than covering laws, their focus of attention could have shifted in a more fruitful direction: toward the investigation of the methods of criticism and interpretation that are actually used by historians. The philosophy of history in the Anglophone world can be greatly stimulated and enriched, I would suggest, once it takes into account these issues and the legacy of the historicist and hermeneutical tradition.

In what follows I would like to vindicate these general claims by putting forward three theses. First, that the covering law theory, even if correct as the sole form of explanation in history, cannot support the general positivist ideal of the unity of science. Second, that the positivist tradition has made its case for the unity of science plausible only by creating a caricature of the chief alternative to it, namely, the method of understanding of the historicist tradition. Third, that the covering law theory is in fact incorrect because covering laws are not the sole form of explanation in history. This would have been clear had the positivists taken better note of the hermeneutical tradition.

HISTORICISM AND THE UNITY OF SCIENCE

It is one of the most striking features of the dispute about covering laws that philosophers rarely asked themselves what was at stake. What difference did it make whether there was only one form of explanation, one kind of methodology, in history? Why not two, three, four, or however many forms of explanation and methodologies? Behind the positivist campaign in behalf of covering laws there was an ideal which had captivated and enthralled the positivists since the days of Comte: the unity of science. Somehow, and for some mystical reason not fully clear to its advocates, science had to be a unity.

In all the sciences, there had to be a single form of explanation, a single kind of methodology. However different their terms or subject matter, the human and natural sciences had to share one and the same logical structure. From our contemporary perspective, which has grown used to scientific specialization and pluralism, it is hard to fathom the hold the ideal of the unity of science had over the positivist mind. To us, there does not seem anything amiss with having many forms of science, and so many different kinds of explanation and methodology. It seems that such methodological pluralism helps to expand the reach of science and to ensure its growth. And is that not, after all, the ultimate goal of positivism?

Whatever the motivation behind the unity of science, it has been a very controversial ideal. The chief source of opposition against it came from the historicist tradition, and more specifically, the historicist's claim for the autonomy of history. It was a mainstay of the historicist tradition from Ranke to Weber that history is indeed a science, though it has its own *sui generis* methods and forms of explanation distinct from the natural sciences. Among these methods are those of the criticism and interpretation of texts, and among these forms of explanation was the method of understanding or *Verstehen*, which insists upon reconstructing the life of the past from within and according to its own terms. Despite the historicists' staunch opposition to positivism, it is noteworthy that the positivists rarely explicitly mention the historicists in their later campaign for covering laws.[3] After reading positivist polemics one's first impression is likely to be that the only source of resistance to their ideals comes from metaphysics, which for them is tantamount to superstition and obscurantism.[4]

But, as in politics, so in philosophy, one's real enemy never remains hidden for long. Sure enough, in his 1942 article "The Function of General Laws in History" Hempel eventually does betray, if only tacitly and inadvertently, that his ultimate target is the historicist tradition. Without mentioning names or texts, at the very close of his paper Hempel takes aim at the historicist belief in the autonomy of history. He notes that even if there were distinctive historical laws – i.e., laws whose *terms* are specifically historical – this still would not warrant the doctrine of the methodological autonomy of history.[5] There is no warrant for such a doctrine, he argues, because the form of these historical laws would still conform to the covering law paradigm. Again betraying, if only implicitly, the ultimate target of his essay, Hempel also criticizes what he calls *"the method of empathetic understanding,"* which is an allusion, of course, to the method of *Verstehen* of the hermeneutical tradition. Hempel, after all, was a German who knew his compatriots all too well.

Why did Hempel disguise the ultimate target of his article? The explanation is obvious: it helped him win his case. Had Hempel mentioned explicitly any of the major historicists and their writings, it would have been plain that he had a much more difficult case to argue. "The method of empathetic understanding," it would have been clear, is a bogeyman, a doctrine that no one really wanted to hold, least of all anyone in the historicist tradition. It would also have been obvious that there is much more to the methods, and forms of explanation, of history than covering laws.

That there is still something wrong, deeply wrong, with the covering law theory becomes apparent as soon as we consider one of the commonplaces of the historicist tradition: that the past is gone and never to return. Because the past is gone, the historicists stress, it has to be painstakingly reconstructed by the critical examination of sources, by the sifting and sorting of documents, texts, inscriptions, and remains. It is the cardinal sin of covering law theory that it never really acknowledges this commonplace; instead, *it treats the past as if it were given*. After all, the covering law theory is a thesis about the explanation of past *actions* and *events*. It assumes that we know these actions and events, and it then tells us about the logic of the explanation of them. But this fails to address the important and big question: *by what methods does the historian reconstruct the past?* It is, of course, through methods of criticism, i.e., through enquiry into the dating, authenticity, and sources of documents; it is also through methods of interpretation, i.e., through techniques determining the meaning of texts, often written in foreign or ancient languages. It is crucial to take these methods of criticism and interpretation into account in determining the scientific status of history, not least because the claim to such status in the nineteenth century rested upon the rigorous and exacting use of these methods. No one claimed that history was a science because of its discovery or application of covering laws; rather, these claims were made because of the painstaking use of methods of criticism and interpretation. It should be plain, though, that these methods, while they sometimes apply general laws, do not consist in them alone. For the domain of these methods is not actual events and actions but more typically *what is said* about events and actions in historical documents. Rather than applying covering laws, what one is doing is assessing evidence, determining meaning, interpreting texts. It is of course precisely with regard to the criticism and interpretation of texts that the hermeneutical tradition has its point or rationale.

So to see what is wrong with covering law theory, let us grant Hempel his central thesis: that covering laws are the *sole* form of explanation of historical events and actions. However true this might be for history understood *a parte objecti*, i.e., history as the totality of past human actions, it is obviously not true for history understood *a parte subjecti*, i.e., history as the totality of what human beings have *written* about the past. Even if all actions have to be explained by covering laws, it hardly follows that the sole or chief methodology of history lies in the formulation and application of covering laws. Such explanation is a goal that the historian reaches only at the end of his enquiries; before he gets there, he first has to apply methods and techniques to assess the authenticity of documents and to interpret their meaning; and in engaging in these activities he is not only formulating and applying covering laws.

What this means, more simply put, is that Hempel's argument in behalf of covering laws does not guarantee his ideal of the unity of science. However correct Hempel's argument might be about the explanation of actions, it does not undermine the historicist's doctrine of the autonomy of history. For that doctrine is made chiefly in behalf of the methods of criticism and interpretation, which have no known analogue in the natural sciences.

What could Hempel say against this? He could resort to semantic gerrymandering, of course, claiming that the criticism and interpretation of documents is not a form of explanation in the proper sense; but this really does not work, because there are perfectly plausible senses of the word "explanation" that apply to the activities of criticism and interpretation. When we assess documents and interpret texts we are also answering the question "Why?" in a straightforward way just as we are in applying a covering law to an action. Hempel could also say that criticism and interpretation are not scientific methods. But this is not an advisable strategy, and for two reasons. First, the methods of criticism and interpretation, rigorously applied, do match many of the criteria of scientific method advanced by positivists themselves, namely, intersubjective testability, strict assessment of evidence, limiting conclusions to evidence, and so on.[6] Second, if Hempel were to push his case against the scientific status of these methods, he has to admit he is engaging in a kind of historical skepticism.

When we look at the debate over covering laws from a broader perspective, it is difficult to resist the conclusion that both the positivists and their opponents committed a classical confusion. It is the simple confusion that Collingwood warns us against in *The Idea of History*, but which he himself seems to commit. The confusion is between history understood as past actions and events, and history understood as the *study* or *record* of such past actions and events. "History" in English, *"histoire"* in French, and *"Geschichte"* in German, are all infected with this ambiguity. History can be the past of human beings or the knowledge they attempt to acquire of their past. The conflict between the historicists and the positivists arose not least because they were talking about history in very different senses: the positivists developed their covering law theory to apply to history in the sense of past actions; and the historicists developed their techniques of critique and interpretation to apply to the records and documents concerning these actions.

To be fair to the positivists, it was not only they who rode roughshod over this distinction. When Collingwood states that the essence of human action is thought he gives it a characterization that would better apply to history *a parti subjecti* rather than *a parti objecti*. History understood as past actions and events cannot be reduced down to thought alone, because there are so many other factors entering into the causes of these actions and events, even though their explanation would indeed have to take into account thought as one of the causes. But there is a sense in which history understood as the *knowledge* of past actions and events is a matter of thought because it involves thinking and reflection upon these past actions and events. Collingwood was led to his identification of history with thought because, perfectly correctly, he took sources – history as knowledge – as the true starting point of history. However, he drew the false conclusion that because these sources consist in thought, the actions and events which they are about also consisted in it.

THE CARICATURE OF *VERSTEHEN*

Although the positivists largely concealed their opposition to the historicist tradition, they would now and then, if only as an afterthought, engage in a critique of the historicist method: the method of understanding or *Verstehen*. Important though such a critique was for them to make their general case for the unity of science, the positivists, it must be said, failed to rise to the occasion. Rather than examining the method in detail by studying the writings of its chief expositors – Droysen, Dilthey, and Weber – the positivists made things easy for themselves. They created a caricature. They had a hollow victory because they attributed to their opponent a position that no one would want to defend. Such an easy victory brought its own risks with it. While they celebrated their triumph over a paper dragon, the positivists exposed their flanks. For other important claims of the historicists, which call into question positivist doctrine, were simply ignored.

Since it is a caricature, the positivist interpretation of the historicist theory of understanding is easily summarized. Basically, the positivists construe understanding to be a method of intuition whereby the historian empathizes, sympathizes, or imaginatively relives the experience of someone else in the past. To understand the past is therefore to relive it, to have an experience like that undergone by someone in the past. All the positivist accounts of the method stress its intuitive, imaginative, or empathetic element, which they oppose to the discursive use of concepts, judgments, and reasoning. The positivists also claim that the historicist methodology presupposes a dualistic metaphysics, according to which the method of understanding applies to the mental realm whereas the methods of the natural sciences are valid for the material world. This interpretation reappears constantly, with little variation, in positivist writings.[7] The same account of the method has been given by analytic philosophers,[8] though they usually focus on Collingwood's version of the method, his theory of re-enactment, which was inspired by the historicists.

Given this account of the method, it should be obvious that it is open to telling objections. First, a method of intuition is unreliable because we could be reading our own contemporary feelings, attitudes, and values into the past. Obviously, it is one thing for me to imagine *myself* as a soldier at the battle of Waterloo; it is another thing entirely to have had something like the experiences of a French dragoon at that battle. No matter how much I study the history of the battle I cannot ever have the same kind of experience as its participants because I cannot abstract entirely from my historical conditioning or know in sufficient depth the historical conditioning behind the life of the dragoon who participated in the battle. Second, even if we could have accurate intuitions of life in the past, they would not constitute an *explanation* of the past; for we still have to confirm or test these intuitions; and we do so by articulating them, by formulating hypotheses and generalizations, and then testing them against other empirical data. At best, it seems, the method of understanding is not a form of explanation but simply a heuristic device for suggesting and discovering hypotheses that can become generalizations. But the more we engage in the process of formulating hypotheses and testing them against experience, the more we see that the method of understanding presupposes the same procedures that we use in the natural sciences. So, in sum, the method of understanding suffers from a dilemma: the more it is unlike the natural sciences and simply a method of intuition, the less reliable and accurate it becomes; but the more reliable and accurate it becomes, the more it is like the methods of the natural sciences.

If this were the sum total of the method of understanding, it would be difficult to disagree with these objections. But the problem is that this was decidedly *not* the method of understanding as it was set forth by its chief proponents, Droysen, Dilthey, and Weber. There are three basic errors behind the positivist interpretation. First, that the method is entirely intuitive or empathetic. Second, that it presupposes a dualistic metaphysics. Third, that it was intended to exclude the use of covering laws or causal forms of explanation. Although these errors are not willful distortions – the positivists simply did not know the texts well enough to have even twisted them – they are *gross* misunderstandings for the simple reason that the historicists themselves anticipated them and explicitly and emphatically protested against them. Let me deal with each of these misinterpretations in a little detail.

If we examine the writings of Droysen, Dilthey, and Weber, it becomes immediately clear that none of them think that the intuitive component of understanding alone is sufficient for explanation. Like the positivists, they stress that, on its own, empathy is subjective and risky business, and that it is at best a heuristic device, the source of hypotheses that have to be checked against experience. Rather than regarding understanding as an act of intuition or a form of immediate experience, they see it as a complex intellectual operation, involving concepts, judgments, and reasoning.

In his brief outline of the theory of understanding in the beginning of *Wirtschaft und Gesellschaft* Weber is very clear that empathy, though a great aid in interpreting the meaning of an action, is not always possible, let alone necessary. He writes: "the ability to imagine one's self performing a similar action is not a necessary prerequisite to understanding; 'one need not have been Caesar in order to understand Caesar'."[9] Weber then goes on to argue that it is necessary to confirm any intuition about the subjective meaning of a person's action by placing it in a wider context and comparing it with the concrete course of events (97). "The rational understanding of motivation," he explains, "consists in placing the act in an intelligible and more inclusive context of meaning" (95).

The same line of argument already appears in Droysen's *Historik*.[10] True to name, understanding is for him a fundamentally intellectual operation. It is a discursive activity that involves concepts, judgments, and inferences. We understand something, he writes, when we place something individual under a universal that explains why it happens; all understanding involves universality and necessity, which are the distinguishing characteristics of thought (H 27). Although Droysen describes understanding in intuitive terms as a flash of insight, these passages should not be taken out of context.[11] When we read him more closely we see that such flashes presuppose, or are the result of, processes of reasoning and inference, whether conscious or subconscious, on the part of the reader or listener. Hence he is careful to distinguish between "the logical mechanism of understanding" and "the act of understanding," where the latter (the act) is the result of the former (the mechanism) (§11). Droysen explains the act of understanding in essentially holistic terms. The relation between individual and universal is for him that between part and whole. When we understand someone, he writes, we take the individual expression to be an example, a single instance, or a part of the whole character or person (§10). We cannot understand a single word, or a single sentence, on its own, but we must see it as part of a whole, whether that is the whole discourse, the historical context or the language in general (L 28). Droysen does not think, however, that such holistic understanding is simply a matter of placing the part within a whole, of subsuming the individual under a universal, as in the case of a covering law. For he stresses that understanding involves a constant movement back and forth between part and whole, where knowledge of one depends on and grows with the other. "The individual is understood in the whole, and the whole is understood from the individual" (§10). This is the famous "hermeneutical circle," of course, already pointed out by Schleiermacher and Boeckh, now endorsed and propagated by Droysen. Because of the circularity in knowledge of whole and part, Droysen says that the method of historical understanding is not exclusively inductive or deductive; rather, it is a combination of both (§10).

A similar view is apparent in Dilthey's chief exposition of the doctrine of understanding, his late fragments "Entwürfe zur Kritik der historischen Vernunft" in *Der Aufbau der geschichtlichen Welt in den Geisteswissenschaften*.[12] For Dilthey no less than Droysen, understanding is fundamentally an intellectual activity. Dilthey attributes a specific form of analogical or inductive reasoning to the elementary forms of understanding. He is explicit that they are a form of inference or reasoning, and he attempts to find for them "a logical construction" (210, 212). Although he does not go into such detail, the reasoning he attributes to elementary understanding has the following structure: (1) There is a uniform connection between a specific kind of expression E and the mental state M that it expresses. (2) There is in this specific case C an expression of kind E. (3) Therefore, in case C, E is an expression of the mental state M. In the most elementary form of understanding we take some particular externalization – a sentence, an action or a gesture – and apply some more general law to it, so that we see it as an instance of that law. More complicated forms of understanding arise when we consider not only one particular externalization but many different kinds of externalization, and when we have to consider the changing circumstances and precise initial conditions under which the general law applies (211).

Not only did Dilthey analyze understanding into basic intellectual operations, he also explicitly denied that understanding is entirely a matter of intuition and imagination. He held understanding to be the result of careful methodological investigation, and he condemned the attempt to base it on intuition alone as "aesthetical mysticism" and "enthusiastic obscurity."[13] Although, like the positivists, he held that imagination and sympathy are important aids to understanding, he never believed that they were by themselves sufficient to establish an interpretation. While he acknowledged that the interpreter often *begins* with some feeling or insight, he stressed that he should never *end* with it. At the beginning of enquiry, the interpreter's intuition has the status of only a hypothesis or conjecture, which he must test, correct, or modify in the light of further evidence. Rather than relying on flashes of inspiration, the interpreter must follow a combined inductive and deductive procedure, whereby he formulates his ideas about the whole after carefully studying each of the parts, and whereby he reinterprets the parts in the light of his knowledge of the whole. Here again was the "hermeneutical circle," which Dilthey, like Droysen, would invoke time and again. He did not regard this circle as "an offense to logic," however, but as involved in all enquiry, whether in the natural or human sciences.

No less a misinterpretation is the positivist claim that *Verstehen* is based upon a dualistic metaphysics. The positivists depict the historicist's distinction between *Geisteswissenschaften* or *Kulturwissenschaften* and *Naturwissenschaften* as essentially metaphysical, as if the former sciences should hold for mental life and the latter for physical nature. Since the mental and physical are so different from one another, it seems that each should be investigated according to a distinct kind of methodology. Since the positivists were either physicalists or anti-metaphysical, they were completely opposed to any such distinction.

This interpretation is so far from accurate, however, that the very opposite is closer to the truth. Rather than upholding dualism as the basis of their method, Droysen and Dilthey oppose dualism because they think that it will undermine understanding. Although both state that the method of understanding involves inferences about a person's mental life from their words and actions, they stress that such inferences require that there be an inner unity between the mental and the physical. They realize all too well that if the mental and physical were heterogeneous, then it would be impossible to ground inferences about the mental on a physical basis. Important for both Droysen and Dilthey is the concept of expression, according to which mental life must embody itself in an outward form. Actions and words are not simply the effects of an internal mental cause, where cause and effect are distinct events; rather, they are the determinate form in which the mental exists; without its embodiment in words and deeds, the mental is only an abstraction. Ultimately, Droysen's and Dilthey's conception of the mind is much closer to Aristotle than to Descartes. It makes the soul the form of the body, the general ways in which it acts and talks in certain circumstances.

It should be noted in this context that Dilthey's famous distinction between the *Geisteswissenschaften* and *Naturwissenschaften* was more phenomenological than metaphysical. It was based upon a distinction between inner and outer *experience* rather than the mind and the body. In his *Einleitung in die Geisteswissenschaften* Dilthey was at pains to stress that the distinction between these sciences is not *ontological*, i.e., it is not between distinct kinds of substance, such as the mind and body. In general, Dilthey rejected mental-physical dualism; he regarded the distinction between mind and body as artificial, an abstraction from the living unity of a human being, whose mental and physical functions are inseparable (14–15). One might object that Dilthey's distinction between inner and outer *experience* is already a kind of metaphysical dualism. It is important to see, however, that Dilthey did not see the distinction between inner and outer experience as fundamentally a distinction between different forms of mental activity, or still less different forms of consciousness. As he later explained the distinction in his *Beiträge zum Studium der Individualität*, it was basically a distinction between different forms of *content*, the different kinds of *objects of awareness*. The aim of the different social-historical sciences is not to provide a description of mental events or activities as they pass through consciousness – hence there is no inference to a hidden mysterious realm – but to identify and analyze the content within our inner experience.

Finally, it is also a misinterpretation to think that the historicists opposed their method of understanding to the use of causal laws. Here again, the very opposite is the case. In *Wirtschaft und Gesellschaft* Weber argued explicitly that the interpretation of someone's actions could be confirmed only when it was placed in a causal context. It is insufficient, he assumed, simply to intuit that someone has a motive; it is also necessary to demonstrate that the person acted on it; and such a demonstration involves showing that the person's action conforms to some regular or law-like form of behavior.[14] While understanding the meaning of someone's actions is irreducible and cannot be replaced by causal regularities, it is still necessary, Weber contended, to place the person's action in a general context which includes such regularities.

The same argument appears in Droysen, who understood the causal explanation of action as one of the necessary forms of its interpretation. Although Droysen denies that causal explanation is a sufficient condition for the understanding of a human action, he does regard it as a necessary condition. In his *Grundriß der Historik* he distinguishes between four different forms of interpretation or understanding.[15] First, there is *pragmatic* interpretation, which reconstructs causal context behind an event (§39). Second, there is the *interpretation of conditions*, which analyzes the specific conditions – whether physical or moral – that make an action possible (§40). Third, there is *psychological* interpretation, which determines the motives for a person's action (§41). Fourth and finally, there is *interpretation of ideas*, which determines the general principles or ideals behind someone's action (§42). Although Droysen writes of them as different kinds of interpretation, it is clear that he thinks all of them are necessary for a full understanding of human action.

Dilthey, for his part, never questioned the value of determining causal laws in the human sciences. In his *Einleitung in die Geisteswissenschaften* he argued that the social-historical sciences use methods of abstraction, and attempt to formulate general laws, no less than the natural sciences (27). The historical and social sciences need to use methods of induction and generalization just like the natural sciences (42). Since human beings are so different from one another and their interactions so complex, Dilthey doubts that laws in the historical and social sciences will ever have the same precision as those in the natural sciences (37); but he does not question, and indeed stresses, the importance of general causal laws in the social-historical sciences (27). They need to determine the interconnections within elements of a whole, and these interconnections are formulable in terms of cause and effect (44).

EXPLANATION AND INTERPRETATION IN MAX WEBER

It might seem from everything that I have said so far that the positivist has a perfectly plausible reply to this defense of the theory of *Verstehen*. Namely, the theory of *Verstehen* is really just a disguised or mystical form of covering law theory; it is covering law theory with bells and whistles (feelings and intuitions) attached. The reasoning behind the rebuttal goes something like this. Granted that the champion of *Verstehen* did not advocate the credibility and reliability of sheer intuition and empathy, granted that he had to admit the need to confirm intuitions and feelings by discursive means, and granted that chief among these discursive means were causal laws, it follows that the theory of *Verstehen* amounts to little more than the covering law theory. Since most of the work of justification and explanation is still done by covering laws, the positivist has been vindicated after all; and since the positivist does not contest that most explanations *begin* with intuitions and feelings, just that they should not *end* with them, there is little ground for the dispute with the historicist. So, it turns out, what is good in the theory of *Verstehen* is already in covering laws; and what is new in the theory – the element of intuition and feeling – is not good at all, except, of course, as a kind of propaedeutic device.

This reply does not really work, however, because it assumes, wrongly, that *all* the work of conceptual elaboration of intuition and feeling is performed by covering laws. Although the champions of *Verstehen* insist that their intuitions and feelings be formulated in more discursive terms, they do not think that these discursive terms are exhausted by covering laws, or indeed any form of causal explanation. If we examine carefully what some of the foremost exponents of the theory of *Verstehen* regard as an interpretation of human action, we find that it has very little to do with causal explanation at all, let alone covering laws. This becomes clear if we look at the writings of the most subtle and sophisticated exponent of the theory of *Verstehen*: Max Weber.

In his later methodological writings, especially *Wirtschaft und Gesellschaft*, Weber developed an important distinction between interpretation and explanation. *Explanation* for Weber is essentially the causal account of a human action. Weber affirms in principle with the naturalist that all human actions are in principle causally explicable, and he even denies that there is any difference in principle between purposes and causes: a purpose is for him simply "the representation of an effect that is the cause of an action." Reasons, for Weber, function as causes when they are the motives for action. Weber's advocacy of the causal explanation of human actions makes it seem as if he is a positivist; and indeed on just these grounds he has often been read as such. However, this interpretation of Weber is, I believe, a serious mistake. It is clear from *Wirtschaft und Gesellschaft*, and some of the earlier methodological writings, that Weber thinks that causal explanation is a necessary but never a sufficient condition for the complete understanding of a human action. Besides the causal explanation of an action there is also what he calls its interpretation. While explanation of an action involves the principle of causality, *interpretation* involves the application and assessment of norms. For Weber, it is one thing to explain an action according to its causes; and it is quite another to assess its rationality according to norms. Here Weber falls back upon the neo-Kantian distinction between the *quid juris?* and the *quid facti?* To illustrate his point, he asks us to suppose that psychology has advanced so far that it is possible to assess the precise neurological causes behind the reasoning of a mathematical theorem; that never suffices to determine whether or not that theorem is true. Why? Because there is a fundamental distinction in principle between determining causes and assessing validity, which no amount of causal explanation will ever surmount. As Weber puts it in his "Roscher und Knies": "There is absolutely no bridge that leads from the purely empirical analysis of a given reality with the means of causal explanation to the affirmation or denial of the validity of some judgment of value."[16] Hence, for Weber, the fundamental distinction between causal explanation and interpretation is that between distinct kinds of activity: explaining according to general laws and evaluating according to general norms. These are distinct because laws attempt to explain what *is* whereas interpretation attempts to assess what *ought to be*. Hence the distinction between explanation and interpretation has nothing whatsoever to do with an ontological distinction between kinds of being, no matter how we construe these forms of being, whether they are the mental and physical, the inner and outer, the noumenal and phenomenal, the archetypical or ectypical. Everything that falls within the realm of being – in all these different forms – is explicable according to the law of causality, but matters of value simply do not fall into any realm of being at all.

As I have explained Weber's position so far, it seems as if the distinction between explanation and interpretation amounts to little more than the familiar distinction between causal and normative accounts of human actions. This distinction is very common today, and it has been explored at great length in contemporary discussions.

Ultimately, it goes back to Weber's neo-Kantian predecessors, Wilhelm Windelband and Heinrich Rickert. What is new and interesting in Weber's approach, however, is not this distinction itself but how he formulates it and the specific account he gives of normative interpretation. *For Weber, the normative interpretation of an action involves the hypothetical attribution to an agent of a process of practical reasoning.* We assume that the agent's action is rational; and then we attempt to reconstruct it according to a practical syllogism. We can have a better idea of Weber's meaning when we consider his own example of how he would interpret a specific human action.[17] If we want to understand, for example, the battle of Königgrätz in 1866, we have to reconstruct the ideal strategy of both Moltke, the Prussian commander, and Benedek, his Austrian opponent. In other words, we have to imagine how each would have acted if he had complete knowledge of his own situation and that of his opponent, if he had total command over his troops, and so on. On the basis of this reconstruction we can compare what should have happened with what in fact did happen, and then better determine the real causes of Moltke's victory and Benedek's defeat.

The crucial point to see here is that understanding action involves *a hypothetical reconstruction of the agent's reasoning.* To understand the agent means to attribute to him a pattern of reasoning; it is to see whether and how it complies with definite norms; it is in effect to follow a practical syllogism. So when Weber stresses the difference between interpretation and explanation what he has in mind is, in part, the difference between practical reasoning and causal explanation. To reason practically presupposes the application of causal laws, to be sure, but it is not one and the same as explaining an action by applying a universal law to it. When I reason "I want X; Y is the only means toward X; therefore, I should pursue Y," I assume that Y is the sufficient or necessary cause of X; but the reasoning itself is not the same as that of "covering law": "Whenever conditions X hold, then Y happens; conditions X now obtain; therefore Y will happen."

For these reasons, Weber attacks any attempt to conflate interpretation with causal explanation. To make such a conflation is for him the old sin of psychologism. When I reconstruct an agent's reasoning and make it comprehensible to myself, he argues, I do not therewith assume that the agent has actually as a matter of fact reasoned in this manner, either consciously or subconsciously. To make this assumption would be like confusing the laws of logic, which have a solely normative validity, with the processes of reasoning. Weber makes this point forcefully in *Wirtschaft und Gesellschaft*: "The meaning [*Sinn*] of a piece of reasoning is not 'psychic'. The rational reflection of an agent whether a definite action according to specific interests is necessary to achieve certain ends or not is not one whit more understandable through any psychological considerations" (§1.I.10).

The final fruit of his theory of interpretation was his famous theory of ideal-types, which has now become a mainstay of sociology. The theory of ideal-types is notoriously complex, not least because there are many kinds of them; but one of the main forms of ideal-types is that which involves the attribution of practical reasoning to agents.

I think I have said enough here to give you a rough idea of what Weber means by interpretation. My main point is that interpretation differs from explanation as the process of practical reasoning does from causal explanation. If it is implausible to reduce practical reasoning down to explanation – and I cannot see how that could be done – the covering law theory fails even as an account of human action itself, let alone as a model for the unity of science.

Let me conclude with a final historical note. Weber's theory of interpretation, which he had developed by 1914, was well ahead of its time. Collingwood, whose knowledge of the German tradition was meager and distorted by Croce, arrived at a position close to Weber's only in the 1940s; but then it had all the weaknesses of the early formulations of the doctrine of *Verstehen* that Weber had already seen and eliminated by the early 1900s.[18] The rational core of Collingwood's theory was rescued by some analytic philosophers in the 1960s and 1970s – Alan Donagan, William Dray, and Rex Martin – by using normative concepts akin to those Weber had already proposed in 1914.[19] This illustrates all too well, I believe, the viciousness of the distinction between analytic and continental philosophy and what happens when philosophers fail to talk with one another. Alas, philosophers who ignore past discussions all too often, with great difficulty and labor, only re-invent the wheel.

NOTES

1. The original edition was published in London, by Hutchinson & Co., in 1951. A revised edition was published in 1958. It was first published in the United States in New York by Harper & Row in 1960. By 1966 it had already gone through several printings. The references in parentheses in the text are to the Harper & Row edition.
2. Carl Hempel, "The Function of General Laws in History," *Journal of Philosophy* 39 (1942): 35–48. Later published in *Theories of History*, ed. Patrick Gardiner (New York: Free Press, 1959), 344–56. All citations to Hempel's article are to the Gardiner edition.
3. So concealed was the presence of the historicist tradition in positivist writing that in 1961 Maurice Mandelbaum, who was thoroughly versed in historicist literature, found it necessary to inform his Anglophone audience that the covering law theorists were rebelling against the historicist tradition. He thinks that their critics have rarely taken this into account. See his "Historical Explanation: The Problem of 'Covering Laws,'" in *The Philosophy of History*, ed. Patrick Gardiner (Oxford: Oxford University Press, 1974), 51–65, 53.
4. In this vein, see Otto Neurath, "Sociology and Physicalism," in *Logical Positivism*, ed. A. J. Ayer (New York: Free Press, 1959), 282–317.
5. Hempel, "The Function of General Laws in History," 356.
6. See Herbert Feigl, "The Scientific Outlook: Naturalism and Humanism," in *Readings in the Philosophy of Science*, ed. H. Feigl and M. Brodbeck (New York: Appleton-Century-Crofts, 1953), 11–14.
7. See Hempel, "The Function of General Laws in History," in Gardiner, *Theories of History*, 352–3. A similar account appears in Neurath, "Sociology and Physicalism," 295, 298. See also Edgar

Zilsel, "Physics and the Problem of Historico-Sociological Laws," in *Readings in the Philosophy of Science*, ed. H. Feigl and M. Brodbeck (New York: Appleton-Century-Crofts, 1953), 721. Although Popper distanced himself from the positivists, he shares with them a similar account of *Verstehen*. See *The Poverty of Historicism* (London: Routledge, Kegan & Paul, 1957), 138. Similar objections to the method appear in the work of Ernest Nagel, who was a sympathizer with positivism. See his *The Structure of Science* (New York: Harcourt, Brace & World, 1961), 480–5.

8 See Patrick Gardiner, *The Nature of Historical Explanation* (Oxford: Oxford University Press, 1952), 128–33; W. H. Walsh, *Philosophy of History* (New York: Harper & Row, 1960), 43, 50, 57; and J. W. N. Watkins, "Ideal Types and Historical Explanation," in Feigl and Brodbeck, *Readings*, 740.

9 Max Weber, *The Theory of Social and Economic Organization*, ed. Talcott Parsons (New York: Free Press, 1947), 90. See too Weber's "Ueber einige Kategorien der verstehenden Soziologie," *Logos* IV (1913): 261–2.

10 There are two editions of the *Historik*, which, despite the common name, are based on different texts. There is Rudolf Hübner's edition, *Historik: Vorlesungen über Enzyklopädie und Methodologie der Geschichte* (Munich: Oldenbourg, 1937), which is chiefly based on the final 1882/1883 version of Droysen's lectures (all references to this edition are designated by "H"). There is also Peter Leyh's edition, *Historik: Die Vorlesungen von 1857* (Stuttgart-Bad Cannstatt: Frommann-Holzboog, 1977), which, true to title, is based on the first 1857 version of the lectures (all references to this edition are designated by "L"). In addition to these sources, there is also the *Grundriß der Historik*, a compendium published by Droysen himself, which went through several editions in his lifetime (1858, 1867, 1875, 1882) (this work is simply cited according to the paragraph numbers [§] of the final 1882 edition). The 1882 edition is collated in Hübner, and all editions are noted in Leyh.

11 As Wach does, *Das Verstehen* III, 180–1, when he stresses the mystical aspect of understanding. Wach conflates Droysen's position with Ranke's; and though he sees the important distinction between act and mechanism, he does not realize its full implications.

12 See Dilthey, *Gesammelte Schriften* (Göttingen: Vandenhoeck & Ruprecht, 1968), VII, 191–251.
13 Dilthey, *Gesammelte Schriften*, XIV/2, 650–8.
14 Weber, *Social and Economic Organization*, 97, 99–100.
15 Droysen gives a detailed account in L 159–216 and H 156–87.
16 Weber, "Roscher und Knies und die logischen Probleme der historischen Nationalökonomie," in *Gesammelte Aufsätze zur Wissenschaftslehre* (Tübingen: J. C. B. Mohr, 1973), 61.
17 See *Wirtschaft und Gesellschaft* §1, I, 11.
18 This point was not lost on one of Weber's better Anglophone critics. See W. G. Runciman, *A Critique of Max Weber's Philosophy of Social Science* (Cambridge: Cambridge University Press, 1972), 30–1.
19 See Alan Donagan, *The Later Philosophy of R. G. Collingwood* (Oxford: Clarendon Press, 1962); William Dray, *Laws and Explanation in History* (Oxford: Oxford University Press, 1957); and Rex Martin, *Historical Explanation* (Ithaca, NY: Cornell University Press, 1977).

7 Hermeneutics

Nietzschean Approaches

Paul Katsafanas

The term "hermeneutics" appears only three times in Nietzsche's notebooks and never in his published works. Nonetheless, Nietzsche's texts are fertile sources of ideas, concepts, and arguments that intersect with the hermeneutical tradition. This chapter will chart several key points of contact between Nietzsche and the hermeneutical tradition.

Taken broadly, hermeneutics is the interpretation of meaningful entities. This raises two sets of questions. First, what is the *range* of hermeneutics? That is, what are the appropriate objects toward which an interpretive stance should be directed? Second, what is the *nature and methodology* of interpretation? What are we doing when we interpret phenomena? What kinds of explanation are provided? What kinds of understanding are achieved?

Nietzsche addresses both sets of questions. To the first, concerning hermeneutics' range, his answer appears to be: everything. It is not just texts, works of art, and so forth that demand interpretation, but something like the totality of human experience. Nietzsche's texts are replete with remarks on the pervasiveness of interpretation. Within a few dozen pages of *Beyond Good and Evil*, for example, he tells us that physics is "only an interpretation" of the world (BGE 22); that the Cartesian cogito "contains an interpretation of the process, and does not belong to the process itself" (BGE 17); that philosophical concepts and "world-interpretations" are constrained and channeled by the grammatical structure of the thinker's language (BGE 20); that modern morality represents "an odd narrowness of interpretation" (BGE 32); that an action's intention is "merely a sign and a symptom that still requires interpretation" (BGE 32); and one could go on and on.[1]

If the range of hermeneutics is the whole of human experience, hermeneutic's methods are equally broad. Nietzsche tells us that the philosopher

> must have been critic and skeptic and dogmatist and historian and also poet and collector and traveler and solver of riddles and moralist and seer and "free spirit" and almost everything in order to pass through the whole range of human values and value feelings and to be *able* to see with many different eyes and consciences, from a height and into every distance, from the depths into every height, from a nook into every expanse. (BGE 211)

For, if we seek understanding, we should aim for

> resolute reversals of accustomed perspectives and valuations ... to see differently in this way for once, and to *want* to see differently, is no small discipline and preparation of the intellect for its future "objectivity" ... There is *only* a perspective "knowing" and the *more* affects we allow to speak about one thing, the *more* eyes, different eyes, we can use to observe one thing, the more complete will our "concept" of this thing, our "objectivity," be. (GM III:12)[2]

Interpretation, whether of values or other entities, requires comprehensive knowledge, diverse abilities, and the capacity to switch between divergent perspectives.

As these tantalizing remarks indicate, Nietzsche is deeply concerned with the way in which human beings interpret phenomena. But, as I'll explain below, he also wants to draw attention to the ways in which seemingly uninterpreted phenomena, seemingly given experiences, have already been interpreted. And he wants to highlight the ways in which some of these interpretations have been *damaging*: "Wherever the theologians' instinct extends, *value judgments* have been stood on their heads and the concepts of 'true' and 'false' are of necessity reversed: whatever is most harmful to life is called 'true'; whatever elevates, enhances, affirms, justifies it, and makes it triumphant is called 'false'" (A 9).[3] Many of his works are devoted to this task.

So we have three points: the *range* of interpretation is something like the totality of human experience; the *methods* of interpretation include capacious knowledge as well as reversals of perspective; and interpretive skill is needed because many of our current interpretations are profoundly *damaging*. In this chapter, I'll provide a brief overview of these matters. I'll begin with a traditional way of classifying Nietzsche in relation to hermeneutics: he is often seen as offering a hermeneutics of suspicion. Finding this characterization potentially misleading, I then provide, in the second section, a discussion of Nietzsche's interpretive stance. The third section reviews Nietzsche's philosophical methodology and his objections to more traditional philosophical approaches. The fourth section discusses Nietzsche's interpretation of modernity as a whole as tending toward nihilism. The fifth section offers some brief reflections on the way in which Nietzsche influenced other thinkers in the hermeneutical tradition.

A HERMENEUTICS OF SUSPICION?

When Nietzsche is put in relation to the hermeneutical tradition, he is often characterized as offering a "hermeneutics of suspicion." The phrase derives from Paul Ricœur, who famously claimed that Nietzsche, along with Marx and Freud, belonged to a "school of suspicion." I'll begin my discussion by considering whether and in what sense this label might be helpful.

Ricœur says that what's distinctive of Nietzsche, along with Freud and Marx, is that "all three clear the horizon for a more authentic word, for a new reign of Truth, not only by means of a 'destructive' critique, but by the invention of an art of *interpreting*."[4] These thinkers inaugurate a new interpretive method that consists in demystifying phenomena and revealing their true meanings. Thus, simplistically, Nietzsche tries to show that what look like attempts to serve God or secure human flourishing are really just attempts to express and maintain power. What makes this a distinctive interpretive method, for Ricœur, is the way in which it works back from and undoes falsification: "the man of suspicion carries out in reverse the work of falsification of the man of guile."[5] Nietzsche, for example, "looks for the key to lying and masks on the side of" those who propound values.[6] So we first locate the ways in which phenomena have been deliberately obscured; we then try to clear away these distortions, working in reverse.

How accurate is this as a characterization of Nietzsche? In one sense, it's clearly true that Nietzsche adopts a suspicious stance toward phenomena that other philosophers take at face value. Nietzsche certainly does reject the stock interpretations of morality, agency, metaphysics, and so on; he certainly thinks these are superficial and need to be corrected.[7] But being suspicious of past philosophical interpretations is hardly distinctive; one of the abiding tropes in philosophy is the presentation of oneself as correcting all the failings of previous philosophers. Moreover, Ricœur's claims about the correction of deliberate falsification are exaggerations: while Nietzsche sometimes does present himself as revealing the way in which phenomena have been *willfully* misdescribed, this comprises only a small portion of his writings (e.g., a few sections of the *Genealogy* and *The Antichrist*). In terms of sheer volume, this material is swamped by the writings that aim at correcting errors, revealing misconceptions, putting forth new ideals, diagnosing cultural pathologies, and so forth. With a few key exceptions, Nietzsche thinks that falsification and distortion are rarely *deliberate*.

So we need to be more precise about what a hermeneutics of suspicion would be. Brian Leiter articulates a common interpretation of it: he writes that a hermeneutics of suspicion identifies the "causal forces that *explained* the conscious phenomena precisely because they laid bare the true *meaning* of those phenomena: I don't *really* want lots of money, I want the *love* I never got as a child; survivors have no moral claim on an inheritance, but it is in the interests of the ruling classes that we believe they do, and so on."[8] In other words, the hermeneutics of suspicion is often interpreted as a stance which discounts the agent's conscious understanding of a phenomenon and instead uncovers the *real and conflicting* cause of that phenomenon.

This, however, is too simplistic. We can see this already in the clichéd examples that Leiter offers: the idea that avowed motives often differ from attributed motives is just a truism, familiar since antiquity. If all that it takes to offer a hermeneutics of suspicion is to reiterate this truism, then every theologian who emphasizes the hidden sinfulness of human beings, every philosopher who worries about whether purportedly altruistic acts are actually selfish, every economist who distinguishes between expressed and revealed preferences, every novelist whose characters are not paragons of self-understanding should count. Clearly Nietzsche is doing more than this.

Now, at one level it's obvious that Nietzsche is interested in the distinction between the way things seem to a subject and the way things seem to a more perceptive, more historically sensitive observer. Thus, Ricœur writes that Nietzsche makes "the decision to look upon the whole of consciousness primarily as 'false' consciousness."[9] Certainly, there is some truth to this: Nietzsche writes, "actions are *never* what they appear to be [...] all actions are essentially unknown."[10] "We are necessarily strangers to ourselves, we do not comprehend ourselves, we *have* to misunderstand ourselves, for us the law 'each is furthest from himself' applies to all eternity" (GM Preface 1). So Nietzsche does suggest that self-ignorance and perhaps even self-deception are pervasive.

But there are two ways of misinterpreting this. First, we might think, with Leiter and others, that Nietzsche is discounting the conscious interpretations and treating the non-conscious meanings as the *true* or *real* meanings. But this simply doesn't fit with his texts, which consistently emphasize the importance of conscious misinterpretations:

> important as it may be to know the motives from which
> humanity has acted so far, it might be even more essential to

> know the *belief* people had in this or that motive, i.e. what humanity has imagined and told itself to be the real lever of its conduct so far. For people's inner happiness and misery has come to them depending on their belief in this or that motive – *not* through the actual motives. The latter are of second-order interest. (GS 44)[11]

This is just one passage, but it is characteristic of Nietzsche's works: the fact that a conscious interpretation is distorting, superficial, or falsifying does not entail that it can be ignored, that we could understand the agent in isolation from these distortions. A few sections later, Nietzsche writes that

> what things are called is unspeakably more important than what they are. The reputation, name, and appearance, the worth, the usual weight and measure of a thing – originally almost always something mistaken and arbitrary, thrown over things like a dress ... has, through the belief in it and its growth from generation to generation, slowly grown onto and into the thing and has become its very body: what started as appearance in the end nearly always becomes essence and functions [*wirkt*] as essence! [...] Let us not forget that in the long run it is enough to create new names and valuations and presumptions in order to create new "things." (GS 58)

People are interpreting animals, and the interpretations often distort their object. But these distortions are not idle: they influence the nature of the interpreted object. To conceive of ourselves as sinful, for example, doesn't make it so: but it does alter our relationship to our own activities, the emotions that we experience, the cultural institutions that we take part in, the values that we embrace, and so on.

So the first problem with characterizing Nietzsche as offering a hermeneutics of suspicion is that this is easily misconstrued as the claim that conscious interpretations should be discounted or ignored. On the contrary, they have immense importance.

Second, the claim can suggest that Nietzsche is interested in uncovering just any causal forces that are operative. But what he's especially interested in is the way in which normatively characterized phenomenon – moralities, social practices, customs, ideals – are misinterpreted by their bearers.[12] I'll explain this below.

NIETZSCHE'S INTERPRETIVE STANCE

I've suggested that the characterization of Nietzsche as offering a hermeneutics of suspicion, while accurate if interpreted in certain ways, is liable to lead to misunderstandings. In this section, I'll review some general features of Nietzsche's interpretive stance. Along the way, I'll note that many of these features are shared by other members of the hermeneutical tradition.

Rejection of Pre-Interpreted Phenomena

First, Nietzsche denies that there are any non-interpreted givens from which we can construct presuppositionless philosophical or scientific accounts. He claims that there are no "immediate certainties" and mocks the idea that knowledge can get "hold of its object purely and nakedly" (BGE 16). Even our most basic relationship to the world, via sense-perception, is mediated by value judgments:

> There is no doubt that all sense perceptions are wholly permeated with *value-judgments*... [*gänzlich durchsetzt sind mit Werthurtheilen*...]. (KSA 12: 2[95])[13]

He suggests that the world presents itself as alluring and aversive, as useful and resistant, as threatening and charming. It incorporates evaluative characteristics as a result of the way in which it relates to our activities and interests. We cannot, he suggests, get past this to some perspective-free way of accessing the world.

And what's true of the world in general is true of the self in particular:

> There are still harmless self-observers who believe that there are "immediate certainties"; for example, "I think," or as

the superstition of Schopenhauer put it, "I will"; as though knowledge here got hold of its object purely and nakedly as "the thing in itself" without any falsification on the part of either the subject or the object. But that "immediate certainty," as well as "absolute knowledge" and the "thing in itself," involve a *contradictio in adjecto*. I shall repeat a hundred times; we really ought to free ourselves from the seduction of words! Let the people suppose that knowledge means knowing things entirely; the philosopher must say to himself: When I analyze the process that is expressed in the sentence, "I think," I find a whole series of daring assertions that would be difficult, perhaps impossible, to prove; for example, that it is I who think, that there must necessarily be something that thinks, that thinking is an activity and operation on the part of a being who is thought of as a cause, that there is an "ego," and, finally, that it is already determined what is to be designated by thinking – that I know what thinking is [...] In place of the "immediate certainty" in which the people may believe in the case at hand, the philosopher thus finds a series of metaphysical questions presented to him, truly searching questions of the intellect; to wit: "From where do I get the concept of thing? Why do I believe in cause and effect? What gives me the right to speak of an ego, and even of an ego as cause, and finally ego as the cause of thought?" (BGE 16)

What presents itself as immediate is, in fact, mediated by conceptual distinctions, metaphysical assumptions, and so on. Thus, after reviewing various examples of purportedly given phenomena, such as experiences of the *will* or the *I*, Nietzsche claims that

> individual philosophical concepts are not anything capricious or autonomously evolving, but grow up in connection and relationship with each other; that, however suddenly and arbitrarily they seem to appear in the history of thought, they nevertheless belong just as much to a system as all the members of the fauna of a continent. (BGE 20)

In these passages, Nietzsche argues that apparently given phenomena – sensory experiences and perceptions of the fact that I am thinking, for example – have a host of presuppositions about the nature of agency, thinking, subjectivity, causality, and thinghood. Were my concept of agency different, Nietzsche emphasizes, I would not perceive my own thinking in the same way. If this is right, then my current conceptual repertoire influences even the most basic perceptions.

The examples above focus on perceptual concepts and philosophical concepts, but for Nietzsche this is a fully general point. Changes in conceptual repertoires lead to changes in purportedly immediate experiences, thereby revealing these experiences not to be immediate at all.

Holism

As the passage from BGE 20 suggests, Nietzsche's rejection of immediate certainties is built upon a form of holism. In fact, he embraces at least two forms of *holism*. He is a holist about *meaning*; and he is a methodological holist about physical and social phenomena.

With regard to meaning, Nietzsche holds that the meanings of concepts are interdependent. Although the above passages focus on specifically philosophical concepts, Nietzsche elsewhere generalizes the point. As he puts it in his notebooks, "An isolated judgment is never 'true,' never knowledge; only in connection and relation of many judgments is there any surety" (KSA 12[7]:4).

Moreover, his approach to studying physical and social phenomena is holistic: as I'll discuss in the following sections, he believes that these phenomena can be grasped and understood only in their historical and social contexts.

Perspectivism

The holism leads into a related topic: perspectivism. I've elsewhere argued that Nietzsche's perspectivism is best understood as a development of Kant's view.[14] According to Kant, the way in which we cognize the world depends upon the pure concepts of the understanding, or categories, which are specifications of our most fundamental concepts and the relations among them. Kant argues that these concepts and relations are uniform for all rational agents (*Critique of Pure Reason* A80/B106 ff.). Nietzsche accepts the Kantian claim that concepts structure experience. However, he rejects the view that there is one set of concepts and conceptual relations that we necessarily impose upon our experience. Instead, he argues that there are many different, mutually incompatible systems of concepts. We have no way of assessing these systems from an external, neutral vantage point in order to determine which is best. Thus, he claims that the "perspective," or set of relatively fundamental concepts and conceptual relations, differs across historical time; these perspectives include classificatory and evaluative concepts; and, while some perspectives can be shown to be internally inconsistent, to occlude phenomena that other perspectives reveal, and so on, none can be shown to be best.[15]

Nonetheless, we take these perspectives to present us with immediate, unbiased presentations of objects. We fail to see the way in which the perspectives are local and contingent. For the perspectives are ensconced even in our language:

> The word and the concept are the most manifest ground for our belief in this isolation of groups of actions: we do not only *designate* things with them, we think originally that through them we grasp the *true* in things. Through words and concepts we are still continually misled into imagining things as being simpler than they are, separate from one another, indivisible, each existing in and for itself. A philosophical mythology lies concealed in *language* which breaks out again every moment, however careful one may be otherwise.[16]

Our language, our concepts, our distinctions are taken to map onto the structure of the world; whereas, in fact, Nietzsche thinks the world as we experience it is partially constituted by these concepts themselves.

Given that our experiences are partially constituted by these perspectives, Nietzsche believes that understanding physical and social phenomena requires attention to the perspective of which they are a part. This is perhaps where he comes closest to the traditional debates within hermeneutics. Around the turn of the nineteenth century, there was sustained debate about whether the human sciences required different methodological approaches than the natural sciences. Some of the philosophers most closely associated with the hermeneutical tradition, including Dilthey, advocated a distinct, hermeneutical approach to the human sciences. Put simply, these thinkers argued that the human sciences were distinctive in that they concerned meanings that would be lost or occluded by a natural scientific approach. Nietzsche is not directly engaged with this debate. He sees the natural sciences as continuous with the human sciences. But this is not for the familiar reason – it is not because the human sciences need not concern themselves with meanings. Rather, it is because he sees the natural sciences, too, as concerned with meanings. So, while thinkers like Helmholtz argue that human sciences deal with value whereas natural sciences deal only with "dead, indifferent matter," Nietzsche sees the natural sciences as tacitly concerned with value as well: not in the sense that values are the explicit object of concern, but in the sense that the allegedly value-free distinctions and concepts with which (say) the physicist operates presuppose and reinforce evaluative views.[17] Thus, in *Beyond Good and Evil*, Nietzsche writes that

> It is perhaps just dawning on five or six minds that physics, too, is only a world-interpretation and exegesis of the world (to suit *us*, if I may say so!) and *not* a world-explanation. (BGE 14)

He continues:

> "Nature's conformity to law," of which you physicists talk so proudly, as though – why, it exists only owing to your interpretation and bad "philology." It is no matter of fact, no

> "text," but rather just a naively humanitarian adjustment and perversion of meaning, with which you make abundant concessions to the democratic instincts of the modern soul! "Everywhere equality before the law – Nature is not different in that respect, nor better than we": a fine instance of secret motive, in which the vulgar antagonism to everything privileged and autocratic – likewise a second and more refined atheism – is once more disguised. (BGE 22)

Analogously, in the *Gay Science*, Nietzsche criticizes the "faith with which so many materialistic natural scientists rest content nowadays, the faith in a world that is supposed to have its equivalent and its measure in human thought and human valuations ... That the only rightful interpretation of the world should be ... one that permits counting, calculating, weighing, seeing, grasping, and nothing else" (GS 373).

Regardless of whether Nietzsche's claims about physics are defensible, they do illustrate his general point: there is no set of concepts or distinctions that is wholly free of evaluative implications and assumptions.

Concepts and Language

Nietzsche extends these reflections on concepts and language to an analysis of conscious thought. He maintains that conscious thought is itself dependent on concepts:

> Man, like every living being, thinks continually without knowing it [*denkt immerfort, aber weiss es nicht*]; the thinking that rises to *consciousness* is only the smallest part of all this – the most superficial and worst part – for only this conscious thinking *occurs in words, which is to say signs of communication* [*denn allein dieses bewußte Denken* geschieht in Worten, das heisst in Mittheilungszeichen], and this fact uncovers the origin of consciousness. In brief, the development of language and the

development of consciousness (*not* of Reason but merely of the way Reason enters consciousness) go hand in hand. (GS 354)

Here, Nietzsche claims that conscious thinking is linguistically articulated. Elsewhere, I have argued that he means, by this, that conscious thinking is conceptually articulated.[18] But, for the reasons discussed in the previous section, the meanings of concepts are not transparent to agents. We fail to recognize the way in which our thoughts are channeled by linguistic structures and concepts. Accordingly, Nietzsche takes conscious (that is, linguistic/conceptual) experience to falsify and distort non-conscious thought. Different conceptual schemes would reveal different aspects of non-conscious thought; none would present it as it is pre-conceptually. Thus, "the world of which we can become conscious is merely a surface- and sign-world, a world generalized and made common [*eine Oberflächen- und Zeichenwelt, eine verallgemeinerte, eine vergemeinerte Welt*]" (GS 354). Consciousness is a "simplifying apparatus" (KSA 11: 34[46]), which "involves a vast and thorough corruption, falsification, superficialization, and generalization" (GS 354).

NIETZSCHE'S METHODOLOGY

Genealogical Investigation of Perspectives

The picture that emerges from Nietzsche's writings is one in which we must give up the idea that there are any simply *given* phenomena: concepts, propositions, and indeed even our experiences have meaning only in relation to the perspectives of which they are a part. How, then, are these phenomena to be understood? Nietzsche's answer is well-known: we must engage in genealogy.

Nietzsche attributes the general point to Hegel. He says that Hegel is one of only three Germans who made substantial philosophical contributions.[19] Specifically, he notes "Hegel's astonishing move, with which he struck through all logical habits and indulgences when he dared to teach that species concepts develop *out of each other*" (GS 357). In other words, Hegel saw that concepts are not fixed and immutable, but are things with histories; he saw that grasping the meaning of a concept required situating it in its own conceptual scheme.

But there is a crucial difference between Nietzsche and Hegel. Hegel has a vindicatory story according to which, in broad outlines, inadequate conceptual schemes are sublated by progressively more adequate ones. Although there are controversies about how to read the transitions between conceptual schemes that Hegel discusses in the *Phenomenology* and elsewhere, one reading is that the progression is rational: the felt inadequacy of a given conceptual scheme motivates the introduction of a new conceptual scheme, which resolves the tensions or contradictions in the former scheme. Whether this is the best way of reading Hegel does not matter; what does matter is that Nietzsche rejects it. For Nietzsche sees shifts between conceptual schemes as mostly arational. We should not expect rational progressions in conceptual transitions: we should not expect supplanting perspectives to resolve tensions in the supplanted perspectives. In the *Genealogy*, for example, Nietzsche investigates the transition between an ancient warrior morality and Judeo-Christian morality. Rather than tracing the transition to conceptual inadequacies in the former, he believes a host of social and psychological factors ranging from the desire for political power, the desire for vindicatory self-conceptions, and fantasies of revenge on an oppressive ruling class to self-deception about the nature of agency explain the transition. These factors are highly contingent and likely unrepeatable: there is no expectation that societies with similar structures would undergo analogous transformations. In that sense, the explanation is quite local. Moreover, the supplanting moral scheme does not resolve tensions within the former scheme; on the contrary, Nietzsche is at pains to present the later moral scheme as even more conflict-ridden, distorting, and inadequate than the former.

Genealogy thus reveals that transitions between conceptual schemes and the persistence of these schemes are explained by arational social and psychological processes. But genealogy also helps us to grasp the phenomena in which we are interested. Take morality: absent genealogy, we might erroneously assume that morality is a unified phenomenon, with parts that cohere, with a unified goal, a unified meaning. Nietzsche instead presents it as an amalgam of disparate parts, welded together only by historical accident. Nietzsche makes the same point about social phenomena in general: he thinks that understanding any particular social phenomenon (punishment, judgments of responsibility, moral codes, political ideals, etc.) requires situating that phenomenon in its historical context. Consider his famous remarks on punishment: he writes that while the "custom," "act," and "drama" of punishment is relatively constant across societies, "the meaning, the purposes, the expectation associated with the performance of such procedures" is "fluid" (GM II: 13). The mechanisms of punishment (constraint, infliction of suffering, etc.) are relatively constant; but the meaning is not. For

> the concept "punishment" possesses in fact not one meaning but a whole synthesis of "meanings": the previous history of punishment in general, the history of its employment for the most various purposes, finally crystallizes into a kind of unity that is hard to disentangle, hard to analyze and, as must be emphasized especially, totally indefinable. (Today it is impossible to say for certain why people are really punished: all concepts in which an entire process is semiotically concentrated elude definition; only that which has no history is definable.) (GM II: 13)

The same point applies to other social practices. When we examine what initially looks like a unified, stable phenomenon, we find discontinuities, amalgamations of loosely related purposes, and the grafting of disconnected practices onto one another. Thus, Nietzsche writes that one of the dangerous errors of philosophers is

> their lack of an historical sense, their hatred of the very idea of becoming, their Egypticism. They think that they show their

> *respect* for a thing when they dehistoricize it, *sub specie aeterni* – when they turn it into a mummy. All that philosophers have handled for thousands of years have been concept-mummies; nothing real escaped their grasp alive. Whenever these venerable concept-idolaters revere something, they kill it and stuff it; they threaten the life of everything they worship. (TI III: 1)[20]

This is one reason why a genealogical approach is needed. Genealogy traces the contingent historical connections between phenomena, showing how they emerged, were transformed, and persisted.

Assessing Perspectives

Assume that we conduct a detailed historical and genealogical investigation of a perspective, getting it clearly into view. What next? Nietzsche suggests that the articulation of the perspective sometimes enables us to critique it. In fact, he presents this as his real aim: "my real concern was something much more important than hypothesis-mongering, either my own or other people's, on the origin of morality ... what was at stake was the *value* of morality" (GM Preface 5). So genealogy somehow enables critique. But how, exactly?

Although there are different interpretive options, I think the most defensible reading is a roughly Hegelian one: Nietzsche appeals solely to *immanent critique*. On this interpretation, we have to show that a perspective is defective in terms of standards that the inhabitants of the perspective would themselves accept. Perspective A is better than perspective B if you can show an inhabitant of perspective B that she has reason to switch to perspective A.

This criterion is often interpreted solely in epistemic terms. On this reading, the transition from B to A involves some kind of epistemic gain: it resolves a contradiction to which B succumbs, or explains a phenomenon that B occludes, or resolves a tension within B, and so on. So, for example, *The Genealogy* argues that Judeo-Christian morality has inconsistent values, incoherent conceptions of agency and responsibility, and so on. We can recognize this from within the Judeo-Christian perspective; and we can thus see that we have reason to modify or abandon it.

But what about situations in which we're faced with two incommensurable perspectives, each with its own flaws, with neither one resolving the tensions within the other? This is, more or less, the scenario Nietzsche presents us with in the *Genealogy*. True, Judeo-Christian morality is presented as leading to pathology, self-deception, and a hindrance of human flourishing; but the archaic warrior morality looks oppressive, superficial, and damning for the bulk of humanity. Epistemic criteria won't provide good grounds for shifting from one to the other; both contain internal tensions and contradictions.

Crucially, Nietzsche also appeals to evaluative criteria in assessing perspectives. Roughly, he tries to show that certain perspectives should be rejected because they undermine or conflict with "will to power." He often expresses this point by claiming that a given perspective is counter to *life* or *health*; but those notions are defined in terms of will to power. Thus, he writes that modern morality is "hostile to life" and "negates life,"[21] that it undermines "the highest power and splendor actually possible to the type man" (GM Preface 6), and so on. How should these remarks be taken? As I interpret him, Nietzsche argues for a conception of agency according to which each action aims at power; given this, moral interpretations which occlude this connection, or which lead us astray from our aims, are to be rejected. Thus, these critiques in terms of power are still immanent critique, because the standard of will to power is (purportedly) present in every perspective.[22]

So we can critique perspectives on immanent grounds, and these grounds can be both epistemic and evaluative. This will enable us to show that certain perspectives are preferable to others. However, Nietzsche does not think that this will give us a unique final perspective. He thinks there will be different, mutually incompatible perspectives that are equally well justified. Or, put differently: there are better and worse perspectives, but we have no reason to believe that there is any *best* perspective. Notice, too, that this critique is always historically situated. We do not generate and assess perspectives *ex nihilo*. We start with our own perspective, and move on (or not) from there.

Does Nietzsche Have a Specific Hermeneutical Theory?

Given all of this, Nietzsche rejects the idea that there are unitary, neatly distinguishable natural, social, and evaluative phenomena: what looks unified from one perspective will not from another. But does Nietzsche advocate any specific method for studying these phenomena? Does he, as Ricœur and others suggest, endorse some explicit hermeneutical strategy?

As I read him, he doesn't. Nietzsche rejects ahistorical approaches to these phenomena. Aside from that, though, he does not offer any specific set of procedures that one must follow. He is always open to revision: he treats his own hypotheses as provisional. Thus, after offering a genealogy of the transition from Homeric morality to Judeo-Christian morality, he appends a note suggesting that someone organize a "series of academic prize essays" on the history of morality, open to philologists, historians, professional philosophers, doctors, and physiologists (GM I:17). The suggestion seems to be that these studies could supplant his own.

We can make a few additional generalizations, though. For one thing, Nietzsche is interested in normatively characterized phenomena. Although this is probably obvious to most readers, Nietzsche is concerned with practices in which agents adopt norms, principles, values; in which they adopt normatively laden concepts such as obedience and guilt; and in which their own perspectives on these phenomena make a difference in determining what these phenomena are.

Additionally, Nietzsche does not suggest that interpretation of these phenomena requires identifying some *best* interpretation and showing that and why it is superior to erroneous interpretations. Rather, he tries to offer *better* explanations. He tries to show that interpretation A is better than interpretation B in that A reveals things that B conceals, or accounts for factors that B overlooks, or makes sense of contradictions and tensions in B, or reveals otherwise hidden connections, or makes better sense of the agents' motivations, etc. So, the person who understands some area, who has knowledge of it, is best understood as the person who has a systematic understanding of a series of related facts, who sees how these facts connect; often the connections will not be logical entailments, and often seeing the connections will require both historical sensitivity and interpretive skill.

INTERPRETING HISTORY, INTERPRETING MODERNITY

With these remarks on interpretation, language, and thought at hand, we can examine one of the most familiar features of Nietzsche's philosophy: his claims about the death of God and impending nihilism.

Nietzsche treats human beings as fundamentally driven by a desire for interpretations of their experience that render experience meaningful. Consider Nietzsche's first book, the *Birth of Tragedy*.[23] There, he writes that "the Greek knew and felt the terror and horror of existence" (BT 3); in particular, the Greek recognized that "despite all its beauty and moderation, his entire existence rested on a hidden substratum of suffering" (BT 4). The Olympian gods were designed to address this need: "that he might endure this terror at all, he had to interpose between himself and life the radiant dream-birth of the Olympians" (BT 3). The Olympian gods were intended for "seducing one to a continuation of life" (BT 3).

Analogous points are made in the *Gay Science*. In a section entitled "The teachers of the purpose of existence," Nietzsche writes:

> At present, we still live in the age of tragedy, in the age of moralities and religions. What is the meaning of the ever-new appearance of these founders of moralities and religions, of these instigators of fights about moral valuations, these teachers of pangs of conscience and religious wars? ... It is obvious that these

> tragedies, too, work in the interest of the *species,* even if they should believe that they are working in the interest of God, as God's emissaries. They, too, promote the life of the species *by promoting the faith in life.* "Life is worth living," each of them shouts, "there is something to life, there is something behind life, beneath it; beware!" ... Life *ought to* be loved *because* – ! ... The ethical teacher makes his appearance as the teacher of the purpose of existence in order that what happens necessarily and always, by itself and without a purpose, shall henceforth seem to be done for a purpose and strike man as reason and an ultimate commandment. (GS 1)

Here, Nietzsche claims that the essential feature of religions and moralities is that they provide an explanation or meaning for otherwise meaningless events. In its most general form, this is the belief that life has some meaning or purpose. In more particular contexts, it is the belief that certain actions or pursuits are worthy and others worthless.

Analogously, at the end of the *Genealogy*, he writes:

> [Man] did not know how to justify, explain, affirm himself: *he suffered from the problem of his meaning.* He suffered otherwise as well, he was for the most part a diseased animal; but the suffering itself was not his problem, rather that the answer was missing to the scream of his question: *"to what end* suffering?" Man, the bravest of animals and the one most accustomed to suffering, does *not* negate suffering, he wants it, he even seeks it out, provided one shows him a meaning for it, a to-this-end of suffering. *The meaninglessness of suffering, not suffering itself, was the curse thus far stretched over humanity.* (GM III: 28)

In these passages, Nietzsche again emphasizes the profound desire that we have to interpret our existence in a way that renders it meaningful. He claims that particular moral systems, from the morality of the ancient Greeks, to that of the early Christians, to that of modernity, are responsive to this need.

He worries, though, that we are on the cusp of a crisis. The systems that formerly answered this need are becoming unsustainable. Briefly, his point is that we have come to value truth for its own sake, as opposed to merely for the sake of other ends; when this commitment to truth becomes sufficiently strong, Nietzsche claims that it will undermine the purported grounds for our traditional values (see GM III). He tells us that "the whole of our European morality" is on the verge of "collapse" (GS 343), for "the deeper one looks, the more our valuations disappear – *meaninglessness approaches!*" (KSA 11:25[505]). For truthful inquiry reveals that these moral systems have been supported on extraordinarily thin grounds.

Suppose this is right. Nietzsche worries that with the collapse of ideals, we will enter a phase of nihilism. Although Nietzsche discusses several different types of nihilism, the one that is relevant here is anomie: social pressures, convention, emotional attachments, and so forth may keep us attached to certain values for a time, but these values lack any coherent justification. As a result, our commitments are at risk of becoming attenuated: we may cease to treat these values as overriding and authoritative. We see them as optional, as capable of being abandoned. Custom, habit, and inertia might preserve vestigial forms of these values, but the sense of their importance, the sense that they override competing pressures, will dissipate.

When this occurs, the desire for interpretations that render existence meaningful or affirmable goes unmet. Thus, Nietzsche endeavors to give some new interpretations: he considers efforts to curtail or circumscribe the will to truth, efforts to enact an aesthetic justification of existence, efforts to affirm the eternal recurrence of one's life, and struggles to inaugurate new ideals (GS Preface 4, GS 107, BGE 59, GM III). I lack the space to explore the details here, but the common thread is readily apparent: Nietzsche wants to find a way of preserving these meaning-conferring interpretations in historical and social circumstances that render them dubious.

NIETZSCHE'S INFLUENCE

In closing, a very brief word on the powerful and pervasive influence of Nietzsche's thought. Georg Simmel describes Nietzsche as the Copernicus of philosophical ethics, effecting a transformation in philosophy as profound as that of Copernicus in astronomy.[24] The list of thinkers influenced by him encompasses nearly all of the notable German and French philosophers of the twentieth century, including many who play active roles in the hermeneutical tradition: Adorno, Camus, Deleuze, Foucault, Heidegger, Horkheimer, Jaspers, Sartre, Scheler, Weber, and the list could go on. Many of these thinkers are covered by other chapters in this volume, so let me close by mentioning just one: Michel Foucault, who is especially close to Nietzsche.

Foucault's methodological approach is in many respects Nietzschean: like Nietzsche, Foucault devotes many of his works to revealing the historically contingent and fluid nature of concepts, social institutions, and values that have traditionally been taken as necessary and fixed. Like Nietzsche, Foucault tries to reveal the way in which purportedly universal truths about human beings and human nature are, when examined carefully, contingent expressions of the evaluative beliefs of particular cultures. Like Nietzsche, Foucault's critical analyses of present conditions often reveal the way in which these present conditions are damaging or oppressive. And, like Nietzsche, Foucault believes that these damaging effects often require careful study: they are not obvious at first glance; uncovering them requires attentive, prolonged investigation of social institutions and practices.

But there are differences. One that stands out right away, when comparing the two thinkers, is the level of historical detail and erudition in Foucault's studies. Nietzsche's historical texts – *The Birth of Tragedy, The Genealogy, The Antichrist* – are brilliant but, with a few exceptions, are largely unmoored from concrete, detailed historical evidence. The evidence may be there in the background – Foucault may be right that genealogy "depends on a vast accumulation of source material" – but, if Nietzsche has this evidence, he certainly doesn't present it.[25] So, whereas Nietzsche spends a few pages on the changing forms and meanings of punishment (*Genealogy of Morals* II), Foucault provides over three hundred pages, replete with detailed evidence, on the emergence of the modern penal system.[26]

In addition, Foucault's distinction between archaeology and genealogy involves something of a departure from Nietzsche. In most of his texts, Foucault advocates an "archaeological" approach.[27] He maintains that philosophical and scientific systems, as well as knowledge claims in general, are governed by principles that operate non-consciously. Thus, studying what individuals consciously think will give us only part of the picture; we also need to examine the unconscious structures within which these conscious thoughts arise. Archaeology attempts to uncover these structures, revealing the way in which they constrain thought within particular perspectives (or "epistemes," as Foucault calls them). Whereas archaeology reveals these principles, in late works Foucault presents genealogy as playing a more critical role: it shows the *effects* of these contingent principles on the present, and thereby seeks to undermine or destabilize them.[28]

CONCLUDING REMARKS

This chapter has outlined the ways in which Nietzsche's concerns intersect with those of the hermeneutical tradition. I began by arguing that while characterizing Nietzsche as offering a hermeneutics of suspicion is not wrong, it is easily misinterpreted. More concretely, I have argued that Nietzsche's interpretive stance has several key features: he rejects immediate givens, endorses holism and perspectivism, and sees conscious experience as structured by concepts and language. Methodologically, Nietzsche inaugurates a genealogical approach to studying objects of philosophical concern, and offers a series of thoughts and arguments on perspectives and the ways in which they might be assessed. I reviewed the way in which he takes religious, moral, and philosophical systems as aspiring to provide an interpretation of existence that renders it meaningful, while seeing this demand as unmet by modernity. In closing, I offered some brief reflections on Foucault's Nietzschean approach to interpretation.

NOTES

1 Friedrich Nietzsche, *Jenseits von Gut und Böse* 1886. *Beyond Good and Evil*, trans. Walter Kaufmann (New York: Random House, 1967). Hereafter cited as BGE followed by section number.
2 Friedrich Nietzsche, *Zur Genealogie der Moral* 1887. *On the Genealogy of Morals*, trans. Walter Kaufmann and R. J. Hollingdale (New York: Random House, 1967). Hereafter cited as GM followed by part and section number.
3 Friedrich Nietzsche, *Der Antichrist* 1895. *The Antichrist*, trans. Walter Kaufmann and R. J. Hollingdale (New York: Random House, 1967). Hereafter cited as A followed by section number.
4 Paul Ricœur, *Freud and Philosophy*, trans. Denis Savage (New Haven: Yale University Press, 1965), 33.
5 Ricœur, *Freud and Philosophy*, 34.
6 Ricœur, *Freud and Philosophy*, 34.
7 For discussion of these points, see Paul Katsafanas, *The Nietzschean Self: Moral Psychology, Agency, and the Unconscious* (Oxford: Oxford University Press, 2016).
8 Brian Leiter, "The Hermeneutics of Suspicion: Recovering Marx, Nietzsche, and Freud," in *The Future for Philosophy*, ed. Brian Leiter (Oxford: Clarendon Press, 2006), 74.
9 Ricœur, *Freud and Philosophy*, 33.
10 Friedrich Nietzsche, *Morgenröthe* 1881, Section 195. *Daybreak*, trans. R. J. Hollingdale (Cambridge: Cambridge University Press, 1982), 116.
11 Friedrich Nietzsche, *Die fröhliche Wissenschaft* 1882/1887. *The Gay Science*, trans. Walter Kaufmann (New York: Random House, 1974). Hereafter cited as GS followed by section number.
12 True, Nietzsche occasionally gestures at non-normative, physiological explanations of particular actions. But these claims about physiology are most notable for their emptiness: Nietzsche makes no concrete claims about the connection between particular physiological states and particular actions.

13 Friedrich Nietzsche, *Sämtliche Werke, Kritische Studienausgabe in 15 Bänden*, ed. G. Colli and M. Montinari (Berlin: Walter de Gruyter, 1967–1977). Hereafter cited as KSA followed by volume, notebook, and entry number.
14 See *The Nietzschean Self*, ch. 3.
15 Nietzsche's talk of perspectives sometimes focuses on these kinds of conceptual changes, and sometimes on affective changes. Thus, he will point out that an individual's "perspective" can shift when the individual begins to experience different affects. As these points are less relevant for our purposes, I here focus solely on the points about concepts.
16 Friedrich Nietzsche, *Menschliches, Allzumenschliches 1878. Human, All too Human*, trans. R. J. Hollingdale (Cambridge: Cambridge University Press, 1996), Volume II, Part 2, Section 11.
17 Hermann von Helmholtz, "On the Relation of Natural Science to Science in General," in *Science and Culture: Popular and Philosophical Essays*, ed. David Cahan (Chicago: University of Chicago Press, 1995), 76–95, at 81.
18 See *The Nietzschean Self*, chs. 2–3.
19 Kant is credited with a second insight, specifically the one mentioned above about concepts structuring experience. The third is Leibniz, whom Nietzsche credits with the discovery of the unconscious.
20 Friedrich Nietzsche, *Götzen-Dämmerung 1889. Twilight of the Idols*, trans. Walter Kaufmann, in *The Portable Nietzsche* (New York: Viking, 1968). Hereafter cited as TI followed by part and section number.
21 Friedrich Nietzsche, *Nietzsche Contra Wagner 1895. Nietzsche Contra Wagner*, trans. Walter Kaufmann, in *The Portable Nietzsche* (New York: Viking, 1968).
22 Paul Katsafanas, *Agency and the Foundations of Ethics: Nietzschean Constitutivism* (Oxford: Oxford University Press, 2013), ch. 6.
23 Friedrich Nietzsche, *Die Geburt der Tragödie aus dem Geiste der Musik 1872. The Birth of Tragedy*, trans. Walter Kaufmann, in *Basic Writings of Nietzsche* (New York: Modern Library, 1967). Hereafter cited as BT followed by section number.
24 Georg Simmel, *Friedrich Nietzsche – Eine moralphilosophische Silhouette*, in *Aufsätze und Abhandlungen, 1894 bis 1900*, ed. H. Dahme and D. Frisby (Frankfurt am Main: Suhrkamp, 1992), 124.

25 Michel Foucault, "Nietzsche, Genealogy, History," in *The Foucault Reader*, ed. Paul Rabinow (London: Penguin, 1984).
26 Michel Foucault, *Surveiller et punir* (Paris: Gallimard, 1975) (*Discipline and Punish*, trans. Alan Sheridan, New York: Pantheon, 1977).
27 Michel Foucault, *L'archéologie du savoir* (Paris: Gallimard, 1969) (*The Archaeology of Knowledge*, trans. Alan Sheridan, New York: Harper & Row, 1972).
28 See, for example, Foucault, *Discipline and Punish*.

8 Hermeneutics and Psychoanalysis

Sebastian Gardner

THE AMBIGUITY OF PSYCHOANALYSIS

The relation of hermeneutics to psychoanalysis is close yet uneasy. Its crux lies in the distinctive and peculiar combination of conceptual commitments found in psychoanalytic explanation. Freud famously accords a presiding role to the practice of interpretation, whereby psychoanalysis is distinguished sharply from other schools of psychology, but he also denies that mental life is constituted throughout by meaning: interpretation may be the "royal road"[1] leading to a new realm of psychological facts and therapeutic technique, but psychoanalysis does not confine itself to meanings and their relations.

This duality reflects another, closely associated ambiguity. The central *explananda* of psychoanalysis – dreams, symptoms, parapraxes, disturbances of affect, sexual perversions, and so on – present themselves as situated on the exact border between the personal and sub-personal. They belong on the one hand within the orbit of individual life, in a way that neural processes and the modules of cognitive science do not, yet they also signal points at which self-consciousness gives way to motivational forces which are no longer determinately personal but rather animal or even mechanical. Hence Freud's requirement that a special receptive stance, suspending the stamp of reflective personality, be adopted toward one's own mental life in order to release the initial data from which unconscious meanings can be extracted.[2]

Freud's inaugural hypothesis concerning the meaning of dreams postulates processes of "condensation" (*Verdichtung*) and "displacement" (*Verschiebung*). These bear loose comparison with

---

I am indebted to audiences at Bonn Universität and University College Dublin for comments on an earlier version of this chapter.

metaphor and other poetic-linguistic operations,[3] but they also, as Freud explains them, implicate concepts of mental *force* and mental *location* – the "economic" and "topographical" points of view.[4] This conception of the dream-work, which transforms "latent" content into "manifest" content, implies that thought and meaning, in addition to playing their familiar rational roles, are also objects of quasi-mechanical manipulation within the psyche. Behind the dream-work lie other, more comprehensive principles of unconscious mental life, which Freud collectively gathers under the heading "primary process" – the pleasure principle, and the "special characteristics" intrinsic to the system *Ucs.*, including timelessness and absence of contradiction[5] – and which again are essentially non-hermeneutical in character.

These assumptions are strictly necessary for Freud's dream interpretations: without the hypothesis of a mental apparatus which structures thought in accordance with principles that could not figure in self-conscious thinking, and shapes the mind's contents independently of any end that the agent could avow, the lateral connections Freud traces between words, ideas, memory-images and so on would simply not add up. Nor would it be possible to conceive dreams as meaningful wholes, that is, essential unities of latent and manifest content which can be translated into one another in the manner of texts, and regarded as expressions of emotion and desire.[6]

Individual psychopathology, and phenomena such as dreams, which ordinary psychological understanding is able to describe without pretending to explain, are what allows psychoanalysis to get its original explanatory purchase, but they do not of course exhaust its range. Having established what he takes to be the fundamental principles of mental functioning, Freud turns to the spheres of social and cultural life and makes deep incursions into the humanities and human sciences. A full account of Freud's interpretative ventures and the special problems which attend them (in particular with regard to artworks) is not possible here, but significant distinguishing features of the psychoanalytic treatment of socio-cultural phenomena include

(1) its illumination of their deep roots in psychic life, which allow social and cultural practices to sustain and reproduce themselves in ways that public reason seems unable to account for, and (2) its power to rationalize not only normal but also pathological social forms. These features are chiefly responsible for the high interest which Freud holds for critical theory in the work of Fromm, Horkheimer, Adorno, Marcuse, and Honneth, who employ psychoanalysis to address the problems posed by ideological subjection, voluntary servitude, fascism, alienation, and so on.

Psychoanalysis thus in one respect offers itself to hermeneutical thought as an ally in the vindication and elaboration of concepts of meaning and understanding, which it shows to have greater scope than previously envisaged, contra reductive naturalistic forms of explanation in psychology and the human sciences; forms of psychology that by contrast merely analyse ordinary psychological understanding – as is the case when cognitive competences are decomposed into their functional elements – do not hold similar hermeneutical interest. Yet at the same time psychoanalysis poses a challenge by virtue of its apparent implication that meaning and understanding are precisely not self-sufficient in the way supposed by at least strong hermeneuticists such as Gadamer. Even when psychoanalytic explanation deals with the most quintessentially rational and meaning-constituted objects of enquiry – works of art, religious beliefs and practices, the normative social bond – it remains committed to showing that these derive ultimately from sources which, whatever they amount to exactly, cannot be regarded as securing their own intelligibility in the way that thinkers in the hermeneutical tradition, from Herder onwards, have standardly maintained with regard to *Bildung*, tradition, objective spirit, and suchlike. It is notable that Freud has no general theory of interpretation, either philosophical or psychological, and that it is not through reflection on the nature of understanding as such that he arrives at his conception of psychological interpretation. Freud's indifference to considerations central to philosophical hermeneutics is reflected in his attitude to language, to which he attaches importance only in so far as it provides (1) the mechanism and marker of consciousness,[7] and, consequently, (2) the unique medium of therapeutic technique. Freud conceives therapy, furthermore, as directed to the bare hedonic end of reducing suffering: the idea that self-understanding, or interpretative self-constitution, is an end in itself which constitutes the final goal of therapy, is not found in Freud himself.

One conclusion which has been drawn is that psychoanalysis and hermeneutics are in fact irreconcilable. The real and abiding significance of psychoanalysis, it has been argued, lies in its demonstration of the explanatory superficiality of hermeneutical notions in contrast with robust, physically identified causes.[8] Freud's avowed positivism gives some grounds for this, but he also disclaims any direct access to the organic substrate of mental activity: in *The Interpretation of Dreams* Freud makes clear that his explanatory goals presuppose the autonomy of the psychological, at least as a methodological principle.[9] Proponents of natural-scientific readings of Freud, while acknowledging that the tendency of their approach is to reduce psychoanalysis to an anticipation of cognitive science and neuropsychology, have defended it nonetheless by arguing that hermeneutical construals fare worse in salvaging its truth-content. It is argued that, given the hermeneuticist's (alleged) dissociation of meaning from the controls of causal reality, it becomes impossible to say in what, other than subjective gratification, the correctness or validity of a psychoanalytic interpretation might consist.[10] What may consequently be recommended, on the scientistic view, is a splitting of Freud's legacy into, on the one hand, a genuinely scientific research program, which is presently underway and making actual progress but has largely left Freud's ideas behind; and, on the other, a loosely formulated psychological wisdom which has humanistic value but lacks strict truth and must submit itself to scientific regulation.

There is a great deal to be said about the general problems which flow from this dissociation of fact from value, and of scientific from ordinary understanding of human beings, but a more direct response is available. The charge of substituting confabulations of meaning for empirical reality rests on a confusion, in so far as what is assumed in hermeneutical readings of Freud is simply that interpretation provides the core means by which psychoanalysis traces the contours of mental phenomena – an epistemological claim to which questions of underlying causal ontology are secondary if not irrelevant, and which could not be controverted without impugning the entire apparatus of common sense psychology. It is true of course that, just as some naturalists perceive intentional idioms as inimical to genuine explanation, at least some hermeneutical readers of Freud contest the general metaphysics of scientific realism ("positivism" or "objectivism"). But the fact that psychoanalysis raises so acutely the question of the relation of meaning and causality – and thereby re-occasions the ancient quarrel of scientific realists and hermeneuticists – does not mean that it should be expected to contain the resources for resolving this wholly general philosophical issue. The real question is whether psychoanalytic interpretation, equipped with its basic assumptions concerning the shape of the mind, is arbitrary in ways that ordinary psychological interpretation is not. Critics of hermeneutical readings of Freud have not shown that this is the case.

If we are to give an account of psychoanalysis which conserves its hermeneutical dimension, then two questions need to be addressed. First we must ask to what extent psychoanalysis is committed implicitly, by virtue of the role it accords to interpretation, to the standpoint of philosophical hermeneutics, and if so, whether making this commitment explicit entails revisions to psychoanalytic theory. One possibility, accordingly, is that hermeneutical reflection reveals the need for an overhaul of psychoanalytic theory that purges it of elements which fail to agree with the general conception of psychological life as constituted throughout by practices of understanding and interpretation. We will see that this is the option developed by Habermas.

The second question is whether, assuming some sort of challenge to be posed, psychoanalysis forces adjustments on hermeneutics. The possibility to be explored here is that psychoanalysis shows its limitations as a general approach to human understanding, or at the very least, the need to draw a distinction within hermeneutics between two different tasks and types of theory or interpretative practice, one pitched at self-consciously articulated meaning and the other at its non-conscious underpinnings. This we will see is roughly the answer returned by Ricœur.

THE PROBLEM FACING A HERMENEUTICAL CONSTRUAL OF FREUD: SARTRE AND WITTGENSTEIN

To get the task into better focus, we may look at two early critical appraisals of Freud: Sartre's treatment of psychoanalysis in his short essay on the emotions from 1939, and Wittgenstein's remarks on Freud from the 1940s as reported in *Lectures and Conversations*. Both Sartre and Wittgenstein decline to take at face value Freud's self-affiliation to the natural sciences, and have some sympathy with Freud's project, but proceed to identify, from different angles, one and the same deep conceptual problem for psychoanalytic explanation as construed hermeneutically.[11]

1. Here is what Sartre says on the subject of psychoanalytic symbolism:

> The psychoanalytical interpretation considers the phenomenon of consciousness as the symbolic realization of a desire repressed by censorship. Let us note that for consciousness this desire *is not implicated in its symbolic realization*. Insofar as it exists by and in our consciousness, it is only what it appears to be: emotion, desire for sleep, theft, phobia of bay-trees, etc. If it were otherwise and if we had some consciousness, *even implicit*, of our real desire, we should be *dishonest*; the psychoanalyst does not mean it that way. It follows that the signification of our conscious behaviour is entirely external to the behaviour itself, or, if one prefers, the *thing*

signified is entirely cut off from the *thing signifying*. The behaviour of the subject is, in itself, what it is (if we call "in itself" what it is *for itself*), but it is possible to decipher it by appropriate techniques as a written language is deciphered. In short, the conscious fact is to the thing signified as a thing, the *effect* of a certain event, is to that event, for example, as the traces of a fire lit on the mountain are to the human beings who lit the fire. Human presences are not *contained* in the ashes which remain.[12]

Freud, as Sartre understands him, wishes to conceive the conscious phenomena for which he offers psychoanalytic interpretations – affects and desires, and the instances of behavior which express them – as essentially *unified* with their underlying unconscious motivation, in just the way that the ordinary course of mental life presents us with intelligible wholes. But this cannot be done, Sartre argues, because the essential principle of all such unities, namely the subject's *taking-X-as-meaning-Y*, is necessarily missing; if it were present, then we would have make-believe, "dishonesty," or some other non-psychoanalytic mental configuration. The underlying problem, which Sartre expands on in his critique in *Being and Nothingness*,[13] is that Freud employs at one and the same time two incongruent models of the human subject, one that affirms its absolute unity and another that distributes its contents over a manifold of psychic parts. The first model affirms a One over the Many, and is in play when Freud asserts that X *means* Y; the second affirms a mere Many without a unifying One, and is employed when Freud tries to tell us what X's meaning Y *consists in*, and why we should accept the attribution. Freud's naturalism, Sartre argues, abets this incoherence.

Sartre does not, however, regard Freud's undertaking as an overall failure. Though he rejects Freud's claim to have provided a theoretical solution, he believes that psychoanalytic conceptualization nonetheless succeeds in bringing to light the paradoxical character of human motivation, and this *explanandum* furnishes the subject matter for Sartre's own hermeneutical project: his attempt by means of "existential psychoanalysis" to understand the individual as an irreducible whole, an entity which is meaningful all the way down.[14]

2. Wittgenstein's remarks are only fragments, and he should not be regarded as engaging in a systematic critique of Freud, but two things that clearly draw his attention in *The Interpretation of Dreams* (the only Freudian text named) are the question of criteria – When should interpretation stop? What gives one interpretation the right to exclude alternatives? – and the more fundamental question of whether the concept of meaning has coherent application to dreams at all. Also in question, therefore, are Freud's notions that dreaming evinces thinking, employs symbols, fulfills wishes, and so on, along with his reapplication of these psychological schemas to symptoms and public behavior.

Observing that Freud's dream symbols fall between nature and convention, Wittgenstein says:

> Consider the difficulty that if a symbol in a dream is not understood, it does not seem to be a symbol at all. So why call it one? But suppose I have a dream and accept a certain interpretation of it. *Then* – when I superimpose the interpretation on the dream – I can say "Oh yes, the table obviously corresponds to the woman, this to that etc."[15]

This might be taken, not as a dismissal of psychoanalytic interpretation but as a basis for validating talk of dream-symbolism indirectly, in so far as the meaning of dreams may be regarded as a function of our later reflection on them; Wittgenstein at any rate seems to intimate that this approach could be adopted without incoherence. What however emerges clearly from Wittgenstein's discussion is his view of the speculative and philosophically driven character of Freud's full psychology: dreams do indeed puzzle us and invite interpretation, but what fundamentally underwrites Freud's ideas, Wittgenstein maintains, is a demand for complete explanation, a conviction that mental events are sufficiently determined; only this philosophical prejudice could justify the various auxiliary ideas introduced by

Freud, in particular the notion of mental force which underpins his conception of wish-fulfillment.[16]

The upshot is, Wittgenstein implies, a compromised style of theorizing: Freud is drawn to the possibility, which nothing in ordinary psychological understanding precludes a priori and which its open-endedness perhaps invites, of making deeper sense of the mind by exploiting, not experimental methods, but the kinds of non-propositional pattern-making that we are familiar with from aesthetic contexts; hence the affinity of dream-interpretation with judgments of correctness in the interpretation of music, painting, and so on. Freud however seeks to convert his interpretative suggestions into *doctrines*, and, having come so far, is obliged to take further scientistic turns in order to substantiate speculations which have outrun their warrant; at which point he betrays the original impulse which sponsored his reflections. What results is a mere "mythology," albeit a powerful one.[17]

Wittgenstein's reservations rest on a conception of meaning forged in the intersubjective context of natural language, while Sartre's turn on the intra-subjective self-relation, but they concur in finding Freud's hermeneutical conceptualization of the phenomena less than fully intelligible. Both accept that there is an authentic element motivating psychoanalytic reflection, but consider it occluded in Freud's theorizing: what begins as a legitimate attempt to locate a type of meaning to which natural science is necessarily blind, is forced into scientistic directions, and ends in absurdity.

A defender of Freud may seek to meet these objections. The effectiveness of Sartre's argument is limited, not by his Cartesian commitment to the transparency of the mental, which he suspends for the sake of argument, but by his strong assumptions concerning what might be called its architecture: Sartre assumes the full determinacy of mental life and transitivity of mental connections, as if assimilating the mind *in toto* to a single practical syllogism.[18] Since this is not an assumption that common sense psychology agrees with, Freud can reject Sartre's objection as relying question-beggingly on a rationalistic, or Kantian, idealization of the mental.

The Freudian reply to Wittgenstein is that the general view of meaning which would make it necessary to treat symbolism as the mere *outcome* of interpretative activity, and not as its independently real object, is unduly restrictive, and overly driven by a concern for empirical anchoring, in a way that gives excessive weight to skeptical worries. To be sure, if psychoanalysis were in the business of setting up psychological attributions *ab initio* – or of making them criteriologically impregnable in the face of other-minds skepticism – then it can be agreed that it would run afoul of Wittgenstein's conditions. But in fact psychoanalysis takes ordinary psychology's attributions for granted, without either contesting or seeking to revalidate them: its aim is rather to elaborate, deepen, and build on them,[19] and there is no obvious reason why this "second wave" of interpretation should be bound by the same rules as govern the ground-floor of interpersonal understanding.

These replies reduce the force of the Sartre-Wittgenstein objection, but without altogether meeting their challenge. For what has been said is only that certain strong, philosophically committed views of psychological understanding – Sartre's idealization or Wittgenstein's semi-verificationism – must be rejected in order for psychoanalytic enquiry to be launched. But this is not to say what alternative conception would positively serve Freud's purposes. With this question in mind, we turn to the constructive proposals of Habermas and Ricœur.

THE MAJOR THEORETICAL PROPOSALS: HABERMAS AND RICŒUR

Habermas and Ricœur's main writings on Freud, respectively *Knowledge and Human Interests* [*Erkenntnis und Interesse*] and *Freud and Philosophy*, both landmarks in the philosophy of psychoanalysis, appeared in the 1960s, and arose in different philosophical settings. Habermas belonged to the Frankfurt School and Ricœur's associations were with Husserl. Neither critical theory nor phenomenology as such being the present topic, our focus is confined to the significance of their thought for a hermeneutical construal of psychoanalysis. The main contrast lies between Habermas's attempt to resolve the problem by making psychoanalysis an unequivocally hermeneutical discourse, eliminating the ambiguity altogether, and Ricœur's strategy of setting psychoanalysis' dual commitments in a broader philosophical context, which allows what seems a problem peculiar to psychoanalysis to be regarded as the resurgence of a more fundamental philosophical opposition, the resolution of which is not a task which Freud alone can be expected to fulfill.

1. Habermas' discussion is explicitly reconstructive, and aims to sift out what is cogent and philosophically defensible in Freud while discarding what belongs to his "scientistic self-misunderstanding" (on this point concurring with Sartre and Wittgenstein). This does not mean, however, that the metapsychology should be rejected, or paraphrased away, as other, softer hermeneutical readings of Freud recommend.[20] To the contrary, it is here that Habermas finds the deepest points of contact with his own program of regrounding critical theory. Metapsychology is, Habermas states, "a *general interpretation of self-formative processes*":[21]

> The model of the three mental agencies, id, ego, and super-ego, permits a systematic presentation of the structure of language deformation and behavioural pathology. Metahermeneutic statements can be organized in terms of it. They elucidate the methodological framework in which empirically substantive interpretations of self-formative processes can be developed.[22]

Habermas's reconstruction of psychoanalysis proceeds on the basis that communicative action provides the measure of rationality. It takes as primary the dialogic situation,[23] artificially reproduced in the therapeutic context, of one person's failure to make sense to another, with the distinguishing feature that here the inability to make oneself intelligible to the other corresponds to, and arises from, an avowed failure to make oneself intelligible to oneself. Habermas's key claim is not merely that the intrasubjective disturbance can be *modeled* on intersubjective breakdown, but that it *consists* in communicative failure. That is to say, we are to abandon the realist conception of the unconscious as a set of phenomena defined by the difficulty they pose for cognition, and instead regard it as *constituted* by abortive communicative action. This is developed into the following picture:

> The object domain of depth hermeneutics comprises all the places where, owing to internal disturbances, the texts of our everyday language games are interrupted by incomprehensible symbols. These symbols cannot be understood because they do not obey the grammatical rules of ordinary language, norms of action, and culturally learned patterns of expression [...] [S]ymptoms are signs of a specific self-alienation of the subject who has them. The breaks in the text are places where an interpretation has forcibly prevailed that is ego-alien even though it is produced by the self. Because the symbols that interpret suppressed needs are excluded from public communication, *the speaking and acting subject's communication with himself is interrupted*. The privatized language of unconscious motives is rendered inaccessible to the ego.[24]

Habermas suggests that even psychoanalysis' aspiration to general laws – the feature which does most to make its discourse look like scientific causal hypothesizing – can be salvaged: these offer "a narrative background" or "dramatic model" with reference to which "interrupted self-formative processes can be filled out and become a complete history."[25]

The dynamic unconscious has, according to Habermas, not had to produce meanings *ex nihilo*, as Sartre and Wittgenstein assume, rather it has deformed meanings previously in circulation. Thus Habermas may agree with Sartre that Freud's mental partition fails to elucidate the incoherence within the subject, while asserting that its correct explanation lies in distorted self-communication, and answer Wittgenstein by granting that the usual conditions for meaning are not met, and then maintaining that this is not because language is absent but because its condition is defective. It follows from Habermas's account that what may seem to be sheer force operative in psychic life is such only in appearance; in reality it consists in a failure, or refusal, to articulate meaning.[26] Habermas may accordingly be described as defending a *privative* conception of the unconscious.[27] These are the essential points on which Ricœur differs from Habermas.

2. Salient in Ricœur's account of Freud are (1) his characterization of psychoanalysis, alongside Marx and Nietzsche, as engaged in a "hermeneutics of suspicion,"[28] (2) his claim that psychoanalysis has immediate philosophical import, and (3) his attribution of a non-hermeneutical "realism" to Freud.

The first of these, though well known, is problematic. The hermeneutics of suspicion designates not a special *technique* of interpretation but a special *goal* of hermeneutical enquiry, namely, of deciphering and unmasking. This assumes that the discourse under examination does not mean what it says, or means more than it says. How does this "prejudice" or pre-judgment, of disbelief or refusal to take at face value, arise? It cannot be prompted by anything at the surface of the discourse, since this is held to be self-concealing. It seems that some *pre*-hermeneutical hypothesis must be already *in situ*. In the case of Marx and Nietzsche, the relevant suspicion-grounding hypotheses are perhaps not hard to locate, but psychoanalysis is not premised on the *falsity* of the mental as ordinarily conceived: what motivates it is the failure of common sense psychology to make sense of some of what it is presented with, not the presumed falsity of common sense psychology, and this generates a need for explanation, not a ground for suspicion. To this extent Gadamer's objection that Ricœur fails to differentiate a distinctive sub-species of hermeneutics appears justified.[29]

The better point of entry to Ricœur is his claim that Freud's ideas have direct impact on two high-level, inter-connected assumptions of modern philosophy: that consciousness and self-consciousness are irreducible, and that individual human subjects possess a deep autonomy which also occupies a privileged position in philosophical reflection. Situating psychoanalysis at the same level as Descartes and Kant, Ricœur declares:

> The reading of Freud is also the crisis of the philosophy of the subject. It imposes the dispossession of the subject such as it appears primarily to itself in the form of consciousness. It makes consciousness not a given but a task. The genuine *cogito* must be gained through the false *cogitos* that mask it [...] And so I say that Freud can be read just as our colleagues and teachers read Plato, Descartes, and Kant.[30]

What does this "dispossession" consist in? The answer lies in what Ricœur calls Freud's realism, by which he means that, in characterizing the unconscious economically and topographically, Freud accords the mental the same *degree* of reality as external physical objects, and of a partially analogous *kind*. At a minimum this means that at least some of the entities which compose the mind are experienced unconsciously in a quasi-objectual manner: they exist *for the subject* as having the features which Freud's economic-topographical descriptions pick out.[31] The image of the unconscious as composed of a kind of affective stuff, which Habermas eliminates, is to that extent restored: mental opacity is unlike the obscurity which texts present, for the mind is pictured as set over *against itself* in a way which contrasts with mere cognitive deprivation. On this basis Ricœur can assert that consciousness, having discovered that "its immediate self-certainty was mere presumption," "must be lost in order that the subject may be found."[32]

Ricœur does not grant Freud a one-sided victory over traditional philosophy, as a naturalist might. Rather his claim is that the antinomy of the objective reality of the mental *versus* self-conscious subjectivity manifests itself *within* psychoanalysis: this is what its mixed discourse commits it to. As regards the further question of what, granting the antinomy, is to be done about it, Ricœur's answer is that it has no purely theoretical solution and remains a task for the practice of reflection, which is guided by the "limit-idea" of its overcoming.[33]

Ricœur's proposal may be understood in the following terms. Discussion of psychoanalysis, including that of Habermas, proceeds on the assumption that it presents us with a problem that demands a theoretical solution. Ricœur's radical alternative is to suppose that what appears to reflection as its own *conceptual* problem, in fact represents a *real opposition* within its object – meaning not simply that the phenomena exhibit different kinds of first-order properties, some meaning-constituted and others not, but that this very heterogeneity reflects a more basic underlying schism in our constitution. The "enigma of Freudian discourse" then becomes, as Ricœur puts it, a constitutive "paradox of reflection," grounded in the nature of its object, human existence.[34]

In order for this to qualify as a positive solution, more must of course be said to recommend it, both as a reading of Freud and as a general philosophical strategy, and here two things can be said quickly. One is that Ricœur's solution will appeal to anyone who, like Ricœur himself, is impressed by the claim of classical German philosophy that human reality stands under an overarching opposition of Freedom and Nature, or spirit and nature – a notion which goes against the grain of philosophical hermeneutics, which has largely followed Herder in regarding Kant's dualism as a mistake. The other is that plausibly the antinomy is attested *a posteriori*. Integral to the ambiguous character of psychoanalysis' primary *explananda* is an internal dissonance: the reflexive perplexity of the Ratman or Wolfman involves a positive apprehension of inner incoherence, which goes beyond mere failure of rational competence.

FREUD'S REALISM: THE "MENTAL APPARATUS" AS A CONTAINER OF MEANING

Habermas and Ricœur are guided to a considerable extent in their treatments of Freud by broader agendas – Habermas is seeking to reconstruct critical theory, and Ricœur to measure the claim of phenomenology to comprehensive philosophical truth – and they introduce concepts which do not belong to Freud's own conceptual repertoire. Let us now go back to Freud and try to determine, in terms closer to his own, what philosophical factors drive his theory construction. The story of Freud's own development is a large and well-trodden area,[35] and I will confine myself here to a specific angle, which helps us to locate the difficulty in marrying psychoanalysis to hermeneutics.

1. Broadly speaking, behind Freud's innovations lie two great nineteenth-century legacies: the tradition of classical German philosophy, and that of empirical psychology, which provide respectively the bare concept of the dynamic unconscious, and the notion (widely if not universally accepted in late nineteenth-century psychological theory) that particular attributions of unconscious mental states can be warranted on strictly empirical grounds.[36] In "The Unconscious" and his other key metapsychological papers of 1915, as in almost all Freud's writings, only the intellectual authority of the latter tradition is acknowledged, although the legacy of the former is presupposed. Also in the foreground is Freud's confidence that the metaphysical integrity of the mental is attested in conscious experience: conscious mentality as such does not, Freud implies, pose any puzzle. On this basis Freud is able to present the possibility of psychoanalytic *Wissenschaft* as turning on a single, essentially simple consideration:

> Our right to assume the existence of something mental that is unconscious and to employ that assumption for the purposes of scientific work is disputed in many quarters. To this we can reply that our assumption of the unconscious is *necessary* and *legitimate*, and that we possess numerous proofs of its existence.

> It is *necessary* because the data of consciousness have a very large number of gaps in them.[37]

Once the conceptual possibility of unconscious mental states has been granted, the way to psychoanalysis is clear, Freud argues, for the manifest existence of "gaps" in conscious mental life provides sufficient reason for positing causes outside it. That these causes must be mental rather than physical follows from the fact that they are adduced to explain lacunae in consciousness, which means restoring its continuity, something which descriptions of brain and other physiological states cannot do. But since *ex hypothesi* the contents of consciousness are unable to supply the missing links, or indeed to account for the original existence of the gaps, we are entitled to infer that the interpolated causes have a specific nature and type of causality of their own – in other words, that the mental has varieties, of which its familiar conscious instances are only one.[38]

Freud thus takes himself to have arrived, by a relatively direct, quasi-conceptual route at the theoretical picture which emerges from his interpretative studies of mental phenomena. Freud believes his argument conforms with accepted, abductive modes of scientific reasoning, which is plausible, and in addition he is confident of having shown the concept of unconscious mentality to be unproblematic, despite the intense dispute which had earlier surrounded it. The only philosopher who exerted direct personal influence on Freud (and commanded his admiration), Franz Brentano, had in fact explicitly rejected the concept as both unnecessary and incoherent. Understanding Freud as replying to Brentano, I will try to show, gives reason for thinking that Ricœur's account of Freud is essentially correct.

The parameters of Freud's 1915 argument become more distinct if we consider it in the light of Brentano's *Psychology from an Empirical Standpoint*, first published in 1874. Brentano's aim in this influential work, which does not belong to the hermeneutical tradition but shares some of its philosophical motivation,[39] was to establish psychology on an autonomous footing and to elevate its scientific standing: the proper position of psychology in the order of justification of human knowledge, Brentano asserts, is foundational (a claim which no doubt appealed to Freud).[40] This involves gaining at the outset an accurate understanding of what fundamentally distinguishes mental from physical phenomena. Brentano's answer to this question is often said to be the possession of intentionality – a mental phenomenon is one that has "content" or "reference to something as an object" – but this is strictly inaccurate, for Brentano defines a mental phenomenon as one which not only possesses intentionality but in addition has *real* or *actual*, as opposed to merely phenomenal, existence.[41]

Brentano grounds this realism concerning the mental on the epistemological fact that we enjoy certainty regarding our mental states. This allows him to claim for psychology exactly the same legitimating ground as other sciences – namely, data or "presentations" in consciousness – but, if Brentano is right, without obliging it to follow their model of theorizing. Whereas all other sciences rest on theoretical *inferences* from what is given in experience – the data of *outer* consciousness, which have merely *phenomenal* existence – to their *unobservable* causes, psychology arrives at an explanatorily final reality through mere *description* of what is perceived, in *inner* consciousness. Consistently with this position, Brentano launches an extended attack on the hypothesis of unconscious mental phenomena, talk of which, he argues, may be reduced without remainder to that of mere dispositions to conscious states.[42]

Now, when Freud asserts the existence of unconscious mental states, he is clear that they are to be understood in unqualifiedly realistic terms, and the point is of course crucial, since a dispositional analysis along the lines recommended by Brentano would stymie psychoanalytic theorizing at the outset, by making it impossible to postulate a source of mental agency independent of the conscious subject. Freud accordingly deserts Brentano's thesis of the explanatory finality of the mental qua conscious, and maintains instead that our epistemic relations to inner-mental and outer-physical reality are symmetrical:[43] contra Brentano, who had argued that, if the principles of reasoning which take us from sense impressions to the entities and forces of chemistry and physics are duplicated internally, then we are led, if anywhere, to something not merely unconscious but also *non-mental*. If inner perception were inner *observation*, Brentano argues, then the phenomena observed would fail to qualify as mental rather than physical;[44] symmetry of inner and outer perception would reduce mental phenomena, like physical phenomena, to mere "signs" of a reality which causes them.[45] Brentano's point here recalls Sartre's objection to Freud: the allegation is again that slackening the relation of the mental to conscious presentation results in absurdity.

Freud's reply, the hermeneutical dimension of his thought here coming to the fore, is that Brentano has a false or at any rate incomplete picture of what it is for there to be data or "presentations" in consciousness. It is not that there is *no* quasi-perceptual aspect to conscious mental states, but that when such acquaintance is present, it necessarily involves understanding. Ordinary instances of emotion show this: a feeling of joy or sorrow involves taking the mental episode in question as having that particular determinate meaning. If this is correct, then it is possible to see how, when we extrapolate interpretatively from the data of consciousness to the unconscious, we are not deserting the field of psychology: what may legitimately be supposed is that different species of mentality exhibit different ratios of interpretable content and perceptual presence, and that the mental states which comprise the contents of *Ucs*. lie at one end of the spectrum; they construe the self and its world in ways which preclude the possibility of their direct manifestation or reflective retrieval. Certainly these unconscious construals present the subject with objects – of a more or less phantastical kind – but they do so without *themselves* being the object of any higher-level presentation, and hence without any accompanying *judgment*.[46] These complex features are not possessed by all species of the mental, and if Brentano builds them into his analysis, then it is because he confuses the reality of the mental in general with the certainty of its conscious instances. A correct psychological realism, in Freud's view, leads by default to the unconscious.

2. To this extent Freud's realism and his hermeneuticism are in one another's service. To now bring into view the other side of Ricœur's picture – the respect in which Freud's realism departs from the hermeneutical standpoint – we may turn to a later paper, in which Freud resumes his implicit dialogue with Brentano.

In "Negation" (1925) Freud offers an account of the logical function of negation. In the following passages we see the characteristic pattern of Freud's reasoning, in which the motive of interpretation – to achieve a better understanding of what is given – combines with speculative ambition:

> The manner in which our patients bring forward their associations during the work of analysis gives us an opportunity for making some interesting observations. "Now you'll think I mean to say something insulting, but really I've no such intention." We realize that this is a repudiation, by projection, of an idea that has just come up [...]
>
> Thus the content of a repressed image or idea can make its way into consciousness, on condition that it is *negated*. Negation is a way of taking cognizance of what is repressed; indeed it is already a lifting of the repression, though not, of course, an acceptance of what is repressed [...]
>
> Since to affirm or negate the content of thoughts is the task of the function of intellectual judgement, what we have just been saying has led us to the psychological origin of that function. To negate something in a judgement is, at bottom, to say: "This is something which I should prefer to repress." A negative judgement is the intellectual substitute for repression; its "no" is the hall-mark of repression, a certificate of origin – like, let us say, "Made in Germany." With the help of the symbol of negation, thinking frees itself from the restrictions of repression

and enriches itself with material that is indispensable for its proper functioning [...]

The study of judgement affords us, perhaps for the first time, an insight into the origin of an intellectual function from the interplay of the primary drive impulses [*Triebregungen*]. Judging is a continuation, along lines of expediency, of the original process by which the ego took things into itself or expelled them from itself, according to the pleasure principle. The polarity of judgement appears to correspond to the opposition of the two groups of drives [*Triebgruppen*] which we have supposed to exist. Affirmation – as a substitute for uniting – belongs to Eros; negation – the successor to expulsion – belongs to the drive towards destruction [*Destruktionstrieb*].[47]

A recurring clinical datum – the phenomenon of sincere but self-ignorant disavowal: "I've really no such intention" – is brought under an interpretation – the repressed is able to figure in consciousness on the condition of its negation – prompting a complex hypothesis which again initially follows Brentano and then departs from him. Freud agrees with Brentano that judgmental affirmation and negation are acts of acceptance and rejection, continuous with the emotions of love and hate. But he then hypothesizes, contradicting Brentano, that (1) both judgmental and conative-affective negation (and affirmation) are a *single* type of mental act,[48] (2) the judgmental form of negation is derivative from and *dependent* on its primary conative-affective form, and (3) both forms have a single *source*, which may be conceptualized in two different ways, either at the level of (phantasies of) bodily processes or at that of drives.

Freud's hypothesis concerning judgment *überhaupt* recommends itself by virtue of the way in which it deepens the original interpretation concerning the role of negation in facilitating a return of the repressed, while also cohering with other parts of psychoanalytic theory. What makes the speculative extrapolation in "Negation" particularly interesting for present purposes is that it shows Freud seeking to, as it were, get behind the back of meaning. Freud's aim is to grasp the source of judgment, not for the sake of hermeneutical completeness – he does not suggest that the logical function of negation itself sets any problem of understanding, for which his account might provide a (psychologistic) solution – but in order to achieve a fundamental insight into the "proper functioning" of conscious intellectual life, which we do by forming a unitary concept of what grounds and contains meaning. Freud's ultimate theoretical concern, led by his realism, is therefore with, as I put it earlier, the "shape" of the mental apparatus. In grasping it, we break out of the hermeneutical circle, or at any rate reach its outermost sphere, the unmoving prime mover of the mental.[49] And we can see how this promises to solve the Sartre-Wittgenstein problem: if Freud's conjectures concerning the underlying shape of the psyche allow us to conceptualize a *new way* in which a subject may mean something, then Freud's claims are not properly measured by any antecedently formed conception of what this consists in. Put differently, the particular kind of "depth" interpretation offered by Freud does not amount only to an extension of hermeneutical range, rather his foundational claim is that the mind *has* depths in a sense not previously recognized.

Now it may be objected that even at the end of the day Freud remains within meaning, in so far as his life and death drives have "aims" (*Triebziele*), and the corporeal processes and phantasies which express them have a rudimentary teleological organization. This raises a difficult, broad question concerning the demarcation of meaning from whatever is held to stand in contrast with it, concerning which different hermeneutical thinkers take different positions. But it is worth noting that at this point we are presented with a further possibility, intimated (but not developed) by Ricœur.[50] If drives and embodiment do not merely ground and contain meaning, but are themselves imbued with it, then meaning bleeds all the way down into nature, just as late eighteenth- and early nineteenth-century *Naturphilosophie* had proposed. In Sections V–VI of *Beyond the Pleasure Principle* (1920), Freud shows his willingness to entertain and defend the unmistakeably *naturphilosophisch* notion that our drives inhere in organic life as such (and indeed originate in its very differentiation from the inorganic).[51] In so doing he distances himself from hermeneutical orthodoxy. But Freud may also be regarded as returning to an early point in the history of hermeneutics, later abandoned. Friedrich Ast, writing in 1808 under the influence of Schelling, asserts the unity of the modern hermeneutical project with the philosophy of nature: no understanding and interpretation of alterity is possible, Ast declares, "without the unity and identity of all that is spiritual and the original unity of all things in spirit."[52] In speculative moments, Freud agrees with Ast that, in order to make sense of human beings, we must offer an interpretation of nature as a whole.

NOTES

1. Freud's famous phrase, applied to dream-interpretation, in *The Interpretation of Dreams*, in the *Standard Edition* of Freud's works (London: Hogarth Press and Institute of Psycho-Analysis, 1953), ed. James Strachey, 24 vols., vol. V, 608. References to this edition, giving volume and page number, are henceforth prefixed SE.
2. SE IV:100–2.
3. See John Forrester's detailed account of the ways in which linguistic themes inform Freud's development, *Language and the Origins of Psychoanalysis* (New York: Columbia University Press, 1980).
4. "The Unconscious" (1915), Pts. II–IV, SE XIV:172–85.
5. "The Unconscious" (1915), Pt. V, SE XIV:186–9.
6. See SE V:339–40.
7. Concerning the relation of "word-presentations" to consciousness, see SE XIV:200–3. Freud's account falls short of any full philosophical thesis concerning the linguistic nature of thought.
8. See Adolf Grünbaum, *The Foundations of Psychoanalysis: A Philosophical Critique* (Berkeley: University of California Press, 1984), and Patricia Kitcher, *Freud's Dream: A Complete Interdisciplinary Science of Mind* (Cambridge, MA: MIT Press, 1993).
9. SE V:536 and XIV:168.

10 See Grünbaum, *The Foundations of Psychoanalysis*, Introduction, "Critique of the Hermeneutical Conception of Psychoanalytic Theory and Therapy."
11 Heidegger criticizes Freud in terms that overlap with Sartre's and Wittgenstein's: see his *Zollikon Seminars* from 1964 and 1966, ed. Medard Boss, trans. Franz Mayr and Richard Askay (Evanston: Northwestern University Press, 2001), esp. 20–4, 113–21, and 168–70.
12 Jean-Paul Sartre, *The Emotions: Outline of a Theory* (1939), trans. Bernard Frechtman (London: Routledge, 2002), 44–5.
13 Jean-Paul Sartre, *Being and Nothingness: An Essay on Phenomenological Ontology* (1943), trans. Hazel Barnes (London: Routledge, 1995), 50–4.
14 Sartre, *Being and Nothingness*, 560–75. Sartre practices existential psychoanalysis in his biographies of Baudelaire, Genet, and Flaubert. Heidegger's hermeneutic of *Dasein* is transposed into psychoanalysis by Ludwig Binswanger and Medard Boss. Sartre's commitment to the hermeneutical standpoint is more limited than Heidegger's: Sartre grants no privileged role to language (*Being and Nothingness*, 372–4), subordinates being-for-others to the structures which define the *pour-soi*, and regards intersubjective meaning as a contradictory phenomenon.
15 Ludwig Wittgenstein, *Lectures and Conversations on Aesthetics, Psychology, and Religious Belief*, ed. Cyril Barrett (Oxford: Blackwell, 1966), 44.
16 Wittgenstein, *Lectures and Conversations*, 42–4, 49–50.
17 Wittgenstein, *Lectures and Conversations*, 52.
18 Sartre affirms this implication in *Being and Nothingness*, 464, 557–64: there is an "original choice of self."
19 Analytic philosophy has pursued this idea by conceiving of psychoanalysis as an extension of common sense psychology: see Richard Wollheim, *Freud*, 2nd edn. (London: Fontana, 2008), Supplementary Preface.
20 E.g., Roy Schafer, "Narration in the Psychoanalytic Dialogue," *Critical Inquiry* 7:1 (1980): 29–53.
21 Jürgen Habermas, *Knowledge and Human Interests* (*Erkenntnis und Interesse*, 1968), trans. Jeremy Shapiro (Boston: Beacon, 1971), 254.

22 Habermas, *Knowledge and Human Interests*, 258.
23 Habermas, *Knowledge and Human Interests*, 252.
24 Habermas, *Knowledge and Human Interests*, 226–7; see also 256–7, where Habermas records his indebtedness to Alfred Lorenzer, whose hermeneutical theory is stated comprehensively in *Die Wahrheit der psychoanalytischen Erkenntnis. Ein historisch-materialistischer Entwurf* (Suhrkamp: Frankfurt am Main, 1974). Lorenzer incorporates – especially with his Kleinian concept of "scenic understanding" (110–15) – elements not taken up by Habermas.
25 Habermas, *Knowledge and Human Interests*, 259–60. It is notable that Habermas – in contrast with other critical theorists, whose readings of Freud are not similarly austere and who characteristically approve Freud's drive theory – does not look to psychoanalysis for substantive explanation of the social world: its chief role is to provide a validating *model* for ideology-critical reflection. Habermas's remarks in *Theory of Communicative Action*, vol. 2, *Lifeworld and System* (1980), trans. Thomas McCarthy (Boston: Beacon, 1987), 99–100, show Freud to have been displaced by Mead.
26 Habermas's account of the relation of causality to meaning in psychoanalysis is complex: see *Knowledge and Human Interests*, 256–7, 271–2, and Grünbaum's corresponding criticisms in *The Foundations of Psychoanalysis*, 9–15. On the question of what inner nature amounts to for Habermas, see his comments in reply to Thomas McCarthy, in John B. Thompson and David Held, eds., *Habermas: Critical Debates* (Cambridge, MA: MIT Press, 1982), 342–5.
27 Habermas, *Knowledge and Human Interests*, 241–2: the act of repression is reduced to "a banishment of need interpretations," a "*splitting-off of individual symbols from public communication.*"
A profound challenge to Habermas's assumption that linguistic communication is where we are most truly at home is posed by Lacan, who agrees that language is the key to the unconscious, but claims that we are necessarily alienated in and by it: in acceding to the "Symbolic" order and uniting herself communicatively with others, the subject divides herself. Language is therefore the *source* of the intra-subjective disturbance posited by Habermas.
28 See Paul Ricœur, *Freud and Philosophy: An Essay on Interpretation* (*De l'interprétation. Essai sur Freud*, 1965), trans. Denis Savage (New Haven: Yale University Press, 1970), 25–7, 33–5,

53–5, 59–64. Also important are the essays in *The Conflict of Interpretations: Essays in Hermeneutics*, trans. Willis Domingo (Evanston: Northwestern University Press, 1974), Pt. II, and *On Psychoanalysis* (Cambridge: Polity, 2012). Ricœur criticizes Habermas's theory in "The Question of Proof in Freud's Writings" (1977), in *On Psychoanalysis*, 11–49.

29 Hans-Georg Gadamer, "The Hermeneutics of Suspicion," in *Hermeneutics: Questions and Prospects*, ed. Gary Shapiro and Alan Sica (Amherst: University of Massachusetts Press, 1984): *every* form of hermeneutics is "a form of overcoming of an awareness of suspicion," in so far as we must *always* look for "the *real* meaning of an utterance" (54, 63).

30 Ricœur, *The Conflict of Interpretations*, 161–2.

31 Ricœur, *Freud and Philosophy*, Bk. II, Pt. I. Cf. Richard Wollheim, "The Mind and the Mind's Image of Itself," in *On Art and the Mind: Essays and Lectures* (Cambridge, MA: Harvard University Press, 1974), 31–53.

32 Ricœur, *The Conflict of Interpretations*, 103, 172.

33 See Ricœur, *Freud and Philosophy*, 60, 65–7, and "The Unity of the Voluntary and the Involuntary as a Limit-Idea" (1951), in *Philosophical Anthropology*, trans. David Pellauer (Cambridge: Polity, 2015), 53–71.

34 Ricœur, *The Conflict of Interpretations*, 173.

35 See Joel Whitebook, *Freud: An Intellectual Biography* (Cambridge: Cambridge University Press, 2017).

36 See my "The Unconscious: Transcendental Origins, Idealist Metaphysics and Psychoanalytic Metapsychology," in *The Impact of Idealism: The Legacy of Post-Kantian German Thought*, vol. I, *Philosophy and Natural Sciences*, ed. Karl Ameriks (Cambridge: Cambridge University Press, 2013), 134–65. Herder, romantic hermeneutics, and *Geisteswissenschaften* theory are not prominent influences on Freud.

37 SE XIV:166.

38 E.g., SE XVIII:24: consciousness is "not the most universal attribute of mental processes, but only a particular function of them."

39 See Joseph Margolis, "Reflections on Intentionality," in *The Cambridge Companion to Brentano*, ed. Dale Jacquette (Cambridge: Cambridge University Press, 2004), 131–48. Concerning Brentano's view of hermeneutical issues, see Klaus Hedwig, "Brentano's Hermeneutics," *Topoi* 6 (1987): 3–10.

40 Franz Brentano, *Psychology from an Empirical Standpoint* (1874), trans. Antos Rancurello, D. B. Terrell, and Linda McAlister, ed. Oskar Kraus and Linda McAlister (London: Routledge, 1973), Bk. I, Ch. 1.
41 Brentano, *Psychology*, 92 and 98: "Knowledge, joy and desire really exist. Color, sound and warmth have only a phenomenal and intentional existence"; mental phenomena alone "possess *actual existence* [*wirkliche Existenz*] in addition to intentional existence."
42 Brentano, *Psychology*, Bk. II, Ch. 2.
43 SE XIV:171: "In psycho-analysis there is no choice for us but to assert that mental processes are themselves unconscious, and to liken the perception of them by means of consciousness to the perception of the external world by means of the sense organs." See also SE V:615–16.
44 Brentano, *Psychology*, 128.
45 Brentano, *Psychology*, 19.
46 Brentano, *Psychology*, 141–2, 153–4, 198–9.
47 "Negation" (1925), SE XIX:235–9 (translation modified). A similar idea figures in Wittgenstein's *Philosophical Grammar*, ed. Rush Rhees, trans. Anthony Kenny (Oxford: Blackwell, 1974), 58: "(Compare William James on the feelings that correspond to words like 'not,' 'but' and so on.) / ('Not' makes a gesture of rejection. / No, it *is* a gesture of rejection. To grasp negation is to understand a gesture of rejection.)"
48 Brentano rejects this move in his 1911 Supplementary Remarks, *Psychology*, 288.
49 The notion of mind as a container becomes extremely important in the post-Freudian theory of Melanie Klein and Wilfred Bion.
50 Noted but not endorsed by Ricœur: *Freud and Philosophy*, 312–13.
51 SE XVIII:36–9.
52 Friedrich Ast, *Grundlinien der Grammatik, Hermeneutik und Kritik* (Landshut: Jos. Thomann, 1808), §70, 167–8. See also Ast's proposal for a *naturphilosophisch* grounding of language, §§3–5.

9 Hermeneutics and Phenomenology

Benjamin Crowe

While his intellectual legacy is hotly contested (and not only because of his deep involvement in the cultural politics of the Third Reich), Martin Heidegger (1889–1976) is a towering figure in twentieth-century hermeneutics. Working in a climate shaped by the historicist tradition, Heidegger creatively adapted ideas from Dilthey, Husserl, Nietzsche, and others to develop a new *phenomenological* conception of hermeneutics that influenced some of the century's most prominent figures. Heidegger dubbed his philosophical approach "phenomenological hermeneutics" in 1919 and went on to develop what he called a "hermeneutics of facticity" familiar to readers of his *magnum opus, Being and Time* (1927), as the "analytic of Dasein."[1] Working within the "historical I," Heidegger's aim is to bring "to light [*zu Tage*]" the categories that are "*alive in life itself* in an original way," i.e., to explicate the structures that constitute our most immediate experience of the world as meaningful. Crucially, Heidegger contends that our understanding of ourselves and of anything else at all is deeply historically situated; "life," he observes in a text from the early 1920s, "moves at any time within a certain state of *having-been-interpreted* [*Ausgelegtheit*] that has been handed down to it." More critically, Heidegger describes how this historical situatedness not only enables understanding, but also forecloses possibilities or allows them to slide into a kind of innocuous obviousness. Hence, as he spells out in some of the concluding sections of *Being and Time*, genuine historical understanding must be understood as *repetition* (*Wiederholung*), as a kind of struggle with the past aimed ultimately at liberating the meaning of the past for a new future. Heidegger's famous and contentious readings of the history of philosophy and of religious thought, as well as of poets like Hölderlin and Rilke, exemplify this approach to hermeneutics.

Hans-Georg Gadamer (1900–2002) was part of a cohort of brilliant students who experienced the development of Heidegger's phenomenological hermeneutics first-hand in the early 1920s. Starting with his earliest works on Plato and Aristotle, Gadamer develops his own approach that, like Heidegger's, emphasizes the ubiquity of understanding in human life. In his enormously influential *Truth and Method* (1960), Gadamer takes the experience of truth in our encounters with great works of art and literature as a model for the kinds of insights that are distinctive to humanistic disciplines (*Geisteswissenschaften*).[2] He argues that tradition furnishes the conditions for understanding, which he conceptualizes as a dialogical process that culminates in a "fusion of horizons." Importantly, the nature of this dialogical process cannot be reductively captured in procedural terms. Throughout his long career, Gadamer defended his approach in debates with the likes of Jürgen Habermas and Jacques Derrida. Gadamer's hermeneutics influenced Anglophone philosophers like Richard Rorty, John McDowell, and Alasdair MacIntyre and impacted work in fields outside of philosophy.

In what follows, I aim to explicate some of the fundamental insights and arguments behind the revolutionary approach to hermeneutics inaugurated by Heidegger and brought to maturity by Gadamer. Regarding Heidegger, I will focus primarily on his work in the decade leading up to the publication of *Being and Time*. As Gadamer himself observes, it is the "early Heidegger" who most emphatically and explicitly framed his project as hermeneutics (*TM* xxxvi). Further, the term (though, I would argue, neither the basic idea nor the associated practice) drops out of Heidegger's philosophical vocabulary shortly after the appearance of *Being and Time*. Finally, it was precisely during this explosively creative period in his career that Gadamer encountered Heidegger, taking part in some of the courses in which Heidegger's new conception of hermeneutics first sees the light of day.[3] Regarding Gadamer, I draw entirely from

Truth and Method. Unlike his former teacher's *magnum opus* (i.e., *Being and Time*), whose publication was forced upon Heidegger as he was still organizing his thoughts, *Truth and Method* is a polished work, the mature fruit of decades of reflection.

It is also important to note that, with one or two exceptions, I will not examine instances of the hermeneutical practice of either philosopher. This is partly because, as Gadamer avers, their hermeneutics is "not primarily a prescription for the practice of understanding, but a description of the way interpretive understanding is achieved" (*GW* 271; *TM* 266). Both were brilliant and exciting interpreters of some of the key texts in the history of philosophy, as well as of Greek poetry and the oeuvres of modern poets such as Hölderlin, Rilke, Trakl, and Celan. Indeed, the sheer size of their ventures into the art of reading and explicating texts is quite remarkable, and a much larger study – which would doubtless be quite valuable – would be required in order to even begin to do justice to their phenomenological hermeneutics in action.

HEIDEGGER'S BREAKTHROUGH: THE PHENOMENOLOGICAL HERMENEUTICS OF FACTICITY

According to most accounts, it was in 1919 at the latest that Heidegger discovered the philosophical project that was to occupy him, under one guise or another, for the rest of his life.[4] Over the decades, Heidegger experimented with a variety of names for the subject matter of his inquiries: "factical life," "life-experience," "Dasein" or "being-here," "human Da-sein," the "worlding of the world," "being itself [*das Sein selbst*]," the "truth of being," the "fourfold [*das Geviert*]," the "topos of being." What these terms aim to capture is the most basic layer of human experience, the place where intelligibility is first constituted and made possible. On Heidegger's account, this deep structure is a complex pattern of multiple historically evolving ways of inhabiting a network of meaning or significance (*Bedeutung*). This pattern is itself comprised of category-like structures, familiar to readers of *Being and Time* as "existentialia," that make possible all meaningful engagement with things. Rather than concepts or schemata employed by a subject to organize her experience, or "synthetic form(s) of consciousness" as on the neo-Kantian model with which Heidegger was deeply familiar and which dominated German academe in this period (see *GA 56/57* 160/136),[5] these structures "are *alive in life itself* in an original way: alive in order to 'form' life on themselves" (*GA 61* 88/66).[6] They form the centerpiece of what might be called Heidegger's deepest philosophical conviction, namely that "[l]ife as such is *not* irrational (which has nothing whatever to do with 'rationalism'!)" (*GA 56/57* 219/187).

That is, life as a whole is a meaningful shape (*Gestalt*) long before the theoretical attitude typically adopted by scientists and philosophers has even come into existence. Life is *always already* meaningful – we quite literally *find* ourselves caught up in it, and it is only for this reason that we are able to analyze it scientifically, shape it with our activities, or represent it with our arts. In turn, each "life-world," or specific, concrete form of life in general, has its own "determination of sense." Thus, for Heidegger, ordinary human life has meaning, and this meaning is not *conceptual*. From a fairly early stage, Heidegger begins to describe the project of investigating and articulating this fundamental layer of meaningfulness as *hermeneutics*. Unfortunately, he typically offers no account of why he has selected this designation, and when he does, the accounts are fragmentary or provisional. For example, in the special "War Emergency Semester" course of 1919 he asserts that "[t]he experiencing of life that seizes hold of it and is carried along by it is the understanding intuition, the *hermeneutical intuition*, the originary phenomenological back-and-forth formation of concepts from which all theoretical objectification, indeed every transcendental positing, falls out" (*GA 56/57* 117/99), without lingering to explain why this intuition is *hermeneutical*. Perhaps the thought is something like this: just as the conscientious reader will give herself over to the work she is reading, trying to let it speak in its own terms without the distortions of her own expectations, so too the person investigating the primal layer of human existence must immerse himself in the subject matter, explicating it "from the inside," as it were, without theoretical commitments as to what will come to light.

In the summer 1921 lecture course on Augustine's *Confessions*, he labels the categorical structures discussed above "hermeneutical concepts" (*GA 60* 232), also without explanation. However, in the summer course for 1923 (in which Gadamer participated), Heidegger is comparatively more explicit about his reasoning. He provides a very brief overview of the history of hermeneutics in § 2, in which he anticipates Gadamer in some ways by hearkening back to an earlier period – particularly in theology (Augustine, other Patristics, and Luther) – in which hermeneutics "had formerly been viewed in a comprehensive and living manner" (*GA 63* 14/10). He says that he has chosen this term for his own enterprise, despite some inadequacies, because in terms of the "object" it indicates that "this object has its being as something capable of interpretation and in need of interpretation and that to be in some state of having-been-interpreted belongs to its being" (*GA 63* 15/11). I will say more below about this "having-been-interpreted" and its significance for Heidegger's overall project. According to Heidegger, we need to understand "from out of facticity itself [...] *in what way* and *when* it calls for the kind of interpretation put forth" (*GA 63* 15/12). That is, the hermeneutics in question is *phenomenological* (*GA 56/57* 131; *NB* 16/121). It is an interpretation that allows its subject matter to show itself according to its own sense. Further, the possibility of this interpretation rests on the fact that "[i]nterpreting is a being which belongs to the being of factical life itself" (*GA 63* 15/12).

At this point, Heidegger makes an interesting point that anticipates some of Gadamer's key insights in *Truth and Method*:

> The chance that hermeneutics will go wrong belongs in
> principle to its ownmost being. The kind of evidence found in its
> explications is fundamentally labile. To hold up before it such an

> extreme ideal of evidence as "intuition of essences" would be a misunderstanding of what it can and should do. (*GA 63* 16/12)

A crucial feature of Heidegger's new hermeneutics of life, which he returns to again and again in this period, is that the categorical structures do not emerge into view by observing the life-world from a detached, neutral, noncommittal point of view. Instead, hermeneutics participates in the "historical I." In part, as with the traditional art of textual interpretation, this means putting forth an initial hypothesis about the meaning of what one is encountering. Again in the summer 1923 course, Heidegger observes that the initial framework, the "as what" that is put forth at the start of the investigation, is like a card being staked in a game – a *gambit* (*GA 63* 18/14). As Steven Crowell has observed in a recent study, the Heideggerian phenomenologist must put herself in play, must stake herself, in the exercise of explicating life's deepest structures.[7] Heidegger typically makes this point by highlighting the "hermeneutical situation" of any assay into phenomenology, by which he means the complex of cultural tendencies, contemporary issues, and ways of viewing the past that are in turn individualized in a deeply personal manner by the phenomenologist herself. Even more fundamentally, as mentioned previously, hermeneutics helps bring to fruition the tendency of facticity to understand itself and to discourse about itself. It seeks to do so in a way that does not involve the imposition of some conceptual framework "from above," which only serves to alienate facticity from itself (*GA 63* 15/12).

The "Natorp Report" of late 1922 provides some further insights into why Heidegger chose to designate his approach as "hermeneutics." The enterprise is the "interpretation of the sense of this being with respect to its basic categorial structures," which collectively comprise "the modes in which factical life temporalizes itself, unfolds itself, and *speaks* about itself (*kategorein* [predicating in terms of categories]) in such temporalizing and unfolding" (*NB* 16). Heidegger emphasizes the origins of the term "category" in Greek law, particularly in the role of the "accuser" or advocate for the prosecution who *addresses* the court and *speaks about* the accused. The categories of life, in other words, are ways in which life articulates itself, makes itself known, or addresses itself to itself. Like speech acts or written words, these structures of intelligibility can be interpreted or rendered explicit. "In other words, as the ontology of facticity, philosophy is at the same time the interpretation [*Interpretation*] of the categories of this addressing and interpreting [*Auslegen*]" (*NB* 16). Hence, this "fundamental research" can fittingly be called "the *phenomenological hermeneutics* of facticity" (*NB* 16).

Heidegger's enterprise then, is one of *articulating* or making explicit the structure of the immediate, meaning-laden experience of the world. Such an "understanding of life," Heidegger tells us, "is *hermeneutical intuition* (making intelligible, giving meaning)" (*GA 56/57* 219/187). The aim is bringing "to light [*zu Tage*]," "exhibiting [*am Tage*]," or placing "into the light of day [*Täglichkeit*]" the "categories" that are "*alive in life itself* in an original way" (*GA 61* 62/47; 88/66).

All understanding, including the understanding achieved in the hermeneutics of facticity, turns out to involve a prior involvement and familiarity with the matter in question, which Heidegger describes in *Being and Time* as a "pre-intention [*Vormeinung*]." On the basis of this projected significance, we can then develop more explicit kinds of understanding in which we actually express and conceptualize the things in question (*SZ* 148ff.). It is this explicit articulation of what has already been opened up for us in understanding that Heidegger calls "interpretation [*Auslegung*]" (*SZ* 148). In hermeneutics of facticity, as in any other interpretation, one must secure an initial purchase on the phenomenon in question. This is something that is "constitutive – and indeed in a decisive manner – of interpretation" (*GA 63* 16/13). Again, this initial grasp on the subject matter is a "projection," a sketch, as Aristotle puts it in *Nicomachean Ethics* I.7. As such, it is neither fixed nor final, but can be questioned, abandoned, or revised as the situation demands.

It is, however, indispensable. The "hermeneutical situation" is, as previously described, the entire complex that structures and makes possible any interpretation. This "situation" has three elements: (1) fore-having, (2) fore-sight, and (3) fore-conception. All share the character of "fixing in advance [*Vorhaften*]" the possibilities available for understanding (*GA 17* 110). The explicit appropriation of some previously understood object always takes its point of departure from a certain "point of view" (*SZ* 150/191). "This fore-sight 'takes the first cut' out of what has been taken into our fore-having, and it does so with a view to a definite way in which this can be interpreted" (*SZ* 150/191). As Heidegger notes, all of this entails that understanding has a *circular* structure, a kind of back-and-forth that he had first alluded to all the way back in the "War Emergency Semester" of 1919, when he first described his enterprise as hermeneutical. The key thing to note is that this circularity does not vitiate the understanding that is achieved, but rather *makes it possible to understand anything at all in the first place*. Handled properly, the circle enables "a positive possibility of the most primordial kind of knowing" (*SZ* 153/195).

The realities of the "hermeneutical situation," and the circular structure of understanding that depends upon it, point to the historically conditioned nature of human existence. For Heidegger, this historical conditioning is not an occasional impediment to reflective transparency nor something to be overcome in the name of objectivity. On the contrary, "historicality is a determining characteristic for Dasein in the very basis of its being" (*SZ* 20/41–2). All meaning, along with the processes of the creation, discovery, and transmission of meaning, is historical. The way Heidegger understands this historicality, as well as its implications for interpretative understanding, both profoundly impacted his own hermeneutics and came to be of paramount significance for Gadamer, as the latter readily acknowledges.

At one level, "history" refers to the structure of our unfolding sense of ourselves, the familiarity with our own lives that "stretches" between birth and death.[8] "History" is not to be taken here in the sense of "source-criticism" or "historical writing." Rather, it is "co-living life," the way in which life is understandable from out of itself (*GA 58* 159–60). Having a "self" is a matter of having a unifying understanding of life-experience, though one that is not simply available at any point in time, but which is enacted during the course of a life. Our basic familiarity with ourselves is something that unfolds over time through the continuing interpretation of particular experiences in light of our expectations. Life, he says, always has a certain "direction," which it "grows into," and yet "gives to itself" (*GA 61* 94/70). "History" in this fundamental sense is a matter of "appropriating oneself out ahead of oneself [*sich Vorneigen*] from out of an originating [*herkommende*] life experience" (*GA 58* 165).

A unified meaning comes about in two phases or moments that are not successive but rather together comprise this, most basic, sense of "history" for Heidegger. First, a "horizon of expectation" is generated by one's prior experience and the active "projecting" of possibilities taken over from one's cultural inheritance. Second, one's "past" is interpreted in light of this horizon of expectation. The result of this process is a fluid self-interpretation that lends pattern and "connectedness" to one's life. Past and future are here woven together into a cohesive "rhythm." This is the "horizon" in which I am actually understandable to myself. This means that we *are* history, in the sense that the ways in which things show up to us as meaningful owes much to what has come before us, while these meanings are only actual in our projects and activities, and we, in turn, shape the history that will root the future. History is "an immediate living reality" (*GA 60* 33). Put simply, "[w]e are history, i.e., our own past. Our future is lived from out of the past. We carry the past with us" (S 174).[9]

The "past" of the self is not, however, exhausted by the events of a life that form a total life-story. The past is also "there" as tradition. We find ourselves always already within a communal tradition that is comprised of practices, concepts, norms, and linguistic usages, which forms the meaningful content of our individual lives. As he makes the point in *Being and Time*:

> Dasein has grown into and grown up in a traditional interpretation of Dasein. This understanding discloses and regulates the possibilities of its being. Its own peculiar past, and that always means that of its "generation," does not *follow after* Dasein, but rather in each case goes on ahead of it. (*SZ* 20/41)

This is the second sense of "history" that Heidegger emphasizes in his hermeneutics of facticity, namely, history as "tradition" (*Überlieferung*). The possibility (or set of possibilities) with which a person identifies, which gives pattern and meaning to a person's life, is not created out of thin air. Instead, it is found within the complex web of ideals, practices, patterns, and concepts that constitute a *tradition*. The cohesiveness of an individual life is, then, dependent on its link to a tradition. To put it slightly differently, one only has a self – and this includes all of one's activities, including that of achieving understanding – *as* a member of a community and as the recipient of a particular cultural inheritance. As he puts it in the "Natorp Report," "[f]actical life moves at any time within a certain state of *having-been-interpreted* [*Ausgelegtheit*] that has been handed down to it, and it has reworked or worked out anew" (*NB* 6/116). This understanding has been "deposited" in language (in a broad sense), not simply as a way people in the past understood things that we can now examine and investigate, but in "one's current understanding of being" and "whatever possibilities and horizons for fresh interpretation and conceptual articulation may be available" (*SZ* 167–8/211).

This sense of history as a tradition that is always already operative in the present, and which conditions the direction of the future is also something that Heidegger comes to view from a critical perspective.[10] Indeed, the attentive reader finds very little of Heidegger's alleged conservatism in the texts. What electrified generations of students was not a defense of the status quo or atavistic longing for the alleged glories of the Second Empire, but rather a genuinely revolutionary call to liberate the present from the burden of tradition while at the same time unlocking the radical possibilities passed over in the contemporary reception of the tradition. Tradition, in its present operation, is not something simply to be followed or blindly accepted. On the contrary, as it is an activity that unfolds in the history of the present, hermeneutics is necessarily a critical enterprise. This is because the historical process inevitably involves what Heidegger calls a "fading of significance [*Verblassen der Bedeutsamkeit*]" (*GA 59* 37). (In a 1921–1922 lecture, Heidegger illustrates the point with the very concept of history, as well as with concepts like "definition" and "philosophy" (*GA 61* 21–22/18).) Tradition ossifies into a kind of self-evidence, where alternative conceptions or interpretations take on the cast of idle "prattle [*Geschwätz*]." Notably, this also goes for "the attempt to bring itself to understanding in its conditioned status" (*GA 61* 1/3). This generates a disjunction for Heidegger: "either we live, work, and do research relative to unexamined needs and artificially induced dispositions, or we are prepared to grasp concretely a radical idea and to achieve our existence in it" (*GA 61* 70/53).

While tradition makes things familiar to us and available to us, it also obscures and occludes, foreclosing possibilities. As he puts it in 1922:

> Life is always stuck fast in, and pushed around by, inauthentic traditions and customs of one sort or another. Out of them develop certain yearnings, and in them the paths along which such yearnings are to be satisfied have been mapped out for one's concern. Life conceals itself from itself. (*NB* 11/118)

The problem is not that we are historically conditioned; rather, the concern here is with the way this conditionedness is typically enacted along these pre-arranged tracks. Elements of tradition take on a "shadowy life [...] that has hardened into a long, degenerate, and spurious tradition, and that has never been appropriated in an original manner" (*GA 9* 3/3). Life is "loaded down [*Belastung*]" with tradition (*GA 9* 34/29). In the summer semester of 1923, Heidegger articulates this phenomenon in terms of "the today [das Heute]" – the immediate milieu into which tradition has congealed at a given time and which influences intellectual discourses (GA 63 33/27) and even a culture's relationship to its own past (GA 63 35–36/28).

It is for this reason that the project of achieving self-understanding in the hermeneutics of facticity must contain an essential *negative* moment. "Hermeneutics carries out its tasks only on the path of destruction" (NB 20/124), which Heidegger describes as

> the authentic path upon which the present needs to encounter itself in its own basic movements, doing this in such a way that what springs forth for it from its history is the permanent question of the extent to which it itself is worried about appropriating radical possibilities. (NB 21/124)

The critical hermeneutics of "destruction" is meant to forge a unity between the creative, "systematic" approach of phenomenological research and the revolutionary interpretation of some of the most important texts in the history of philosophy. In this regard, it is intended as an alternative to historicist reconstruction as well as to the neo-Kantian approach (which was highly influential in the first several decades of the century), on which traditional texts are read as responses to perennial philosophical problems.[11] "[P]henomenological method already works with the aid of a *critical destruction* of objectifications which are always ready to accumulate on the phenomenon" (GA 58 255). It does so by making it possible for us to uncover meanings concealed in contemporary discourse and culture, including the way in which the past is received and interpreted in the present. Further, in light of the historical nature of human existence, this enterprise necessarily means a confrontation with tradition (GA 59 29). Thus the "[b]asic sense of phenomenology" includes "carrying out a destruction in the history of the spirit" (GA 61 132/98).[12] Rather than simply "enlarging knowledge about the past," the confrontation with tradition is meant to force "the present back upon itself in order to intensify its questionability" (*NB* 4/113). "Understanding consists not merely in taking up the past for the sake of a knowledge that merely takes note of it, but rather in *repeating* [*wiederholen*] in an original manner what is understood in the past in terms of and for the sake of one's very own situation" (*NB* 4/114).

Before turning to Gadamer's philosophical hermeneutics, I will leave the final word on his own approach to Heidegger (this time, from an address on Dilthey given in Kassel):

> What is required of philosophical research is that it be a critique of the present. In disclosing the past in an original manner, the past is no longer seen to be merely a present that preceded our own present. Rather, it is possible to emancipate the past so that we can find in it the authentic roots of our existence and bring it into our own present as a vital force. Historical consciousness liberates the past for the future, and it is then that the past gains force and becomes productive. (*S* 174f.)[13]

GADAMER'S PHILOSOPHICAL HERMENEUTICS

In 1960, after over three decades of teaching at Marburg, Kiel, Leipzig, Frankfurt, and, finally, Heidelberg (where he remained for the rest of his life), during which he published essays as well as his *Habilitation* thesis on Plato, Hans-Georg Gadamer published *Truth and Method*. With the appearance of this monumental work Gadamer became the most influential living expositor of the hermeneutical tradition in philosophy. Years of reflection had brought Gadamer to the convictions that (1) hermeneutics is a field of problems that spans the whole of philosophy and that (2) the positivist and historicist models of understanding, the twin legacies of the nineteenth century, not only stood in the way of this recognition but fundamentally misrepresented the nature of human understanding. In *Truth and Method*, Gadamer undertakes to defend both of these points by showing how "[u]nderstanding must be conceived as a part of the event in which meaning occurs, the event in which the meaning of all statements – those of art and all other kinds of tradition – is formed and actualized" (*GW* 170; *TM* 164–5). While he is deeply critical of the epistemological obsessions of the neo-Kantians and the legacy of what he deems to be the "Historical School," Gadamer nevertheless establishes this claim through a transcendental account of the structure of understanding that is profoundly indebted to Heidegger's "hermeneutics of facticity."[14] According to Gadamer, it was Heidegger who first grasped "that we study history only insofar as we are ourselves 'historical' means that the historicity of human Dasein in its expectancy and its forgetting is the condition of our being able to re-present the past," and that human historicity is not a barrier to understanding but rather its indispensable condition (*GW* 266; *TM* 262).

Gadamer's radical expansion of the scope of hermeneutics and his other departures from the hermeneutical tradition can be illustrated by many points he makes during the long argument of the book. Perhaps most straightforwardly, by rendering it a critical or transcendental project, philosophical hermeneutics is not a method or procedure for getting "correct" understandings of texts (*GW* 300; *TM* 295). The investigations are not meant to establish a theory that can then serve, in applied form, to set hermeneutical practice on a course that is "technically correct" (*GW* 271; *TM* 266). Instead, what Gadamer aims to achieve is self-understanding, something that "would benefit the art of understanding at most indirectly" (*GW* 271; *TM* 266). Thus, hermeneutics is "not primarily a prescription for the practice of understanding, but a description of the way interpretive understanding is achieved" (*GW* 271; *TM* 266). It is worth noting that, despite this delimitation of the scope of his enterprise, Gadamer nevertheless pauses the argument at various points to reflect in a more practical register on the art of interpretation. More interesting than these moments, however, are those in which Gadamer carries out hermeneutics in its Gadamerian mode. I will briefly illustrate one of these latter moments and its significance within the argument of *Truth and Method* below.

Historicism can be broadly construed as the approach to history that acknowledges the finite, conditioned nature of any period's scope of vision and aims at precise, objectively correct reconstruction of the cultural products of a period. This approach is the product of what Gadamer sometimes calls the "Historical Enlightenment," meaning the great flowering of historiography in nineteenth-century Germany (with Ranke and Droysen as leading figures). Historicism shares with positivism the view that proper methodology secures the correctness of results, whereas positivism tends to include the additional claim that only the methods of the natural sciences fit the bill. It is this twin legacy of the Enlightenment and its aftermath that Gadamer takes as his principle foil in *Truth and Method*. Historicism reflects this legacy with its "prejudice against prejudice itself, which denies tradition its power" (*GW* 278; *TM* 273) by treating past cultures as naively self-enclosed and best understood through the superior, objective lens of current methodologies.[15] Gadamer tries to unravel this underlying prejudice by reminding the readers that prejudice means originally pre-judgment or "a provisional legal verdict before the final verdict is reached, not necessarily a judgment that is false" (*GW* 275; *TM* 270). The Enlightenment "prejudice against prejudice," on the other hand, grew out of rationalism. Descartes' methodological doubt exemplifies this more basic rationalist move; by suspending the affirmation of all pre-conceived opinions, it is possible to begin "from scratch," as it were, employing a method that founds all of our judgments securely (see *GW* 275; *TM* 271). Eventually, this *a priori* suspicion of tradition, supported by the brilliant polemics of figures like Hume, Voltaire, and Diderot, rises to the point of a rupture or alienation in relation to tradition that characterizes the historical consciousness of the nineteenth century (*GW* 279–280; *TM* 275).

Gadamer's claim is that "[t]he overcoming of all prejudices, this global demand of the Enlightenment, will itself prove to be a prejudice, and removing it opens the way to an appropriate understanding of the finitude which dominates not only our humanity but also our historical consciousness" (*GW* 280; *TM* 276). Gadamer argues this point by turning one of the key insights of historicism back on itself, namely, that reason is always historically conditioned. "In fact," he observes, "history does not belong to us; we belong to it" (*GW* 281; *TM* 276). Moreover, the recognition of authority is itself an act of rationality, rendering the supposedly radical opposition between the authority of tradition and the authority of reason a false dilemma (*GW* 283–4; *TM* 279). Thus, the work of scholars in the humanistic disciplines [*Geisteswissenschaften*] cannot be artificially isolated from their historical being, from their belonging to the unfolding of the very tradition that they study (*GW* 286–7; *TM* 282).

Hence, "[t]he effect [*Wirkung*] of a living tradition and the effect of historical study must constitute a unity of effect, the analysis of which would reveal only a texture of reciprocal effects" (*GW* 287; *TM* 282–3). Put most directly, Gadamer's thesis is that "[m]odern historical research itself is not only research, but the handing down of tradition. We do not see it only in terms of progress and verified results; in it we have, as it were, a new experience of history whenever the past resounds in a new voice" (*GW* 289; *TM* 284). Cutting to the heart of the epistemological model at the root of the historicist tradition, Gadamer maintains that historical understanding is not the activity of an isolated subject striving to understand an alien object from out of the distant past, but rather "a process of transmission in which past and present are constantly mediated" (*GW* 295; *TM* 290). History [*Geschichte*] is an event [*Geschehen*] rather than an object of study or a particular methodology for coming to terms with such an object. Historical and cultural research *presupposes* tradition, in the sense of the preconceptions that enable understanding, and, at the same time, *produces* it.

On the basis of this critical revision of historicism, Gadamer derives a new imperative:

> Historical consciousness must become conscious that in the apparent immediacy with which it approaches a work of art

or a traditionary text, there is also another kind of inquiry in play, albeit unrecognized and unregulated. If we are trying to understand a historical phenomenon from the historical distance that is characteristic of our hermeneutical situation, we are always already affected by history. It determines in advance both what seems to us worth inquiring about and what will appear as an object of investigation, and we more or less forget half of what is really there – in fact, we miss the whole truth of the phenomenon – when we take its immediate appearance as the whole truth. (*GW* 305–6; *TM* 300)

With its overly naive reliance on method for achieving the "correct" understanding of a historical phenomenon, historicism masks the formative activity of tradition, which Gadamer labels "effective history [*Wirkungsgeschichte*]" (*GW* 305–6; *TM* 300–1). What is needed is another type of historical consciousness, "historically effected consciousness [*wirkungsgeschichtliches Bewußtsein*]," or "consciousness of the hermeneutical situation" (*GW* 307; *TM* 301). The label "historically effected consciousness" is meant to point to both "the consciousness affected in the course of history and determined by history and the very consciousness of being thus affected and determined" (*TM* xxxiv; translation modified). This consciousness is fundamentally non-objectifying or non-alienated, since it is part of the situation in question, not an external observer of it. The ideal of total reflective transparency must, however, be abandoned. Critical self-consciousness does not eliminate our dependence on the "hermeneutical situation," but rather embeds us further within it in a productive and conscious manner. Borrowing from Hegel, Gadamer describes how historically effected consciousness brings to light the "substantiality" presupposed by a historically specific shape of consciousness, which means becoming explicitly aware of how the situation furnishes a limiting horizon – "the range of vision that includes everything that can be seen from a particular vantage point" (*GW* 307; *TM* 302).

At the same time, the text speaks to us from its own horizon-bestowing situation into which we must transpose ourselves. This does not mean that we agree with or endorse the meaning that the text is conveying to us (*GW* 308; *TM* 303). Yet, it is a mistake to bracket or isolate the claim of the text methodologically, drawing a rigid line between its horizon and the one from which we are operating. Doing so rests on the false picture that horizons are *closed*, which Gadamer sardonically labels "a kind of Robinson Crusoe dream of the historical enlightenment" (*GW* 309; *TM* 304). The idea that the horizons of past cultures are closed, and that this sets up an insurmountable boundary to understanding, or that the past is "over and done with" from our, supposedly superior, point of view, turns out to be a fiction. Playing with the metaphor of a horizon, Gadamer avers that "[h]orizons change for a person who is moving. Thus the horizon of the past, out of which all human life lives and which exists in the form of tradition, is always in motion" (*GW* 309; *TM* 304).

Understanding is not about transposing ourselves into a totally alien world, be it that of a past culture or the inner recesses of the mind of a genius. Instead, the kind of transposition involved in understanding is a matter of "rising to a higher universality that overcomes not only our own particularity but also that of the other" (*GW* 310; *TM* 305). Our horizon (comprised of prejudices) is not a "fixed set of opinions and validations," which means that it is also not a barrier to grasping the meaning of the past. To the contrary, in our confrontation with the historically other, our own prejudices (both in the standard sense and in the more neutral sense intended by Gadamer) are put under pressure, thus undergoing a kind of continual formation and re-formation. The ultimate lesson is that "*understanding is always the fusion of these horizons supposedly existing in themselves*" (*GW* 311; *TM* 306).[16] While it is certainly true that confronting the past involves the projection of a historical horizon onto it that allows us to articulate the real differences between the past and the present, understanding also involves *superseding* this historical horizon. For Gadamer, the traditional hermeneutical concept of *application* captures this crucial aspect of understanding (*GW* 312–16; *TM* 307–11). Traditional disciplines like legal-juridical and biblical hermeneutics furnish models for how the achievement of a "historical understanding," in the modern or historicist sense, is precisely *not* what one is attempting to achieve in coming to grips with the past.

In a section on Aristotle's *Nicomachean Ethics* which harkens back to the formative role played by his participation in Heidegger's seminars on Aristotle in the early 1920s, Gadamer focuses on the way in which practical wisdom (*phronesis*) exemplifies a kind of knowledge that belongs within a process of becoming, rather than standing over against it as if it were a detached, objective observer (*GW* 317–29; *TM* 312–24).[17] The process of becoming that is in question is the sphere of human praxis, which Aristotle understands in a way that foreshadows the concept of history that emerged from the nineteenth-century "Historical School" and the work of figures like Dilthey and the Baden neo-Kantians (Rickert and Windelband). The sphere of praxis, like that of history, is a domain of "human institutions and human modes of behavior which are mutable" (*GW* 317; *TM* 312). Particularly important for Gadamer is the fact that practical wisdom is concretely engaged in a specific temporally sited situation, and that "it is impossible for ethics to achieve the extreme exactitude of mathematics" due to the nature of its subject matter and its participation in a process of becoming (*GW* 318; *TM* 313). Rather than providing a decision procedure or moral methodology, philosophy on the Aristotelian model aids moral consciousness by "outlining phenomena" and so facilitating self-reflection in the here and now context of action. Such knowledge is not detached from being (or its object) – just as in the case of effective historical consciousness, where the interpreter belongs to the tradition, and understanding is an event within its unfolding history (*GW* 319–20; *TM* 314).

This analysis of Aristotle is a fine exemplar of Gadamerian hermeneutics (in the traditional sense of the art of reading texts) in practice.[18] Gadamer's own "horizon" is comprised of a set of problems about understanding, largely shaped by the dynamics of historiography and philosophical reflection on it in the late nineteenth and early twentieth centuries. Aristotle's horizon, on the other hand, is that of late classical Greece, where the disintegration of the classical *polis* and the question of how knowledge relates to ethical practice had been made key desiderata of philosophy since Socrates. The "fusion" here consists in the articulation of a concept of a distinctive kind of intellectual activity that is situated within a continually changing context. Just like the activity of acquiring historical understanding, that of achieving moral knowledge is conditioned by custom and education. Moreover, as with historical understanding, the full sense of a concept only emerges within the specific situation (*GW* 322–3; *TM* 317).

Following this brilliant exposition of Aristotle's ethics, Gadamer goes on to provide a more detailed account of historically effected consciousness (*GW* 346–86; *TM* 341–62), making it clear that "[t]he purpose of the whole account of the formation and fusion of horizons was to show how historically effected consciousness operates" (*GW* 352; *TM* 346). Here, he emphasizes how, as a mode of consciousness, it partakes of the reflexivity characteristic of all conscious activity. This observation leads Gadamer to turn to Hegel and his account of the "experience [*Erfahrung*]" of *Geist* in the *Phenomenology of Spirit*, in which the reflexive structure of consciousness fuels the dynamic process of self-criticism and revision traversed along the famous "highway of despair."[19] In a way parallel to the Hegelian ideal of Absolute Knowing as the terminus of self-criticism, nineteenth-century historians and philosophers of history conceived of the goal of historical knowledge as "the thoughtful fusion of the whole of tradition with the present" (*GW* 347; *TM* 341). On Gadamer's view, for reasons detailed above, such total transparency is impossible, and historical understanding is most certainly what Hegel would dub a "bad infinity." Summarizing his own account of prejudice and tradition, and reflecting the legacy of Heidegger, Gadamer insists that "[h]istorically effected consciousness is so radically finite that our whole being, effected in the totality of our destiny, inevitably transcends its knowledge of itself" (*TM* xxxiv).

The aspect of Hegel's picture that Gadamer wants to preserve highlights the negative or dialectical structure of experience (*GW* 359–60; *TM* 353–5). The true outcome of experience, rather than self-transparency or certainty of the correctness of one's findings, is a kind of openness to what is different and new, won through the hard lessons of failure. "Thus experience is experience of human finitude [...] In it are discovered the limits of the power and the self-knowledge of his planning reason" (*GW* 363; *TM* 357). This experience, which is the essence of historically effected consciousness, is "hermeneutical experience." Hermeneutical experience is, in the first instance, the experience of *tradition* (*GW* 363; *TM* 358). Rather than being an object of historical curiosity or a puzzle from an alien world, tradition is a Thou; it is something that addresses us like a genuine dialogical partner (*GW* 364; *TM* 358). As such, it demands a non-objectifying form of understanding quite distinct from the historicists' "naïve faith in method" (*GW* 364; *TM* 358). It certainly does not require freedom from all prejudice, which is impossible anyhow (*GW* 365–6; *TM* 360–1). What a cultivated historically effected consciousness requires is an "openness to tradition," comprised of an act of self-limitation that enables genuine understanding.

CONCLUSION

While he famously viewed the traditional arts of the philologist and the historian with no small amount of contempt, Heidegger's phenomenological hermeneutics certainly does not foreclose the possibility of continued reflection on the art of understanding. At the same time, Heidegger succeeded in opening up a radically new dimension of hermeneutical inquiry. While the seeds were planted by Herder, Hegel, and Dilthey, Heidegger's conception of hermeneutics as a phenomenological enterprise intended, like Husserl's phenomenology, to be a "primordial science [*Urwissenschaft*]" of human experience in its totality, took hermeneutics far beyond its traditional purview and upended the terms of the debates occasioned by the rise of historicism. Understanding turns out to be not one sort of cognitive behavior among others, distinguished only by its subject matter and its methodological limitations. Instead, human beings are shown by Heidegger to be *understanding animals* through and through. Life is meaningful in its immediacy, and the structures that render it meaningful can be explicated by means of an engaged interpretation that largely bypasses the epistemological quandaries that occupied Heidegger's predecessors.

Yet, as even a casual glance at the titles of the *Collected Edition* of Heidegger's works makes apparent, this engaged interpretation did not happen in some kind of vacuum, but took the shape precisely of confrontation with texts. Augustine's *Confessions*, Aristotle's *Physics* and *Nicomachean Ethics*, Kant's *Critique of Pure Reason*, Nietzsche's published and unpublished writings, the fragments of the pre-Socratics and the hymns of Hölderlin comprise the field upon which Heidegger's phenomenological enterprise was enacted. While Heidegger's readings of these and other texts have provoked no little controversy, and often bear little resemblance to what historians of philosophy would recognize as being of a piece with their own studies, he nonetheless succeeds in his aim of showing how the philosophical tradition is neither a litany of erroneous views nor a group of time-bound expressions of bygone cultures but rather what he liked to call *Denkwürdigkeiten*, matters worth thinking about.

For Gadamer, Heidegger's revolution inspired a renewed attempt to think through the distinctive role and value of humanistic inquiry in an age that prizes exactitude and results above all else. Humanistic understanding is elevated by Gadamer from being a mere imitator, aspiring to but never quite attaining the precision and objective validity of the sciences. Appropriating Heidegger's insight into the all-pervading activity of understanding and the ways in which history penetrates the present and sketches out the future, Gadamer transforms the humanistic enterprise into the individual and collective event in which meaning emerges from obscurity and human life advances on the endless path of self-understanding.

Like Heidegger, Gadamer did not simply theorize about the art of textual interpretation. Instead, he dedicated his life to enacting, and thus exemplifying, the event of understanding. Not least within *Truth and Method* itself, Gadamer's readings of Plato, Aristotle, the pre-Socratics, and other classics succeed in engaging with the efforts of other scholars while forging entirely novel ways of understanding these thinkers and their intellectual relationships to one another. Gadamer's readings of German-language poets like Celan and Rilke integrate his work on the history of philosophy while likewise challenging aestheticizing tendencies that he had criticized so thoroughly in the opening sections of *Truth and Method*. Just as in Heidegger's case, Gadamer's art of interpretation overcomes the objectifying isolation into which classics are so often imprisoned while preserving the real otherness of the great works and thinkers he examines.

NOTES

1 Martin Heidegger, *Gesamtausgabe*, vol. 2: *Sein und Zeit* (Frankfurt am Main: Vittorio Klostermann, 1977); *Being and Time*, trans. John Macquarrie and Edward Robinson (New York: Harper & Row, 1962) [abbreviated as *SZ*]. Heidegger's early lectures will be cited according to the *Gesamtausgabe*, ed. Friedrich-Wilhelm von Hermann et al. (Frankfurt am Main: Vittorio Klostermann, 1975ff.) [abbreviated as *GA* with volume number].

2 Hans-Georg Gadamer, *Gesammelte Werke*, vol. 1: *Wahrheit und Methode* (Tübingen: J. C. B Mohr [Paul Siebeck], 1993) [abbreviated as *GW*]; *Truth and Method*, trans. Joel Weinsheimer and Donald G. Marshall, 2nd edn. (New York: Continuum, 2002) [abbreviated as *TM*].

3 A key text by Heidegger from this period, the so-called "Natorp Report," composed in the fall of 1922, was shared by Paul Natorp with Gadamer (both were then in Marburg); see "Phenomenological Interpretations in Connection with Aristotle: An Indication of the Hermeneutical Situation (1922)," trans. John Van Buren, in *Supplements: From the Earliest Essays to "Being and Time" and Beyond*, ed. John Van Buren (Albany: SUNY Press, 2002): 111–46 [abbreviated as *NB*]. As a result, Gadamer wrote to Heidegger in Freiburg almost immediately to express his desire to participate in his upcoming seminar on Aristotle. During

the summer of 1923, Gadamer attended all of Heidegger's classes, including the lecture course "Ontology: Hermeneutics of Facticity" (see *GA 63*; *Ontology: Hermeneutics of Facticity* [trans. John Van Buren, Bloomington, Indiana: Indiana University Press, 1995]), as well as a "Phenomenological Practicum for Beginners in Connection with Aristotle's *Nicomachean Ethics*," where comments on Book VI from the "Natorp Report" were likely expanded upon in the classroom. I will discuss at more length below the importance of Aristotle for Gadamer's conception of understanding. During the same summer, Gadamer and his first wife visited the Heidegger family at the famous cabin in Todtnauberg.

4 For an exhaustive archival account of the formative stages in Heidegger's thinking, see Theodore Kisiel, *The Genesis of Heidegger's Being and Time* (Berkeley: University of California Press, 1993).

5 Martin Heidegger, *Towards the Definition of Philosophy*, trans. Ted Sadler (London: Athlone Press, 2000) [translation of *GA 56/57*].

6 Martin Heidegger, *Phenomenological Interpretations of Aristotle: Initiation into Phenomenological Research*, trans. Richard Rojcewicz (Bloomington: Indiana University Press, 2001) [translation of *GA 61*].

7 Crowell distills his powerful reading in *Phenomenology and Normativity in Husserl and Heidegger* (Cambridge: Cambridge University Press, 2013).

8 Charles Guignon has explored this sense of "history" in Heidegger in a number of works. See (1) *Heidegger and the Problem of Knowledge* (Indianapolis: Hackett Publishing Company, 1983); (2) "History and Commitment in the Early Heidegger," in *Heidegger: A Critical Reader*, ed. Hubert Dreyfus and Harrison Hall (Oxford: Blackwell, 1992), 130–42; and (3) "Authenticity, Moral Values, and Psychotherapy," in *The Cambridge Companion to Heidegger*, ed. Charles B. Guignon (Cambridge: Cambridge University Press, 1993), 215–39. My own conception of this aspect of Heidegger's thought owes much to Guignon's reading. For a further discussion that links this sense of "history" to Heidegger's readings of Dilthey and the early Christian tradition, see my *Heidegger's Religious Origins: Destruction and Authenticity* (Bloomington: Indiana University Press, 2006), especially ch. 6.

9 "Wilhelm Dilthey's Research and the Struggle for a Historical Worldview," trans. John Van Buren, in *Supplements: From the Earliest Essays to "Being and Time" and Beyond*, ed. John Van Buren (Albany: SUNY Press, 2002): 111–46 [abbreviated as *NB*].

10 I have examined this critical perspective in more detail in *Heidegger's Religious Origins*, especially ch. 4, as well as in *Heidegger's Phenomenology of Religion: Realism and Cultural Criticism*, ch. 1. An expansive reading of this facet of Heidegger's relationship to the philosophical tradition that spans both *Being and Time* and his work from the 1930s–1950s is Iain D. Thomson, *Heidegger on Ontotheology: Technology and the Politics of Education* (Cambridge: Cambridge University Press, 2005).

11 Several scholars have provided detailed and insightful analysis of Heidegger's relationship to the historicist tradition and to neo-Kantian philosophy of history. For an exemplary account, see Charles R. Bambach, *Heidegger, Dilthey, and the Crisis of Historicism* (Ithaca, NY: Cornell University Press, 1995).

12 In his first Marburg course, Heidegger puts the point this way: "the task of freely giving Dasein to itself and achieving an explication of it is bound up with the task of unsettling [*erschüttern*] contemporary Dasein [...] This is carried out in the manner of a dismantling [*abzubauen*], in which the basic categories of consciousness, person, and subject are led back to their original meaning, in the sense that one shows, through insight into the origin of these categories, that they arise from a totally different basis of ontological experience and that their conceptual tendencies are unsuitable for what we want to bring into view as Dasein" (*GA 17* 113).

13 See some roughly contemporaneous comments, also from the first Marburg course: "In point of fact, destruction is critical. But what is criticized is not the past, which is opened up through destruction. Rather, the critique falls upon the present, upon our contemporary Dascin, to the extent that it is concealed by a past that has become inauthentic. Aristotle or Augustine are not criticized, but rather the present [...] Thus, destruction as critique is critique of the today, which makes visible that which is authentically, originally positive in the past" (*GA 17* 119). Gadamer and other former students recalled how Heidegger's arrival in Marburg had the feel of a hostile takeover, and

that Heidegger made clear his intentions to blow apart the way in which the discipline of the history of philosophy had been pursued at that time.
14 This transcendental register is emphasized in the Foreword to the 2nd edn. (xxix–xxx).
15 For a thorough treatment of this element of Gadamer's framing of hermeneutics, see Georgia Warnke, *Gadamer: Hermeneutics, Tradition, and Reason* (Stanford: Stanford University Press, 1987). See also David Detmer, "Gadamer's Critique of the Enlightenment," in *The Philosophy of Hans-Georg Gadamer*, ed. Lewis Edwin Hahn, The Library of Living Philosophers XXIV (Chicago and LaSalle: Open Court, 1997), 275–86.
16 For a recent explication and defense of Gadamer's notion of the "fusion of horizons," see David Vessey, "Gadamer and the Fusion of Horizons," *International Journal of Philosophical Studies* 17 (2009): 531–42.
17 Among the many good studies of Gadamer's work on Aristotle, see Günter Figal, "*Phronesis* as Understanding: Situating Philosophical Hermeneutics," in *The Specter of Relativism: Truth, Dialogue, and Phronesis in Philosophical Hermeneutics*, ed. Lawrence K. Schmidt (Evanston: Northwestern University Press, 1995), 236–47. Regarding Gadamer's readings of Plato and Aristotle, and the significance of these readings for philosophical hermeneutics as a whole, see Lauren Swayne Barthold, *Gadamer's Dialectical Hermeneutics* (Lanham: Lexington Books, 2010).
18 Catherine Zuckert provides an overview of Gadamer's hermeneutical practice with regard to ancient philosophy in "Hermeneutics in Practice: Gadamer on Ancient Philosophy," in *The Cambridge Companion to Gadamer*, ed. Robert Dostal (Cambridge: Cambridge University Press, 2002), 201–24.
19 There are many studies of Gadamer's readings of and relationship to Hegel. The most detailed one, which likewise situates this relationship within the larger scope of Gadamer's relationship to the German philosophical tradition, is Kristin Gjesdal, *Gadamer and the Legacy of German Idealism* (Cambridge: Cambridge University Press, 2009).

10 Hermeneutics and Critical Theory

Georgia Warnke

Despite differences among the major theorists associated with the Frankfurt School of Critical Theory, the common core of their social criticism as Thomas McCarthy points out is a "critical reconstruction of Enlightenment conceptions of reason and the rational subject ... in which they are recast in sociohistorical terms rather than simply dismantled."[1] From this point of view, the worry about philosophical hermeneutics as developed by Hans-Georg Gadamer is that in its focus on historical tradition it comes too close to simply dismantling rather than recasting these Enlightenment conceptions. In this chapter I want to indicate how the commitment to recasting them motivates Jürgen Habermas's reaction to Gadamer's hermeneutics in the 1970s and Axel Honneth's criticism of it in the 2000s. I begin, however, with the programmatic statements about critical theory that Max Horkheimer makes in the 1930s, as these set the direction for the concerns Habermas and Honneth advance.[2]

HORKHEIMER'S CRITICAL THEORY

The outlines of Horkheimer's attempt at a recasting of reason and the rational subject are perhaps clearest in his 1939 essay, "The Social Function of Philosophy," in which he compares the tasks of philosophy to those of what he here calls the special sciences or, in other words, the empirical natural and social sciences.[3] The problem with these sciences, he claims, is that they focus on human needs, actions, and desires as they emerge within given social and historical conditions without questioning those conditions. As he puts the point, the special sciences are concerned with human life only "in its present form."[4] Horkheimer also suggests that much of contemporary philosophy has a similar purview. Where it does not imagine

237

abstract utopias divorced from any contact with human reality, what we might today call ideal theory, it sees its function as that of serving the sciences and accepting "the tasks set for it by the ever renewed needs of government and industry."[5] Yet Horkheimer insists that historically the thrust of philosophy has been otherwise:

> Philosophy has always set itself against mere tradition and resignation in the decisive problems of existence, and it has shouldered the unpleasant task of throwing the light of consciousness even upon those human relations and modes of action which have become so deeply rooted that they seem natural, immutable and eternal.[6]

As Horkheimer sees critical theory, it is the continuation of this philosophical task of reflecting critically on the world in which we find ourselves. Moreover, critical theory does so in light of the potential for social rationality that world contains. In his essays in the 1930s he follows Marx in looking to the rationality, "if in a restricted sense,"[7] embodied in the technological mastery of nature. "Human work," Horkheimer writes in "Traditional and Critical Theory," has "an element of planning in it."[8] Immanent in it is the idea of a rational society in which the contributions of individual members consciously and transparently complement one another. To the extent that in existing societies they do not, Horkheimer contends it is because these societies entrust technological mastery "to special, mutually opposed interests." Rather than as collective, conscious action, events occur as the blind outcomes of uncoordinated activities and "it is enough for individuals to look out for themselves."[9]

Under these conditions the social and historical world that is the product of human activity and is hence open to transparent collective direction appears, instead, as a kind of second nature, indifferent to human aims, actions, and desires. It is the "sum-total of facts; it is there and must be accepted."[10] Indeed, for Horkheimer, the opposition between the results of collective human activity and what appears to individuals as a set of facts to be passively accepted explains both the dualism in Kant's philosophy between "purely passive sensation and active understanding" as well as his recourse to the transcendental subject as that which pre-forms the sensible appearances for perception behind the back, as it were, of the individual. Critical theory's effort is to capture the kernel of truth in this Kantian dualism while at the same time releasing this kernel from its ideological imprisonment in conceptual mystifications. Critical theory thereby assists in a process of Enlightenment that can connect the "sum total of facts" to collective activity and refashion that activity as the rationally coordinated contributions of consciously acting human beings.

Despite his critique of the special sciences, Horkheimer does not think that philosophy can accomplish this process of Enlightenment on its own. Rather, it needs to coordinate with empirically based, interdisciplinary analyses able to uncover the "concrete relations and tendencies"[11] that point, on the one hand, to rational potentials and, on the other hand, to the factors impeding their realization. In his inaugural address upon assuming the directorship of the Institute for Social Research in 1931, Horkheimer thus calls for the "ongoing dialectical permeation and evaluation of philosophical theory and empirical-scientific praxis,"[12] a permeation that is to include studies of "the economic life of society, the psychological development of its individuals and the changes within specific areas of culture to which belong not only the intellectual legacy of the sciences, art and religion, but also law, customs, fashion, public opinion, sports, entertainment, lifestyles and so on."[13] In "Traditional and Critical Theory" Horkheimer contrasts the intent of these studies to the special sciences or what he here calls traditional theory. While social sciences of the latter type model themselves on the natural sciences and take themselves to be a value-free exploration of a world or second nature independent of them, an empirical-scientific praxis permeated by philosophical concerns with reason is reflexive and thus aware of its implication in the same social and historical world it studies.

Horkheimer notes four interrelated aspects of this awareness. First, as opposed to traditional forms of inquiry, critical theories recognize that their subject matter includes conditions and processes that influence their own projects and agendas; second, they are aware that the conceptions and ideas they employ to understand the social world themselves arise out of it and, third, inasmuch as the "sum total of facts" is produced by human activity, critical theories acknowledge that this activity includes the practice of social science itself. Indeed, to the extent that, as Horkheimer says in "The Social Function of Philosophy," the specialized sciences allow themselves to be guided by human reality as it is, what they take as their value-free neutrality is in fact a non-value-free endorsement of the established social context. In contrast, critical theories recognize their social involvement as well as their non-value-free status as a form of social practice.

A fourth aspect of a critical inquiry's reflexive character is its awareness that the objects of its research can become subjects of knowledge. As a self-conscious form of social practice, critical theory takes up a relation to those groups suffering most from the irrational organization of society. Horkheimer denies that a critical theory can simply register that group's point of view. Rather he writes, "If critical theory consisted essentially in formulations of the feelings of one class at any given moment, it would not be structurally different from the special branches of the sciences."[14] It would be a traditional form of social psychology that took up an external, "objective" perspective on its subject matter without concern for its potential for self-enlightenment. Rather, critical theory takes up what Horkheimer calls a "dynamic unity with the oppressed class."[15] Critical theory's function is not to avoid possible conflict with it but rather to investigate developments in the structure of society and its role in them with the goal of illuminating the possibilities for a more rational future.

As is well-known, Horkheimer's (and Adorno's) confidence in a rational future did not survive the horror of National Socialism. Rather than looking to the reason immanent in human work, their *Dialectic of Enlightenment* now sees this form of reason as the problem. The technological mastery of nature that Horkheimer once associated with the possibility for a rational organization of society he now sees only as domination and, furthermore, as the explanation for "why humanity, instead of entering a truly human state, is sinking into a new barbarism."[16] Yet according to Habermas, Horkheimer was always aware of limits of a definition of reason in terms of technological mastery. For him this "restricted sense" of reason was a by-product of the bourgeois era – even if it was also one that "pointed beyond itself to a post-bourgeois form of society that would redeem the promise once provided by substantive reason."[17] Moreover, if at the start of the 1940s Horkheimer no longer believed in this promise, Habermas thinks his work in the 1950s and 1960s was more ambivalent. Indeed, Habermas finds in Horkheimer's *Notizen* a seed of an idea that he thinks "might have restored to criticism a piece of its self-confidence": namely, the notion that "Language, whether it wants to or not must make a claim to truth" and, moreover, that "Truth in speech accrues not to the isolated, naked judgment, as if it were printed on a piece of paper, but to the speaker's relationship to the world as it is expressed in judgment, focused on this place and referring to a specific object."[18] With these notions Horkheimer points, if vaguely, to the rational basis of speech oriented to mutual understanding, the idea that Habermas pursues in the form of a theory of communicative action that he thinks can redeem the potential for social reason to which critical theory was originally committed. His interest in Gadamer's hermeneutics stems from this pursuit. In Habermas's analysis of it, it too looks to the possibilities of language and mutual understanding even if it stops short of the kind of critical reflection Habermas thinks is necessary.

HABERMAS'S CRITIQUE OF GADAMER

Like Horkheimer, Habermas is interested in the extent to which philosophy and empirically based social sciences can join forces to uncover and explain deficits in social rationality. Moreover, like Horkheimer, he thinks the self-understanding of traditional or what Habermas calls positivistic social sciences is problematic insofar as it neglects their reflexivity and immersion in the same social and human world they study. He finds linguistic approaches to the social sciences equally problematic. Drawing from Ludwig Wittgenstein, such approaches no longer associate the social sciences with the explanations of behavioral regularities that positivistic social sciences see themselves as providing and look rather to understandings of language games comprising "symbolically regulated interactions."[19] Such approaches may thus reflect an advance over positivistic social sciences insofar as they move to the plane of shared or intersubjective meanings. According to linguistic approaches, any attempt to explain the causes for certain behaviors requires that we first determine what those behaviors are and determining what specific behaviors are requires understanding the complex of concepts, actions, and normative expectations – the language game or form of life – in terms of which they have the sense they have. Yet in Habermas's view linguistic approaches conceive of understanding language games only as socialization within them and hence on the model of learning a first language. They thereby assume that we can leave our own language game behind and that our prior socialization within it has no impact on our understanding of a new one. The social scientist becomes a free-floating linguistic analyst who is meant to be able to "slip into the grammar of any language game without being himself bound by the dogmatism of his own."[20] But then the question arises as to how this sort of free-floating is possible. Like positivistic approaches to the social sciences, linguistic approaches thus overlook the social and historical situation of the social scientists themselves who are already socialized into specific language games.

For Habermas, one of the virtues of Gadamer's philosophical hermeneutics is that it begins with this social and historical situation and thereby provides for an alternative to the self-understanding of forms of social science – both positivistic and linguistic – that assume they can extract themselves from it. As Habermas explicates a philosophical hermeneutic it is a reflection upon the experiences of language we gain in the process of exercising our communicative competence. In mastering a language we acquire the capacity both to understand and to make ourselves understood. While hermeneutics develops this capacity as an interpretive discipline, philosophical hermeneutics reflects upon its conditions. What Habermas sees as its "characteristic insight" is the recognition "that the means of natural language are, in principle, sufficient for elucidating the sense of any symbolic complex, however unfamiliar and inaccessible it may initially appear."[21] Our ability to understand language games distant from those in which we are involved depends not on liberation from our own but on translation into it. We are able to learn a foreign language on the basis of the language we already possess and to make sense of the contents it expresses by relating them to the contents we already understand. On the one hand, this process of translation gives priority to our own language and to the interpretive resources it contains. For this reason Gadamer stresses the prejudiced character of understanding. As Habermas explains, hermeneutical understanding "is ... unavoidably prepossessed by the context within which the understanding subject has initially acquired his interpretive schemes."[22] On the other hand, translation expands our original language so that we can express what is expressed in the language we are translating. In so doing, moreover, the language we are translating can illuminate the context and prejudices with which we began and provide for a new perspective on them.

The same complex of prepossession, extension, and illumination holds when translation is necessary for speakers of the same language because their historical distance from one another means that they can no longer understand one another directly. In the cases of both cultural and historical distance translation is less an attempt at accomplishing a one-on-one equivalence of terms than an attempt at communicating and agreeing on meaning. Thus, whereas language games for Wittgenstein form tight complexes of symbols and actions that we must learn as first languages and participate in as natives if we are to understand them at all, according to Habermas, languages for Gadamer form open horizons. Rather than static entities, they are resources and repositories of shared meanings that can expand and fuse with other horizons to allow for mutual understanding both across cultures and historical generations and between ordinary communication partners. As Habermas puts this point:

> In translation we are not concerned with a transformation that permits statements in one language system to be reduced to statements in another. The act of translation points rather to a productive accomplishment to which language always empowers those who have mastered its grammatical rules: assimilating what is foreign and thereby further developing one's own language system. This occurs every day in situations in which the dialogue partners must first find a "common language." This language is the result of having reached an understanding.[23]

The notion of a fusion of horizons signals a second virtue of Gadamer's hermeneutics for Habermas. Insofar as this fusion represents the productive possibilities of not only personal and linguistic but also historical distances in enlarging our understandings of meaning, it depicts a continuing tradition in which the horizons of the present emerge out of the horizons of the past and provide for an expanded perspective on them. At work here is what Gadamer calls effective history. The extension of language systems through translation is mirrored in the extension of the meaning of historical events, actions, texts and the like through the events, actions, texts and the like that follow them. Habermas's example is the Thirty Years War, which becomes the Thirty Years War only after it ends in 1648. Moreover its meaning depends upon the changeable interests and concerns of historians as well as upon the different contexts in terms of which they understand it. It could refer to "the political collapse of the German Empire, the postponement of capitalist development, the end of the Counter-Reformation, the theme of the Wallenstein drama, etc."[24] Because history does not end, nor do the possible contexts and historical narratives on which the fused-horizonal meaning of an event, action, or text depends. We could supply an exhaustive account of their meaning only if we could know not only all the future events, actions, and texts that would follow them and participate in their meaning but also all the concerns and interests of all future historians. Indeed, even history's last historian would be unable to provide an exhaustive account as she would be unable to narrate her last act of accounting.

Habermas denies that this inability to conceive of a complete historical account shows that any – inevitably partial – understanding of textual and historical meaning is therefore arbitrary. Instead, the inability points to what he sees as a third virtue of Gadamer's hermeneutics: the connection it establishes between hermeneutic understanding and "the articulation of an action-orienting self-understanding."[25] The classical hermeneutic circle refers to the process of understanding a text and describes that process as an activity of understanding its initial parts in terms of anticipating the meaning of the whole of the text and continually revising this anticipation of meaning on the basis of an accumulating understanding of its parts. The same holds of past historical events. On the one hand, we understand them *in media res*, as it were, from a present horizon that cannot know their end. On the other hand, we necessarily project this end, and hence the future, as the context for our understanding even as we revise this projection on the basis of ongoing events. Habermas thus declares:

> Every historian is in the role of the last historian ... What he can know historically cannot be grasped independently of the framework of his own life-praxis. In this context, what is in the

future exists only within the horizon of expectations. And these expectations form the fragments of previous tradition into a hypothetical totality of pre-understood universal history. In the light of this history every relevant event can in principle be as completely described as is possible for the practically effective self-understanding of a social lifeworld.[26]

For Habermas, then, the merit of Gadamer's philosophical hermeneutics is that it opens up congealed language games, accounts for the understanding of historical tradition in a way that connects it to its ongoing development and orients social action. Nevertheless, Habermas also thinks that philosophical hermeneutics lacks an adequate recognition of the possibility of rational deficits in a tradition's development. He suggests that Gadamer is justified in emphasizing the capacity of natural languages to extend themselves in encounters with other languages to express whatever they want to express and thereby to forge a common language and come to agreements on meaning. Habermas also suggests that Gadamer is justified in insisting on the capacity of understanding in natural languages to illuminate biases and prejudices that may have accumulated in them along with the interpretive resources they contain. What is less evident to Habermas is the capacity of understanding in natural languages to reflect on possible systematic deformations internal to them. Such deformations cannot be exposed in encounters with other languages that might reveal the biases and prejudices of one's own because the distortion is in the language of encounter itself. Habermas concedes that "within the limits of tolerance of normal everyday communication it is possible for us to determine what we do not – yet – know when we try to make sense of an incomprehensible complex of meaning." Yet, he continues, "This hermeneutic consciousness proves inadequate in the case of systematically distorted communication: incomprehensibility is here the result of a defective organization of speech itself."[27]

As evidence of such defective organization Habermas turns to the case of the pathologically disturbed expressions that Freudian psychoanalytic theory examines. Distortions in communication occur here on three levels: on the level of linguistic symbols insofar as their use deviates from the publicly accepted system of linguistic rules and can affect semantic content, syntax, and complete fields of meaning; on the level of behavior insofar as it becomes inflexible and compulsive; and on the level of the relation between language and behavior insofar as "the usual congruence between linguistic symbols, actions and accompanying expressions has disintegrated."[28] To be sure, Gadamer can argue that our capacity to detect instances of distorted communication already depends upon a background communicative consensus. Freud's detection of distorted communication relies on conventions of language use that we generally share. Yet for Habermas, the difficulty here lies with this background consensus. Evidence of distorted communication means that we cannot assume that it is itself free of systematic distortion. Indeed, Habermas claims that we could identify a legitimate consensus with a given factual agreement only "if we could be certain that each consensus arrived at in the medium of linguistic tradition had been achieved without compulsion and distortion."[29]

Whereas philosophical hermeneutics insists that our immersion in a natural language means that we have no position from which to verify its implication in or lack of internal distortions, Habermas denies that critical social sciences need operate under this constraint. Rather, as an example of such a science, psychoanalysis can look to a theoretical reference system that is geared to the analytic dialogue between doctor and patient and allows for methodological control over that dialogue. The analytic dialogue departs from ordinary communication insofar as analysts do not engage their patients as communication partners capable of expanding the analysts' horizons. Instead, analysts remove themselves from the interactions in order to become objects of transference, the point of which is to open the space for decoding symbols that have become incomprehensible to the patients. Here Habermas appeals to Alfred Lorenzer's account of psychoanalysis as form of linguistic analysis. Within the analytic dialogue, the theory specifies the typical pathological situation as one in which a child experiences and then represses an unbearable conflict. This repression is explained as the elimination of the experience from public communication and the desymbolization of the meaning of the conflict-charged object. The gap in the semantic field that the symbol once occupied is then replaced with a symptom. The analyst facilitates access to the original repressed experience by allowing the scenarios in which the symptom occurs to be played out in the transference relation that the analyst establishes by taking on the role of the conflict-charged primary object. The warrant for the truth of the theory lies in the patient's capacity to recover lost meaning. What Lorenzer calls scenic understanding proceeds, Habermas writes, "from the insight that the patient behaves in his symptomatic scenes as he does in certain transference scenes; it aims at a reconstruction of the original scene which the patient validates in an act of self-reflection."[30]

Habermas's account of psychoanalysis as a critical science coheres with Horkheimer's insistence that critical theories assist in the Enlightenment of their subject matter by reconnecting what appears as a second nature over and against them to possibilities for rational direction. In later work Habermas moves away from psychoanalysis as an example to "reconstructive sciences" that try to make theoretically explicit basic intuitive competences. Reconstructive sciences yield knowledge that is empirical rather than a priori and fallible rather than certain. Nevertheless, Habermas maintains that they can uncover invariant structures and, in particular, that a reconstructive science of communicative competence affords knowledge of the pragmatic conditions presupposed in coming to an understanding with others. Specifically, he claims "anyone acting communicatively must, in performing any speech act, raise universal validity claims and suppose that they can be vindicated."[31] Or as he also puts the point, "We understand a speech act when we know the kinds of reasons that a speaker could provide in order to convince a hearer that he is entitled in the given circumstances to claim validity for his utterance – in short, when we know what makes it acceptable."[32] In making assertions or raising normative claims, speakers take on the burden of being able to provide the reasons for their utterances that hearers can freely accept. Where at least initially they cannot, speakers and hearers may move from ordinary speech to forms of "discourse" in which they explicitly take up the reasons for and against the claim at issue and move toward an agreement based only on the force of the better argument. In considering Gadamer's analysis, Habermas therefore insists:

> A critically enlightened hermeneutic that differentiates between insight and delusion incorporates the meta-hermeneutic awareness of the conditions for the possibility of systematically distorted communication. It connects the process of understanding to the principle of rational discourse according to which truth would be guaranteed only by that kind of consensus that was achieved under the idealized conditions of unlimited communication free from domination and could be maintained over time.[33]

HONNETH'S CRITIQUE OF GADAMER

Both psychoanalysis and reconstructive sciences indicate for Habermas that what he sees as Gadamer's "accurate critique" of the self-understanding of certain social scientific approaches should not have led him to oppose hermeneutic understanding to "methodical knowledge as a whole."[34] Rather, by emphasizing the former at the expense of the latter and by neglecting the potential of critical forms of inquiry – those that Horkheimer also highlights – Gadamer skews the relation between the ongoing development of a tradition and rational reflection upon it. Honneth is equally suspicious of the way he thinks Gadamer rejects possibilities for reflection. In "On the Destructive Power of the Third: Gadamer and Heidegger's Doctrine of Intersubjectivity," Honneth focuses on Gadamer's account of experience and especially on the set of parallels Gadamer establishes between the experience of historical tradition and the experience of reciprocal recognition between an "I" and a "thou." On the one hand, this set of parallels is "a methodological turning-point of the greatest utility" for Honneth inasmuch as it allows for a normative assessment of different approaches to historical tradition. On the other hand, he finds it "astonishing" that Gadamer prioritizes an immediate form of reciprocal recognition that is free from the intervention of what Honneth calls "a third" or generalized other.[35]

As Honneth explains, in turning to experience Gadamer's argument is with Hegel. To be sure, Gadamer sees in Hegel's account of the dialectic an insight into the importance of negative experiences. Positive experiences are crucial to the natural and social sciences insofar as they serve to confirm hypotheses. At the same time, Gadamer stresses the sort of experiences that we go through or suffer. In such cases – the cases in which we can be said to "have an experience" – experiences interrupt our normal routines, thwart our expectations and expose mistakes in the assumptions we previously held. Their importance for both Gadamer and Hegel is that they thereby expand our knowledge. Insofar as we are brought up short by assumptions we held that prove unsustainable in the face of events, we learn more not only about those events but also about our previous assumptions. Hegel sees a progressive suffering of negative experiences as a reflexive process that includes the capacity for rational self-correction and ultimately leads to absolute knowledge. Gadamer draws two different conclusions. First, in repeatedly suffering negative experiences we move not to absolute knowledge but rather to insight into our continuing fallibility. Through experiences we develop a readiness for yet further experiences. Second, because we expand our knowledge through negative experiences that we endure or go through, knowledge is something that happens to us, rather than something we can control.

Were Gadamer's argument against Hegel a direct one, Honneth thinks that he would move from these conclusions about the consequences of experience to identifying our understanding of historical tradition with experience. In this case, we would find that in understanding tradition "we do not hope reflexively to attain ... a determinate cognition or insight but rather the converse: an expansion of our knowledge accomplishes itself in us, an expansion that is fundamentally open to renewed correction and thus knows no closure."[36] In experiencing tradition our knowledge expands in a way we cannot prompt or guide and, insofar as history continues, it also remains incomplete. Nevertheless, Gadamer conceives of historical tradition as a set of voices that can address us and that we can also fail to hear. Tradition thus possesses the character of a thou and our relation to it takes on the character of an intersubjective relation. Consequently, Gadamer explores three possible modes of intersubjective relation and links them to three possible ways of understanding historical tradition. In each case he tries to show that two ways are deficient while only one allows for a genuine encounter.

The first mode of relating to a thou that Gadamer discusses he sees as an objectivizing one. We treat others as objects that are of interest to us only as impediments or aids to our own ends. In so doing, as Honneth interprets Gadamer's point, we make a cognitive and moral error. The I limits its understanding of the other to those assets that serve the I's purposes and it thereby treats the other only as a means rather than as an end in itself. Equally importantly for Gadamer according to Honneth, "the I ... imagines itself in the role of a completely independent subject, one that is wholly unaffected by the preceding actions of others and thus one that is without any intersubjective past."[37] On this mistaken assumption, the I acknowledges no dependence on others or involvement with them. The corresponding mode of historical consciousness reflects a positivistic self-understanding. Gadamer emphasizes the cognitive and normative error it sustains in distancing itself from the tradition and taking itself to be uninvolved with it. An objectivizing approach to historical tradition treats it as an external object and devotes itself to tracking its causal regularities. The effect of such an approach is to deprive the thou and the tradition of what Honneth terms its "surprise-value." As he writes, "Bound fast by a few fixed properties, the other ... can no longer contribute to the unsettling or refutation of presuppositions about it."[38] The I or the interpreter is left with the complacency of its own presuppositions.

A second mode of relating to the thou Gadamer characterizes as authoritarian solicitude where again the error is both cognitive and moral. The I makes the cognitive error of taking the other to be the same as oneself and assuming that it therefore knows the other as well or better than the other understands itself. Here the I simply substitutes itself for the thou and in so doing errs morally in abstracting out of a reciprocal relationship. With an empathetic response that thinks it already knows what the other is feeling, the I relates, in fact, only to itself and fails to respond to the other at all. The corresponding form of understanding tradition signals the scientistic hermeneutics or linguistic analysis that Habermas associates with Wittgenstein and Honneth with Wilhelm Dilthey. In a cognitive error, a scientistic hermeneutics assumes that it possesses an understanding of the tradition uncurtailed by its own historical starting point and that it can therefore achieve an internal understanding of any historical situation as if it were its own. The normative failure here, as in the objectivizing attitude, is one of refusing to open oneself to the "surprise value" of the tradition. What concerns Gadamer about both authoritarian solicitude and scientistic hermeneutics, Honneth maintains, is "the tendency to 'reflect-oneself-out'" of a genuine interaction.[39] The I or interpreter distances itself from the immediacy of the other or historical tradition and relates only to itself.

Only on a third and highest level are these errors corrected according to Honneth's account of Gadamer. On this level, the relation between I and thou is one of "radical openness" in which both I and other allow themselves a genuine connection to one another and can therefore engage in the kind of reciprocal encounter in which each relates immediately to the other rather than reflecting out of the relationship. On the corresponding level of our relation to tradition, the same immediacy applies. Recognizing our prior connection to the tradition, we open ourselves up to it and the claims it makes. Because of the parallel to the relationship to the thou, the highest mode of relation to tradition thus will involve not the reflexive knowledge to which Hegel points but rather an immediate engagement with it. This engagement allows for the other's or tradition's "surprise value" and, hence, for the experiences that this "surprise value" can provoke. As Honneth writes:

> In this way, the drawing of correspondences that Gadamer had carried out on all three levels ends exactly at the point at which the experience-character of all historical understanding becomes transparent: one can speak of an appropriate attitude toward historical tradition only if the tradition is conceived like an interaction partner, over against which it is necessary to open oneself, trustingly, in understanding. Any intrusion by reflection would therefore be only disruptive, since it would remove the ground from the prior bond (between subject and history), on the presupposition of which the necessary trust can first be advanced. Though the philosophy of reflexion would have it otherwise, the understanding of history is thus an accomplishment that happens, not a reflexive act of appropriation.[40]

In Honneth's view, this conclusion shares an assumption with Heidegger that any move away from an immediate openness to the other is a move toward *das Man*. It reflects out of a direct relation to a particular or concrete other in favor of a relation to a more generalized other who could be anyone. Yet Honneth argues that the insistence on the former as the sole authentic relation to the other is plausible only with regard to those to whom we are particularly close and even in those cases it has its limits. For even within close relationships we can always judge our actions and interactions according to socially generalized norms and standards of behavior that can provide a corrective to merely receptive openness. Such judgments Honneth sees as the power of the third, as judgments, in other words, from the perspective of an impartial party or generalized other. If this perspective is available even within close personal relationships its appropriateness is even clearer in more distant and anonymous ones. Here we cannot require a trusting openness to others; rather we rely on an attitude more like mutual respect. The conclusion for our relation to historical tradition follows for Honneth: it too must be subject to two forms of understanding. We might identify one of these with the openness to experience corresponding to relations to those to whom we are closest. The other, however, would incorporate the generalized perspective of the impartial third. It would be relation precisely "reflected out" of an immediate engagement and able to take a more distanced stance. Honneth writes, "History is appropriately made present only when the two standpoints of the 'concrete' and the 'generalized' other continually and reciprocally correct one another."[41]

CONCLUSION

The starting point for critical theory as Horkheimer establishes it is the capacity for critical reflection to disclose deficits in social reason and to assist in a process of Enlightenment that can overcome them. Following Horkheimer, both Habermas and Honneth see Gadamer's attitude toward reflection as a problem. Challenging what he sees as the precedence Gadamer gives to the authority of the tradition, Habermas claims that "reflection does not wear itself out on the facticity of traditional norms without leaving a trace. It is condemned to operate after the fact; but, operating in retrospect, it unleashes retroactive power."[42] Challenging what he sees as the misplaced precedence Gadamer gives to immediate experience, Honneth emphasizes the importance of the capacity to moderate our trusting openness to our traditions and to reflect on them in light of generalized norms.

To be sure, Gadamer is not without a response to his critics. I want to conclude this chapter by looking at his response to Habermas's analysis, which also suggests the reply he might give to Honneth.

A first objection Gadamer raises is to Habermas's depiction of his hermeneutics as a resource for considering the "positivistic ossification of sociological logic."[43] In Gadamer's view, by depicting philosophical hermeneutics in this way, Habermas restricts its scope to the methodological concerns of the social sciences and neglects what Gadamer takes to be more properly at its center: namely, experiences such as those we have of art. Characteristic of these experiences, he maintains, is that we are moved, stirred, shocked, or otherwise engaged in ways that can be neither stimulated nor enhanced by methods or procedures. The same holds of our experiences of tradition and other people for Gadamer. These have the power to affect us profoundly, to undermine our assumptions and presumptions and to transform what we thought we knew. Precisely these possibilities are lost when we insist, as Habermas does, according to Gadamer, on "raising understanding up out of a prescientific exercise to the rank of a self-reflecting activity."[44] They would also be lost for Gadamer were we to try to reflect out of an immediate experience of art, tradition or the other and take the generalized perspective of the impartial third, as Honneth recommends. In our self-involved concern with our own knowledge we split ourselves off from an engagement with the very world we seek to understand. For Gadamer, the result of doing so can only be what he calls an "alienated understanding."[45]

A second objection Gadamer raises against Habermas's analysis focuses on the premise he takes from Horkheimer: the potential for a rational society as anticipated in human work or the pragmatic structure of communication oriented to understanding. Here, as Gadamer sees it, the idea is that individuals and societies can become fully transparent to themselves, that critical sciences can assist in reconnecting unconscious motives and compulsions to their sources and opening ideological justifications to the light of day. On the one hand, Gadamer denies that such sources and ideologies are beyond the grasp of hermeneutic inquiry. Instead, they represent prejudices and relations of power that are taken up and illuminated in our ongoing experience. Indeed, he argues that we could regard psychological compulsion and ideology as outside of the scope of hermeneutic understanding only if they were outside of language altogether, an eventuality Habermas's own account seems to deny.

On the other hand, Gadamer rejects the possibility of full transparency. Here he distinguishes between hermeneutic or "effective reflection" and the form of reflection that Habermas and Honneth emphasize but that, because it distances itself from direct experience, Gadamer can see only as "making everything an object and creating the conditions for science in the modern sense."[46] He sees hermeneutic reflection as differing in two ways. First, it underlines our inability to limit in advance what we can come to understand. To the extent that we are open to experience our prejudices and pre-understandings are always in play and what we expected or thought we knew can always be shattered by the "surprise value" of what we openly encounter. Second, "effective reflection" acknowledges that because we are always already immersed in language, we cannot lay all its contents out in front of us to be exhaustively explored at once. Rather, Gadamer writes, "reflection on a given pre-understanding brings before me something that otherwise happens behind my back. Something – but not everything."[47] We can come to grasp the unsustainable character of some of our prejudices only to the extent that we remain open to experience and only on the basis of prejudices that, at least for the time being, we do not question. Moreover, when we do question the latter it is on the basis of the authority of still others that we are not currently putting in question.

Hence, while Habermas emphasizes reason over authority and Honneth reflection over experience, Gadamer maintains that these dichotomies are not as stark as they perhaps suppose. We can always question the authority of aspects of our tradition, but we do so on the basis of other aspects – inherited ideals, principles, and the like – that we do not question. Similarly, we can reflect on our experiences but only if we do not begin by distancing ourselves from them. Nevertheless, if these dichotomies are less stark than Habermas and Honneth suppose, the distance between Gadamer and his Frankfurt School critics remains. In *Truth and Method*, he follows his analysis of negative experience with an account of dialogue that emphasizes the capacity of participants to consider the challenges to their understanding of the subject matter at issue that their interlocutors present and together with them to rethink what they thought they grasped. Indeed, Gadamer insists upon the "discipline of questioning and inquiring," and calls it "a discipline that guarantees truth."[48] In this regard he anticipates the account of communicative reason that Habermas develops. Nevertheless, for Gadamer questioning remains tied to the immediate experience that Honneth seeks to moderate. Questions, Gadamer insists, are not the product of critical reason but rather arise out of experiences, including experiences of others, that bring us up short. To this extent, what he sees as genuine dialogue in the openness of participants to one another, Honneth finds normatively undirected and Habermas thinks fails to find a way "to differentiate between insight and delusion."

NOTES

1 See Thomas McCarthy, "The Idea of a Critical Theory and its Relation to Philosophy," in *On Max Horkheimer: New Perspectives*, ed. Seyla Benhabib, Wolfgang Bonß, and John McCole (Cambridge, MA: MIT Press, 1993), 127–52.

2 Habermas's and Honneth's concerns about Gadamer's hermeneutics are complemented by concerns Karl-Otto Apel, loosely associated with the Frankfurt School, also raised. As does Habermas, Apel looks to psychoanalytic theory to question Gadamer's reliance on pre-understandings arising from historical tradition. As is Honneth, Apel is skeptical of Gadamer's satisfaction with a view of understanding as "the happening of truth." See Karl-Otto Apel, *From a Transcendental-Semiotic Point of View*, ed. Marianna Papastephanou (Manchester: Manchester University Press, 1998), 183–215.

3 Max Horkheimer, "The Social Function of Philosophy," in Horkheimer, *Critical Theory* (New York: Herder and Herder, 1972), 253–72.
4 Horkheimer, "The Social Function of Philosophy," 256.
5 Horkheimer, "The Social Function of Philosophy," 262.
6 Horkheimer, "The Social Function of Philosophy," 257.
7 Max Horkheimer, "Traditional and Critical Theory," in Horkheimer, *Critical Theory*, 200.
8 Horkheimer, "Traditional and Critical Theory," 200
9 Horkheimer, "Traditional and Critical Theory," 213.
10 Horkheimer, "Traditional and Critical Theory," 199.
11 Horkheimer, "The Social Function of Philosophy," 269.
12 Max Horkheimer, "The State of Contemporary Social Philosophy and the Tasks of an Institute for Social Research," in *Critical Theory and Society: A Reader*, ed. Stephen Eric Bronner and Douglas MacKay Kellner (New York: Routledge, 1989), 31.
13 Horkheimer, "Contemporary Social Philosophy," 33.
14 Horkheimer, "Traditional and Critical Theory," 214.
15 Horkheimer, "Traditional and Critical Theory," 215.
16 Max Horkheimer and Theodore W. Adorno, *Dialectic of Enlightenment*, ed. Gunzeln Schmid Noerr, trans. Edmund Jephcott (Stanford: Stanford University Press, 2002), xiv.
17 Jürgen Habermas, "Remarks on the Development of Horkheimer's Work," in *On Max Horkheimer*, 55.
18 Habermas, "Development of Horkheimer's Work," 61.
19 Jürgen Habermas, *On the Logic of the Social Sciences*, trans. Shierry Weber Nicholsen and Jerry A. Stark (Cambridge, MA: MIT Press, 1988), 117.
20 Habermas, *Logic of the Social Sciences*, 136.
21 Jürgen Habermas, "The Hermeneutic Claim to Universality," in *Contemporary Hermeneutics: Hermeneutics as Method, Philosophy and Critique*, ed. Josef Bleicher (London: Routledge and Kegan Paul, 1980), 182.
22 Habermas, "The Hermeneutic Claim to Universality," 183.
23 Habermas, *Logic of the Social Sciences*, 146–7.
24 Habermas, *Logic of the Social Sciences*, 156.
25 Habermas, *On the Logic of the Social Sciences*, 162.
26 Habermas, *On the Logic of the Social Sciences*, 160.
27 Habermas, "The Hermeneutic Claim to Universality," 191.

28 Habermas, "The Hermeneutic Claim to Universality," 192.
29 Habermas, "The Hermeneutic Claim to Universality," 205.
30 Habermas, "The Hermeneutic Claim to Universality," 193.
31 Jürgen Habermas, "What is Universal Pragmatics," in *On the Pragmatics of Communication*, ed. Maeve Cooke (Cambridge, MA: MIT Press, 1998), 28.
32 Jürgen Habermas, "Actions, Speech Acts, Linguistically Mediated Interactions and the Lifeworld," in *On the Pragmatics of Communication*, 232.
33 Habermas, "The Hermeneutic Claim to Universality," 205.
34 Habermas, *On the Logic of the Social Sciences*, 167.
35 Axel Honneth, "On the Destructive Power of the Third: Gadamer and Heidegger's Doctrine of Intersubjectivity," *Philosophy and Social Criticism* 29 (2003): 6. See also David M. Rasmussen, "Hermeneutics and Public Deliberation," *Philosophy and Social Criticism* 28 (2002): 506–7.
36 Honneth, "On the Destructive Power of the Third," 9.
37 Honneth, "On the Destructive Power of the Third," 10.
38 Honneth, "On the Destructive Power of the Third," 10.
39 Honneth, "On the Destructive Power of the Third," 11.
40 Honneth, "On the Destructive Power of the Third," 12–13.
41 Honneth, "On the Destructive Power of the Third," 20.
42 Habermas, *On the Logic of the Social Sciences*, 170.
43 Hans-Georg Gadamer, "On the Scope and Function of Hermeneutical Reflection," in Gadamer, *Philosophical Hermeneutics*, ed. and trans. David E. Linge (Berkeley: University of California Press, 1977), 26.
44 Gadamer, "Scope and Function," 27.
45 Gadamer, "Scope and Function," 27.
46 Gadamer, "Scope and Function," 27.
47 Gadamer, "Scope and Function," 38.
48 Hans-Georg Gadamer, *Truth and Method*, 2nd revised edn., trans. Joel Weinsheimer and Donald G. Marshall (New York: Continuum, 1989), 491. See also Kristin Gjesdal, "Between Enlightenment and Romanticism: Some Problems and Challenges in Gadamer's Hermeneutics," *Journal of the History of Philosophy* 46 (2008) and Richard J. Bernstein, "What is the Difference That Makes a Difference? Gadamer, Habermas, and Rorty," in *Hermeneutics and Modern Philosophy*, ed. Brice R. Wachterhauser (Albany: SUNY Press, 1986), 343–76.

11 Hermeneutics
Francophone Approaches
Michael N. Forster

Germany's enormous contributions to hermeneutics – here understood as the theory and methodology of interpretation, of coming to understand – are well known and are covered extensively in the secondary literature. The same cannot be said of French contributions. However, France has in fact been a rich source of hermeneutics – rarely under that name, to be sure, but nonetheless in substance. This chapter will focus on the two centuries of which this is most true: the eighteenth and the twentieth.

FRENCH CONTRIBUTIONS IN THE EIGHTEENTH CENTURY

A casual glance at the long eighteenth century might seem to show that, in sharp contrast to the great flowering of hermeneutics that took place then in Germany with thinkers such as Ernesti, Herder, Schleiermacher, and Boeckh, France contributed little to the discipline. *In a way* that is true: the sorts of ambitious systematic approaches to hermeneutics that we encounter in Germany are absent there. Moreover, this difference may seem to be explicable in terms of several contrasts between the two countries: German Protestantism versus French Catholicism, German anti-dualism concerning the relation between thought (or concept) and language versus French dualism, and German anti-universalism concerning human mental life versus French universalism. But the casual impression in question is misleading. For the very roots of German hermeneutics turn out to have been largely French.

As I have shown in detail elsewhere,[1] German hermeneutics rested on two revolutions against common assumptions of the Enlightenment: First, it rested on a new philosophy of language which argued, in opposition to the Enlightenment's usual assumption of a sharp dualism between thought or concept and language such that thought and concept could in principle occur without language, the latter only serving as an aid to remembering and a means of communicating the former, that (1) thought is essentially dependent on and bounded by (some of the German thinkers involved even went as far as to say: identical with) language, and (2) concepts or meanings consist, not in the sorts of items, in principle independent of language, with which much of the philosophical tradition has equated them – such as things referred to (Augustine), Platonic forms, or the subjective "ideas" championed by Port Royal, Locke, Hume, and Condillac – but in *word-usages*.

Second, it rested on a rejection of the sort of universalism concerning beliefs, concepts, values, sensations, and so on – the assumption that these have been more or less the same at all times and places – that the Enlightenment had tended to adopt in favor of anti-universalism: the view that on the contrary these things vary profoundly from historical period to historical period, culture to culture, and even individual to individual. This second move showed that the task of interpretation was a vastly more difficult one than Enlightenment thinkers had commonly assumed it to be, thereby leading German hermeneutical theorists to attempt to find solutions to the challenges involved, attempts which centrally appealed to the new philosophy of language just mentioned.

Now the *first* of these moves was mainly a German achievement: Thesis (1) was introduced by Leibniz, then taken over by Wolff and the Wolffians, before being adopted and radicalized by Herder, Hamann, Schleiermacher and others. (It is, indeed, also to be found in Condillac in a certain form, but this hardly constitutes an exception to the rule since Condillac clearly borrowed it from Wolff.) And thesis (2) was first introduced by Spinoza, then taken over from him by the German theorists of biblical interpretation Wettstein and Ernesti, and then finally borrowed from them and radicalized by Herder and Hamann.[2] But the *second* move, anti-universalism, is a different matter entirely: it was largely a French achievement and was exported from France to Germany.[3]

Herder obscured this debt to the French in his *This Too a Philosophy of History for the Formation of Humanity* (1774) – arguably the first, most radical, and best known statement of the anti-universalist position in the German tradition – by accusing Montesquieu, Voltaire, and Hume of having championed, or at least tended toward, a false universalism. But the real founders of anti-universalism had in fact been French: especially Montaigne in his *Essais* (1580), followed by his relative La Mothe le Vayer in such works as his *Petit traité sceptique sur cette commune façon de parler: "N'avoir pas le Sens commun"* (1646). Moreover, in their youth, Montesquieu and Voltaire had actually continued and extended this anti-universalist position – for example, Montesquieu in his *Lettres persanes* (1721) and Voltaire in his *Essai sur la poésie épique* (1728), both of which works had emphasized deep mental differences between different cultures and periods (the former especially moral differences, the latter mainly differences in literary genres). And Condillac in his *Essai sur l'origine des connaissances humaines* (1746) had then extended this project to the level of words and concepts, arguing (in the footsteps of Locke) that (complex) concepts vary significantly between different peoples and even between different individuals.[4]

A tendency to universalism really only emerged in the *later* works of Montesquieu and Voltaire, such as Montesquieu's *De l'esprit des lois* (1748) (with its thesis that there are just three or four possible types of constitution and moral outlook) and Voltaire's *Essai sur les mœurs et l'esprit des nations* (1756) and *La philosophie de l'histoire* (1765) (to which Herder was mainly responding in *This Too a Philosophy of History*) with their implications of universalism in the moral and other domains. The Scotsman Hume had then joined this late French universalist project in works such as *An Enquiry concerning the Principles of Morals* (1751) and *Of the Standard of Taste* (1757).

Nor is this indebtedness of German hermeneutics to the French tradition for its anti-universalism merely generic in nature; it also takes more specific forms. Let me briefly give two examples of this.

Ernesti essentially founded the hermeneutical tradition in Germany with his great work on biblical hermeneutics *Institutio interpretis Novi Testamenti* (1761). In this work he distinguished between two sorts of deep variation or originality that are to be found in words/concepts: (1) that which derives from differences in culture or period, and (2) that which derives from extraordinary individuals.[5] Under Ernesti's influence, the recognition of these two distinguishable sources of variation in words/concepts then became fundamental to the whole German hermeneutical tradition; for example, it recurs in Herder, Friedrich Schlegel, Schleiermacher, and Boeckh. But it was actually *Condillac* who, partly under the influence of Locke, had first argued that different nations develop different forms of language and (complex) ideas and that different individuals do so too, namely in a chapter of his *Essai sur l'origine des connaissances humaines* (1746) titled "Le génie des langues":

> One only needs to study a man for a while to learn his language; I say *his language*, because each has his own [...] The character of peoples shows itself even more clearly than that of individuals [...] If the genius of languages begins to form itself in accordance with that of peoples, it only manages to develop through the help of great writers [...] Nations can only have superior geniuses after their languages have made considerable progress [...] If great talents owe their development to the palpable progress that the language made before them, language in its turn owes to these talents new steps of progress.[6]

And it is virtually certain that Ernesti took this thesis over from Locke and Condillac, because he cites Locke explicitly in connection with national originality,[7] and concerning individual originality he writes entirely in Condillac's manner of a "genius of each author [*scriptoris cuiusque ingenium*]."[8]

The second more specific debt in question concerns the role of (literary) genres in interpretation. Herder, in a series of writings that centrally included the *Critical Forests* (1769) and *Shakespeare* (1773), came to recognize, not only that understanding a work (of literature) always requires identifying its genre correctly (i.e., the set of purposes and rules that constitutes its genre), but also that this task is often much more difficult than it has usually been assumed to be because genres that share the same name (e.g., "epic poetry" or "tragedy") and a few other relatively superficial characteristics in common, and which consequently appear at first sight to be identical, are often in fact significantly different from each other in their constitutive purposes and rules between one historical period and another, one culture and another, one individual author and another, and even one work of an author and another, so that the interpreter of a work, if he is to interpret it correctly, often needs to (1) get to know a genre with which he is not yet familiar and (2) resist strong temptations to assimilate it falsely to another genre or genres with which he is more familiar – tasks that, according to Herder, can only be accomplished by means of scrupulous empirical research (especially on the work itself, but also on its social context and the developmental history of genres that lies behind it). After Herder, other theorists in the German hermeneutical tradition, especially the Schlegel brothers and Boeckh, inherited this approach to genre, making it central to their own hermeneutics as well. But it was actually *Voltaire* who had originally developed this approach to genre, namely in his *Essai sur la poésie épique* (1728), where he had illustrated it mainly with the example of epic poetry (especially that of Homer, Trissino, Camoëns, Tasso, de Ercilla, Milton, and himself in his *Henriade*) but also with the example of tragedy (especially that of Sophocles, Corneille, Racine, Shakespeare, and Addison).[9] Herder then essentially took over this approach from Voltaire in his *Critical*

Forests and *Shakespeare,* where he likewise focused on epic poetry and tragedy as his examples.

FRENCH CONTRIBUTIONS IN THE TWENTIETH CENTURY

The long nineteenth century was less eventful for hermeneutics in France. But the twentieth century saw the development of a lively interest in the subject (albeit rarely under that name). Some of the developments that occurred in the twentieth century were derivative and others were misguided, but a considerable residue of original and defensible thought on the subject remains. So I would like here to survey some of the main developments that took place and to sift them according to those categories. (For the most part I will proceed, not chronologically, but in a way that groups similar or related approaches together.)

Jean-Paul Sartre in *Being and Nothingness* (1943) and in his massive multi-volume biography of Flaubert, *The Family Idiot* (1971), develops and applies an approach to language and interpretation that basically goes as follows: Language is fundamental to thought, and while essentially a social institution, also gets appropriated and reformed in original ways by individuals.[10] Accordingly, the interpretation of an original author must aim to achieve not only a thorough knowledge of his historical context, background culture, and background language, but also a thorough insight into the individual character of his own use of language and mode of thought.[11]

This position is extremely sensible. But it is not original. For it is very similar to the hermeneutical approach that Schleiermacher had already developed in the nineteenth century,[12] and that was then continued and disseminated by his pupil Boeckh, which likewise emphasized the importance of complementing a thorough attention to historical context, background culture, and background language with a close consideration of the author's individual use of language and mode of thought. Moreover, in an even more striking anticipation of Sartre's project, nineteenth-century Germans who were influenced by this hermeneutical approach, such as Haym, Dilthey, and Unger, had already written detailed biographies of writers (especially philosophers) in which they had implemented it. Sartre presumably borrowed his approach from this German tradition.[13]

A much more original aspect of Sartre's position is a central role that he accords to interpretation, or its subject matter meaning, in the early existentialism that he develops in *Being and Nothingness*. For this early existentialism centrally includes what one might call a hermeneutical theory of radical freedom. Fichte had argued in his subjective idealism that human beings enjoy a very radical sort of freedom because they *create the world*.[14] In *Being and Nothingness* Sartre rightly rejects this sort of position as extravagant and untenable, but he also substitutes for it a more plausible variant that preserves much of its radicalism: although we do not create the world itself, we do create the *meanings or interpretations* through which we become acquainted with it (following the tradition of Herder, Hegel, and Heidegger, Sartre believes that *all* of our experience is meaning-laden), and since we always have a free choice as to which these meanings or interpretations are to be, we are at least completely responsible for the world *as we know it*.

This is a very interesting position, and one for which Sartre argues with subtlety. Whether it is tenable in the end is another matter, though. For example, one might worry that it exaggerates the degree of control that we enjoy over our own interpretations of the world (this indeed seems to have been one of Sartre's own reasons for eventually becoming disillusioned with it). And one might also be concerned that whatever freedom we *do* have to choose interpretations often merely amounts to a freedom to choose *false* ones.

Another more original aspect of Sartre's position in the area of hermeneutics is one that he added to the basic hermeneutical approach described above during his Marxist period, beginning with *Search for a Method* (1957).[15] In this work he argues that if Marxism is to provide an adequate explanation of ideology, it cannot rest content with appealing to socio-economic classes and their interests but must bridge the gap to the individuals who compose these classes, and that in order to do so it needs to call on such auxiliary disciplines as a psychoanalysis of individuals' unconscious. This theoretical step was not completely new; Engels had already proposed integrating the unconscious into a Marxist explanation of ideology in his book *Ludwig Feuerbach* (1886). But it is at least *more* original than Sartre's fundamental Schleiermacherian approach to hermeneutics, and it opens up some intriguing prospects.

Another significant contributor to hermeneutics in France is Paul Ricoeur (who, unlike most of the other thinkers discussed in this chapter, not only contributes to hermeneutics but also uses the *name* freely). Ricoeur presents his own hermeneutics most fully in *The Conflict of Interpretations* (1969).[16] It is very eclectic (despite his own frequent protests to the contrary), combining approaches from Schleiermacher, Dilthey, Heidegger, Gadamer, Hegel's *Phenomenology of Spirit*, Freud, structuralist linguistics, and religion.

As he explains his own approach to hermeneutics concisely in "The Task of Hermeneutics" (1973),[17] it seeks to advance beyond what he considers to be the unduly subjective-epistemological approaches of Schleiermacher and Dilthey and the more adequate objective-ontological approaches of Heidegger and Gadamer to a position that allows for more critical "distanciation" from the tradition than Gadamer had accepted, focuses on texts rather than on other forms of expression, and has a strong religious tendency.[18]

While giving up Gadamer's reverence for tradition is no doubt a good idea, overall this program is not very philosophically attractive. It takes over too much from predecessors in an uncritical way, the arguments that motivate its transitions between their positions are not compelling ones, its focus on texts to the exclusion of such things as discourse and art is an impoverishment, and its insertion of religion into hermeneutics represents a marked step of regress in comparison with earlier hermeneutical theorists such as Herder and Schleiermacher (who, although, like Ricoeur, both Protestant believers, had the good sense to keep religious assumptions out of interpretation).[19]

Ricoeur does also incorporate a number of more attractive principles into his hermeneutics, though. These include the following: (1) He emphasizes that it is an important function of interpretation to overcome distance between the cultural epoch to which a text belongs and the interpreter himself.[20] (2) He insists that interpretation confronts not only pre-given linguistic-conceptual structures but also their inflection by individual subjects.[21] (3) He argues that interpretation must deal not only with sub-sentential and sentential meaning but also with the linguistic structures that enable it.[22] And (4) he argues that one of the main functions of interpretation is not only to achieve an understanding of other people but also, thereby, a better *self*-understanding.[23]

These principles are all very sensible. However, they are not original. For example, principles (1) and (2) were already central to the hermeneutics of Herder and Schleiermacher; principle (3) was already prominent in the hermeneutics of Schleiermacher and Friedrich Schlegel; and principle (4) was already salient in the hermeneutics of Herder and Hegel.

Ricoeur's most important contribution to hermeneutics arguably instead lies in a certain move that he makes in *Freud and Philosophy* (1965)[24] and then continues in *The Conflict of Interpretations* (1969): he develops the concept of a "hermeneutics of suspicion" to connote three radical strands of thought from the nineteenth century, namely Marx's theory of ideology, Nietzsche's method of genealogy, and Freud's theory of the unconscious,[25] thereby making clear not only that these approaches bear a significant generic resemblance to each other, but also that they can all be seen as attempts to deepen hermeneutics in a certain way.

As Ricoeur conceives the "hermeneutics of suspicion,"[26] its defining feature lies roughly in a thesis that the *surface* meanings and thoughts that a person expresses (and perhaps certain aspects of his behavior which at first sight seem to be meaningless as well, e.g., Freud's parapraxes) often serve as representative-but-also-masking proxies for *deeper* meanings and thoughts which are in some degree hidden (even from the person himself), which are quite different from and indeed often quite contrary to the surface meanings and thoughts involved, and which the person has some sort of motive for concealing in this way (both from others and from himself).

Three paradigmatic examples of such a position are Marx's theory that ideologies such as Christianity are rooted in class interests; Nietzsche's theory that Christian morality, with its overt emphasis on such ideals as "love" and "turning the other cheek," is in fact motivated by hatred and resentment (*Ressentiment*); and Freud's theory that a broad range of both apparently meaningful and apparently meaningless behaviors express unconscious motives and meanings.

What warrants classifying such theories as forms of *hermeneutics* is the fact that in each case they offer not only deeper *explanations* of the surface meanings and other phenomena involved but deeper explanations in terms of underlying *meanings*.

In my view, these theories do in fact constitute a major development in the field of hermeneutics, indeed an enormous one.[27] Ricoeur has therefore performed a valuable service in coining the concept of a "hermeneutics of suspicion" and thereby drawing attention to the similarity between these theories and their potential for radicalizing hermeneutics.

Ricoeur's main achievement in this area was, I would suggest, just that. In keeping with his general eclecticism, he also tries to incorporate a version of the hermeneutics of suspicion – in particular, a version of Freud's theory – in his own hermeneutics.[28] But whether this further move achieves much for hermeneutics may reasonably be doubted.

Another French thinker who is significant for hermeneutics is Jacques Derrida, especially in a series of writings that he began publishing in 1967.[29] Derrida encapsulates his theory of meaning and interpretation in the concepts of an open-ended "iterability" – a word that he uses in the double sense of *other* and *again*[30] – and "différance" – a word that he uses in the double sense of *differing* and *deferring*.³¹ In its former, synchronic aspect, this is largely just a way of repeating Saussure's sound and important point that meaning only arises through a system of linguistic oppositions.³² In its latter, diachronic aspect, it is largely just a way of repeating Gadamer's conception that meaning is not something original and discrete but instead something that only arises through an open-ended process of (re)interpretation (Derrida's writings on this whole subject appeared just a few years after the publication of Gadamer's *Truth and Method* in 1960).³³

However, as I have argued in other works,³⁴ Gadamer's conception is untenable: counterintuitive, ungrounded, and indeed implicitly incoherent. Briefly, the main problems with it are as follows: First, he vacillates between three mutually inconsistent versions of his main claim: (a) there is no such thing as an original meaning, (b) there is but we cannot know it, and (c) there is but it is of no possible interest to us. Second, his core argument for the most important of these versions, version (a), is that when an author writes or says something, this gives rise to an interpretation that means something a bit different from it, then another that means something a bit different again, and so on ad indefinitum, so that there can be no original meaning but only an open-ended sequence of meanings-relative-to-an-interpretation. However, this argument is not only a complete non sequitur, but also implicitly incoherent, since it presupposes in its premises just the sorts of original meanings that it then goes on to deny in its conclusion. Making matters even worse in a way, Derrida provides even less of an argument in support of the conception in question than Gadamer had done. In short, except for its sound Saussurean component, Derrida's theory is a house built on sand.

Derrida also has a number of more promising ideas about interpretation, though. One of these is a thesis that texts, especially philosophical ones, typically contain hidden contradictions, which interpretation should reveal. (Derrida famously calls this revelation "deconstruction," and practices it on many philosophers from the tradition, including Rousseau and Hegel for instance.³⁵) This thesis is true of many texts, including philosophical ones, and is very important. It is not a new thesis; for example, Friedrich Schlegel had already articulated it in the late eighteenth and early nineteenth centuries, and had indeed already applied it to philosophers as Derrida does. But Derrida's commitment to it is at least far superior to dubious contrary ideas about the need to exercise "charity" in interpretation, and in particular to avoid imputing logical inconsistencies to texts, that are currently widespread among Anglophone philosophers and historians of philosophy.³⁶ (Anglophone historians of ideas, such as Lovejoy and Skinner, have done much better here, though.)

Derrida is also significant for his advocacy of "decentering" in interpretation. He means different things by this in different contexts, some of them defensible but others not. Sometimes he just means acknowledging the (alleged) state of affairs that there is never an original, discrete meaning to interpret due to the sort of situation that Saussure and Gadamer had described.³⁷ But this is in part problematic for the reasons already mentioned above. However, at other times he instead means interpreting texts with a focus on aspects of them that they themselves present as having only marginal importance (for example, aspects that carry an implicit political or social ideology).³⁸ Such interpretations can indeed sometimes be legitimate, illuminating, and important.

Another French thinker who has made significant contributions to hermeneutics (though he only uses the name sparingly) is Roland Barthes, whose intellectual background lay in structuralist linguistics.

One of Barthes' central ideas in this area is "the death of the author," an idea that he first developed under the influence of structuralist linguistics in an essay bearing the same title that was first published in English in 1967.³⁹ (Versions of the same idea were also championed at around the same time by other prominent French thinkers similarly influenced by structuralist linguistics, including Derrida and Foucault.⁴⁰) Barthes's idea essentially holds that it is a mistake ever to impute what is expressed in a text to an individual author or his intentions; instead, it is always the result of a confluence of grammatical forms, terms, formulas, tropes, and so on that derive from the common language.[41]

This idea amounts to a huge exaggeration and distortion. For much of what is expressed by texts *is* imputable to individual authors and their intentions (think, for example, of the many linguistic, conceptual, and thought-innovations that were introduced by Plato or Shakespeare). But it is at least useful as a counterweight to equally one-sided author-centered positions which ignore the large role played in texts by inherited linguistic conventions. Avoiding both the Scylla and the Charybdis here – or, in other words, recognizing that texts involve neither just "individuality" nor just "universality," but a *synthesis* of the two – was in fact already one of the most driving and praiseworthy ambitions behind Schleiermacher's hermeneutics.[42]

Much more fruitful for hermeneutics are two of Barthes's other innovations: his introduction of a *structuralist reading of texts* and his development of a broader *semiology*. In both of these domains he not only makes important theoretical contributions but also demonstrates their fruitfulness by developing impressively illuminating interpretations that apply them.

Let us begin with his *structuralist reading of texts*. His theory and practice in this area are well exemplified by two works from 1970: *S/Z* (which takes as its example Balzac's novella *Sarrasine*) and *L'analyse structurale du récit* (which focuses on passages from the *Acts of the Apostles*).[43] While Barthes vacillates in these texts between a Derridean rejection of the notion of a text's original meaning(s) and a more traditional commitment to it (at least in the case of "classical" texts), he seems in the end to prefer the latter position, and to regard structuralist interpretation, not as a substitute, but as a sort of preparation, for more traditional forms of interpretation.[44] This is certainly his best position.[45]

So understood, the basic idea behind such structuralist readings is to focus on deep formal features of texts that enable or support their semantic content. These deep formal features include, for instance, recurrent large-scale oppositions in a text between such things as death versus life, masculine versus feminine, and active versus passive (as in the novella *Sarrasine*); patterns of appearance and disappearance of characters in a narrative (as in the *Acts of the Apostles*); certain patterns of use of proper names for individuals, places, and so on (e.g., the way in which in the classic novel a proper name functions to embody a person, turning him or her into something more than a mere collection of described characteristics and activities); and the communication of ideas through formal structures (e.g., the way in which in the novella *Sarrasine* the male character's name "Sarrasine," by sounding feminine and having its second *s* sound like the *z* in the name of the effeminate castratus Zambinella, hints at Sarrasine's own effeminate and "castrated" character; the enfolding of *Ike* in *like* in the American presidential campaign slogan "I like Ike"; or the reflection in the *Acts of the Apostles* of its central theme of the dissemination of the word of God in a constant use of recursive forms of indirect discourse).

This approach to interpretation actually bears only a rather tenuous resemblance to the structuralist linguistics that inspired it (e.g., while its emphasis on oppositions does constitute a point of similarity, the other features just mentioned do not). Nor is it entirely unprecedented in German hermeneutics (for example, Friedrich Schlegel already noted that the sharply contrasting contents of the philosophies of Spinoza and Fichte – Spinoza's static single substance versus Fichte's active self – are inscribed in the very forms of their philosophical texts). Nonetheless, drawing attention to the importance of identifying such deep formal features as a part of interpretation seems valid and fruitful. Moreover, it is an additional virtue of Barthes's position here that he conceives the features in question as cultural and variable, rather than as innate or common to all texts.[46] So this looks like a genuine contribution to hermeneutics. Indeed, it is tempting to suggest that it should be classified as a fifth essential aspect of interpretation in addition to the four aspects that had already been identified by Boeckh (historical, linguistic, individual, and generic interpretation).

Equally impressive are Barthes's contributions to the development of a broader *semiology*. His most purely theoretical contribution in this area is his *Elements of Semiology* (1964).[47] In this book he picks up and develops Saussure's idea that linguistics should be considered merely part of a broader science of semiology, which Barthes understands to include not only language but also such non-linguistic forms of expression as road signs, fashion, cuisine, cars, and so on.

This approach implies a significant broadening of hermeneutics beyond the linguistic, and is very plausible. But it is not really a new step in the discipline. For although Schleiermacher and Gadamer had more or less restricted interpretation to language, many other German theorists of hermeneutics had not: for example, Herder (who had also focused on sculpture and music), Friedrich Schlegel (who had also focused on painting and architecture), Hegel (who had also focused on architecture and sculpture), and especially the mature Dilthey (who had also focused not only on the arts, but moreover on a much broader class of "expressions" that included just the sorts of further cases with which Barthes is mainly concerned). Nor is Barthes's attempt in his book to extend key Saussurean linguistic concepts and distinctions to other sorts of signs always convincing. For example, his extension of Saussure's *langue/parole* distinction to non-linguistic cases does not seem very plausible (in part because this celebrated distinction is itself vague and questionable).[48] On the other hand, some other extensions that he proposes seem much more illuminating, for example his extension of the sort of combination of purely positive and (especially) oppositional characteristics that he sees as constitutive of the meaning of linguistic signs for Saussure to non-linguistic signs as well (for instance, Barthes plausibly suggests that in the area of fashion the meaning of a short dress is in part constituted by its contrast to that of a long one).[49] Moreover, the book also makes several further plausible observations that carry important implications for hermeneutics. For instance, it points out that such seemingly non-linguistic cases are often in fact linguistically infused.[50] And it notes that unlike language, non-linguistic signs often have a merely practical function in addition to their function as signs (for example, in the case of food or clothing).[51]

Perhaps even more impressive than this rather abstract book are several works in which Barthes not only theorizes his semiology but also applies it in detail to the interpretation of specific cases, both linguistic and non-linguistic, thereby showing its fruitfulness.[52] One such work is *L'empire des signes* (1970).[53] Here Barthes in effect continues the great interest in cultural otherness that has dominated much French thought since Montaigne in the sixteenth century.[54] The work officially presents itself as a sort of fictional image of Japan. But it turns out that this is more a humble confession of the limitedness of Barthes's information than an accurate description of his intentions or his achievements. For – in sharp contrast to the deliberate fictions of certain French predecessors who had dealt with cultural otherness (e.g., Chateaubriand and Nerval) and the unintentional fictions of others (e.g., Levi-Strauss in his structural anthropology), with which it could easily be confused – the book is in fact a careful and sophisticated piece of anthropological research, albeit research based less on fieldwork than on reading (rather like Ruth Benedict's excellent work on Japan). Some of the book's interpretations concern language, texts, and discourse. For example, Barthes argues plausibly that radical differences between the Japanese language and our European languages contribute to radical differences in thought: grammatical complexity in the personal pronouns in Japanese precludes our Western conceptions of subjectivity; in Japanese the grammatical marking of the distinction between animate versus inanimate, and the fact that fiction normally employs the latter grammatical forms, make fiction a very different sort of genre than it is in the West; and in Japanese the existence of transitive verbs without either subjects or objects (modeled on the Indian *dhyana*) contributes to a very different metaphysical outlook on the world from ours.⁵⁵ Again – very much in the spirit of such earlier hermeneutical theorists of genre as Herder and the Schlegels who had emphasized the variability of genres across time and culture and the problems of misinterpretation to which this leads – Barthes argues in some detail that Japanese haiku poems are precisely *not* supposed to give concise expression to a rich fund of meanings, as westerners usually interpret them, but that they on the contrary have a Zen Buddhist background that makes them aim at stopping discourse and thought, at bringing them to a halt (like a Zen *koan*).⁵⁶ But the greater part of the work is devoted to interpreting *non*-linguistic signs in Japan, such as the layout of a city like Tokyo, whose center turns out to be strikingly inaccessible and empty, and the Japanese practice of elaborately wrapping very modest gifts – both of which cases, on Barthes's interpretation, like the haiku poem, turn out to signify more an absence than a fullness.

Another work that combines semiological theory and practice in an impressive way is Barthes's earlier volume *Mythologies* (1957), which similarly considers a broad range of examples of both linguistic and non-linguistic signification, but this time in contemporary French society and with the addition of a strong sociopolitical dimension to the analysis.⁵⁷ In this work Barthes points out that when one takes into account not only linguistic but also non-linguistic signs, meaningful signs turn out to be an almost ubiquitous feature of our everyday experience: "In a single day, how many really nonsignifying fields do we cross? Very few, sometimes none. Here I am before the sea; it is true that it bears no message. But on the beach, what material for semiology! Flags, slogans, signals, signboards, clothes, suntan even, which are so many messages to me."⁵⁸ And he also offers numerous fascinating interpretations of specific examples of this, both linguistic and non-linguistic, from the French context. The non-linguistic cases include, for instance, a justly famous interpretation of the meaning of wrestling (as contrasted with other martial arts such as boxing and judo) in the essay "In the Ring," and an equally interesting interpretation of the meaning of the Tour de

France bicycle race as a sort of modern epic in "The Tour de France as Epic." In addition, Barthes emphasizes that these and many other forms of sport, entertainment, artifact, and so on typically serve functions of social ideology: communicating a distorted representation of realities that rationalizes the social status quo, in particular by lending it an appearance of permanence and naturalness.[59]

Barthes's book has certain limitations, to be sure. It is less original in approach than it might seem; in particular, both the extension of interpretation to non-linguistic cases of the sorts in question and the explanation of them as social ideology had been strongly anticipated by Adorno's work on "the culture industry" (first presented in Adorno and Horkheimer's *Dialectic of the Enlightenment* [1944]). Also, some of the book's interpretations are a bit too imaginative to be fully convincing as interpretations. Furthermore, the book fails to distinguish clearly enough between meaning-ladenness, distortive meaning-ladenness, and ideologically motivated distortive meaning-ladenness. And finally, its theoretical account of ideology and of the relation of ideology to "mythology" is too thin to be satisfying. Nonetheless, the book remains impressive both as a statement of Barthes' semiological approach and as a demonstration of the fruitfulness of its application to individual cases.

Finally, it seems appropriate to mention the contributions of two thinkers whose original roots were in Eastern Europe but who spent most of their careers in France, became French, and wrote in French. Both of them were representatives of structuralist linguistics and interacted in various ways with both Derrida and Barthes. My brief discussion of them here will be limited to just a single idea of relevance for hermeneutics in each case.

Tzvetan Todorov, who was originally Bulgarian, is especially important for his work on genre, particularly in his book *Genres in Discourse* (1978).[60] Boeckh had already in the nineteenth century recognized that the identification of genre is an essential part of all interpretation (and had accordingly added to Schleiermacher's distinction between three essential parts of all interpretation – historical, grammatical, and psychological interpretation – a fourth: generic interpretation). Subsequently, the twentieth-century Russian literary theorist Mikhail Bakhtin had adopted a similar position.[61] In their wake, Todorov championed this crucially important insight as well. Like Bakhtin, he in particular emphasizes that not only texts (both literary and non-literary) have genres that need to be identified if they are to be understood, but oral uses of language do so too.[62] In addition, he has a number of further interesting insights concerning genre. For example, he notes that although in general genre needs to be distinguished from illocutionary force (a distinction that some of his predecessors, such as E. D. Hirsch, had failed to draw), there are cases, such as prayer, in which they overlap.

Julia Kristeva, another Bulgarian who became French, has also made significant contributions to hermeneutics. Her concept of *intertextuality* is especially important in this connection. She first introduced this concept, under the influence of Bakhtin's conception of the dialogical character of the novel, in the essay "Word, Dialogue, and the Novel" (1966).[63] The concept basically connotes the various ways in which texts (and discourses) largely consist of explicit and implicit incorporations of, and other responses to, other texts (and discourses). This is a broad category that includes various kinds of responses to other texts (and discourses).[64]

That texts involve such features has been recognized for a very long time (see, for example, Protagoras's discussion of Simonides's poem in Plato's *Protagoras*). Nonetheless, it is useful to have them encapsulated together under the single term "intertextuality," since this alerts the interpreter to how widespread they are and sharpens his eye for them.

The concept arguably needs to be revised in one respect, though. When Kristeva originally introduced it, she did so partly in the service of the sort of position, motivated by structuralist linguistics, that was also championed at around the same time by Barthes under the title "the death of the author."[65] However, as I have argued above, this position was a one-sided misrepresentation of the interaction between the communal and the individual (or intentional) that is in fact the usual nature of works. A sensible version of the notion of "intertextuality" therefore ought to drop it. It is to a considerable extent the *author* who decides (whether consciously or unconsciously) what other texts (and discourses) to incorporate and respond to in his work and how to do so.

CONCLUSION

In sum, the French contribution to hermeneutics has been a quite substantial one. Not only did French thought provide one of the two indispensable bases for the great development of German hermeneutics that took place in the eighteenth and nineteenth centuries (namely, anti-universalism), but in addition the twentieth century has seen the development of a rich and lively tradition of thought on hermeneutics in France (even if not usually under that name).

NOTES

1 See M. N. Forster, *After Herder: Philosophy of Language in the German Tradition* (Oxford: Oxford University Press, 2010) and *German Philosophy of Language: From Schlegel to Hegel and Beyond* (Oxford: Oxford University Press, 2011).
2 Concerning this history, see ibid.; also M. N. Forster, "Herder's Doctrine of Meaning as Use," in *Linguistic Content: New Essays on the History of Philosophy of Language*, ed. M. Cameron and R. J. Stainton (Oxford: Oxford University Press, 2015); and M. N. Forster, "German Philosophy of Language before Kant" (forthcoming).
3 Concerning this subject, see M. N. Forster, "Eine Revolution in der Philosophie der Sprache, der Linguistik, der Hermeneutik und der Übersetzungstheorie im späten 18. und frühen 19. Jahrhundert: deutsche und französische Beiträge," in *Friedrich Schleiermacher and the Question of Translation*, ed. L. Cercel and A. Serban (Berlin and Boston: De Gruyter, 2015).
4 It is a minor symptom of how deeply rooted this whole tradition was in France that two very sophisticated variants of it already occurred there by the eighteenth and early nineteenth centuries: an idea, already prominent in Montaigne and then exploited by Montesquieu in his

Lettres persanes, that by investigating the Other and in particular the Other's view of us we can come to a clearer understanding of *ourselves*; and an idea, prominent in Madame de Staël's work on Germany and in de Tocqueville's work on America, that this sort of investigation should not be restricted to "primitive" peoples but should also be extended to "civilized" nations.

5 J. A. Ernesti, *Institutio interpretis Novi Testamenti*, 5th edn. (Leipzig: Weidmann, 1809 [1761]), 48, 54.
6 E. B. de Condillac, *Essai sur l'origine des connaissances humaines* (Paris: Vrin, 2014 [1746]), 287–93.
7 Ernesti, *Institutio interpretis Novi Testamenti*, 48.
8 Ernesti, *Institutio interpretis Novi Testamenti*, 54.
9 Voltaire (actually F. M. Arouet), "Essai sur la poésie épique," in *Œuvres complètes de Voltaire*, ed. L. Moland (Paris: Garnier Frères, 1877), 8:306–14, 317–18.
10 J.-P. Sartre, *Being and Nothingness*, trans. H. E. Barnes (New York: Simon & Schuster, 1956 [1943]), 654ff.
11 See J.-P. Sartre, *L'idiot de la famille: Gustave Flaubert de 1821 à 1857*, esp. vol. 1 (Paris: Gallimard, 1988 [1971]).
12 Concerning this similarity, see M. Frank, *Das Sagbare und das Unsagbare* (Frankfurt am Main: Suhrkamp, 1990).
13 To put this suggestion in more concrete biographical terms: just as Sartre after his stint at the Institut français in Berlin in 1933 wrote *Being and Nothingness* (1943) very much in the spirit of Hegel and Heidegger, so he developed his views on language and interpretation in that work and in subsequent works very much in the spirit of Schleiermacher and his tradition.
14 J. G. Fichte, *The Vocation of Man*, ed. R. M. Chisholm (London and New York: Macmillan, 1985 [1800]). Fichte scholars nowadays tend to dislike this sort of reading of Fichte's position, believing (correctly) that such a position is too crude to be philosophically plausible. But, crude or not, it is clearly at least Fichte's position in the work just cited.
15 J.-P. Sartre, *Search for a Method*, trans. H. E. Barnes (New York: Vintage, 1968 [1957]).
16 P. Ricoeur, *The Conflict of Interpretations: Essays in Hermeneutics*, ed. D. Ihde (Evanston: Northwestern University Press, 1974 [1969]).
17 P. Ricoeur, "The Task of Hermeneutics," *Philosophy Today* 17:2 (1973).

18 For this involvement of religion in hermeneutics, see also Ricoeur, *The Conflict of Interpretations*, esp. 21–4, 171, 195, 332–3.
19 Two further features of Ricoeur's hermeneutics closely related to its involvement of religion are likewise sharply retrograde in comparison with Herder and Schleiermacher: (1) an assumption that in order to *understand* a text, such as the Bible, one must *believe* it (Ricoeur, *Conflict*, 390) (it had been one of Schleiermacher's most important contributions to hermeneutics that he denied this emphatically), and (2) a liberal appeal to what Ricoeur calls "symbolic" meaning in the interpretation of religious texts such as the Bible (see, e.g., Ricoeur, *Conflict*, 269–86) (this blithely ignores Herder and Schleiermacher's salutary warnings against succumbing to the temptation to give unjustified allegorical readings of such texts).
20 Ricoeur, *Conflict*, 4.
21 Ricoeur, *Conflict*, 261, 397–8.
22 Ricoeur, *Conflict*, 55–61.
23 Ricoeur, *Conflict*, 16–18, 169–70, 264–5, 323–30.
24 P. Ricoeur, *Freud and Philosophy: An Essay on Interpretation*, trans. D. Savage (New Haven: Yale University Press, 1970 [1965]).
25 Ricoeur occasionally adds other thinkers to this list as well, e.g., La Rochefoucauld and Feuerbach.
26 See esp. Ricoeur, *Freud and Philosophy*, 32ff.; *Conflict*, 99, 148–9, 330–1.
27 For more discussion of this, see M. N. Forster, "Hermeneutics," in his *German Philosophy of Language*; also "Ideology," in *The Oxford Handbook of German Philosophy in the Nineteenth Century*, ed. M. N. Forster and K. Gjesdal (Oxford: Oxford University Press, 2015); and "Genealogy" and "Genealogy and Morality" in *American Dialectic*, respectively, 1:2 (2011) and 1:3 (2011).
28 See Ricoeur, *Conflict*, 18, 189–90, 244–5, 332–4, 473.
29 One of Derrida's most explicit general discussions of interpretation is "Structure, Sign, and Play in the Discourse of the Human Sciences," in J. Derrida, *Writing and Difference*, trans. A. Bass (Chicago: University of Chicago Press, 1978 [1967]). However, many of his other writings bear on the subject as well.
30 For the concept of "iterability," see esp. J. Derrida, "Signature, Event, Context," in his *Margins of Philosophy*, trans. A. Bass (Chicago: University of Chicago Press, 1984 [1972]).

31 For the concept of "différance," see esp. J. Derrida, "Différance," in his *Margins of Philosophy*, and J. Derrida, *Of Grammatology*, trans. G. Spivak (Baltimore and London: Johns Hopkins University Press, 1974 [1967]).
32 See esp. *Writing and Difference*, 280.
33 See esp. *Of Grammatology*, 66–7, 163, 296, 304, 311–14. Although Derrida does not acknowledge his intellectual debt to Gadamer and the debt has generally been overlooked in the secondary literature, there can be no doubt about it in my view. For example, besides the fundamental similarity in their positions described above, like Gadamer, Derrida stresses the open-endedness of the process in question (*Of Grammatology*, 163), takes the re-presentation of such things as theatrical works as a model for it (*Of Grammatology*, 304), even has a version of Gadamer's strange idea that the interpreter's contribution always gets reabsorbed into the meaning and so vanishes (*Of Grammatology*, 313–14), and also in effect repeats Gadamer's sharp contrast between this whole model of interpretation and Romantic hermeneutics' allegedly misguided contrary conception of interpretation as the recapturing of an original meaning (*Writing and Difference*, 292).
34 See M. N. Forster, "Hermeneutics," in his *German Philosophy of Language*; also and esp., "Gadamer's Hermeneutics: A Critical Appraisal," *Mythos-Magazin* (online), July 2011.
35 For some examples of this approach at work, see *Of Grammatology*, *Margins of Philosophy*, and *Writing and Difference*.
36 Such ideas in Anglophone philosophy often stem from a sort of double error: a principle, espoused by many philosophers in one version or another (including Aristotle, Kant, the early Wittgenstein, and Quine), to the effect that it is impossible to think inconsistently together with an inference from that principle to the inevitable erroneousness of imputing inconsistencies to texts. This is a double error because, first, the principle in question turns out to be mistaken (see on this my *Wittgenstein on the Arbitrariness of Grammar* [Princeton: Princeton University Press, 2004], ch. 5), and second, even if it were true, it would only plausibly apply to *explicit* inconsistencies, whereas the inconsistencies that need to be imputed to texts are usually merely *implicit* ones.

37 See especially "Structure, Sign, and Play in the Discourse of the Human Sciences."
38 Closely related to this strategy of interpretation (or perhaps really just a special form of it) is Derrida's strategy in the interpretation of visual art of focusing on such seemingly marginal features of an artwork as the "subjectile" (i.e., the material medium), the "trait" (e.g., the brushstroke), and the "parergon" (e.g., the frame, the title, or the signature). For a helpful account of this, see the discussion of Derrida's theory of art by J. Wolfreys in *Understanding Derrida*, ed. J. Reynolds and J. Roffe (London: Continuum, 2004), ch. 10.
39 R. Barthes, "The Death of the Author," *Aspen Magazine* 5:6 (Fall and Winter 1967). Reprinted in French in R. Barthes, *Œuvres complètes* (Paris: Seuil, 2002), vol. 3, 40–5.
40 See Derrida, *Writing and Difference*, 226–7; M. Foucault, "What is an Author?" (1969), in M. Foucault, *Language, Counter-Memory, Practice: Selected Essays and Interviews by Michel Foucault*, ed. D. F. Bouchard (Ithaca, NY: Cornell University Press, 1980).
41 This position is also reflected in Barthes's privileging of impersonal over author-centered interpretations in works such as *Mythologies* and *L'empire des signes* (discussed below).
42 Concerning this project of Schleiermacher's, see M. Frank, *Das individuelle Allgemeine: Textstrukturierung und -interpretation nach Schleiermacher* (Frankfurt am Main: Suhrkamp, 1985). The title of Frank's book reflects this project.
43 Both of these texts are reprinted in Barthes, *Œuvres complètes*, vol. 3.
44 See, e.g., Barthes, *Œuvres complètes*, 1021 (an interview from 1971, where, incidentally, Barthes also seems open to using the name "hermeneutics" in this context). The slightly earlier text *Système de la mode* (1967) – reprinted in Barthes, *Œuvres complètes*, vol. 2 – exhibits this sort of project as well, beginning with structuralist chapters and then culminating in semantic ones. See there also Barthes's more explicit commitments to such a project at 1079, 1080–2, 1089ff.
45 For a similar view, see Ricoeur, *Conflict*, 55–61.
46 See, e.g., *Œuvres complètes*, vol. 3, 470, 989.
47 R. Barthes, *Elements of Semiology*, trans. A. Lavers and C. Smith (New York: Hill & Wang, 1977 [1964]).
48 Concerning the point in parentheses, see Ricoeur, *Conflict*, 84–6.

49 Barthes expands on this example in *Système de la mode* (1967) where he distinguishes between *genres* of fashion items (as reflected in the general names of types of such items) and *variants* that pertain to them (i.e., roughly, properties that are expressed by adjectives) and argues that oppositions or exclusions are essential to *both* of these (see esp. 992–7, 1009). He also notes that not all of the relevant oppositions are binary as they are in the case of the short and long dress (1064).
50 Compare *Système de la mode*, 898–9, 1296–7. This point helps to explain that book's focus on fashion-*writing*.
51 Compare *Système de la mode*, 964–6, 1162–3.
52 In these works he focuses on impersonal or collective rather than individual forms of expression, in keeping with his dubious idea of "the death of the author" (hence, for example, his liking for the term "mythologies"). However, such a focus could be legitimate even without the dubious idea in question, in which case it would concern a sort of special case rather than presenting a paradigm, as it were.
53 Reprinted in Barthes, *Œuvres complètes*, vol. 3.
54 See Barthes, *Œuvres complètes*, 1007–8.
55 Barthes, *Œuvres complètes*, 354–5.
56 Barthes, *Œuvres complètes*, 403–15. In other contexts Barthes sometimes expresses misgivings about the concept of genre (see, e.g., Barthes, *Œuvres complètes*, 56–7), but for reasons which seem to me inadequate.
57 R. Barthes, *Mythologies*, trans. R. Howard and A. Lavers (New York: Hill & Wang, 2013 [1957]).
58 Barthes, *Mythologies*, 221.
59 This idea is also prominent in Barthes's somewhat later work *Système de la mode*, which diagnoses fashion(-writing) as a site of illusions about times, places, occupations, individual women, and so on that serve an ideological function. For example, Barthes argues there that fashion's (or fashion-writing's) representation of individual women is typically self-contradictory in such a way that it ideologically bridges the gap between what its consumers' lives are really like and how they want them to be (1146–60).
60 T. Todorov, *Genres in Discourse*, trans. C. Porter (Cambridge: Cambridge University Press, 1990 [1978]).

61 See M. M. Bakhtin, "The Problem of Speech Genres," in his *Speech Genres and Other Late Essays*, ed. C. Emerson and M. Holquist (Austin: University of Texas Press, 1986).
62 Todorov, *Genres in Discourse*, 9–10. See Bakhtin, "The Problem of Speech Genres."
63 J. Kristeva, "Word, Dialogue, and the Novel," in her *Desire in Language: A Semiotic Approach to Literature and Art*, ed. L. S. Roudiez (New York: Columbia University Press, 1980); see esp. 64–8. Barthes endorses this concept as well; see, e.g., Barthes, *Œuvres complètes*, vol. 3, 463, 1012.
64 Following Bakhtin, Kristeva even suggests that this phenomenon is part of the very nature of language itself ("Word, Dialogue, and the Novel," 67–8), though she also (again in "Word, Dialogue, and the Novel") argues that it tends to be suppressed in certain literary genres (e.g., epic), only becoming fully developed in others (e.g., Socratic dialogue, Menippean satire, and the modern novel).
65 See, e.g., Kristeva, "Word, Dialogue, and the Novel," 68.

12 Hermeneutics
Non-Western Approaches
Kai Marchal

Practices of interpretation can be found in any civilization.[1] As soon as human beings were able to speak about their dreams, the need arose to interpret these fleeting images. Similarly, there was a desire to establish the meaning of oracle bones, natural events (earthquakes, eclipses, storms), and other divinatory signs. The statements of kings and priests were so ambiguous that fearless interpreters had to be found to expound their words. In later ages, written documents (laws, chronicles, sacred scriptures) required sophisticated techniques of textual analysis. The demand for clarification led to the writing of commentaries and activities like collecting, editing, annotating, and translating. In their commentarial efforts, moreover, interpreters often engaged with difficult religious, metaphysical, and ethical problems. We find similar developments in Ancient Greece, Egypt, and Israel, but also in Mesopotamia, Persia, among the Maya, as well as in India, China, and many other cultures across the globe.

Yet, when philosophers and other theorists in Western academia ponder the task of hermeneutics today, they mostly focus on theories and conceptual frameworks that originate in Europe. They read texts like the Platonic dialogues, Aristotle's *De interpretatione*, Augustine's *De Doctrina Christiana*, Schleiermacher's lectures, or Hans-Georg Gadamer's *Truth and Method*. Only rarely, however, do they examine the ancient Chinese commentator Wang Bi's (226–249) reflections about the art of interpretation, Hillel the Elder's (c. 110 BCE–10 CE) list of interpretative techniques for the Jewish *Torah*, al-Ghazālī's (1058–1111) *Ihya' ulum al-din* ("The Revival of the Religious Sciences"), or even Motoori Norinaga's (1730–1801) methodological reflections on the interpretation of Ancient Japanese poetry. Indeed, few of these texts are even known to non-specialists.

For most philosophers and academics, "hermeneutics" – in its disciplinary self-understanding, the theory and methodology of interpretation – is largely constituted by European or North-American approaches.

This chapter seeks to explore a simple question: Is modern hermeneutics necessarily a Western phenomenon? Hans-Georg Gadamer was himself doubtful of the possibility of bridging the differences between Western and non-Western thinking: "The enigmatic statements of profundity and wisdom which were developed in other cultures, especially those in the Far East, stand in an ultimately incommensurable relation to what is called Western philosophy, especially because science, in the name of which we ask, itself is a Western discovery."[2] Still, it is not clear how well Gadamer actually understood these other perspectives. In recent decades, numerous philosophers and scholars, both in Western and non-Western countries, have engaged in intercultural dialogue in an attempt to re-conceptualize hermeneutics (particularly philosophical hermeneutics) from the perspective of non-European traditions of thought. In our increasingly globalized world in the twenty-first century, the need to re-think the problem of interpretation from a broader, not merely European perspective is more urgent than ever.

In the following, I will therefore introduce some of the most important non-Western perspectives on hermeneutics. I will then focus on the case of China, especially the history of Confucian interpretative traditions. Then, I will summarize the global reception of philosophical hermeneutics (Heidegger and Gadamer) and, finally, discuss some of the theoretical implications of global approaches to hermeneutics.

Certainly, many of the non-Western interpretative traditions, venerated by generations of readers, were marginalized with the advent of modernity and the introduction of new knowledge systems (often during the time of Western colonial rule). Moreover, it is often pointed out that these traditions were either religious in nature or of merely local importance; they are thus best studied not as part of a universal inquiry into the problem of understanding, but rather in the context of the respective national philologies or so-called "area studies." Similarly, philosophers trained in the West continue to hold deep suspicions of fields like "comparative philosophy" or "global philosophy" (both are thought to lack a solid methodological foundation or to be simply not relevant).[3] Therefore, they prefer to relegate the task of understanding the Other to philologists, anthropologists, ethnologists, or specialists in religious or cultural studies. Such judgments, however, typically are not based on solid knowledge, but on prejudices and vague assumptions. Many philosophers do not perceive how contingent factors influence their judgments, such as the fact that they belong to Western culture(s) where familiarity with Greek thinkers like Aristotle is assumed, while ignorance of Buddhist thinkers like Śāntarakṣita (the eighth-century Indian thinker) is largely accepted.[4] In our increasingly globalized world, however, philosophers can only continue to do this at their own peril.

There is another important issue. In contemporary academia, words like "the West," "Islam," "Hinduism," and "National Studies" have become highly controversial. They are often inscribed with specific political connotations and, in many places across the globe, autochthonous interpretative traditions have become objects of highly politicized debates and even violent struggle. A chapter on "non-Western hermeneutics" may thus appear rather problematic. After all, is not the word "non-Western" itself a kind of embarrassing shorthand for a multiplicity of cultures and worldviews which do not have much in common? (This word is surely not part of the self-understandings of many people in Colombo, Tokyo, or Muscat.)[5] One also needs to be aware of the various pitfalls of the Orientalist imagination, not to mention the temptations of political correctness. Nor do I want to deny my own situatedness (as a German philosopher and Sinologist based in Taipei, Taiwan) or the profusion of existing literature in academic fields ranging from Egyptology, Assyriology, and African Studies to Tibetan Studies, Japanology, and Sinology

HERMENEUTICS: NON-WESTERN APPROACHES 289

that no single individual could hope to know sufficiently over a lifetime. Thus, my aim here is not to carry out the near Herculean task of conducting a systematic survey of non-Western approaches of reading and understanding, but rather to stimulate the reader to further inquiry.

NON-WESTERN INTERPRETATIVE TRADITIONS

The trajectories of interpretative traditions outside the West have followed different patterns. Many cultures have sophisticated models of canonical exegesis and commentarial literature whose historical roots sometimes date back to the earliest periods of their recorded histories. In India, for example, Sanskrit scholars began producing an impressive body of literature, including not only extensive studies of grammar and lexicography, but also rhetoric (alaṅkāraśāstra) and hermeneutics (Mīmāṃsā), as early as the fourth century BCE. In Jewish culture, commentaries in the *midrash* employ highly specialized approaches to recover meaning from the Torah. Prominent scholars like Rabbi Akiva (c. 50 – c. 132) and Rabbi Ishmael (90–135) attempted to establish rules for interpreting the sacred text. In the Arab world, exegetical traditions centered around the *Qur'an*, that was first memorized and written down by various Companions of the Prophet Muhammad (c. 570–632). Over the centuries, numerous scholars have investigated the language of this scripture, and theologians have debated the nature of God's teachings and have tried to restore the literal meaning (zahir) and the inner, spiritual meaning (haqiqa) of various passages. As in Jewish culture, philosophers in later centuries explored the tensions between reason and revelation. In early Japan, scholars of language and literature often concentrated on the study of Chinese texts. Only later, beginning in the seventeenth century, did they turn their attention to Japanese texts like the *Nihon Shoki* (*The Chronicles of Japan*, 720) or the *Man'yōshū*, the oldest extant collection of Japanese poetry. Much more can be said about these traditions, but also about Mesopotamia (a particularly important case), the Maya, and the Aztecs.[6]

One may be tempted here to argue that there are a number of commonalities between these interpretative traditions. Those might include the following: a strong emphasis on the sacred nature and absolute authority of certain texts; the interconnectedness of philological, religious, and philosophical problems (assuming these aspects can be distinguished); a belief in the need for transmitting texts (and the authority to interpret them) from teacher to student; a belief that readers can have immediate access to the original meaning of texts; and the tendency to reject the present in the name of an idealized past. Nonetheless, such evaluations may easily lead to overgeneralizations and misinterpretations. In fact, the very notion of *comparing* those interpretative practices from our point of view is potentially misleading.[7] One thing we can say with some plausibility is that all these traditions have certain affinities to familiar philological endeavors in the European *Geisteswissenschaften*. Thus, as the Sanskrit scholar Sheldon Pollock puts it, we need "to know how philology has made our world, not just in Europe, but everywhere."[8]

THE CASE OF CHINA

Instead of continuing to generalize, I want now without further ado to discuss one case in more depth: China. Chinese culture or civilization is often considered to embody the very idea of Otherness. There is a long history of Orientalist scholarship chasing China's ghost-like presence, in which the country appears as the diametrical opposite to what Western readers already know. Quite a few scholars have committed what the Sinologist Andrew Plaks has aptly called the "antipodal fallacy."[9] Nevertheless, it would likewise be wrong to assimilate Chinese perspectives entirely to our own worldview or to overlook certain deeper differences between the so-called West (North America and Europe) and China in cultural and historical terms, some of which come to the fore in matters of reading and understanding.

Many of those who encounter China's intellectual universe for the first time react like James Legge, the famous nineteenth-century translator of the Chinese classics. When Legge published the prolegomena to the first volume of the *Classics* in 1861, he found Confucius's teachings rather disappointing and lacking in any concern for what he perceived as religious or universal matters. The Victorian missionary-cum-sinologist was only able to appreciate Confucian ideas *on their own terms* after associating with Chinese scholars on a more personal level.[10]

The Chinese have always privileged texts over other media, especially those which are connected to Confucius (551–479 BCE) and have been canonized by emperors since the Han dynasty (206 BCE – 220 CE). An essential idea in China's pre-modern worldview – shared by Confucians, Buddhists, and even some Daoists – was that there are certain texts that contain ultimate values and, therefore, need to be respected by every human being. The *Spring and Autumn Annals*, a historical record of Confucius's native state, was part of the *Five Classics*, the traditional Confucian canon (which also comprises the *Book of Changes*, the *Record of Ritual*, the *Book of Odes*, and the *Book of Documents*). Later, this canon also included the *Analects* (*Lunyu*), the putative record of Confucius's conversations with his disciples. The "scholar-officials" (*ru*) served both as guardians of the canonical texts and as administrators, civil servants, and ministers. Until the abolition of the civil examination system in 1905, debates regarding these "classics" (*jing*) on doctrinal questions and larger issues of interpretation permeated the intellectual life of China.

The *Analects* is not only the most important "classic" in Chinese civilization; it is also one of the most influential texts in human history. Several aspects of China's long history of interpretive practice can be elucidated through a closer analysis of this text and its countless commentaries and sub-commentaries. Like the *Spring and Autumn Annals*, the *Analects* is a rather sparse text. Readers not versed in Chinese culture often dismiss it as a mixture of exhortations and austere words of wisdom. In fact, Confucius's sayings and his interactions with his disciples are far from trivial, but rather require a sustained effort of interpretation.

First, there is the performative dimension of the *Analects*. Like countless other thinkers in China, Confucius gave expression to his ideas in the course of teaching. Any communication – oral or written – is understood as being closely connected to a person's character. Thus, whenever Confucius offers ethical advice to his disciples, its very meaning (and validity) cannot be dissociated from the circumstance of its articulation.

Second, according to many later commentators, the reader of the *Analects* needs to engage with the text through a process of dialogic understanding. Through close interaction with "the Master" via the text, the learner transforms the disciples' questions into his own questions and is educated by Confucius's answers. Yet, Confucius's goal was never to treat a matter exhaustively or to impose a definite meaning on his disciples. He sought rather to suggest a space for thought and to stimulate their imagination (complicated rhetoric could actually be an obstacle).[11] This attitude was pervasive and can also be found, for instance, in Zen Buddhism. As the Sinologist Christoph Harbsmeier observes: "Ideally, classical Chinese texts sow the seeds of meaning in the reader rather than transmitting explicitly the fruits of thought. Thus ancient Chinese texts cultivate an implicit mutual understanding."[12]

Third, this essential fluidity of meaning is also the reason it would be a misunderstanding to attribute a sort of "intentionalist hermeneutics" to the Confucian tradition. When "scholar-officials" throughout the ages thought about how to understand a particular text, they often invoked Mengzi (370 – c. 290 BCE), the second most important thinker after Confucius. In explaining how to read the *Odes*, he stated: "Meet what was [originally on the poet's] mind with [i.e. in terms of] your own intentions" (*yi yi ni zhi*). In other words, Mengzi wants his disciples to understand literary texts with reference to their own existential situation, not merely to recover authorial intention. More broadly, each interpreter needs to read the text anew and to engage in a continuous, creative transformation of the past. Indeed, personal engagement is more important than mere intellectual understanding.

Thinkers of later centuries (many of whom contemporary scholars would not hesitate to qualify as "philosophers") deployed very sophisticated exegetical techniques to interpret obscure passages in the *Analects* and other canonical texts. Often, they conveyed their own philosophical, metaphysical, or ethical understanding in the genre of the interlinear commentary.[13] For example, Wang Bi represents an important shift in Chinese interpretative history by articulating a deepened awareness of the instability of meaning. Under the influence of Daoism, Wang assumed language to be a rather unreliable tool; the "intentions" (*yi*) of the sage Confucius, which are embodied in texts like the *Analects*, cannot be easily transmitted to later generations. Thus, they need to be recovered by means of non-discursive insight into the *Dao* ("the Way"). In the end, any particular perspective gleaned from particular discourses needs to be transcended.[14]

Zhu Xi (1130–1200), the most prominent representative of Neo-Confucianism, frequently expressed his suspicion about claims of canonical authority. He believed that the authority to evaluate texts needed to be shifted from the court, or other political authorities, to Neo-Confucian scholars. It is possible to acquire a thorough understanding of texts, including those from a distant past; the reader only needs to apply them to his or her own existential situation and to overcome prejudices – in Zhu's words, to "void the mind" (*xu xin*). Zhu's "method of reading books" (*dushu fa*) has often been praised as the most systematic attempt in pre-modern China to tackle the problem of understanding. While he places high demands on the reader and describes reading as a form of ethical self-cultivation (*gongfu*), he also highly values the autonomy of the reader. He thus never simply asks for passive acknowledgment of the tradition (or authorial intent). For Zhu Xi, reading is not only a way of connecting with the world of past sages like Confucius, but also enables the reader to gain holistic insight into the present world and to respond aptly, and in accordance with the Confucian virtues, to any situation that arises.[15]

MODERN HERMENEUTICS IN EUROPE AND BEYOND

We would do well at this point to return for a moment to the history of European hermeneutics. Theologians in the Medieval Period mainly formulated their hermeneutic insights without thinking about how history and the contingencies of time put limitations on their quest of making sense of texts. Over the course of the eighteenth and nineteenth centuries, however, the problem of historicity became more prominent. The discovery of Asia and its religions fundamentally challenged the still widely accepted Judeo-Christian worldview, even among philosophers. Sanskrit was now thought to be the world's oldest language instead of Hebrew; the Bible had much older competitors from China and India; and European civilization suddenly appeared as a local phenomenon in a dramatically expanded and increasingly complex world.[16] In response to Immanuel Kant's project of re-founding modern rationalism, German romantic thinkers like Johann Georg Hamann, Johann Gottfried Herder, and Friedrich Schlegel insisted on the radical diversity of cultures, the dependence of thought on language, and the limitations that historical developments place upon human agency. Against this backdrop, Friedrich Schleiermacher developed his project of a universal hermeneutics rooted in an awareness of the limitations of any interpretative understanding of human life.[17]

Yet, the horizon of modern hermeneutics has narrowed since the late eighteenth century. In 1772, the young Herder praised John Zephaniah Holwell's (1711–1798) *Shastah*, and in his later search for humanity's origin, he introduced Indian Brahmins to his readers. Moreover, in his letter to Abel-Rémusat, Wilhelm von Humboldt developed his own theory of the Chinese language.[18] By contrast, most representatives of twentieth-century hermeneutics no longer seriously engaged with non-European cultures, but highlighted the Greek roots of European culture instead. One obvious reason for this change was the strong influence of G. W. F. Hegel's model of *Philosophiegeschichte* over the course of the nineteenth century, a model that provides only marginal room for Chinese or Indian ways of thinking. Moreover, the increasing professionalization of the humanities and the rise of specialized philologies made philosophers less inclined to ponder non-European languages or to engage with texts from the Arab world, India, or China.

The case of twentieth-century philosophical hermeneutics is somewhat different. Martin Heidegger was one of the few twentieth-century philosophers willing to explore new perspectives of thinking and to look beyond the European history of philosophy. In his attempt to disentangle himself from the European *Seinsgeschichte*, he occasionally referred to texts like the *Daodejing* and sought a dialogue with Buddhist monks, Chinese translators, and Japanese philosophers, as in his famous text "A Dialogue on Language between a Japanese and an Inquirer" (written between the years 1953 and 1954, but only published in 1959).[19] Still, Heidegger was also convinced that Asian languages were ultimately inaccessible and never made an effort to actually learn languages like Sanskrit or Ancient Chinese. While he repeatedly gestured toward a future East–West dialogue, he "never thought of modifying his central ideas in light of the insight from other traditions."[20] Instead, he was convinced that a fundamental renewal of philosophy can only be achieved through a reversal of European traditions.

Similarly, Hans-Georg Gadamer (trained both in Greek and Latin classics and in philosophy) largely focused on the European history of understanding. In contrast to his teacher Heidegger, who wanted to discard Western metaphysical thinking once and for all, Gadamer turned to Plato and emphasized the degree to which "we" (if we happen to be European or belong to the Anglo-American world) are tied to our heritage. Gadamer certainly spoke about the need for engagement with non-Western thinking and yet (as already indicated) sometimes dismissed it as not relevant at all. Indeed, he has been frequently criticized for erasing alterity by insisting on the need to achieve a "common language." Ultimately, there may be deeper, potentially incommensurable differences between European (North

American) and non-Western cultures that cannot be captured in a dialogic interplay.[21]

Today, Heidegger's thinking remains a locus of strong disagreement among philosophers. Gadamer is also frequently read in divergent ways. Both philosophers have nonetheless clearly had an enormous impact on debates about cross-cultural dialogue, not only in the West, but also in the Arab world, Iran, India, China, Japan, and many other countries. The year 1929 marks an important watershed in the soon-to-be global history of philosophical hermeneutics: The Japanese philosopher Watsuji Tetsurō (1889–1960), in an essay written in that year, engaged with Heidegger's account of *Dasein* and language to re-examine the question of Being through the Japanese language.[22] In the following decades, Heideggerian and, some time later, Gadamerian ideas spread around the globe in a complex process of reception and transfer of ideas that is still not well understood. Conferences like the first East–West philosophers' conference (held in Hawaii in 1939) helped initiate intercultural exchanges. In the Arab world, Abdur Rahman Badawi (1917–2002) was one of the first to engage Heidegger's work in the 1940s. Later, Henry Corbin and Nasr Abu Zayd reconstructed Ibn Arabi's thought from a Heideggerian perspective, while scholars such as J. L. Mehta and Wilhelm Halbfass explored Hindu thought in a similar manner. In China, Taiwan, and Singapore, the Chinese words *jieshixue* and *quanshixue* (for the word "hermeneutics") became popular in the early 1990s. Philosophers such as Wu Kuang-ming, Wang Qingjie, and Zhang Xianglong engaged with Heidegger and Gadamer to open up new vistas for Daoism and Confucianism.[23]

CONCLUDING OBSERVATIONS

These still-evolving non-Western accounts of hermeneutics have emerged in different places, and in different languages. Although a fusion of horizons has been achieved to at least some extent on a global level, intercultural dialogue is still often characterized by its contingency: The ever-growing interconnectivity of people is occurring in increasingly fragmentized ways; philosophical theories are being imported into very different contexts, yet often threaten to erase traditional knowledge; and texts are now read by many more readers, who nonetheless are more interested in the re-assertion of their own cultural horizons than the horizons of the texts' originators. The historical conditions of many of these cross-cultural interactions are favorable to the further expansion of Anglophone culture(s) of scholarship. That said, there are reasons to think that a truly global hermeneutic consciousness should reflect the historicity of the present moment, despite all its confusing hybridity.

Clearly, thinkers in Tibet, India, Japan, and elsewhere tend to conceive of the project of hermeneutics from the perspective of their own questions. The example of China is quite telling, as its intellectual traditions often provide the background for the reception of non-Chinese thought (similarly to how Indian Buddhism was integrated into the Chinese worldview from the third century BCE). Many Chinese philosophers unfold their understanding of European philosophical problems in terms that are familiar to them; and Gadamer's claim that understanding is necessarily determined by the past actually encourages his readers to do so. His critique of the Cartesian subject and his transformation of Aristotle's concept of *phronesis* into a comprehensive account of hermeneutic experience are therefore re-interpreted against the backdrop of Confucian interpretative traditions.[24] To be sure, there are quite a few analogies between philosophical hermeneutics and the Chinese traditions. For example, as the Sinologist John Makeham points out: "Although lacking any attendant phenomenological agenda (not to mention a concept of being), the goal of Zhu Xi's hermeneutics is also concerned less with understanding as a mode of knowing than as a mode of experiencing: learning to be a sage."[25] Similarly, the writings of Buddhist thinkers like Fazang (643–712) – who contended that human beings always interpret their world and who also gave prominence to the problems of temporality and finitude – have been read as an alternative *Buddhist* account of hermeneutics.[26] Furthermore, the philosopher Jay L. Garfield has argued that we can meaningfully integrate insights from Tibetan and Indian Buddhism into a renewed understanding of the hermeneutic circle and hermeneutic distance.[27] Similar arguments can be found in texts written in Chinese, Japanese, and other languages, although most readers of this companion will not be in a position to read them (few have been translated into languages like English, French, or German).

In non-Western cultures, central aspects of modern hermeneutics, the question of language, problems of understanding, meaning, finitude, and temporality, have often been conceived differently. Unfortunately, beyond participating in discussions on multiculturalism and Otherness, many Western philosophers are not yet willing to engage in an open-ended and equal exchange with scholars from countries like India, Egypt, Thailand, or Korea (where social, political, or cultural conditions often also undermine the possibility of cross-cultural exchange). It may be tempting to conclude, then, that there is simply no escape from the global reach of European thought. As the postcolonial theorist Dipesh Chakrabarty remarked: It is "impossible to *think* of anywhere in the world without invoking certain categories and concepts, the genealogies of which go deep into the intellectual and even theological traditions of Europe."[28] Nonetheless, the language of hermeneutics has become universal, if one may say so, by being translated into very different discourses and horizons. In the end, the most important advantage of engaging hermeneutic thinkers from the Arab world, India, or China may simply be that we become aware of the Others' understanding of ourselves against the backdrop of their traditions. We may even become open to the possibility of a radically different outlook on things. To ignore such an outlook means to also ignore the requirements of our global present.

NOTES

1 While preparing this chapter, I have learned a great deal from discussions with Ching Keng, Philippe Brunozzi, Joachim Gentz, Leigh Jenco,

Johannes Kaminski, Malcolm Keating, Lin Chen-kuo, Lin Wei-chieh, Mathias Obert, and Dennis Schilling. Moreover, I am especially indebted to Michael N. Forster and Kristin Gjesdal, as well as many of the contributors to this volume, for their insightful comments on an earlier draft. I also want to thank Christopher Reid for carefully polishing my English.

2   Hans-Georg Gadamer, "Begriffsgeschichte als Philosophie," in *Gesammelte Werke*, vol. 2 (Tübingen: J. C. B. Mohr (Paul Siebeck), 1986), 77.

3   Many philosophers – in line with Donald Davidson – are not convinced of the possibility of radically different conceptual schemata and think that conceptual relativism is incoherent. For a defense of the position that any account of similarities across or within forms of life should be particularized, while there can never be total incommensurability, see Lin Ma and Jaap van Brakel, *Fundamentals of Comparative and Intercultural Philosophy* (Albany: SUNY Press, 2016), 149–77. Compare also Michael N. Forster, "On the Very Idea of Denying the Existence of Radically Different Conceptual Schemes," *Inquiry*, 41:2 (1998): 133–85. The voices calling for greater diversity in philosophy – as it is practiced in Western academia – have become louder in recent years. See, e.g., Thom Brooks, "Philosophy Unbound: The Idea of Global Philosophy," *Metaphilosophy*, 44:3 (April 2013): 254–66.

4   The philosopher and Buddhist scholar Jay Garfield puts it well: "When we do that, we distinguish living philosophy from dead ideas on the basis of an arbitrary criterion of cultural proximity, and in doing so, license an intellectual attitude toward that which we designate as distant that we would never permit toward that which we regard as proximate." Jay L. Garfield, *Engaging Buddhism: Why It Matters to Philosophy* (Oxford: Oxford University Press, 2015), 334.

5   More specifically, the question of whether Islam belongs to the West has become extremely politicized in the recent past. There is actually strong evidence that the Qur'an needs to be understood against the backdrop of late Mediterranean antiquity and is, thus, best interpreted as an "Oriental-European text"; see Angelika Neuwirth, *Der Koran als Text der Spätantike. Ein europäischer Zugang* (Berlin: Verlag der Weltreligionen, 2010), 67.

6   A helpful overview of various interpretative traditions worldwide can be found in Sheldon Pollock, Benjamin E. Elman, and Ku-ming Kevin Chang

(eds.), *World Philology* (Cambridge, MA and London: Harvard University Press, 2015). Compare also Mordechai Z. Cohen and Adele Berlin (eds.), *Interpreting Scriptures in Judaism, Christianity, and Islam: Overlapping inquiries* (Cambridge: Cambridge University Press, 2016); and countless other monographs. As space here is limited, I do not say much about literary genres and literary hermeneutics in a global context. See, e.g., Zhang Longxi, *The Tao and the Logos: Literary Hermeneutics, East and West* (Durham, NC and London: Duke University Press, 1992); and David Damrosch, *How to Read World Literature?* (Oxford: Wiley-Blackwell, 2017).

7 As soon as we make comparative judgments of the sort "Whereas we in the West have conceptualized the issue of X, scholars and thinkers in the non-West have never been aware of it," we risk falling victim to the logic of essentialization and saying more about the difference between an imagined West (and non-West) than about these specific practices. Comparative judgments are unavoidable, but should be made at a much later stage of engagement with the Other. James Elkins, in the context of Chinese art history, puts it very well: "Philosophically speaking, comparisons, parallels, and analogies are forms of difference, and difference is what allows understanding in the first place." James Elkins, *Chinese Landscape Painting as Western Art History* (Hong Kong: Hong Kong University Press, 2010), 45.

8 See Pollock et al., *World Philology*, 24.

9 Andrew Plaks, "Why the Chinese Gods Don't Suffer," in *Studies in Chinese Language and Culture: Festschrift in Honour of Christoph Harbsmeier on the Occasion of His 60th Birthday*, ed. Christoph Anderl and Halvor Eifring (Oslo: Hermes Academic Publishing 2006), 124. The most famous representative of such an "Orientalist" interpretation of Chinese culture is the Sinologist and philosopher François Jullien. For an insightful critique of Jullien's approach, see Haun Saussy, *Great Walls of Discourse and Other Adventures in Cultural China* (Cambridge, MA and London: Harvard University Press, 2001).

10 See Norman J. Girardot, *The Victorian Translation of China: James Legge's Oriental Pilgrimage* (Berkeley, Los Angeles, and London: University of California Press, 2002), 58–61.

11 The art of rhetoric in pre-modern China was about the rules and techniques of writing and the structuring of arguments. For an

overview, see Christoph Harbsmeier, "The Rhetoric of Premodern Prose Style," in *The Columbia History of Chinese Literature*, ed. Victor H. Mair (New York: Columbia University Press, 2002), 881–908. By contrast, the Chinese rarely showed interest in rhetoric as the art of public speech (though they were quite interested in the art of persuading rulers). Still, in Harbsmeier's words, "there was no discipline of rhetoric in pre-modern China comparable in scope and systematicity to that of Aristotle, Cicero, and Quintilian" (Harbsmeier, "Chinese Rhetoric," *T'oung Pao*, Second Series, Vol. 85, Fasc. 1/3 (1999), 114–26; here: 115–16).

12 Harbsmeier, "The Rhetoric of Premodern Prose Style," 882.
13 See, for example, John B. Henderson, *Scripture, Canon and Commentary: A Comparison of Confucian and Western Exegesis* (Princeton: Princeton University Press, 1991); Steven van Zoeren, *Poetry and Personality: Reading, Exegesis, and Hermeneutics in Traditional China* (Stanford: Stanford University Press, 1991); and Joachim Gentz, *Das Gongyang zhuan: Auslegung und Kanonisierung der Frühlings- und Herbstannalen (Chunqiu)* (Wiesbaden: Harrassowitz, 2001).
14 For an overview of Wang Bi's hermeneutic approach to the *Analects*, see Rudolf G. Wagner, "Making Sense: Wang Bi's Commentary on the *Lun Yu*," in *Zhong Ri sishu. Quanshi chuantong chutan* (Taipei: Taiwan daxue chuban zhongxin, 2008), vol. 1, 109–58.
15 See John Makeham, *Transmitters and Creators: Chinese Commentators and Commentaries on the* Analects (Cambridge, MA: Harvard University Asia Center and Harvard University Press, 2004).
16 See, for example, Urs App, *The Birth of Orientalism* (Philadelphia: The University of Pennsylvania Press, 2010); and Bradley L. Herling, *The German Gita: Hermeneutics and Discipline in the Early German Reception of Indian Thought* (New York and London: Routledge, 2006).
17 Compare Michael N. Forster, *German Philosophy of Language: From Schlegel to Hegel and Beyond* (Oxford: Oxford University Press, 2011).
18 See Jean Rousseau and Denis Thouard (eds.), *Lettres édifiantes et curieuses sur la langue chinoise. Un débat philosophico-grammatical entre Wilhelm von Humboldt et Jean-Pierre Abel-Rémusat (1821–1831), avec une correspondance inédite de Humboldt (1824–1831)* (Paris: Presses Universitaires du Septentrion, 1999). For a German

translation of von Humboldt's famous letter (written in French) and a critical analysis, see Christoph Harbsmeier, *Wilhelm von Humboldts Brief an Abel-Rémusat und die philosophische Grammatik des Altchinesischen* (Stuttgart-Bad Cannstatt: Friedrich Frommann, 1979).

19 See Heidegger, *On the Way to Language*, trans. Peter D. Hertz (New York: Harper San Francisco, 1982 [1971]), 1–54. For a very insightful analysis of the various misunderstandings and misrepresentations that are characteristic of Heidegger's attempt to engage Japanese and Chinese thinking, see Lin Ma, *Heidegger on East-West Dialogue: Anticipating the Event* (New York and London: Routledge, 2008).

20 Ma, *Heidegger on East-West Dialogue*, 166.

21 In the English-speaking world, philosophers and theorists like Charles Taylor, Fred Dallmayr, Raimon Panikkar, Bhikhu Parekh, and Roxanne Euben consider a Gadamerian "dialogic approach" to be helpful for achieving genuine cross-cultural consensus in a global world. For insightful discussions of Gadamerian hermeneutics from an intercultural perspective, see Andreas Vasilache, *Interkulturelles Verstehen nach Gadamer und Foucault* (Frankfurt and New York: Campus Verlag, 2003); and Ma and van Brakel, *Fundamentals of Comparative and Intercultural Philosophy*.

22 An English translation of Watsuji Tetsurō's text ("The Japanese Language and the Question of Philosophy") can be found in Michael F. Marra (ed.), *Japanese Hermeneutics: Current Debates on Aesthetics and Interpretation* (Honolulu: University of Hawaii Press, 2002), 51–91.

23 See Kata Moser, "La réception arabe de Heidegger," *Bulletin Heideggérien* V (2015): 4–16. The first translation of Heidegger's writings into Arabic appeared in 1963; yet, the first complete Arabic translation of *Being and Time* only came out in 2013. Compare also Henry Corbin, *Creative Imagination in the Sufism of Ibn Arabi* (Princeton: Princeton University Press, 1969); Nasr Abu Zayd, *Rethinking the Qur'an: Towards a Humanistic Hermeneutics* (Utrecht: Humanistics University Press, 2004); Wilhelm Halbfass, *India and Europe: An Essay in Understanding* (Albany: SUNY Press, 1988); Rita Sherma and Arvind Sharma (eds.), *Hermeneutics and Hindu Thought: Toward a Fusion of Horizons* (Dordrecht: Springer Netherlands, 2008); J. L. Mehta, *India and the West: The Problem of Understanding* (Atlanta: Scholars Press, 1985); Kuang-ming Wu,

On the "Logic" of Togetherness: A Cultural Hermeneutic (Leiden, New York and Köln: Brill, 1998); Xianglong Zhang, *Haidege'er sixiang yu Zhongguo tiandao* [Heidegger and China's Way of Heaven] (Beijing: Sanlian chubanshe, 1996); and Qingjie Wang, *Jieshixue, Haidege yu Ru Dao jin shi* [Hermeneutics, Heidegger and a New Interpretation of Confucianism and Daoism] (Beijing: Zhongguo renmin daxue chubanshe, 2004).

24 See, e.g., Lin Wei-chieh, *Zhu Xi yu jingdian quanshi* (Taibei: Taiwan daxue chuban zhongxin, 2008).

25 Makeham, *Transmitters and Creators: Chinese Commentators and Commentaries on the* Analects, 197.

26 See Mathias Obert, *Sinndeutung und Zeitlichkeit: Zur Hermeneutik des Huayan-Buddhismus* (Hamburg: Meiner Verlag, 2000); and Donald S. Lopez, Jr. (ed.), *Buddhist Hermeneutics* (Delhi: Motilal Banarsidass, 1993). Similar things have been said about Confucian thinkers like Zhang Xuecheng (1738–1802), see, e.g., Wu Chan-liang, "Historicity, Tradition, Praxis, and Tao: A Comparison of the World Views of Zhang Xuecheng and Modern Philosophical Hermeneutics," in *Interpretation and Intellectual Change: Chinese Hermeneutics in Historical Perspective*, ed. Ching-i Tu (New Brunswick and London: Transaction Publishers, 2005), 227–44. Yet, other scholars have questioned such comparisons by pointing out, for example, that Qing dynasty *kaozheng* scholarship may not have much in common with nineteenth-century historicism in Europe at all (Michael Quirin, "Scholarship, Value, Method, and Hermeneutics in *Kaozheng*: Some Reflections on Cui Shu (1740–1816) and the Confucian Classics," *History and Theory* 35:4 (1996): 34–53). For a critical discussion of certain misunderstandings see also Kathleen Wright, "Hermeneutics and Confucianism," in *The Routledge Companion to Hermeneutics*, ed. Jeffrey Malpas and Hans-Helmuth Gander (London and New York: Routledge Press, 2014), 674–91.

27 See Jay L. Garfield, *Empty Words: Buddhist Philosophy and Cross-Cultural Interpretation* (Oxford: Oxford University Press, 2002).

28 Dipesh Chakrabarty, *Provincializing Europe: Postcolonial Thought and Historical Difference* (Princeton: Princeton University, 2007 [2000]), 4.

13 Hermeneutics and Literature
Jonathan Culler

For Hans-Georg Gadamer, the most eminent theorist of twentieth-century hermeneutics, literature offers the paradigmatic case for hermeneutics: as the form of writing that most demands interpretation, it is also the form where the claim of the past on the present is most fully experienced. Thus, "Historical understanding proves to be a kind of literary criticism writ large."[1] The interpretation of literary texts becomes paradigmatic for the interpretation of other texts. It is somewhat ironic, therefore, especially since both Heidegger and Gadamer value poetry very highly, that the tradition of modern hermeneutics has not figured significantly in the study of literature. Explaining why this might be so is one of the major tasks of this chapter. From antiquity through the Middle Ages, however, ancient hermeneutics does have an impact on thinking about literature; and one can also argue that a new conception of literature that arises at the end of the eighteenth century plays an important role in the development of modern hermeneutics. That history will be another focus of this chapter.

HERMENEUTICS AND POETICS

As a framework for this discussion, let me note that in literary studies there is a distinction between hermeneutics and poetics that is in principle quite simple and straightforward. Given a text, hermeneutics asks what it means, seeks to discover a meaning – whether some original meaning or a meaning it has for readers in today's circumstances, or often some combination of the two – what this text is "really about" as we say. Poetics, on the other hand, asks what are the rules and conventions that enable the text to have the meanings and effects it does for readers, for those who participate in the tradition to which it relates. In other words, poetics starts with texts and their significance and asks about their conditions of possibility or intelligibility rather than asking what the text really means. In this, poetics is analogous to linguistics, which does not undertake to discover the true, deeper meaning of English sentences but asks what are the rules and conventions of the language that make it possible for these sequences of noises or letters to function as they do, as meaningful utterances. Roland Barthes, for instance, distinguishes criticism (*la critique*) from a poetics he calls *une science de la littérature*: the former attempts to work out the meaning of a text, placing it in a context, applying a particular language to it, whereas the latter will not attribute or even discover a meaning but will describe the logic by which readers generate meanings that are acceptable in terms of the conventions of literature, just as sentences of a language are accepted by the linguistic intuitions of speakers.[2]

In this schema, then, poetics and hermeneutics are working in different directions: hermeneutics from text toward a meaning and poetics back from effects or meanings to the conditions of possibility of such meanings. This distinction is clear in theory but often muddied in practice, for those setting out to interpret may need to try to describe the conventions that enable them to posit a particular meaning, and those who claim to do poetics, not hermeneutics, are frequently tempted, not just to offer interpretations as they proceed, but to conclude that what this text is really about is the nature of literature itself, the codes and conventions one has identified along the way.[3] The enterprise of poetics, in its diverse guises, is crucial to literary studies, whose goal, after all, is (or should be) to understand how literature works, not to come up with new interpretations of individual works; but projects in poetics frequently find themselves enlisted as methods of interpretation: so Northrop Frye's *Anatomy of Criticism*, which sought to provide a comprehensive theoretical framework for thinking about literature and its possible forms, gave rise to "myth criticism." But despite critics' inclinations to put everything to work in the service of interpretation, the opposition between poetics and hermeneutics helps to make sense of the variety of projects undertaken as literary criticism.

In the Western tradition, both poetics and hermeneutics date from ancient Greece. Aristotle's *Poetics* gives what was to become an authoritative account of the forms of mimetic literature and their rules of construction and provided a framework of genre theory which came into prominence with the Renaissance. Hermeneutics emerges at much the same time, with the need to interpret the Homeric epics, explicating their archaic language but especially defending them against critiques by Plato and others that they contained claims that were theologically and morally inappropriate or false by determining what they were really saying. Allegorical interpretation, from the fifth century BCE to the Stoic and Neoplatonic schools and even later, sought to reveal the truths behind the fables. Porphyry, a third-century philosopher who also wrote philological commentary on Homer, produced what has been called "the earliest surviving interpretive critical essay in the European tradition," an extensive interpretation of Homer's episode of the Cave of the Nymphs in book 13 of the *Odyssey* as an allegory of the soul's fall into the world.[4] With the advent of Christianity, the rehabilitation of pagan myths and poetic fables became even more important, as the study of classical texts became central to education, a fundamental part of *grammatica*, and students needed to be protected against the allurements of pagan antiquity by explanations of what they should learn from these texts. The tradition of medieval commentary provided not only information about the organization and rhetorical devices of texts but also interpretations highlighting their pedagogical and moral utility.[5] As Augustine put it, "what they [the pagans] have said should be taken from them as from unjust possessors and converted to our use."[6] Allegorical interpretations treated the Homeric gods as representing particular virtues or powers, as in an elaborate twelfth-century interpretation by William of Conches:

> Consider Jupiter cutting off his father's testicles and throwing them in the sea so that Venus is born. This is nothing but that

the testicles signify the fruits of the earth, through which, in the course of time, the seed from the bowels of the earth is diffused more and more. Jupiter cuts off the testicles of Chronos, and this is nothing but that the warmth of the upper element ripens the fruits and makes them ready for cutting off and gathering. The fruits are cast into the sea, that is into the hollow maw of the human belly, and thus Venus – that is, sensual delight – is born.[7]

The practice of commenting on sacred texts, in both the Jewish and Christian traditions, contributed to the hermeneutic resources of literary criticism. Christian hermeneutics developed the conception of the four-fold meaning of scripture, summed up in the couplet of Augustine of Dacia: "Littera gesta docet, quid credas allegoria, / Moralis quid agas, quid speres anagogia" (The literal reading teaches what happened, the allegorical what you ought to believe, the moral what you should do, and the anagogical what you should hope for). Although theologians denied the appropriateness of applying techniques of scriptural exegesis to secular literature, Dante in the *Convivio* writes of his own poems: "the interpretation should be both literal and allegorical. For the understanding of this, it should be realized that texts can be understood and should be explicated primarily on four levels."[8] In practice, though, Dante seldom moves beyond an allegorical interpretation. What literary criticism derives from biblical hermeneutics is above all the idea of finding ways to make a particular text yield an appropriate sort of meaning, one roughly known in advance. As John of Salisbury wrote, "examine Virgil or Lucan, and whatever philosophy you may profess, there you will find its foundation."[9]

For most of its history, however, Western discussion of literature is beholden not to hermeneutics but to generic categories based on mimesis – genres differing according to what is represented. Such poetics, in the sense of a general account of literary possibilities and the rules or conventions of each, is central to the Western tradition of criticism, as Aristotle's *Poetics* for many centuries provided norms for the evaluation of drama. Linked with the generic orientation of poetics are writings about poetry, such as Horace's *Ars Poetica* and Geoffrey de Vinsauf's *New Poetries*, which offer advice to poets while discussing techniques of composition and rhetorical strategies but do not discuss the interpretation of poetry.

Criticism of the Renaissance turns aside from the interpretive aspects of medieval hermeneutics and devotes much energy to the recovery of classical texts and exploration of the possibilities of national, vernacular literatures and their relation to the classical past and its models. Critical writing of the seventeenth and eighteenth centuries continues the evaluative mode but also foregrounds discussions about the relation of literature to audiences and about concepts of taste. John Dryden defines criticism as "a standard of judging well, the chiefest part of which is to observe those excellencies which should delight a reasonable reader."[10] Alexander Pope's substantial and much cited *Essay on Criticism*, while discussing at length conflicts about the evaluation of poetry, does not even mention the problem of working out what a poem means or the possibility of interpretation; and Samuel Johnson's essays on literature, which often closely scrutinize literary techniques (he devotes an entire Rambler essay, "The Pauses in English Poetry, Adjusted," to pauses in Milton's blank verse[11]), offer evaluations of various aspects of works, while speaking of authors, their character and their achievement, but his writings lack a hermeneutical dimension.

LITERATURE AND HERMENEUTICS IN THE NINETEENTH CENTURY

The revolution in the concept of literature that occurs in that generally revolutionary time of the late eighteenth and early nineteenth centuries breaks with a conception of literature linked to generic norms. The shift from a concept of literature as mimesis – an imitation of action – to a concept of literature as expression of an author undermined the primary strain of evaluative criticism: assessment of works in terms of the norms of genres, of verisimilitude, and appropriate expression. Nonetheless, most discussion of literature remains evaluative rather than interpretive until at least the mid-twentieth century, and such writing about literature as is not primarily evaluative treats it as a historical phenomenon, to be related to its context of production: a product of literary influences and of the spirit of the age. There is almost no interpretation of particular works in the writings about literature of eminent figures in the history of criticism: Coleridge, Matthew Arnold, Sainte-Beuve, Taine, Emerson, Friedrich Schlegel, Goethe. (In fact, the term *hermeneutics* does not even figure in the twenty-two-page index of the bulky *Literary Criticism: A Short History* by Wimsatt and Brooks and only once in the volume on the late eighteenth century of René Wellek's *History of Literary Criticism*.) And one can add that literary education prior to the mid-twentieth century involved little interpretation: students translated, imitated, memorized literary works, learned about authors and about literary history, but were not asked to produce interpretations.

However, this change in the conception of literature – from imitation of action to expression of an author – is closely associated with the development of modern hermeneutics in that it inspired German thinkers to propose a general hermeneutics, as opposed to the special hermeneutics that had focused on biblical or Classical texts. Johann Gottfried Herder, an early proponent of a philosophical hermeneutics, was a poet, critic, and mentor to the young Goethe and major figure in German romanticism and *Sturm und Drang*. Inspired by the genius of Homer, Pindar, biblical poetry, and folk literature, he wrote a little book celebrating Shakespeare, urging he not be judged against Aristotelian norms for tragedy: we must "explain him, feel him as he is, use him, and – where possible – bring him to life for us Germans."[12] His *Fragments on Recent German Literature* stress the differences among languages and cultures, challenging the Enlightenment notion that humanity is everywhere the same; on the contrary, Herder sees the tremendous differences among peoples of different ages and nations. His *Treatise on the Origin of Language* argued that language was of human rather than divine origin and that since language shapes thought, each language and era has its own spirit, which should not be judged by standards of another. Grammatical or philological hermeneutics must therefore be supplemented by a process of *Einfühlung*, a feeling one's way into the thought of an author.[13]

Friedrich Schleiermacher, whose lectures outlined a complex model for modern hermeneutics, was part of the Jena circle of writers and critics, deeply concerned with the translation and comparative study of foreign literatures, especially (ancient) Greek, and with championing new German literature. The comparative perspective, part of the anthropological current that emerges in the eighteenth century, brought recognition of the diverse ways in which different cultures make sense of the world. There is need for a new hermeneutics because distance separating reader from text is not just a matter of language and grammar but also of different conceptual frameworks.[14] Hermeneutics could not be just a philological science, construing ancient texts, but must become an art identifying the genius of each language and age and should focus on the individual author as creator of the text; the search for meaning involves reconstructing the author's internal and external world and the process of creation. Schleiermacher maintains that "grammatical" interpretation, in which "the person ... disappears and only appears as organ of language," needs to be complemented by a mode of interpretation focused on the author, which he calls "technical" (from *techne*, art) or, later, "psychological," in which "language with its determining power disappears and only appears as the organ of the person, in the service of their individuality."[15] The combination of these two modes of interpretation yields understanding that is directed toward thought, which is always the thought of someone whose thinking is shaped by a concrete cultural linguistic horizon.

Schleiermacher's work offered the foundations for a balanced text-based hermeneutics, oriented toward discourse of all sorts but shaped by the emerging conception of literature as the expression of an author, and might well have contributed to a reorientation of literary criticism, but much of his hermeneutic theory remained unpublished, passed on primarily by students; and, despite his influence, the hermeneutic tradition developed in a different direction.

THE TWENTIETH CENTURY

Once the mimetic model of literature is displaced by an expressive model, the question arises, what does the work express: the thinking of the author, the spirit of the age, the historical conjuncture, the conflicts of the psyche, the functioning of language itself? Such conceptions of what a text might express have become in our day the basis of so-called "schools" of criticism or critical approaches to literature. But arguments about what sorts of meaning works might be taken to embody or express seldom draw upon the hermeneutic tradition. One reason is that hermeneutics itself had changed. The dominant modern line, which runs through Dilthey to Heidegger and Gadamer, focuses on the understanding of understanding. Dilthey, who worked to give historical studies a firm foundation by distinguishing its mode of knowledge (*Verstehen* – understanding) from that of the sciences (*Erklären* – explanation), stressed the psychological side of Schleiermacher's theory. Schleiermacher takes the likelihood of misunderstanding to be the starting point for hermeneutics: "strict practice assumes that misunderstanding results as a matter of course."[16] But Heidegger treats understanding not as an epistemological matter but as ontological, a form of being in the world. This strand has not contributed centrally to literary studies.[17] As Gadamer writes, "The purpose of my investigation is not to offer a general theory of interpretation and a differential account of its methods." "I did not wish to elaborate a system of rules to describe, let alone direct, the methodological procedures of the human sciences. Nor was it my aim to investigate the theoretical foundation of work in these fields in order to put my findings to practical ends." The focus is "not what we do or what we ought to do, but what happens to us over and above our wanting and doing."[18]

With the rise of Anglo-American New Criticism, whose revolutionary effect was to make the single poem the privileged object of study and make the goal of literary investigation the determination of the way in which its various parts contributed to the complex meaning of the whole, the question of what sorts of evidence should be privileged came to the fore, as object of often fierce debates, but the tradition of hermeneutics played no role here.

One famous exchange, in the early 1950s, between Cleanth Brooks, a leading New Critic, and Douglas Bush, a literary historian, about the interpretation of Andrew Marvell's "An Horatian Ode upon Cromwell's Return from Ireland," bears especially on how far historical information about the political attitudes of the man, Andrew Marvell, can be held to determine the meaning of the poem, whose attitude toward both Cromwell and the recently executed Charles I is subtle and difficult to grasp.[19]

Marvell wrote "An Horatian Ode Upon Cromwell's return from Ireland" after Oliver Cromwell, who had previously led the Parliament to victory in the English Civil War and brought about the execution of Charles I, had ruthlessly put down an Irish rebellion. For Bush, the issue is clear: we need to work out what the statements of the poem must have meant in their historical context and avoid importing our own prejudices as modern readers. Brooks, while conceding the interest of historical evidence, argues that interpreting the poem is not a matter determining the author's intention. Here's a problematical passage in the poem, a crux for their argument:

> And now the Irish are asham'd
> To see themselves in one Year tam'd:
> So much one Man can do,
> That does both act and know.
> They can affirm his Praises best,
> And have, though overcome confest
> How good he is, how just,
> And fit for highest trust.

Is this facetious, sardonic, ironic, or a serious claim about the Irish? Brooks argues that if the poem is any good, this passage must make sense dramatically. As a straightforward claim – that the defeated Irish confess how good he is, how just – it would be foolish, a blemish on the poem as a whole, which Brooks sees as a complex, balanced, portrait full of judicious but often double-edged praise of Cromwell. Brooks hears a grim irony here: the Irish who have been crushed confess (with a sword at their throat) how good and just he is.

Bush calls this a "desperate solution." Nothing in the wording carries "the faintest trace of irony; it is as straightforward a statement as we could have, however little we like it" (349). He is not worried about how it fits into the poem or whether it is a blemish: "we really must accept the unpalatable fact that Marvell wrote as an Englishman of 1650; and, in regard to what seems to us a strange assertion, we must say he is indulging in some wishful thinking – Cromwell is so great a conqueror that even the Irish must share English sentiment and accept the course of history" (349).[20]

Brooks insists that, considering the poem as a critic, one must focus on whether its elements contribute to an artistic unity – a matter that does not bother the literary historian: "If we unify the poem," Brooks writes, "by saying that it reflects the uncertainties and contradictions of a man who was uncertain and self-contradictory, and sometimes foolish ... then we may have a useful historical document but I am not sure that we have a poem" (356). While Bush focuses on what historical evidence can tell us about what Marvell thought at the time when he wrote the Ode, for Brooks this is a "coarse method" that will not tell us what the poem says because (1) even if we knew what Marvell the man thought of Cromwell at the moment he was writing the poem, the man is not the same as the poet (who is, for instance, composing a Horatian Ode); and (2) even if we knew what Marvell the poet intended to say in his poem, this would not prove that the poem actually said this. There is the problem of the role of the unconscious in the process of composition and the possibility of the poet's having written better than he knew. We must maintain the distinction between the total attitude as manifested in the poem and the attitude of the author as man and private citizen. We are trying to read the poem and thus appeal "to the full context of the poem itself," not to Marvell's mind. For Brooks, it is a problem of poetic organization not of biography or history.

Bush disputes what he calls "such an arbitrary doctrine of criticism" (341). He quarrels with Brooks' identification of ironies and ambiguities, casting himself as a historian for whom the text means what it says (given historical knowledge) and accuses Brooks of forcing the poem to fit the prejudices of a good modern liberal, for whom it goes without saying that a smart sensitive fellow like Marvell could not have admired "a crude, ruthless man of action like Cromwell, who must have been something like a Puritan Stalin" (342).[21]

This seems a situation – a quarrel about how to determine the meaning of a text – that calls for hermeneutic theory. A philological hermeneutics, focused on how to determine the true, original meaning of sacred texts or legal texts – how to overcome the distance that separates us from the language of those texts by construing their grammar and lexicon – might provide some instruction, but a philosophical hermeneutics focused on the structure of understanding offers little help. As Peter Szondi remarks, "the fact that a specifically literary hermeneutics scarcely exists today stems rather from the nature of the hermeneutics that actually does exist." "Hermeneutics was once exclusively a system of rules, while today it is exclusively a theory of understanding."[22] With the move from rules or procedures for the determination of meaning to reflection on the character of understanding it no longer seeks to provide instruction about how to interpret. Both Brooks and Bush, a Gadamerian might say, are performing acts of *Horizontverschmelzung*, a fusion of horizons, only the horizons of expectation with which they approach this text are different, involving different conceptions of a literary work's relation to a historical context.

The most fundamental contribution of Anglo-American New Criticism was not techniques of close reading, as is often supposed, but its success in establishing the presupposition that the standard by which any contribution to literary studies was to be judged was whether it enables us to produce new and superior interpretations of particular literary works, and that therefore the goal of literary studies is the production of interpretations of literary works. This is a major shift in the treatment of literature, which was previously subject to evaluation much more than interpretation. And criticism as a professional activity becomes dissociated from the reading of literature: readers find interest and pleasure in many aspects of literary works, but do not generally seek to generate interpretations.[23]

Szondi notes that the age of interpretation has inherited little from hermeneutics, except the notion of the hermeneutic circle, which often serves as an excuse for failure to reflect on the nature of one's evidence (why worry, if circularity cannot be avoided?).[24] In the era of interpretation most questions about interpretation are not so straightforward as in the quarrel between Bush and Brooks. As I mentioned, once literature is conceived as fundamentally expressive, the question of what literary works express can receive a variety of answers, which give rise to competing critical approaches or schools. In addition to New Critical readings, which aim to demonstrate the contribution of different aspects of the work to an "organic whole" dramatically embodying a complex attitude, Marxist, psychoanalytic, feminist, deconstructive, ecological readings all espouse different views of what sort of meanings should be teased out of works, what they are fundamentally about. (One might imagine an analogy to the target languages of four-fold interpretation of the Bible.) These are often presented as different "approaches" to a work, not mutually exclusive therefore, but still competing for the attention of critics and readers: a competition based on different views of what is most important both in the production of literature and in its place in our lives.[25] Many critical arguments in recent years bear on how far particular works of the past embody a critique of ideologies and social practices of the day and, if they do, how far such implications are a matter of subversion or of containment – the containment of subversive energies by channeling them into literature. Students of literature would be interested in arguments about why one method or orientation might be superior to others, which philosophical hermeneutics has not attempted to supply, or in arguments about how to determine whether an interpretation is a misreading. To sustain claims for the interpretation that they themselves are proposing, critics need to be able to argue that some interpretations, at least, are misreadings; otherwise, they feel vulnerable to the charge that in literary studies anything goes, and that one reading cannot be deemed superior to another. Again, twentieth-century philosophical hermeneutics has not offered much assistance here. Gadamer's *Truth and Method* seems to show no interest in the question of how to distinguish valid interpretations from invalid ones, if indeed it would recognize this distinction.

The most prominent hermeneutical venture into the realm of literary criticism is E. D. Hirsch's *Validity in Interpretation*, which at first sight seems to be an attempt to solve the problem of how to determine the validity of an interpretation and to adjudicate disputes such as the argument between Bush and Brooks. Hirsch is highly critical of the New Critical notion of the *intentional fallacy* – the notion that one does not determine the meaning of a text by consulting the author, by making the author's intention the standard for judgment. He argues that in fact the act of interpretation only makes sense if one assumes that a text has a meaning that one is trying to recover and that meaning is to be identified with the author's intended meaning. There must be something that interpreters could be right or wrong about, a meaning that is unchanging, otherwise chaos reigns. Hirsch distinguishes this original meaning, which is the object of *understanding*, and what he calls *signification*, the product of *interpretation*, what the text might signify for interpreters. Of course, many have criticized the attempt to make this distinction between meaning and signification, arguing that anything posited by a present-day interpreter as the original meaning is already a function of the interpreter's present situation, from which there is no escape (taking without knowing it a Gadamerian line: all understanding is interpretation). But the more important critique of Hirsch, as offered by David Hoy, for example, is that ultimately Hirsch's model does not provide guidance for interpretation: it can't be "cashed in" as Hoy puts it, because his authorial intention turns out to be the intention manifested in the text and not something that could be known independently and deployed as a standard for evaluating what one says about the text.[26] Hirsch writes that the author whose intention is the meaning of the text is "the speaking subject":

> The speaking subject is not, however, identical with the subjectivity of the author as an actual historical person ... The speaking subject may be defined as the final and most comprehensive level of awareness determinative of verbal meaning. In the case of a lie, the speaking subject assumes that he tells the truth, while the actual subject retains a private awareness of his deception.[27]

The historical person may have inner thoughts about the meaning of the text but "this level of awareness is as irrelevant as it is inaccessible." Ultimately, Hirsch's actual position is not so very different from Wimsatt's, whose notion of the intentional fallacy he had attacked, nor from that of Gadamer, whom he also criticizes (at least, not so different from the Gadamer who writes about Celan).[28] But for the most part, literary critics have assumed that Hirsch was directing them to try to discover what the historical author intended and make that the standard of validity, and they have resisted that directive, for the reasons that prevent Hirsch from actually insisting on the intention of the historical individual.

Resistance to identification of the meaning of the text with the intention of the author has been widespread in literary studies. The Dilthey-Gadamer tradition that makes understanding another person the model for understanding of a text made it unlikely that literary criticism would seek to learn from modern hermeneutics;

critics have preferred to draw upon evidence about the language of the text and various contexts, past and present, in which it might be situated. Two celebrated essays of the late 1960s, "The Death of the Author" (Barthes) and "What is an Author?" (Foucault), decline to treat the author of a work as the determiner of its meaning and stress that the author-figure is a cultural construction, different from the biographical individual – a construction serving ideological functions. For Barthes, Foucault, and French structuralism generally, meaning is generated by impersonal systems – linguistic, psychic, socio-historical – that work through individuals.

Their contemporary, the French philosopher Paul Ricoeur, argues that structuralism and hermeneutics are in principle complementary rather than opposed, although the hermeneutic tradition needs to be transformed so that it can enter into productive dialogue with modern disciplines concerned with the interpretation of texts. Exploring a range of topics central to literary studies, including metaphor, the symbol, narrative temporality, and Freudian interpretation, Ricoeur denounces the "ruinous distinction" between explanation sought in the natural sciences (*Erklären*) and understanding appropriate to the human and social sciences (*Verstehen*).[29] He maintains that there can be no structural analysis without hermeneutic comprehension, which provides the ground on which structural homologies can be discerned.[30] There is a dialectic of understanding and explanation.

In promoting a hermeneutics that might integrate structural analysis, Ricoeur set aside what he called the "hermeneutics of suspicion," which has been important in literary and cultural studies. The "three masters ... of the school of suspicion," Marx, Nietzsche, and Freud, offer mutually exclusive procedures of demystification in which the deficiencies of any thinker's self-understanding is the major target.[31] A range of modern disciplines and modes of thought – linguistics, psychoanalysis, Marxism, feminism, and various historicisms – provide evidence that people are opaque to themselves, not understanding their own motivation and the forces, linguistic, psychological, socio-political, that operate through them, so interpretation cannot remain satisfied with their own accounts of their intentions or commitments. Such criticism seeks explanation as much as understanding: to determine what are the factors that produced the text, made it the way it is, is to reveal its true significance. Susan Sontag's celebrated opposition to interpretation takes this mode as the norm: "The modern style of interpretation excavates, destroys, it digs 'behind' the text to find a sub-text which is the true one."[32]

Literary studies seldom speak of the hermeneutics of suspicion, because the term both implies that a psychological attitude lies behind interpretive method and suggests a unity where there is great diversity of concerns: feminist critics are suspicious in quite different ways from psychoanalytic, historicist, or ecological critics. But Rita Felski recommends Ricoeur's term as an antidote to the aura of the popular term *critique*, whose smug authority it helps to demystify.[33]

The one strand of interpretive criticism explicitly related to philosophical hermeneutics is the so-called aesthetics of reception. Hans Robert Jauss, in particular, made a method of criticism out of hermeneutical theory – specifically, what Gadamer calls *wirkungsgeschichtliches Bewusstsein* ("historically-effected consciousness," or "consciousness exposed to the effects of history") – attempting to describe, for any given work, the horizon of expectation within which it was created and the subsequent history of its reception. For Jauss, the work does not have an inherent meaning but functions as an answer to questions posed by the horizon of expectations, which can be reconstructed, but which also changes through time as a work is received and as the literary context and assumptions about genres change. Jauss's program for interpretation through the analysis of reception is ambitious, including not only the study of the history of responses to a particular work and the reconstruction of the horizon of expectations responsible for those responses, but also the investigation of how the interaction of expectations and innovatory works leads to changes in literary canons and aesthetic norms. But despite disclaimers, his formulations frequently suggest that the reason for undertaking the reconstruction of horizons is to discover the original meaning of a particular work and thus to provide a historically authorized interpretation. For example, his work on Goethe's *Iphigenie* seems largely aimed at showing that it was a truly original and interesting play: "As an implicit answer and thus above all as a moment of the social process, the meaning of Racine's or Goethe's *Iphigenie* can be ascertained only from the receptive consciousness of their time through objectively verifiable stages of reflection."[34]

A much more elaborate analysis of one of Baudelaire's *Spleen* poems illustrates what he takes to be the different levels or processes of aesthetic understanding and interpretation: first, an initial reading, focused on the reader's step-by-step aesthetic experience of the text; then a retrospective interpretation, transforming the modern reader's initial experience into a totalizing interpretation; and finally the reconstruction of the historico-literary context in which the poem appeared and exploration of the history of the reception of the poem that situates and refines the interpretation just produced.[35] Jauss thus seeks to integrate a wide range of historico-literary research on the work's relation to varying horizons of expectations with an emphasis on the role of the reader in concretizing meanings. It is a method that seeks to include many of the different sorts of activities in which critics have engaged, declining to choose between the meaning of the work for its original audience and the aesthetic experience of readers today, but the stress on the activity of the reader comes at a price of positing "the reader" and thereby assuming more unanimity among readers of a given moment than could be documented.

Modern philosophical hermeneutics, with its focus on the nature of understanding, might seem to have a greater affinity with poetics than with an interpretive literary criticism, since poetics is interested in the conditions of possibility of literary works and their intelligibility. But most projects in poetics seem rather foreign to the concerns manifest in, say, *Truth and Method*. For instance, narratology is concerned with how to describe narrative, and the variety of narrative techniques, what sort of model of author-narrator-focalizer-narratee-reader is most appropriate (Should we posit a narrator for every narrative? Does a single narrative imply more than one narrative audience? How does focalization work?). In the study of poetry there are major issues involving prosody: appropriate models for meter, the relation between rhythm and meter, the relations between prosody and meaning, and questions about how to conceive of the "speaker" which poems often induce us to posit. Such investigations may enable interpretations but they are above all attempts to comprehend how understanding takes place in particular domains. In short, what literary studies require is not reflection on the nature of understanding in general but work on the ways in which particular literary forms or genres function and are understood. Although Herder and Schleiermacher inaugurated modern hermeneutics in proposing a general hermeneutics in place of the special hermeneutics focused on particular sorts of discourse, perhaps literary studies would be better served by a special hermeneutics, or a dialectic of hermeneutics and poetics.

NOTES

1 Hans-Georg Gadamer, *Truth and Method*, trans. Joel Weinsheimer and Donald Marshall (New York: Continuum, 2004), 35.
2 Roland Barthes, *Critique et vérité* (Paris: Seuil, 1966), 62–3.
3 In Barthes's most explicit attempt at a poetics of literature, he insists that he will describe the codes responsible for the intelligibility of Balzac's novella "Sarrasine," not produce an interpretation; but he nonetheless concludes that "*Sarrasine* represents the disturbance of representation." *S/Z* (Paris: Seuil, 1970), 222.
4 Robert Lamberton, *Homer the Theologian: Neoplatonist Allegorical Reading and the Growth of the Epic Tradition* (Berkeley: University of California Press, 1989), 120. He continues: "If we think of Aristotle's *Poetics*, Horace's *Ars Poetica*, Longinus's *On the Sublime* as the seminal works of ancient literary criticism, it is primarily because of their vast influence. The interpretive tradition in ancient criticism has

not fared as well, and today is largely lost or ignored." For the text, see Porphyry, *On the Cave of the Nymphs*, trans. Robert Lamberton (Barrytown: Station Hill Press, 1983).

5 See *Medieval Literary Theory and Criticism: The Commentary Tradition*, ed. A. J. Minnis and A. B. Scott (Oxford: Oxford University Press, 1988).

6 Saint Augustine, *On Christian Doctrine*, trans. D. W. Robertson (Indianapolis: Bobbs Merrill, 1980), 75.

7 Quoted in E. R. Dronke, *Fabula: Explorations into the Uses of Myth in Medieval Platonism* (Leiden and Köln: Brill, 1974), 26. For a succinct discussion of such practices, see Peter Szondi, *Introduction to Literary Hermeneutics*, trans. Martha Woodmansee (Cambridge: Cambridge University Press, 1995), 5–13.

8 Dante Aligheri, *Il Convivio*, book 2, chap. 1. https://digitaldante.columbia.edu/library/dantes-works/the-convivio/book-02/.

9 John of Salisbury, *Metalogicon*, I.24, quoted in *The Cambridge History of Literary Criticism*, vol. 2, ed. Alistair Minnis and Ian Johnson (Cambridge: Cambridge University Press, 2005), 23.

10 "The Author's Apology for Heroic Poetry and Poetic Licence," *Essays of John Dryden*, ed. W. P. Kerr (Oxford: Clarendon Press, 1926), vol. 1, 179.

11 Samuel Johnson, Rambler # 90. www.johnsonessays.com/the-rambler/english-poetry-adjusted/.

12 Johann Gottfried Herder, *Shakespeare*, trans. Gregory Moore (Princeton: Princeton University Press, 2008), 2.

13 Andrew Bowie writes, "It is only at the historical moment when the changes in the understanding of language ... first emerge that such a conception of art and literature becomes possible and that the hermeneutic imperative begins to play a central role in philosophy and art." *From Romanticism to Critical Theory: The Philosophy of German Literary Theory* (London: Routledge, 1997), 89.

14 But Michael Forster maintains that "almost everything that is distinctive and important in Schleiermacher's hermeneutics had in fact already been developed before him by Herder." *After Herder* (Oxford: Oxford University Press, 2010), 137.

15 Friedrich Schleiermacher, *Hermeneutics and Criticism and Other Writings*, ed. Andrew Bowie (Cambridge: Cambridge University Press, 1998), 94. As Szondi and others have noted, the term *psychological* has

led to a misunderstanding of Schleiermacher's hermeneutics, which relies on public evidence to formulate hypotheses about authorial intention.
16 Schleiermacher, *Hermeneutics and Criticism*, 22.
17 "Hermeneutics remains a path not taken in Anglo-American literary theory," notes Rita Felski. "The tradition of hermeneutical thinking is rarely acknowledged (how often do you see Gadamer or Ricoeur taught in a theory survey?), let alone addressed, assimilated, or argued over." "Critique and the Hermeneutics of Suspicion," *M/C Journal* 15:1 (2012). http://journal.media-culture.org.au/index.php/mcjournal/article/view/431. Gerald Bruns agrees: "Hermeneutics is not obviously compatible with a university career in literary studies. In literary studies we learn mainly new ways to approach old texts, and Schleiermacher is never thought of." *Hermeneutics Ancient and Modern* (New Haven: Yale University Press, 1992), ix–x.
18 Gadamer, *Truth and Method*, xxviii, xxv–xxvi.
19 Cleanth Brooks, "Literary Criticism," *English Institute Essays* (New York: Columbia University Press, 1946), 127–58; Douglas Bush, "Marvell's Horatian Ode," *Sewanee Review* 60 (1952): 363–76; Cleanth Brooks, "A Note on the Limits of 'History' and the Limits of 'Criticism,'" *Sewanee Review* 61 (1953): 129–35. The exchange is collected in *Seventeenth Century English Poetry: Modern Essays in Criticism*, ed. W. R. Keast (Oxford: Oxford University Press, 1962). References to this edition are given in the text.
20 Bush's dubious paraphrase, "accept the course of history," rather different from "confess how good he is, how just," shows he does feel the incongruity of the poem's actual words.
21 Brooks replies, "The title *liberal* alas, is one that I am scarcely entitled to claim. I am more often called a reactionary, and I have been called a proto-fascist" (354). Bush's incorrect inference from Brooks's text to the supposedly liberal opinions of its historical author, Cleanth Brooks, suggests that one cannot presume continuity between what a text says and what the historical individual believes.
22 Szondi, *Introduction*, 1–2.
23 Some readers are especially interested in characters and become very invested in them; others above all follow the plot and do not try to put together a rich conception of the characters; both sorts of readers

perhaps skip paragraphs of description; whereas other readers may be especially interested in the evocations of another time and place. Roland Barthes offers a rather casual typology of readers – fetishist, obsessional, paranoiac, and hysterical – that works as a reminder that non-professional readers have very different sorts of investments in literary works. *Le Plaisir du texte* (Paris: Seuil, 1973), 99–100. And elsewhere he distinguishes five ways of reading: *en piqué*, spearing, picking out flavorful phrases here and there; *en prisé*, savoring, taking in fully a particular development; *en déroulé*, proceeding swiftly and evenly; *en rase-mottes*, nose-to-the ground, taking in every word; and *en plein ciel*, taking overviews, seeing the text in a wider context. *Sollers écrivain* (Paris: Seuil, 1979), 75–6. The point is that actual readers of literature proceed in various different ways and that the concern for totality and the hermeneutic integration of as many aspects of the work as possible into an interpretation is not especially common outside of professional circles.

24 Szondi, *Introduction*, 6.
25 It is worth emphasizing that interpreting literature takes many different forms: with a poem by Paul Celan, one struggles to produce a plausible paraphrase. Interpreting a play or a novel may involve, rather, identifying a major theme, relating it to the author's other works, treating it as a statement about its era, or articulating what we find particularly stimulating in it today.
26 David Hoy, *The Critical Circle: Literature, History, and Philosophical Hermeneutics* (Berkeley: University of California Press, 1978), 32. This is even clearer in a well-known polemic by Steven Knapp and Walter Benn Michaels, which argues that meaning simply is what the author intends, and any other conception of meaning is unintelligible. They explicitly claim that this has no consequences, since it entails nothing about how to discover this meaning – just that when you make a claim about the meaning of a text you are by definition referring to what the author intended. "Against Theory," *Critical Inquiry* 8 (1982): 723–42.
27 E. D. Hirsch, *Validity in Interpretation* (New Haven: Yale University Press, 1967), 243–4.
28 Discussing Celan, Gadamer takes a surprisingly anti-intentionalist position: "But is it necessary to have knowledge of what the poet himself thought about a poem? All that matters is what the poem

actually says, not what its author intended and perhaps did not know how to say. Of course a hint from the author regarding the raw material of his subject 'matter' can be useful even for a perfectly self contained poem, and can guard against misunderstanding. But such hints remain a dangerous crutch." *Gadamer on Celan: 'Who Am I and Who Are You?' and Other Essays,* trans. Richard Heinemann and Bruce Krajewski (Albany: SUNY Press, 1997), 68. Elsewhere he writes, "The text which is written down is accessible, in its full meaning, across space and time, to everyone who knows the script and language." "The Eminent Text and its Truth," *Bulletin of the Midwest Modern Language Association* 13 (1980): 4.

29 Paul Ricoeur, *From Text to Action,* trans. Kathleen Blamey and John Thompson (Evanston: Northwestern University Press, 1991), 53.
30 See Paul Ricoeur, "Stucture et herméneutique," in *Le Conflict des interprétations* (Paris: Seuil, 1969), 33–4, 57–9, 63.
31 Paul Ricoeur, *Freud and Philosophy: An Essay on Interpretation* (New Haven: Yale University Press, 1970), 32–4.
32 Susan Sontag, *Against Interpretation* (New York: Dell, 1966), 6.
33 Felski, "Critique and the Hermeneutics of Suspicion."
34 Hans Robert Jauss, "De l'Iphigénie de Racine à celle de Goethe," in *Pour une esthétique de la réception* (Paris: Gallimard, 1978), 249.
35 Hans Robert Jauss, "The Poetic Text within the Change of Horizons of Reading: The Example of Baudelaire's 'Spleen II,'" *Toward an Aesthetic of Reception,* trans. Timothy Bahti (Minneapolis: University of Minnesota Press, 1982), 139–88.

14 Hermeneutics and Law
Ralf Poscher

Hans-Georg Gadamer thought that hermeneutics in general had something to learn from legal hermeneutics.[1] This claim is highly plausible because today at any rate there is hardly another field of hermeneutics of comparable social importance, with a similar institutionalized practice or a similar number of people professionally involved. It is no surprise that something can be learned from the most professionalized hermeneutical practice that impacts and shapes almost every aspect of our social lives. I disagree with Gadamer not that something can be learned, but what can be learned.

In a nutshell, Gadamer thought that what can be learned from the law is that an application element must be integrated into the concept of interpretation.[2] For Gadamer, hermeneutics is a monistic practice consisting of interpretation, which has some application element incorporated into it. Contrary to this monistic account, what can be learned from law is that hermeneutics is a set of distinct practices that are of variable relevance for different hermeneutical situations. All of these distinct hermeneutical practices involve distinct theoretical issues, most of which can be linked to particular debates in analytic philosophy. This also holds true for Gadamer's application element. On the one hand, Gadamer's achievement is to have highlighted this as an important element, not just of legal hermeneutics. On the other hand – as Emilio Betti has already rightly noted[3] – his account of application is highly equivocal. If my count is correct, it confounds at least four theoretically distinct aspects.

In the following, I wish to show that legal hermeneutics has always been acutely aware of the complexity of hermeneutical practices and that most of the relevant distinctions are deeply rooted not just in the legal methodological but also in the doctrinal and even institutional tradition. Very much in the spirit of Gadamer, the chapter will proceed in accordance with the different hermeneutical activities on which a lawyer must rely when she applies the law to a given case. Thus, it will show that legal interpretation, rule-following, legal construction, association, the exercise of discretion, and judgments on the significance of a legal provision are all distinct activities that can be involved. To prove the point that this complex conception of hermeneutics is not specific to the law, but applies to hermeneutics in general, some parallels in the field of the hermeneutics of art shall be noted.

LEGAL INTERPRETATION: AN INTENTIONALIST ACCOUNT

The most basic operation when a lawyer approaches a case is to identify the legal norm applicable. The norm is usually communicated by a text – be it the text of a precedent or a statute, an act of parliament, a constitution, or an administrative directive or bylaw. So the first thing a lawyer must do is to find the text of the precedent or code relevant to her case and use it to identify the legal norm. For example, Art. 5 par. 3 of the German constitution simply reads: "Art and science [...] are free." How does the lawyer, dealing with a police prohibition against a staging of *Macbeth*, on the ground that it is regarded as a critique of the president, get from the text of Art. 5 par. 3 to the legal norm that the state must refrain from infringing on the exercise of art? Semantically, the text does not even state a norm, but a fact!

The basic hermeneutical operation allowing an interpreter to glean the meaning from a set of signs can be explained by an intentional account along the lines of Grice and Davidson.[4] There seems no alternative to basing meaning in a fundamental sense on communicative intentions. No non-natural meaning can exist without at least presupposing communicative intentions. The famous lines drawn in the sand by the waves[5] that resemble letters have no meaning. We can assign meaning to them only by presupposing some kind of hypothetical speaker.[6] If the waves form the signs "I love you," we might suppose a mundane context like a couple on a romantic walk and one of them stating her or his affection.

Unlike natural signs, which acquire their "meaning" from non-intentional causal relations between an object and its environment, non-natural signs acquire their meaning through the intentions that a speaker or author connects with an utterance. Like smoke, shouting the English word "fire" also signals fire. But it does so, not because of the causal relation between the shout and the fire, but because of the intentions of the person shouting. Thus, meaningful utterances are a special kind of intentional action. They intend to communicate propositional content via utterances – be they sounds or signs, or any other kind of communicative means.[7]

This is not to say that intentionalism leaves nothing to be explained. As a mentalist theory of meaning, intentionalism explains meaning via mental representations in the form of communicative intentions, and thus, still needs to be supplemented with a theory of mental content.[8] However, there seems to be no way around the intentionalist account of meaning.[9] However a theory of mental content might approach its subject, it must be able to give a viable account of intentions in general, and communicative intentions in particular, to fulfill its explanatory task. Communicative intentions are the kind of mental content that make utterances meaningful.

This also means that any attribution of meaning to an artifact for theoretical reasons requires the attribution of intentions, since this is the only way meaning comes into the world. These intentions do not have to be actual intentions, but we cannot make sense of an artifact having meaning, without at least implicitly presupposing an intentional agent – even if it be fictive or hypothetical.[10]

The same is true of legal texts. Legal methods have always been acutely aware of the fundamental importance of intentions. *Legislative intent* figures in every classical canon of legal interpretation – even if its role is contested.[11] The text "Art and science [...] are free" in Art. 5 par. 3 of the German constitution only has the meaning it has because we attribute to those who ratified it the intention to communicate a legal *norm* and not just a fact.

That the ascription of intentions to collective bodies like parliaments and constitutional assemblies raises issues of collective intentionality shows only two things: First, that we cannot let go of communicative intentions even if it is hard to make sense of collective ones. Second, that legal hermeneutics needs to combine a wide range of theoretical resources. In this case, it draws on the theory of action, where it can make use of reductive accounts of collective intentions to reconstruct our pervasive talk of legislative intent also with respect to group agents like parliaments and constitutional assemblies.[12]

Legal texts receive their meaning from the legislative communicative intentions that gave rise to them. Thence it is easy to explain the nature of interpretation in its most basic form: Interpretation is a special case of empirical explanation. Interpretation is a form of explanation that relates to intentional phenomena, i.e., to someone's beliefs, desires, intentions, hopes, wishes, actions, etc., and secondary to their products, such as tools and – most prominently in the hermeneutical tradition – texts. If we see someone picking up an umbrella, we explain his action by his belief that it is going to rain, his desire not to get wet and his intention to go outside; we, thus, interpret his action.

However, interpretation is not limited to actions; it applies to any object connected to intentions. To take Heidegger's famous example,[13] we interpret a piece of wood connected to a metal bar as a hammer, because someone created it with the intention of fulfilling this purpose. Moreover, if we believe in the objective spirit steering the course of history, we can interpret the course of history, because we conceive of the objective spirit as an intentional agent.

As mental phenomena, intentional phenomena supervene on non-intentional phenomena like neurophysiological brain states and, ultimately, the interplay of sub-nuclear particles. There is a token- but no type-identity between the different phenomena. The same higher order type can be realized by very different lower order ones. Very different types of neurophysiological brain states can instantiate the same type of mental content. Different kinds of explanation draw on different regularities for types at their respective levels of description. The explanations at different levels of description are not reducible to each other due to the lack of type identity. Thus, psychological regularities do not translate into neurophysiological ones, though each psychological phenomenon is instantiated by a neurophysiological token.

An anomalous monism along Davidson's lines allows for different methods[14] for different kinds of causal explanations under different descriptions. Frank Jackson and Philip Pettit framed this in a program theory, according to which higher-order explanations reveal to which type of event some state of affairs is programmed, irrespective of the different microphysical types that might realize the supervening type.[15] However, interpretations as intentional explanations do not just differ from non-intentional ones in terms of the level of explanation – such as biological explanations from physics – but also in terms of the standards involved.[16] Interpretation has been characterized as a normalizing type of explanation because it relies on rational standards[17] like the principle of charity, according to which we must generally interpret the beliefs of an agent charitably with respect to their truth.[18] When we interpret other intentional beings, we – except under special circumstances – rely on the rationality of the agent. Without presupposing a certain degree of rationality, it would be impossible for us to reconstruct the intentions of agents other than ourselves.

Interpretation as an intentional explanation is distinct from other causal explanations because of the standards employed, which are based on rationality.[19] Thus, a non-intentional causal reconstruction of intentions would not count as an interpretation. If we had a mind-reading machine somehow able to reconstruct the intentional content of a speaker's mind from mere natural causes, such as her brainwaves, the results would not be an *interpretation* of the mind it monitors.

Despite the different standards employed, intentional explanations nonetheless remain empirical. It is always an empirical question whether or not someone acted with a specific intention. It is an empirical question whether she picked up the umbrella to use it as a protection against the rain or to take it to the repair shop or wrap it as a gift. What holds for intentions connected to actions also holds for communicative intentions, which are simply intentions connected to a special type of action, namely speech acts.

From an intentional perspective, the interpretation of an utterance in its basic sense is an empirical hypothesis on the communicative intentions that the utterer connected with it. Whether the utterer meant the river- or the savings-bank when she asked him to meet her at the "bank" is an empirical question.

The communicative interpretation of speech acts aims at speaker's meaning in Grice's sense. In communicative interpretation, semantic meaning – sentence meaning in Grice's terms – acts as the main clue to infer the communicative intentions of the speaker. Semantic meaning itself supervenes on the diachronic and synchronic multitude of uses of a term to convey specific meanings. It makes it possible to infer that speakers in general use terms according to their semantic meaning. However, semantic meaning alone might not give us sufficient clues, as in the "bank"-example above. Speakers might not comply with the standard use of terms – consider Davidson's malapropisms – or might employ them to communicate a different intention – consider Gricean implicatures or metaphorical use. Ever since Carl Friedrich von Savigny introduced his canons of interpretation, the semantic ("grammatical"[20]) meaning of the law is among the legal canons for deciphering the intentions of the legislator.

An intentional account of interpretation does not raise issues other than those that must be answered by empirical investigations in general. "The communicative model thus causes no ripples in the smooth waters of science."[21] Intentionalism not only provides us with a basic concept of meaning but also with a basic concept of interpretation that holds no mystery. Intentionalism can provide a precise definition of interpretation as the basic hermeneutical operation with respect to the *genus proximum* of empirical explanation.

This also holds for the law. The first step in legal hermeneutics is to develop – in a fundamental theoretical sense – an empirical hypothesis on the communicative intentions that the legislator connected with a legal text. In the case of the lawyer confronted with the text of Art. 5 par. 3 of the German constitution, semantics gives us the factual statement, that "Art and science [...] are free." The context of the utterance, however, supports the empirical hypothesis that the constitutional assembly intended to communicate the normative principle that "The state shall not infringe upon the exercise of art."

In the arts, communicative interpretation in this intentionalist sense is mirrored by a corresponding approach that stresses authorial intent.[22] This approach is contested, and its limitations are the topic of such literary theories as New Criticism[23] and poststructuralists such as Roland Barthes celebrated the "Death of the Author" (1967). However, the fact that the author's intentions might be difficult to ascertain, that literary hermeneutics go beyond the author's intentions, that perhaps even the most important parts of literary hermeneutics do not rely on them, does not render them irrelevant. In art too the question of what the author intended remains a sensible one allowing for sensible answers. That Picasso wished to communicate the horrors of civil war with "Guernica" seems a legitimate hermeneutical thesis, although it does not exhaust the hermeneutical potential of the canvas. That the reconstruction of authorial intentions does not exhaust hermeneutics, however, is exactly the point of a complex conception. Hermeneutics involve a whole set of practices, but communicative interpretation is one of them – and even a foundational one in the theoretical sense that interpretation presupposes the ascription of non-natural meaning to an utterance by an – actual or presupposed fictive – author.

RULE-FOLLOWING AND THE APPLICATION OF THE LAW

After a communicative interpretation of Art. 5 par. 3 of the German Constitution our lawyer knows that the text "Art is free" was written and promulgated with the intention of communicating the constitutional norm that the state shall not infringe upon the exercise of art. What is the next step? After identifying the norm communicated by the text, she must apply it to her case. This is the first kind of application that Gadamer hinted at with his equivocal notion.

The theoretical background to how to reconstruct what happens when we apply a norm to a case covered by it is the subject of the extended rule-following discussion spurred by Wittgenstein's remarks on the topic and Saul Kripke's[24] skeptical interpretation of them. Wittgenstein rightly pointed out that no kind of interpretation in the sense of substituting one rule formulation with another can ever close the gap between a rule and its application. The effort to close the "gap" between the rule and its application by paraphrasing the rule will just lead to an endless and fruitless series of interpretations. In intentionalist terms: no interpretative reformulation of the communicative intentions can close the gap between the norm communicated and its application. "What this shows, is that there is a way of grasping a rule which is *not an interpretation*, but which is exhibited in what we call 'obeying the rule' and 'going against it' in actual cases."[25] Thus, a faculty other than inferring the intentions of others is needed to apply a rule, and this seems to be the best conception of rule-following: a shared fundamental human faculty.[26]

Understanding a rule is a complex faculty that among other things consists of the ability to paraphrase expressions of the rule. However, understanding a rule above all entails the faculty to apply it in standard cases in various intertwined practices, which include judging others according to rules, as in the case of a court judging the behavior of defendants and parties according to the law. A faculty-based understanding of our rule-following practice resembles Kant's analysis of the faculty of judgment:

> If the understanding in general is explained as the faculty of rules, then the power of judgement is the faculty of subsuming under rules [...] Now if it [logic] wanted to show generally how

> one ought to subsume under these rules, i.e., distinguish whether something stands under them or not, this could not happen except once again through a rule [...] and so it becomes clear that although the understanding is certainly capable of being instructed and equipped through rules, the power of judgement is a special talent that cannot be taught but only be practiced.[27]

So one might speak of a gap between a rule and its application, but there is no gap between *understanding* a rule and knowing how to apply it in standard cases, because being able to apply it to standard cases is precisely what understanding in Kant's and Wittgenstein's sense most importantly entails.

Applying the rule established via communicative interpretation as the content of an utterance demands the use of our faculty of following it. By obeying the rule in a given case, the faculty of following the rule is exercised. Just as abilities are exercised under given circumstances: as a swimmer exercises the ability to swim on various occasions – in a lake on a hot summer day, in a pool for a workout, etc. – or as a jockey exercises the capacity to ride on different horses in different races.

In contemporary pragmatism, the relation between a rule and its application is sometimes reversed even more radically. Rules are regarded merely as the attempt to make our practice in standard cases explicit. Applications do not follow from rules, but rules supervene on applications.[28] This would also explain why we sometimes fail to come up with a rule that covers all of our practice in individual cases, as the Gettier-problems seem to illustrate for the concept of knowledge. Just as Wittgenstein remarked: "A main source of our failure to understand is that we do not command a clear view of the use of our words. – Our grammar is lacking in this sort of perspicuity."[29]

However we conceptualize the relation between understanding a rule and its application – as a grammatical relation in Wittgenstein's sense or as an attempt to make our practice explicit in Brandom's sense – the relation between a rule and its application addresses a different issue than the inference of communicative intentions from an utterance. While the meaning of an utterance is determined by inferring the communicative intentions connected with it, the applications of the rule thus communicated are not extracted from the rule via interpretation or any other inferential means. The rule that is the content of the communicative intention does not "contain" its applications just as the ability to swim does not "contain" a swim in a specific lake.

Communicative interpretation and rule-following are all that is needed in so-called easy cases. Thus the politically motivated police prohibition of the *Macbeth* performance is an easy case of a violation of Art. 5 par. 3 of the German constitution. After the lawyer reconstructed the law-maker's intentions to establish the rule that government infringements on art are prohibited, she must simply employ her rule-following capacity to apply the rule to her case. A theatrical performance is a paradigm instance of art and the prohibition of the show is a paradigm instance of a state infringement. If the lawyer "understands" the rule, she can apply it to the case. In German, there is even a term for the rule-following faculty in legal contexts. The term "Judiz" refers to the ability of an experienced lawyer to deliver a correct judgment on a case intuitively. Note, however, that even in an easy case the application of the law requires two operations: the inference of communicative intentions from a text and the exercise of our rule-following ability.[30]

At least in the performing arts, there are elements of rule applications as well. "Interpreting" a piece of music involves rule-following in conforming to the instructions given in the form of musical notation. If the first movement is to be played *adagio*, it must be slower than the second in *presto*.

LEGAL CONSTRUCTION, THE HERMENEUTICAL CREATION OF LAW

If one were to look at our overall legal practice, quantitatively, easy cases make up almost the totality. Of the billions of contracts concluded any given year only an infinitesimally small number will be brought to the attention of professional lawyers and of these only a small fraction are not easy cases, in which the lawyers are only needed to enforce the payment of a price, a mortgage, or an eviction. However, despite their infinitesimally small quantitative importance, cases in which communicative interpretation and rule-following are insufficient to apply the law are central to law as a professional practice. This is especially true of so-called hard cases in which the further methodic resources do not allow for a determinate legal answer.[31] Hard cases are those on which our higher courts decide, that are published in law reports, and that are as H. L. A. Hart rightly observed "the daily diet of the law school."[32]

Cases can be hard for several reasons. It might be impossible to decipher the communicative intentions of the legislator for epistemic reasons. This might be due to the semantic or syntactical indeterminacies caused by ambiguity, polysemy, multidimensionality, standard relativity, or vagueness; or due to the pragmatic context of the legislative process that conflicts with an otherwise determinate text. Often, though the text of each of the relevant legal provisions for a case is determinate, their relation might not be clear when they point in different directions. Even then, the application of the law may be merely more complicated but still easy since there are a number of priority rules such as the hierarchal ordering of statutes and constitutions, or the *lex-posterior-* or *lex-specialis-*rule. However, if that is not the case, there might be what could be called systematic indeterminacy of the law. The communicative meaning of a specific provision might have to give way to a legal meaning emerging from the resolution of the systematic conflict. In yet other cases, the application of the communicated legal rule does not conflict with other legal norms, but with further intentions of the legislator, with expediencies of rationality or justice. How these cases are to be handled – whether and under what circumstances we can make use of teleological reductions, the absurdity rule, or even Radbruch's famous formula – is highly contested and can thus render them hard. Last but not least, indeterminacy concerns cases that pertain to constellations that were unforeseen or even unforeseeable by the legislator.

Gadamer captured the latter aspect in his idea of the different horizons between the production of a text and its application.[33] In the distance between the two horizons – to continue in the metaphor – cases may arise that leave us uncertain as to whether they fall under a rule or not. Does the answer of an internet search engine to the query "best contemporary politician" fall under the protection of the First Amendment of the US Constitution? When the framers were contemplating free speech, nothing like a computer let alone the internet could even be imagined. It is fair to assume that they would be at least as baffled as we are when confronted with the case: the resulting indeterminacy is not only epistemic. In all cases of indeterminacy, lawyers must have recourse to yet another activity to apply the law to a given case – namely legal construction.

Since the first modern reflections on legal hermeneutics, legal scholars have been aware of the distinction between legal interpretation and legal construction. Savigny distinguished between legal interpretation and "Fortbildung des Rechts," i.e., the doctrinal development of the law, in his early lectures on methodology in 1809.[34] Three years before Savigny published his methodological teachings in 1840,[35] Francis Lieber published his seminal essay "On Political Hermeneutics, or on Political Interpretation and Construction,"[36] in which he distinguished between legal interpretation and construction. Ever since, the distinction has remained a lively topic in the methodological debate in law.[37]

Legal construction amends the law that is indeterminate for the case at hand by a rule that covers it such that it can be applied by mere rule-following. This distinguishes legal construction from legal interpretation. Legal construction creates new law. It is not an empirical but a normative enterprise.

What still makes it an interpretative activity is that its justification must follow the structure of communicative interpretation.

The courts cannot simply amend the law by a rule of their choosing, like a legislator solely following his or her conviction of political rationality. Courts must justify it as an intention that a – fictive – rational legislator could have connected with the text. This places semantic restrictions on legal construction since a rational legislator would not have associated an intention with the text that could not be connected with it by an interpreter. Semantic meaning plays a guiding role in legal interpretation but a limiting role in legal construction. Beyond the requirement to establish a justification that can relate to the text, the details of the justificatory standards for legal construction are specific to a legal culture and can even vary for different areas of the law. The need to maintain an interpretative relation with a text, however, distinguishes legal construction from legislation, though both serve to create new law.[38]

Legal construction is not merely reconstructive but allows for creativity and choice. The results of a search engine can either be included in or excluded from the free speech protection of the German constitution or the First Amendment. They could be brought into connection with the text of both provisions. A rational legislator might have intended to protect the creators of algorithms that produce opinionated content and might have connected this intention with the broad formulations of the free speech protections.

Via legal construction, the law is adapted to the developing exigencies of its time. Legal construction thus relates to another aspect of Gadamer's concept of application and probably that which caught his attention when he looked at the law. Legal construction bridges the horizon of the past legislator to that of the present-day court that has to apply the law to new circumstances.

In the legal literature, this is classically framed by the expression that the text of the law can be smarter than the legislator.[39] This is bolder than Kant's original remark on his interpretation of Plato that we often "understand an author better than he has understood himself"[40] since the former hides the agency of the interpreter behind the personification of the text transforming it into a rational, intentional subject.

In the interpretation of art, construction works in a similar way. Robert Stecker provides a nice example in his book on interpretation and construction in the hermeneutics of art. It is famously disputed whether Jean-Antoine Watteau's painting "The Embarkation for Cythera" shows people arriving at or leaving the island of Venus's birth. Watteau purposely left the answer open. Irrespective of whether the difficulty is merely epistemic, i.e., Watteau had a communicative intention but did not disclose it, or whether he did not specify his intention on this point, someone who wants to give an interpretation of the painting that pertains to the point cannot rely on the intentions of the artist. He must construct the scene as either depicting an arrival or a departure and, thus, implicitly presuppose an intentional subject who painted the scene with either this or that intention. Radical constructivists – as Stecker calls them – claim that every interpretation of art is a construction of the interpreter, moderate constructivists merely allow for constructions to legitimately supplement or substitute interpretations that rely on the communicative intentions of the artist.[41] Be that as it may, my point is simply to show that the distinction between communicative interpretation and construction applies equally to the hermeneutics of art.

There is, however, one striking dissimilarity between construction in the hermeneutics of law and of art. In law construction is mandatory, since every case brought before the courts has to be decided. That holds also for those for which there are no intentions of the legislator to be had. In these cases, abstaining from construction would amount to a denial of justice. In art, whether it seems worth engaging in construction is up to the beholder. Watteau's painting can be just as well enjoyed without it.

ASSOCIATION AND THE CONTEXTS OF DISCOVERY AND JUSTIFICATION

In its relation to the text, construction is distinct from association. In the case of an association, the object offers only an opportunity for the production of meaning on the part of the person perceiving it. There is only a causal relation between the object and the association.

While the object triggers the association, it is not conceptualized as representing the association, or even as containing any meaning at all. The famous madeleine may trigger childhood associations, but these associations can be explained without ascribing these meanings to the madeleine. The madeleine causes the childhood associations, but it does not intend to do so. The same is true of a song that a mother frequently sang to her child. The song does not need to be about childhood to trigger childhood associations.

For an interpretational justification, a merely associative relation is not sufficient. Rather, the justification of an interpretational relation must pertain to a meaning of the text that structurally predates the act of interpretation. In contrast to association, in interpretation the text is not only the trigger but also the measure of the meaning connected with it. It is not enough for a text to cause an idea in the mind of the recipient; the meaning connected with the text must also be intended by its actual or implicit fictive author. In law, association might come into play in what is called the context of discovery.[42] All kinds of associations can come into play when confronted with the task of applying the law to a hard case. In the search engine case, the kind of query in question might remind the lawyer of a great politician in history and his way of dealing with difficult questions. This might spark an idea of how the free speech guarantee may be best adapted to the digital age. For reasons of legitimacy, however, association does not figure in the context of hermeneutical justification of legal decisions. Legal decisions rely on the legitimacy of their source. Thus, their legitimation must be traced back to the source of the law to be applied – be it an actual, fictive or in former times usually divine legislator. By contrast, the content of an association is not intentionally tied to its source, but springs from the associating subject.

In art, however, association is much more often at the center of its reception – beauty is in the eye of the beholder. More often than not, artists create their works with the specific purpose of creating objects of association, which involve the spectator much more than the intentions of the artist. It is this non-interpretative component of hermeneutics in particular that makes the reception of art a much more personal and subjective experience.

EXERCISE OF DISCRETION AND THE GENERALITY OF DESCRIPTIONS

Rule-following is a complex ability that comprises a whole set of activities such as paraphrasing a rule in different formulations or judging whether someone is following it. Lawyers are often engaged in the latter: judging the rule-following behavior of others – paradigmatically the behavior of a defendant by the court. However, the faculty of rule-following is foremost "exhibited in what we call 'obeying the rule' and 'going against it' in actual cases."[43] When lawyers have to apply the law to a case, they often not only have to judge how other addressees of the law have performed, but are addressed by legal rules themselves. They must then use their rule-following faculty to perform an action that is "obeying the rule." A criminal court must not only judge whether the defendant has violated the law but, if so, also obey a legal rule that demands that a sentence be handed down. Usually an obligation fulfilled with professional routine, it can make itself felt if it comes with a moral burden. For example, some judges in the United States complain that inflexible sentencing guidelines force them to hand down sentences that do not do justice to some of their cases.[44]

This kind of application of a norm in the sense of exhibiting rule-following behavior involves a fourth activity that addresses a third aspect of Gadamer's equivocal concept of application. It involves yet another theoretical aspect of legal hermeneutics, relating to what has been called the descriptive inexhaustibility of concrete objects and events due to the ontological density of the world.[45] The Latin dictum *individuum est ineffabile* can be traced back to ancient Greek philosophy and came to prominence in German romanticism, not least through Goethe's repeated references to it.[46] It can be elucidated by contrasting the world with our linguistic representations of it.

None of our linguistic representations of concrete objects and events can describe all their properties with its predicates. This is especially obvious when we take relational properties into account. Each individual object and each individual event is already related in time and space to an infinite number of other individual objects and events. Given their infinity, it would be impossible to describe them in their totality for theoretical reasons. Further, our descriptions are limited by our perception, which is more or less restricted to properties at the level of medium-sized goods.[47] Most importantly, however, we limit our descriptions for pragmatic reasons with respect to our purpose. Even definite descriptions do not demand completeness. Identification is achieved by the singularity of the combination of properties described.

In the legal methodological tradition, Hans Kelsen stressed the limitations of our descriptive means to underscore the inevitability of discretion. Legal norms determine the creation of other norms or acts.

> This determination can never be complete. The higher norm cannot bind in every direction the act by which it is applied. There must always be more or less room for discretion [...] Even the most detailed command must leave to the individual executing the command some discretion. If the organ A orders organ B to arrest subject C, the organ B must, according to his own discretion, decide when and where and how to carry out the order of arrest.[48]

In law, the purpose is to steer the behavior of its addressees in aspects that are relevant to the interests and rights of others. It thus suffices to describe the main properties of the behavior that affects these interests and rights. Thus, no legal rule ever describes the behavior it demands in full ontological detail. It only describes certain aspects of the action and leaves the rest open. It commands the purchaser of a good to pay the agreed price. However, it does not describe the specific banknotes or coins to be used, the time of day they are to be handed over, or what kind of clothes the purchaser must wear on the day of payment.

In all the non-prescribed aspects of the legally required behavior, the addressee of the law has discretion. This also holds insofar as the required action is only described in very general terms. The German police codes empower the police to take "measures" to avert danger without specifying the measures in any way except that they must serve the purpose of averting danger. The police thus has wide-ranging discretion as to the kind of measure to be taken. In the case of an environmental hazard, it can compel the landowner to investigate the source; it can order this to be done by a third party or do it on its own. Sometimes the law explicitly sets boundaries for the discretion with respect to certain actions. Usually, penal norms do not specify fixed sentences, but a certain sentence range such as "one to five years of prison," leaving it to the discretion of the judge to decide on a sentence within the range, as she deems appropriate for the concrete circumstances of the case and the perpetrator. Sometimes the law even goes so far as to grant discretion as to whether to administer the legally conditioned action at all. Under German law, prosecutors and courts in principle have no discretion whether to prosecute a crime that was brought to their attention; they are under what in German doctrine is called the legality principle – they have to prosecute every crime. By contrast, when confronted with a danger to public safety the German police in principle has discretion whether to intervene or instead to hope for the best and sit it out. In German doctrine this is called the opportunity principle. The police are allowed to intervene in a demonstration when participants pose a danger to public safety, but they might also consider it wiser to take the risk of not doing so since a police intervention could turn a menacing, though still peaceful demonstration into an uncontrollable riot.

Whether discretion pertains to an aspect of an application that the law did not address or the generality of the description of the aspects it did address or to an explicit granting of discretion, its exercise is categorically distinct from legal interpretation or construction. Insofar as the law provides discretion, its addressees are not bound by interpretive standards. They are not required to justify their choices with respect to the text, as they must in the case of legal construction. They do not have to argue that the actual or a fictive rational legislator intended to communicate that they had to pay the debt with this and not that 50-euro-note, that the legislator intended to communicate two years when it ordered the sentence to be one to five years, etc. Broadly speaking, one could say that legal construction pertains to the indeterminacy of the law, discretion to its generality. We need legal construction to precisify the law when its description is indeterminate with respect to its applicability to a given case. We exercise discretion insofar as it is determinate that it applies but general in its scope, and we have to choose one of the alternative forms of application that fall under its general description.

Discretion is on the one hand limited by the general description of the rule that is to be applied. This excludes actions that lie beyond the scope of the general description. If the law provides for a sentence between one and five years, the court cannot hand down six years. On the other hand discretion is usually reined in by some secondary legal standards such as the principle of proportionality. Given a sentence range from one to five years a five-year sentence for a first offender in a case that caused only minimal harm would be disproportionate. However, insofar as the discretion is not reined in by secondary standards, its addressee is not bound by the law and her decision bears no interpretative relation to it.

The exercise of discretion cannot be justified according to an interpretative standard, but it might well require justification according to other standards, such as its general rationality, efficiency, or political appropriateness. Exactly along these lines, German administrative law distinguishes sharply between justification of an administrative interpretation of the law controlled by the courts according to standards of legal interpretation and construction on the one hand, and the justification of the exercise of discretion controlled solely within the political hierarchy of the administration itself according to standards of political rationality on the other. The distinction between legal construction and the exercise of discretion is thus even written into our legal institutions.

In literary aesthetics scholars such as Roman Ingarden have highlighted the "spots of indeterminacy of represented objectivities" in literary works, some of which are filled in by the imagination of the reader. In the performing arts discretion shares the same source.[49] Even if she wanted to, a playwright could not determine every aspect of its staging. She has to leave room for discretion and usually will do so abundantly to allow for interesting variations and adaptions of her play to divergent local and temporal contexts. In the performing arts, discretion also serves to bridge the horizons Gadamer was so concerned with and provides room for the adaptation or – as Gadamer would say – application of a play to a different time and place in history. In 2003 John Dew could stage Wagner's Rheingold in Wiesbaden with a Nuclear Power Plant as Walhalla because Wagner's text does not say what Walhalla should look like on stage, leaving it to the discretion and imagination of directors.

However, though discretion shares some of the same functions as construction, they could not be more different in nature – the latter is interpretational, the former is not.[50] As in the case of association, the hermeneutical subject does not have to justify the exercise of discretion with respect to communicative intentions already connected with the text. In contrast to association, however, the exercise of discretion must stay within the boundaries of the text, whereas association can go far beyond it. Further, the exercise of discretion usually has to be justified by some other rational standard,[51] whereas associations need not follow rational patterns at all.

"BUT, AT SOME POINT, THE COLOURING CHANGES":[52] THE SIGNIFICANCE OF SIGNIFICANCE

The last point can be kept short because Betti has already discussed it extensively.[53] It pertains to Gadamer's equivocation of meaning and significance. The equivocation is facilitated by the ambiguity of the German term "Bedeutung," used in both senses. Gadamer insisted that even a legal historian would never be interested in the pure reconstruction of historical facts for their own sake and that any sensible form of historiography would try to understand the meaning of historical facts with regard to their relevance from a contemporary perspective. For Gadamer this shows that the contemporary interests in a text are part of every interpretation of a text.

This argument, however, confuses meaning with significance.[54] The significance of a legal regulation might only be assessed from the ever-changing present perspective. However, this does not automatically affect its meaning. A speed limit on certain roads does not change its meaning by the fact that it has become insignificant due to permanent heavy congestion. As Betti rightly insisted, meaning and significance must be distinguished. Legal interpretation and construction are about the meaning of laws, not about the significance of this meaning.

Nevertheless, in law as well, there are some discussions in which meaning is confounded with significance. In German constitutional law, there is a more-than-a-century-old discussion on constitutional change (*Verfassungswandel*), i.e., on whether and how constitutional provisions can change their "meaning" due to changing political circumstances. It fascinated constitutional scholars in the late nineteenth century that the constitution of the newly founded German Empire played out quite differently from what the text of the constitution seemed to suggest.[55]

One striking example was the development of a federal bureaucracy out of the chancellery. The Chancellor represented presiding – hegemonic – Prussia in the Federal Council, the representative body of the federation's monarchies. The Chancellor was responsible for countersigning federal laws and the exercise of their oversight by the council. Nowhere did the constitution provide for federal ministries. Bismarck, however, built an extensive federal oversight administration around his chancellorship with different departments that became de facto federal ministries. The provisions on the chancellery thus took on an unforeseen significance discussed under the topic of constitutional change as a hermeneutical phenomenon.[56]

In art, the changing significance of works of art is one of the most commonplace experiences in its reception. For decades, no theater in Germany bothered to stage "The Suppliants" of Aeschylus. However, after the height of the so-called refugee crisis in the summer of 2015, even our provincial theater in Freiburg staged it. Even after more than 2,500 years, the significance of a play can change dramatically in just one summer.

SUMMARY

Legal hermeneutics is an internally complex phenomenon sometimes encompassing difficult-to-distinguish, related, and intertwined activities. An analytical perspective that distinguishes the different elements can clarify the complex nature of hermeneutics. It can relate the different elements to different theoretical issues that are not specific to hermeneutics in the philosophy of language, action, rationality, and ontology. The law shows in many of its doctrinal and methodical aspects an intuitive awareness for these distinctions. It distinguishes between interpretation and construction, between interpretation and judicial faculty of judgment ("Judiz"), between construction and association for contexts of justification and discovery, between interpretation and the exercise of discretion, and also between meaning and historical significance. In theoretically following up on the distinctions inherent in legal doctrine and methods, hermeneutics in general can live up to Gadamer's observation that there is something to be learned from looking at the law.

NOTES

1 Hans-Georg Gadamer, *Truth and Method* (New York: Crossroad, 1989), 324–40.
2 Gadamer, *Truth and Method*, 340: "all reading involves application."
3 Emilio Betti, "Hermeneutics as the General Methodology of the Geisteswissenschaften," in *Contemporary Hermeneutics:*

Hermeneutics as Method, Philosophy, and Critique, ed. Josef Bleicher (London: Routledge & Kegan Paul, 1980), 81–4.

4 Herbert P. Grice, "Meaning," in *Studies in the Way of Words* (Cambridge, MA: Harvard University Press, 1989); Donald Davidson, "A Nice Derangement of Epitaphs," in *Truth, Language, and History*, ed. Donald Davidson (Oxford: Clarendon Press, 2009), 89–107; on their similarities and differences: John Cook, "Is Davidson a Gricean?" *Dialogue* 48 (2009): 557.

5 Steven Knapp and Walter Benn Michaels, "Against Theory," *Critical Inquiry* 8 (1982): 727–8.

6 Larry Alexander and Saikrishna Prakash, " 'Is That English You're Speaking?' Why Intention Free Interpretation is an Impossibility," *San Diego Law Review* 41 (2004): 977.

7 This also holds for externalist elements of meaning, which are themselves based on externalist intentions. Michael S. Moore, "Can Objectivity be Grounded in Semantics," in *Law, Metaphysics, Meaning, and Objectivity*, ed. Enrique Villanueva (Mexico City: Rodopi, 2007), 253–4; Michael S. Moore, "Semantics, Metaphysics and Objectivity in Law," in *Vagueness and Law: Philosophical and Legal Perspectives*, ed. Geert Keil and Ralf Poscher, 1st edn. (Oxford and New York: Oxford University Press, 2016).

8 An overview by David Pitt, "Mental Representation," in *The Stanford Encyclopedia of Philosophy*, ed. Edward N. Zalta.

9 For recent general critiques of intentionalist accounts see Jody Azzouni, *Semantic Perception: How the Illusion of a Common Language Arises and Persists* (New York: Oxford University Press, 2013), 265–320. His perceptual account relies heavily on the conscious phenomenology of semantic experiences. Intentionalist accounts should, however, be able to accommodate much of the "data" when subconscious inferences are taken into account – a possibility not finally eschewed but regarded as "empirically unlikely" by Azzouni (*Semantic Perception*, 289). See also Ernest Lepore and Matthew Stone, *Imagination and Convention: Distinguishing Grammar and Inference in Language*, 1st edn. (Oxford: Oxford University Press, 2015), who do still accept the fundamental importance of "direct" communicative intentions but try to broaden the importance of conventional meaning. For a first adaptation of this approach for law see Marcin Matczak, "Does Legal

Interpretation Need Paul Grice? Reflections on Lepore and Stone's Imagination and Convention," *Polish Journal of Philosophy* 10 (2016), available at: https://ssrn.com/abstract=2716629.

10 This is the theoretical reason for approaches like "hypothetical intentionalism." See Brian G. Slocum, *Ordinary Meaning: A Theory of the Most Fundamental Principle of Legal Interpretation* (Chicago: University of Chicago Press, 2015), see also already Andrei A. Marmor, *Interpretation and Legal Theory* (Oxford: Hart Publishing, 2005), 23.

11 For a critical assessment with respect to so-called ordinary meaning see Slocum, *Ordinary Meaning*, 36–91.

12 For two different reconstructions along these lines see Richard Ekins, *The Nature of Legislative Intent* (Oxford: Oxford University Press, 2012); Ralf Poscher, "The Normative Construction of Legislative Intent," forthcoming in *Droit & Philosophie, Annuaire de l'Institut Michel Villey*, 2017, available at: https://ssrn.com/abstract=2861250, with further references to the theoretical critics of legislative intent.

13 Martin Heidegger, *Being and Time*, ed. Joan Stambaugh and Dennis J. Schmidt (Albany: SUNY Press, 2010), § 15, 68–70.

14 Donald Davidson, "Three Varieties of Knowledge," in *Subjective, Intersubjective, Objective*, ed. Donald Davidson (Oxford University Press, 2001), 215–20.

15 Frank Jackson and Philip Pettit, "Structural Explanation in Social Theory," in *Reduction, Explanation, and Realism*, ed. David Charles and Kathleen Lennon (Oxford: Clarendon Press, 1992), 117–26. Further on program explanations, Frank Jackson and Philip Pettit, "Functionalism and Broad Content," *Mind* 97 (1988): 391–7; Frank Jackson and Philip Pettit, "Program Explanation: A General Perspective," *Analysis* 50 (1990): 107–17.

16 Davidson, "Three Varieties of Knowledge," 215.

17 Philip Pettit, "Towards Interpretation," *Philosophia* 23 (1994): 162–6; for a systematic analysis of these rational standards in the history of philosophy Oliver R. Scholz, *Verstehen und Rationalität: Untersuchungen zu den Grundlagen von Hermeneutik und Sprachphilosophie*, Klostermann Rote Reihe (Frankfurt am Main: Vittorio Klostermann, 2016).

18 Davidson, "Three Varieties of Knowledge," 211.

19 On the content/occurrence ambiguity of rational explanations, see Geert Keil, "Beyond Assimilationism and Differentialism: Comment on Glock," in *Welt der Gründe: Vorträge und Kolloquien des XXII. Deutschen Kongresses für Philosophie vom 11. bis 15. September 2011 an der Ludwig-Maximilians-Universität München*, ed. Julian Nida-Rümelin and Elif Özmen (Hamburg: Felix Meiner Verlag, 2012), 920: "In Davidson's theory of action explanation, mental attitudes play a dual role [...] The causal relation holds between two occurrences, that is, between the mental event [i.e. the occurrence of the attitude] and the bodily movement. The relation of rationalization holds between the propositional content of the mental attitude and the description of the action. In the slogan 'reasons are causes' [...] these subtleties get lost."; cf. on this point also Hans-Johann Glock, "Reasons for Action: Wittgensteinian and Davidsonian Perspectives in Historical and Meta-Philosophical Context," *Nordic Wittgenstein Review* 3 (2014): 40f.

20 Friedrich Carl von Savigny, *System of the Modern Roman Law*, trans. W. Holloway (Madras: J. Higginbotham, 1867), 172.

21 Michael S. Moore, "Interpreting Interpretation," in *Law and Interpretation: Essays in Legal Philosophy*, ed. Andrei A. Marmor (Oxford: Clarendon Press, 1995), 5; see also Stanley Eugene Fish, "Intention is all there is: A Critical Analysis of Aharon Barak's Purposive Interpretation in Law," *Cardozo Law Review* 29 (2008): 1116.

22 For literary interpretation see, e.g., Eric D. Hirsch, *Validity in Interpretation* (New Haven: Yale University Press, 1967).

23 John Crowe Ransom, *The New Criticism* (Westport: Greenwood Press, 1979).

24 Saul A. Kripke, *Wittgenstein on Rules and Private Language: An Elementary Exposition* (Oxford: Blackwell, 1982).

25 Ludwig Wittgenstein, *Philosophical Investigations*, ed. Gertrude E. M. Anscombe (Oxford: Blackwell, 1953), § 201.

26 Philip Pettit, *The Common Mind: An Essay on Psychology, Society, and Politics* (Oxford University Press, 1996), 76–108. On the challenges for such accounts to preserve the specific normativity in distinguishing correct and incorrect applications, between following a rule and merely believing that one follows a rule, see Hans-Johann Glock, "Meaning and Rule Following," in *International Encyclopedia of the Social & Behavioral Sciences*, 2nd edn., ed. James D. Wright (Amsterdam: Elsevier, 2015), 842f.

27 Immanuel Kant, *Critique of Pure Reason*, trans. Paul Guyer and Allen W. Wood (Cambridge: Cambridge University Press, 1998), 268 [A133/B172].
28 Robert B. Brandom, *Making it Explicit: Reasoning, Representing and Discursive Commitment* (Cambridge, MA: Harvard University Press, 1994), ch. 1; Robert B. Brandom, "Some Pragmatist Themes in Hegel's Idealism," in *Tales of the Mighty Dead: Historical Essays in the Metaphysics of Intentionality* (Cambridge, MA: Harvard University Press, 2002), 230–4.
29 Wittgenstein, *Philosophical Investigations*, § 122.
30 Ralf Poscher, "Interpretation and Rule Following in Law: The Complexity of Easy Cases," in *Problems of Normativity, Rules and Rule-Following*, ed. Michał Araszkiewicz et al. (Heidelberg: Springer, 2015), 285.
31 In legal theory it is not disputed that hard cases exist, the debate over one-right-answer-theories only concerns their merely epistemic or substantive character. For two versions of the epistemic thesis, see Ronald M. Dworkin, "Is There Really No Right Answer in Hard Cases?" in *A Matter of Principle* (New York: Oxford University Press, 1985), 119–45; Michael S. Moore, "Law as a Functional Kind," in *Educating Oneself in Public: Critical Essays in Jurisprudence*, ed. Michael S. Moore (New York: Oxford University Press, 2000), 228; Michael S. Moore, "Legal Reality: A Naturalist Approach to Legal Ontology," *Law and Philosophy* 21 (2002): 619–705.
32 Herbert L. A. Hart, "Positivism and the Separation of Law and Morals," *Harvard Law Review* 71 (1958): 615.
33 Gadamer, *Truth and Method*, 301–7.
34 Friedrich Carl von Savigny, "Methodologie (Vorlesungsnotizen)," in *Vorlesungen über juristische Methodologie 1802–1842*, ed. Friedrich Carl von Savigny (Frankfurt am Main: Vittorio Klostermann, 1993), 150.
35 Savigny, *System of the Modern Roman Law*, § 50.
36 Francis Lieber, "On Political Hermeneutics, or on Political Interpretation and Construction, and Also on Precedents," *American Jurist and Law Magazine* 18 (1837): 37.
37 E.g. for the contemporary discussion in constitutional law: Keith E. Whittington, *Constitutional Interpretation: Textual Meaning, Original Intent and Judicial Review* (Lawrence: University Press of Kansas, 1999); Lawrence B. Solum, "The Interpretation-Construction Distinction," *Constitutional Commentary* 27 (2010): 95; Randy E. Barnett, "Interpretation and Construction," *Harvard Journal of*

  Law & Public Policy 34 (2011): 65; in private law: Gregory M. Klass, "Interpretation and Construction Distinction in Contract Law," available at: https://ssrn.com/abstract=2913228.

38 Ralf Poscher, "The Hermeneutic Character of Legal Construction," in *Law's Hermeneutics: Other investigations*, ed. Simone Glanert and Fabien Girard (New York: Routledge, 2017), 207/220-2.

39 Karl Binding, *Handbuch des Strafrechts – Band I*, Systematisches Handbuch der Deutschen Rechtswissenschaft (Leipzig: Duncker & Humblot, 1885), 454; Josef Kohler, "Über die Interpretation von Gesetzen," *Zeitschrift für das Privat- und Öffentliche Recht der Gegenwart* 13 (1886): 1–61; Adolf Wach, *Handbuch des deutschen Civilprozessrechts, Erster Band* (Leipzig: Duncker & Humblot, 1885).

40 Kant, *Critique of Pure Reason*, 396 [A314/B370].

41 Robert Stecker, *Interpretation and Construction: Art, Speech, and the Law* (Malden, MA: Blackwell, 2003), 95–152.

42 On the distinction, usually attributed to Hans Reichenbach, *Experience and Prediction* (Chicago: University of Chicago Press, 1938), 6f., but in substance having a much richer genealogy that some authors trace back to ancient Greek philosophy, see Paul Hoyningen-Huene, "Context of Discovery and Context of Justification," *Studies in History and Philosophy of Science Part A.* 18 (1987): 502f.; on the role of the distinction in legal methodology, see Bernhard Schlink, "Juristische Methodik zwischen Verfassungstheorie und Wissenschaftstheorie," *Rechtstheorie* 7 (1976): 101.

43 Wittgenstein, *Philosophical Investigations*, § 201.

44 E.g., Federal Judge J. S. Rakoff, "Mass Incarceration: The Silence of the Judges," *New York Review of Books*, May 21, 2015: "it is we judges who are forced to impose sentences that many of us feel are unjust and counterproductive."

45 Geert Keil, "Über die deskriptive Unerschöpflichkeit," in *Phänomenologie und Sprachanalyse*, ed. Geert Keil and Udo Tietz (Paderborn: Mentis, 2006), 83–125.

46 Keil, "Über die deskriptive Unerschöpflichkeit," 84–7.

47 John L. Austin, *Sense and Sensibilia* (Oxford: Oxford University Press, 1962), 8: "moderate-sized specimens of dry goods."

48 Hans Kelsen, *Pure Theory of Law* (Union: Lawbook Exchange, 2002), 349.

49 Roman Ingarden, *The Literary Work of Art: An Investigation on the Borderlines of Ontology, Logic, and Theory of Literature; With an Appendix on the Functions of Language in the Theater*, trans. George

G. Grabowicz (Evanston: Northwestern University Press, 1986), § 38, 246–54; cf. also David Lewis, "Truth in Fiction," *American Philosophical Quarterly* 15 (1978): 42f.; Keil, "Über die deskriptive Unerschöpflichkeit," 105.

50 Contrary to H. L. A. Hart, "Discretion," *Harvard Law Review* 127 (2013): 652–65, who discusses both phenomena under the topic of discretion. However, he shows at least some sensibility for their differences when he distinguishes them gradually ("Discretion," 665). "It seems to me clear, for example, that where discretion is used in the course of judicial determinations in the attempt to apply rules, the weight of factors such as consistency with other parts of the legal system will be prominent, whereas they may be at their minimum in cases of Avowed Discretion exercised by, say, a rate-fixing body."

51 Cf. Hart, "Discretion," 657, distinguishing the exercise of discretion from personal whim.

52 Max Weber, "The 'Objectivity' of Knowledge in Social Science and Social Policy," in *Collected Methodological Writings*, ed. Hans H. Bruun and Sam Whimster (London: Routledge, 2012), 138: "But, at some point, the colouring changes: the significance of those points of view that have been applied unreflectingly grows uncertain, the way forward fades away in the twilight. The light shed by the great cultural problems has moved on. Then science, too, prepares to find a new standpoint and a new conceptual apparatus, and to contemplate the stream of events from the summits of thought. It follows those stars that alone can give meaning and direction to its work."

53 On his controversy with Gadamer see David C. Hoy, "Interpreting the Law: Hermeneutical and Poststructuralist Perspectives," *Southern California Law Review* 58 (1985): 140–7.

54 Emilio Betti, "Hermeneutics as the General Methodology of the Geisteswissenschaften," in *The Hermeneutic Tradition: From Ast to Ricoeur, Hermeneutics as the General Methodology of the Geisteswissenschaften*, ed. Gayle L. Ormiston and Alan. D. Schrift (Albany: SUNY Press, 1990), 173.

55 Paul Laband, *Die Wandlungen der deutschen Reichsverfassung* (Dresden: Jahn & Jaensch, 1895); Georg Jellinek, *Verfassungsänderung und Verfassungswandlung: eine staatsrechtlich-politische Abhandlung*, ed. Walter Pauly (Goldbach: Keip, 1996).

56 Example taken from Laband, *Wandlungen*, 8–21; cf. also Jellinek, *Verfassungsänderung und Verfassungswandlung*, 26f.

15 Hermeneutics and the Human Sciences

Kristin Gjesdal

The relationship between hermeneutics and the human sciences – the *Verstehenswissenschaften*, as Wilhelm Dilthey would put it in an effort to encompass the full span of disciplines covering human action, expression, and spontaneity – is in part a matter of the relationship between philosophy and its neighboring disciplines. Is philosophy, with its focus on the legitimacy of our knowledge-claims and orientation toward truth, a meta-discipline providing basic epistemological premises for other sciences? Should it be seen, as it often is, as a critical meta-discourse, questioning the procedures that govern other fields of knowledge while itself being immune to first-order queries raised from within these fields? And, if so, who has granted philosophy such a position? Is it the case that philosophy is celebrated, as a beacon of wisdom and authority, across the human and social sciences? Indeed, any philosopher engaging in some level of interdisciplinary collaboration will be well aware that scholars from other fields often view philosophers and their appetite for academic meta-discourse with a good dose of skepticism. Even within philosophy, there is a great deal of disparity when it comes to conceptions of methodology and the positioning of the discipline, be it institutionally or with respect to its intellectual goals and criteria of success. This, in fact, is a point that distinguishes philosophy from what a recent sociological study characterizes as consensus-oriented fields like history and economics, and has even had philosophers ask if there is a crisis in the discipline.[1] However, if philosophers, while far from in unison in their conception of the scientific basis and status of their work, still view their discipline as king among the sciences, one cannot help wondering if there is something slightly quixotic about the entire enterprise – or, at least, if our thinking about the relationship between philosophy and the human sciences is better off if it starts from a more modest attitude and a willingness not simply to *teach*, but also to *learn* from its neighboring disciplines.

Hermeneutics is a field in which this interaction – between philosophy teaching and philosophy learning – has been prominently played out since the mid-eighteenth century. Defined as a theory of interpretation, hermeneutics, in its modern form (which is the focus of this chapter), has an unquestioned home in philosophy. Indeed, for some of its twentieth-century practitioners, the claim is even stronger and philosophy *itself* emerges as emphatically hermeneutical – a proposition that will be discussed in what follows, though, in my view, its status as a subfield *of* philosophy (rather than being identified *with* the field itself) in no way detracts from the relevance of hermeneutical discourse. Hermeneutics, however, is not simply a theoretical exercise. It also encompasses the practice, some will say art, of interpretation. And, if we want hermeneutics to be more than an abstract, philosophical enterprise, if it is to inform our actual efforts in interpretation and communicate with practical-empirical scholarship, then our philosophizing about interpretation must recognize its dependency on what is going on at a practical and concrete level across the human sciences.

It is the goal of this chapter, via a survey of some key positions in modern philosophy of understanding and interpretation, to lay out and discuss the relationship between these two levels of hermeneutical thought. I will propose that across its modern articulations, hermeneutics, rather than endeavoring to provide a top-down theory of science for the human sciences, should begin by contemplating – as part of its answer to questions such as "What is understanding?" "How is understanding best understood?" and "What scientific purchase can we claim for hermeneutics?" – the ongoing negotiations of the relationship between interpretative activity in the human sciences and meta-discussions on the goals, methods, and deeper preconditions for this activity.

QUESTIONING THE STANDARD NARRATIVE

As it marks the beginning of twentieth-century hermeneutics, Martin Heidegger's *Being and Time* represents an attempt to provide an alternative to the neo-Kantianism that was gaining an ever more solid foothold.[2] However, in the 1920s, Heidegger's work is itself an effort not simply to reject, but also to appropriate Kantian philosophy, especially the notion, which Heidegger traces back to the A-deduction of the *Critique of Pure Reason*, of a foundational temporal synthesis facilitating human experience and judgment. This argument, first developed in *Kant and the Problem of Metaphysics* (published in 1929, but initially envisioned as a crucial part of the planned Part Two of *Being and Time*),[3] informs the hermeneutical perspective developed in *Being and Time* and also in the work of Heidegger's student Hans-Georg Gadamer. Gadamer's 1960 *Truth and Method* has come to serve as a seminal text in twentieth-century hermeneutics.[4]

In *Truth and Method*, Gadamer distinguishes between two trends in hermeneutics. On the one hand, there is *methodological* hermeneutics, understood as a critical-epistemological tool for the sciences of interpretation. On the other hand, there is *philosophical* hermeneutics, a branch of thought that is not limited to questions concerning the procedures of the human sciences, but, rather, is driven by a deeper interest in a fundamental human capacity for understanding, as it undergirds tradition and the symbolic expressions and practices that make up its basic fabric. While methodological hermeneutics asks how to best make sense of human (symbolic) expressions within a particular field of meaning, communication, and human practice, philosophical hermeneutics asks how such sense-making, communication, and practice is possible in the first place. So conceived, philosophical hermeneutics is a matter of describing the enabling conditions of human understanding, and ultimately of experience as such.[5]

However, the distinction between methodological and philosophical hermeneutics is not the only key distinction Gadamer draws in *Truth and Method*. Following a line of thought that stretches back to the beginnings of the discipline (again in its modern formulation), he also distinguishes between *special* hermeneutics, which deals with interpretative challenges and techniques within designated disciplines or fields of research (religious and classical texts being two cases in point), and *universal* hermeneutics, which addresses linguistic understanding *überhaupt*.

Deliberately seeking a synthesis of historical and systematic thought, Gadamer argues that universal hermeneutics finds its first spokesman in the ninteenth-century philosopher Friedrich Schleiermacher.[6] Schleiermacher, he argues, was the first to realize that, as a philosophical discipline, hermeneutics should elevate itself above special kinds of texts and instead address symbolic understanding in its generality. Gadamer takes this to be a healthy move and uses a passage from Schleiermacher – "Everything presupposed in hermeneutics is but language" – as the epigram for the important Part Three of *Truth and Method*, in which he, after a lengthy detour through Kant and post-Kantian philosophy, formulates his own theoretical contribution (TM 381; GW I 387).

Gadamer, however, takes only a relative interest in Schleiermacher's work. For Gadamer, Schleiermacher's understanding goes wrong when, in his turn from special to general hermeneutics, he remains stuck in a methodological outlook that, so Gadamer argues, he naively takes over from Kant.[7] Gadamer's point is certainly not that all of Kant's philosophy is wrong. For, as Heidegger had shown, Kant had himself traced experience back to a pre-reflective, temporal synthesis – an insight that is of irreducible hermeneutical value, although, following Heidegger's recommendations, it must be detached from a narrow Kantian framework and led back to human practice and historical being-in-the-world. The problem with Schleiermacher is that he overlooks the promising aspects of the Kantian Critique, what Heidegger had identified as Kant's erstwhile commitment to *metaphysica generalis*, and takes over the less promising aspects of it (an orientation toward transcendental subjectivity and a recasting of philosophy as method).⁸ In this vein, Schleiermacher, on Gadamer's reading, leads the conditions for textual interpretation back to the interpreter herself, thus failing to notice how the very interpretation of texts is enabled by a deeper, hermeneutical responsiveness that resides in the most fundamental practices through which the world is disclosed to beings like us. Gadamer traces this enabling, pre-reflective dimension – understanding (*Verstehen*), as different from interpretation (*Auslegung*) – to a continuum of tradition, as it exists prior to any distinction between interpreter and text.⁹ In Gadamer's eyes, from the point of view of his Hegelian-Heideggerian synthesis, Schleiermacher, in spite of facilitating the move from special to general hermeneutics, puts hermeneutics on the wrong track.¹⁰ Due to a misinterpretation of Kant's conception of genius (TM 188–94; GW I 191–7), Schleiermacher, as Gadamer reads him, imports, into a field that is characterized by participation in a deeper, trans-subjective meaning context (tradition), a set of ideals that are taken over from the natural sciences: value neutrality, disinterestedness, context independence, and an appeal to a universally shared methodology as the ultimate condition for success in interpretation. In Gadamer's words, "it is likely that not until Schleiermacher – with whom hermeneutics became an independent method, detached from all content – could the interpreter claim superiority over his object" (TM 194–5; GW I 198). In effect, Schleiermacher is thus taken to bring to an end a wide-spanning humanism that views tradition as a reservoir of truth and as an arena for human self-formation and meaning (TM 197; GW I 201).¹¹

Gadamer views this as a philosophical mistake. As a response, philosophical hermeneutics – which is how Gadamer designates his project – needs to get beyond the forecourt of epistemology. ("Philosophical hermeneutics" had been Gadamer's initial suggestion for a title to his 1960 book until his publisher came up with *Truth and Method*.)¹² After 150 years of being constrained to methodological thought – from Schleiermacher's lectures in the early 1800s to the 1960 publication of *Truth and Method* – Gadamer seeks to offer an account of understanding as it discloses a world of human meaning prior to the division between the human and the natural sciences (and prior to any disciplinary distinctions or varieties within the human sciences, to any distinctions *in* philosophy and even, as far as textual understanding goes, to any distinction between hermeneutics, criticism, dialectics, stylistic analysis, or other approaches). Thus, *his* contribution, as a meta-theory of understanding, cannot be judged by criteria of success that are taken from any one of these methodologically limited fields (as this, for Gadamer, would be equivalent to mixing up constitutively different levels of philosophical discourse). As he puts it in a much-quoted formulation, he is interested in "something which [...] methodological dispute serves only to conceal and neglect, something that does not so much confine or limit modern science as precede it and make it possible" (TM xxix; GW II 439).

Now, to the general reader, Gadamer's work, with its appeal to a pre-Kantian humanist tradition, has come to incarnate a commitment to the human sciences in a world in which their status is under increasing threat. How, then, can Gadamer, on the one hand, insist that hermeneutics is prior to the division of the natural and the human sciences while, on the other, take a special interest in the humanities? The answer is fairly simple: If a human being is characterized by its understanding attitude to the world, then philosophy has an obligation to ask what understanding is. For Gadamer, this is a most fundamental question in philosophy and, moreover, a question that hermeneutics is uniquely qualified to answer.[13] Vice versa, this is, *pace* methodological hermeneutics, the only or most important question in hermeneutics.

In Gadamer's view, the world-disclosive understanding at stake in hermeneutics cannot be explained by a reference to the powers of a (transcendental) ego. As such, it must be studied as it materializes itself in and across a set of concrete interpretative practices – ultimately tradition itself. As Heidegger had put it: understanding is articulated in interpretation – it does not become something different, but it becomes itself.[14] For Gadamer, however, this point is historicized and located, Hegel in hand, within the dynamic of an organically unfolding tradition that is ultimately understood in light of play and playing.

This is where the human sciences enter the picture. As disciplines of interpretation, they cover the discourses and realms through which human understanding takes place in interaction with the tradition. First, the human sciences address human actions, historical events and expressions, that is, objects that are themselves expressive of a given interpretation of the world (a Medieval image of Christ, for example, articulates a certain image of religion, the human condition, the relationship between the finite and the infinite, and so on). Second, their goal is, broadly speaking, to interpret and make sense of a meaningful material, be it a work of literature, a painting, or a historical event. Across the human sciences, what we encounter are *interpretations* of human spirit – human spirit encountering itself in and through objects that are expressive of human *understanding*. Hence, if we want to know what understanding is, if we want to study the relationship between understanding (as a pre-reflective disclosure of a human world) and interpretation (as an activity in which we deliberately take part), then, on Gadamer's view, we should pay special attention to the human sciences and, more specifically, to the tradition as it is prior to any division into disciplines and special methodologies.

While, on Gadamer's model, philosophy does not provide epistemic guidelines for the other sciences, it nonetheless articulates the most fundamental conditions of experience as they get expressed throughout the different domains of human-historical understanding.[15] At stake, in other words, is a softer, ontologized and also historicized version of a transcendental claim, one that avoids the formalism and subject-centeredness that Gadamer ascribes to Kant and the neo-Kantian hypostatization of epistemology but nonetheless remains committed to the image of philosophy as a search for a priori conditions for experience. Gadamer himself admits to this

Kantian streak, his "using Kant to overcome Kant"-attitude, while writing, in *Truth and Method*:

> it seems [in the context of hermeneutics] a mere misunderstanding to invoke the famous Kantian distinction between quaestio juris and quaestio facti [as this had been the project of the neo-Kantians]. Kant certainly did not intend to prescribe what modern science must do in order to stand honorably before the judgment seat of reason. He asked a philosophical question: what are the conditions of our knowledge, by virtue of which modern science is possible, and how far does it extend? The following investigation asks a philosophic question in the same sense. (TM xxix; GW II 439)

While launching an alternative to neo-Kantianism and its epistemological aspirations, Gadamer, following Heidegger, commits to an apriorism of sorts – though definitely one that differs from the more standard positions we find among the neo-Kantians in Marburg and Heidelberg.

This claim is perhaps provocative (and it goes beyond my reading of Gadamer's work in *Gadamer and the Legacy of German Idealism*).[16] Yet I think it is a helpful point to bring up in this context because it allows us to approach the relationship between hermeneutics and the human sciences with a new question in mind: not simply that of truth versus method, which is how Gadamer's work has often been read, but, rather, that of asking to what extent hermeneutics is best cast from the point of view of an ontological position or, if there are other – better or alternative – ways of approaching this field, and thus also what the relationship between philosophical hermeneutics and the human sciences is. This question needs to be asked precisely because Gadamer, with admirable consistency and passion, seeks to rehabilitate the human sciences (and here he moves beyond Heidegger, who, beyond his first lecture courses, took little to no interest in the humanities as an object of philosophical reflection[17]). But given his ontological framework, the way in which he can think about, conceptualize, and practically engage the human sciences is already set. In his ontological approach, Gadamer takes almost no interest in the different challenges emerging from within the different parts of the human sciences (the human sciences, for him, primarily matter as studies of interpretation). Nor does he acknowledge different subfields of philosophy, let alone of textual interpretation. There is, in his work, a worrisome tendency to identify philosophy with hermeneutics (hermeneutics as ontology) and to see hermeneutics, in turn, as the master discourse of the human sciences. The question posed at the opening of the chapter thus remains: Can the relationship between hermeneutics and the human sciences be adequately explored if philosophers see themselves as holding the one and only key to this broad span of academic fields and subfields? And does it matter much to practitioners of other disciplines whether this key is of an epistemic or of an ontological material? To both these questions, I am inclined to respond with an unreluctant "no."

PROVIDING AN ALTERNATIVE STORY

Three decades passed between Gadamer's first preparations for *Truth and Method* and its 1960 publication. He started working on this magisterial study around 1930, but then got interrupted by the war. Hence, in the period between the beginning and the completion of the project, the political and philosophical landscape had changed dramatically and it was easy, it seems, to forget how Gadamer's project had in fact grown out of, and as a response to, the Marburg environment, where he had initially been a student and had written his dissertation under the guidance of Paul Natorp.[18] And, with that, it was also easy to forget how polemical Gadamer's retrieval of the history of hermeneutics initially had been. His goal in the first parts of *Truth and Method* is, as I see it, not really to provide a history of the discipline, but, rather, to justify the ontological alternative in hermeneutics (and, equally important, the hermeneutical alternative in philosophy) and, in order to do so, philosophical competitors had to be brushed off.[19]

If Gadamer, with his massively influential narrative about the rise of ontological hermeneutics, may be right in emphasizing the difference between methodological and ontological approaches within this field, he is not, for that reason, correct in his description of what a non-ontological hermeneutics amounts to. For Gadamer, all such positions fall into the category of quasi-scientific and ahistorical proceduralism (as described above), as models that, on the condition of an appropriate, disinterested attitude, ascribe to the interpreting subject an ability to create a unity between the diversity of objects to be interpreted as well as to establish the conditions that grant the interpreter access to the meaning of the interpreted material in the first place (i.e., the kind of unity that tradition, in Gadamer's own model, provides). In his view, methodological hermeneutics thus represents yet another version of the combination of subjectivism and formalism that, at least from a Heideggerian standpoint (possibly from a Hegelian standpoint, too), characterizes traditional Kantian philosophy. If this is a projection that may be understandable with reference to the neo-Kantianism that Gadamer had initially sought to overcome, it is nonetheless unfortunate in that it has remained decisive for how philosophers, in the wake of *Truth and Method*, have maneuvered the fields of hermeneutics and the human sciences. The local, historical, and philosophical framework in which Gadamer's hermeneutics was conceived thus came to shape his theory – and these were, it seems, historical conditions that Gadamer took for granted, did not really question, and probably did not see as something that would mark the global aspirations of his contribution.[20]

As a chief spokesman of methodological hermeneutics – and, indeed, the philosopher who introduced the very distinction between explanatory natural science and the understanding sciences – Dilthey's contribution, though itself of a pre-Heideggerian vintage, is fit to challenge Gadamer's narrative, especially its weighing of the alternatives of methodological and ontological positions in hermeneutics (and the identification of *philosophical* hermeneutics with the latter). Dilthey, for a start, does not trace hermeneutics back to Kant only (here I depart from, among others, Rudolf Makkreel's argument).[21] In Dilthey's story, as in Gadamer's, Friedrich Schleiermacher's contribution, his move from special to general hermeneutics, is seen as decisive, and yet this, for Dilthey, is not a move that should be understood only or primarily with reference to a Kantian-epistemological framework. Dilthey, instead, connects hermeneutics back to Herder and his response to the formalism of rationalist school philosophy. (The point here is not that all rationalist school philosophy was, necessarily, formalistic, but that it was *perceived* as being such and thus as calling for alternative philosophical models.[22]) In the mid-eighteenth century, so Herder argues, a new sense had emerged that historical and artistic material required an individualizing approach and that such an approach, in turn, demanded a context-sensitive, historical, and sympathetic kind of interpretation.[23] To the extent that transcendental philosophy was important, it was Fichte and not Kant who would get the place of honor.[24] Many factors contributed to the breakthrough of the Herder-Schleiermacher lineage in the philosophy of interpretation. Of particular importance in this context are the following points: (a) the discussion between Lessing and Winckelmann over the right approach to historical-artistic material (Lessing was worried about Winckelmann's deductive approach and Winckelmann, in turn, was concerned about Lessing's lack of first-hand experience with the works he describes and was pleading for a more empirical approach to sculpture); (b) a broad interest, among German philosophers, in Hume's essays and historical work (but also in the larger, empiricist circles, including Shaftesbury and Henry Home, as well as poets and theologians like Edward Young or Robert Lowth); (c) a turn in natural science from physics to biology as a methodological paradigm; (d) concerns about the formalism, etiquette, and class-coding of the French classicist aesthetics that had been favored by rationalist philosophers (and, as a consequence, its dismissal of all kinds of folk culture and non-classical work, including Shakespeare's drama); (e) worries about European colonialism (its violence and its failure to realize that the concept of humanity extends beyond the inhabitants of modern Europe).

Transcendental philosophy, as one can see, plays less of a role here – and could, indeed, have played no major role since the movements described above crystallize in the 1760s, that is, well before Kant's Copernican turn. (From this point of view, it is rather the case that the mid-eighteenth century saw a host of efforts to synthesize rationalism and empiricism, and Kant's model is only one out of a number of such attempts.) Nor do we encounter a set of positions that seek to explain interpretation by reference to a subjectively held, formally articulated, and ahistorically constructed methodology. At stake, rather, is a "bottom up" (Herder's expression), inductively established, empirically oriented movement that offers systematic reflection on the nature of interpretation and, hand in hand with this, a broad program of practical hermeneutical work encompassing the collection of dying literary forms, translations, intercultural mediation, and a re-evaluation of aesthetic hierarchies of all sorts (European versus non-European art, high-class arts of etiquette and form versus folk songs and poetry, a return to the art forms of indigenous peoples such as the Sami or the Inuit).[25] It is not a matter of sheer historical chance that this is also the early days of linguistics and anthropology, as these disciplines find an early shape in the works of Herder and Humboldt.[26]

For the sake of simplicity (and so as to facilitate a large-span overview), we can follow Dilthey and describe this hermeneutical program as a lineage of thought that extends from Herder, via Schleiermacher, to Dilthey himself (though other philosophers, most prominently the Schlegel brothers, also belong to this picture). In my view, this is a line of thought that offers an attractive, though often overlooked, alternative to Gadamer and his ontological focus, his attempt at sublating specific disciplinary discussions into a circular, hermeneutical model where the general truth content of traditional texts is given expression in and through concrete interpretations that, in turn, are enabled by this very same tradition.[27] Like later hermeneutical positions, the Herder-Schleiermacher-Dilthey lineage in hermeneutics seeks non-formalist, non-objectivizing attitudes in interpretation.[28] But from *its* point of view, tradition (and its unifying tendencies) is not simply world-disclosive, but can also be conservative and stifling (it is, as Herder puts it, with a metaphor that will later resound in Marxian criticism of religion, the opium of a culture).[29] The benchmark of a productive interpretation – of an interpretation that yields new knowledge, understanding, and serves to overcome prejudices – can therefore not lie within the "happening" or "play" of tradition, as Gadamer metaphorically characterizes the hermeneutical experience with reference to canonical works of art.[30] Rather, the Herder-Schleiermacher-Dilthey lineage of thought views interpretation as being enabled through a combination of historical context, criticism, linguistic analysis, and a capacity for a basic sympathy with the point of view at stake, and a back and forth movement between these interpretative strategies.[31] This, and not some kind of naively objectivizing, formalist methodology, is the lesson to be extracted from eighteenth- and nineteenth-century hermeneutics.[32] Gadamer confuses *any* thought about methodology (in general) with what he takes to be varieties of *Kantian-romantic* methodology (in particular),[33] and thus fails to acknowledge other, non-Kantian ways to think about methodology, both broadly speaking and within the specific discourse of hermeneutics.[34]

This, we should note, is not simply a question of getting the history of hermeneutics right or wrong (though that does indeed matter), but, more importantly, one of illegitimately reducing the systematic potential and relevance of this rich philosophical tradition, not only, but perhaps especially, if we are interested in the relationship between hermeneutics and the human sciences.

In the eighteenth-century debates about method, the significant question is not simply that of method versus truth. No, from this point of view, there is another, equally important distinction at stake, namely that between an ontological hermeneutics (widely defined along Gadamer's own lines) as opposed to an empirically informed approach. It is within this latter constellation that we should locate the Herder-Schleiermacher-Dilthey lineage in hermeneutical thought.

To what extent, then, does this lineage allow us to rethink the relationship between hermeneutics and the human sciences? How can it help us reconfigure the relationship between philosophy and the neighboring disciplines?

Like Herder and Schleiermacher, Dilthey combined an interest in hermeneutical theory with sustained hermeneutical practice (crystallizing, most famously, in his important studies of Schleiermacher, Novalis, Goethe, the young Hegel, Hölderlin and others, but also in his pseudonymous work as a critic of contemporary art and literature).[35] In fact, for Dilthey the value of Herder's and Schleiermacher's contributions does not simply rest on the way in which they provide the building blocks for hermeneutical theory, but also on their exemplification of practical-interpretative work, or, stronger still, on the back and forth movements between these levels of discourse. In Herder's case, his early work on art forms that escaped the attention of the educated elites seems especially important (and it would shape the artistic outlook of an entire generation of writers and painters in Germany and beyond).[36] In Schleiermacher's case, his broad-spanning engagement with the New Testament would, in the same vein, change the outlook of modern theology and religious culture. Other contributions from the period include Goethe's cultural emulation project in *West-Eastern Divan*, the Schlegel brothers and their studies of Indian literature, and perhaps even Hegel's fascination with ancient Indian texts and Persian poetry, as a discussion of the latter closes his aesthetics lectures in a spirit that goes beyond his Winckelmannian downplaying of the qualities of Egyptian art (over against classical art) at the beginning of the lecture course.[37]

Dilthey, though, speaks a language that differs from his predecessors in late eighteenth- and early nineteenth-century philosophy. His is indeed a language of method and scientific accountability, broadly speaking (though he does not, for this reason, endorse a position of the kind that Gadamer [and Heidegger] ascribes to him).[38] Again, Herder's contribution is important and will contribute to the shaping of Dilthey's outlook.[39] Herder had begun his reflections on hermeneutical issues by a grand-spanning (but never properly finished) essay on the nature of philosophy, and its confused and confusing position in between the natural and human sciences. He had observed that philosophy, when institutionally threatened, has a tendency to endorse the abstract language of the theoretical natural sciences (mathematics being a prime example), whose claims are necessary and universally valid and whose academic status, as a result, somehow appears to be beyond doubt and need for justification. In this form, philosophy comes to dominate the other humanistic disciplines.[40] In response to this predicament, in an attempt to overcome it, Herder conducts the double move of (a) emphasizing philosophy's affinity with the empirical-natural sciences (his affiliation of it with biology is stylistically reflected in a prose that is brimming with organic metaphors) and (b) stressing the importance of philosophy's reflecting on its own conditions, not as a meta-discipline, but as part of a broader field of academic discourse (for him, this disciplinary modesty is not a hindrance, but a platform for engaging in the interdisciplinary work to which he dedicated his life). When, a century later, Dilthey wrestles with the legitimacy of philosophy – and, more broadly, of the human sciences – it is not surprising that Herder will be one of the philosophers to whom he will appeal. In theory and practice, Dilthey's work is that of a true humanist and, as such, he is worried by a sense that the human sciences, while under increasing pressure from the natural sciences, can no longer point to the classical humanist tradition for their disciplinary justification. How, Dilthey asks, can the humanities be pitched as sciences? How can we, on the one hand, acknowledge their special status and, on the other, still see them as knowledge-producing, capable of arriving at intersubjectively testable results and making progress – i.e., of standing on par with the natural sciences?

Dilthey's philosophical production is but one, sustained effort to answer these questions and justify the relative methodological autonomy of the *Verstehenswissenschaften*. Understood as sciences of interpretation, the humanities enable a systematic exploration of our status as meaning-producing and, as such, as capable of moving beyond or, better, freely and reflectively responding to the law-governed structures of the natural world. Dilthey backs up this standpoint through a theory of the human mind, and much of the controversy around his contribution has centered on the precise status of this dimension of his work. In the literature, there is a tendency, shaped perhaps by Husserl (himself a transcendental philosopher of sorts), to see Dilthey's early theory as psychologistically motivated and only its later configurations as more hermeneutical in spirit (though it is an open question to what extent this periodization really holds and also whether we are justified in drawing such a distinction between the psychologistic and the hermeneutical aspects of his contribution). It is on the basis of this alleged psychologism that Husserl, Windelband, and others accused Dilthey of blurring the boundaries between philosophy and empirical science,[41] though another way of reading it would be, precisely, to see this aspect of his work as also involving his revival of the Herder and Schleiermacher lineage in hermeneutics.

I will not, in this context, enter into a more detailed debate about the major fault lines of modern hermeneutics. Nor will I enter into a more detailed discussion of Gadamer's and Heidegger's criticism of methodological hermeneutics. For our purposes, it suffices to know (a) that the different historical reconstructions of hermeneutics reflect and effectuate different systematical and methodological commitments, (b) that the positions at stake part ways over the status of philosophy vis-à-vis hermeneutics (is philosophy as such best understood as hermeneutics or is hermeneutics a subfield of philosophy?), (c) that they, as such, differ over the question of whether (and in what sense) philosophical hermeneutics provide the meta-discourse of the human sciences and, finally, (d) that this, in turn, reflects a disagreement over whether or not philosophical hermeneutics should be ontological. In this way, the different answers to the question "what is hermeneutics?" generate different responses to the question of whether (or in what sense) the human sciences are truly sciences and, relatedly, what kind of knowledge and education can be gained through involvement in these fields.

CONCLUDING THOUGHTS

I opened this chapter by asking how best to conceive of the relationship between philosophy and the other sciences as it appears through the lens of hermeneutical theory and practice. In its Heideggerian-Gadamerian form, this question is given a global, almost a priori answer: when hermeneutically conceived, philosophy offers an account of the deeper understanding through which our world is disclosed as a world of meaning (thus, as more than a mere environment, i.e., as human). However, once we question the Heideggerian-Gadamerian identification of philosophy with hermeneutics, and hermeneutics, in turn, with ontology, it is no longer clear how best to respond to this question. However, the fact that we do not, within non-ontological hermeneutics, find an absolute response to what philosophy is and how it best serves the other sciences, does not mean that we have no responses at all. And, further, once philosophy is no longer seen as a master discipline, philosophers can reflect, in the spirit of Herder, Schleiermacher, and Dilthey, on the role of their discipline in ongoing interaction with practitioners of other fields of knowledge. Thoroughly historical in their approaches, these philosophers suggest that the role of philosophy, amongst the other sciences, varies between cultures and time periods. Neither a king of the sciences, nor their servant, philosophy turns toward human self-understanding, thinks about thinking, understands understanding – yet does so with reference to how understanding and interpretation take shape throughout the human sciences. It may not be much, but it is, I think, enough to make philosophy one among a broad spectrum of human and social sciences (from whose results it draws and to whom it contributes with its own findings), and hermeneutics an irreducible contribution within this designated field of scholarship and thought.

NOTES

1 For a study of the discipline of philosophy with respect to grant discussions and discussions of scientific standards, see Michèle Lamont, *How Professors Think: Inside the Curious World of Academic Judgment* (Cambridge, MA: Harvard University Press, 2009), 64–8. See also Jason Stanley, "The Crisis of Philosophy," *Inside Higher Ed*, April 5, 2010: www.insidehighered.com/views/2010/04/05/crisis-philosophy, accessed June 2017.

2 For a survey of Heidegger and neo-Kantianism, see Michael Friedman, *A Parting of the Ways: Carnap, Cassirer, and Heidegger* (Chicago: Open Court, 2001), in particular 11–63 and Peter E. Gordon, *Continental Divide: Heidegger, Cassirer, Davos* (Cambridge, MA: Harvard University Press, 2010), especially 52–69. See also Charles Bambach, *Heidegger, Dilthey, and the Crisis of Historicism* (Ithaca, NY: Cornell University Press, 1995). Gadamer even includes Husserl in this movement and characterizes his contribution as "the final and most powerful form of neo-Kantian thought," which will in turn be transformed by Heidegger into philosophy (the contrast between "thought" and "philosophy" is Gadamer's own). Hans-Georg Gadamer, "Hegel and Heidegger," in *Hegel's Dialectics: Five Hermeneutical Studies*, trans. P. Christopher Smith (New Haven: Yale University Press, 1976), 102; "Hegel und Heidegger," *Gesammelte Werke* (Tübingen: J. C. B. Mohr, 1990), vol. III, 89. Further references to this work will be abbreviated GW, followed by volume and page number.

3 Martin Heidegger, *Kant and the Problem of Metaphysics*, trans. Richard Taft (Bloomington: Indiana University Press, 1990); *Kant und das Problem der Metaphysik* (Frankfurt am Main: Vittorio Klostermann, 1973).

4 Hans-Georg Gadamer, *Truth and Method*, trans. Joel Weinsheimer and Donald G. Marshall (New York: Continuum, 2003); *Wahrheit und Methode*, GW I. Further references to *Truth and Method* will be

abbreviated TM. Gadamer's work was discussed by Habermas, Apel, and later generations of critical theorists in Frankfurt (see Georgia Warnke's contribution to the present volume) and has later informed contributions by contemporary philosophers such as Donald Davidson, Charles Taylor, Alasdair MacIntyre, John McDowell, and Robert Brandom. For a solid treatment of contemporary debates in hermeneutics, see Jeff Malpas and Hans-Helmuth Gander (eds.), *The Routledge Companion to Hermeneutics* (London: Routledge, 2015).

5 See for example TM 164; GW I 268. See also "On The Scope and Function of Hermeneutical Reflection" (1967), where Gadamer, responding to Habermas's criticism of *Truth and Method*, writes that "[t]he phenomenon of understanding, then, shows the universality of human linguisticality as a limitless medium that carries *everything* within it – not only the 'culture' that has been handed down to us through language, but absolutely everything – because everything (in the world and out of it) is included in the realm of 'understandings' and understandability in which we move," *Philosophical Hermeneutics*, 25; "Rhetorik, Hermeneutik und Ideologiekritik. Metakritische Erörterungen zu *Wahrheit und Methode*," GW II 237.

6 For Schleiermacher's articulation of his commitment to universal hermeneutics, see Friedrich Schleiermacher, *Hermeneutics and Criticism and Other Writings*, ed. and trans. Andrew Bowie (Cambridge: Cambridge University Press, 1998), 5–7; *Hermeneutik und Kritik*, ed. Manfred Frank (Frankfurt am Main: Suhrkamp, 1993), 75–7. However, even though Gadamer traces general hermeneutics back to Schleiermacher, and Schleiermacher himself claims ownership of this significant move, the notion of universal hermeneutics stretches further back. See Werner Alexander, *Hermeneutica Generalis. Zur Konzeption und Entwicklung der allgemeinen Verstehenslehre im 17. und 18. Jahrhundert* (Stuttgart: M&P, Verlag für Wissenschaft und Forschung, 1993). See also Axel Bühler's discussion of this point in his introduction in Georg Friedrich Meier, *Versuch einer allgemeinen Auslegungskunst*, ed. Axel Bühler and Luigi Cataldi Madonna (Hamburg: Felix Meiner, 1996), vii–cii.

7 For Gadamer's tracing Schleiermacher's hermeneutics back to Kant, see TM 184–97; WM 188–201. In later essays, including an important 1966 response to the reception of *Truth and Method*, Gadamer, again,

associates Schleiermacher's hermeneutics with "the modern idea of science" and emphasizes what he, in a spirit stretching back to Nietzsche's *The Birth of Tragedy*, sees as a peculiar connection between scientism and aestheticism in modern philosophy. See "The Universality of the Hermeneutical Problem," in *Philosophical Hermeneutics*, trans. and ed. David E. Linge (Berkeley: University of California Press, 1977), 7; "Die Universalität des hermeneutischen Problems," GW II, 223.

8   As Heidegger characterizes Kant's erstwhile commitment in *Kant and the Problem of Metaphysics; Kant und das Problem der Metaphysik* § 39: "The Kantian laying of the ground for metaphysics began with the grounding of what underlies authentic metaphysics, or *Metaphysica Specialis* – it began with the grounding of *Metaphysica Generalis*. This, however – as 'ontology' – is already the form which has been consolidated into a discipline, the form of what, in Antiquity and finally with Aristotle, remains established as a problem of [...] authentic philosophizing." Gadamer, on his side, focuses not on the first Critique, but the *Critique of the Power of Judgment*. While seeking to offer a balanced picture of Kant, Gadamer is primarily concerned about what he sees as a romantic hypostatization of Kantian genius (TM 42–101; GW I 48–107).

9   With the English translation of *Truth and Method*: "we are always already situated within traditions, and this is no objectifying process – i.e., we do not conceive of what tradition says as something other, something alien. It is always part of us, a model or exemplar, a kind of cognizance that our later historical judgment would hardly regard as a kind of knowledge but as the most ingenuous affinity with tradition" (TM 282). The translation is a problematically modified version of the original: "Wir stehen [...] ständig in Überlieferung, und dieses Darinstehen ist kein vergegenständlichendes Verhalten, so daß das, was die Überlieferung sagt, als ein anderes, Fremdes gedacht wäre – es ist immer schon ein Eigenes, *Vorbild und Abschreckung*, ein Sichwiedererkennen, in dem für unser späteres historisches Nachurteil kaum noch Erkennen, sondern unbefangenste Anverwandlung der Überlieferung zu gewahren ist" (GW I 286–7, my emphasis). Such insights into the constitutive situatedness in tradition are, in turn, held up against "the dominant epistemological methodologism" (GW I 286–7).

10 It should be noted that both Hegel and Heidegger emerge as critics of romantic aesthetics (of a Jena disposition). Heidegger, though, is favorably disposed toward Hölderlin's and Schelling's versions of Tübingen romanticism. Hegel, on his side, borrows more from the romantics than what he usually is willing to admit. Gadamer draws on their respective criticisms – and the positive, philosophical alternatives outlined – in *Truth and Method*. This, though, does not mean that he is uncritical of Hegel and Heidegger. While he is rather vague in his criticism of Heidegger, his objections to Hegel are clearly articulated and include worries about the notion of the end of art (see for example TM 98–9; GW I 104–6) and what Gadamer calls his (Hegel's) radicalization of logos (see for example "Hegel and Heidegger," 107; "Hegel und Heidegger," GW III 94).

11 Needless to say, this point does not do justice to Schleiermacher's engagement with the tradition or his importance as a Plato scholar. Further, it overlooks his interaction with early modern philosophers, including Leibniz and Spinoza, especially the latter, whom Gadamer takes to figure prominently within the humanistic tradition.

12 Gadamer, "Reflections," 17.

13 It is important, in this context, to realize that Gadamer views hermeneutics as a (dialogical) practice and insists that it emerges out of a dialogue with the past. Given these twin commitments, his hermeneutics is not simply a theory, but also a way of philosophizing – a way of philosophizing in which systematic and historical questions are necessarily intertwined.

14 Martin Heidegger, *Being and Time*, trans. Joan Stambaugh (Albany: SUNY Press, 1996); *Sein und Zeit* (Tübingen: Max Niemeyer, 1993), §32.

15 Gadamer's discussion of his own beginnings in neo-Kantian philosophy (and his teachers, including Natorp and Hartmann) and his almost twenty years in Marburg include "Reflections on my Philosophical Journey," trans. Richard E. Palmer, in *The Philosophy of Hans-Georg Gadamer*, Library of Living Philosophers, vol. XXIV, ed. Lewis Edwin Hahn (Chicago: Open Court, 1997), 3–63 and *Philosophische Lehrjahre* (Frankfurt am Main: Vittorio Klostermann, 1977), 14–111. Se also, Jean Grondin, *Hans-Georg Gadamer: A Biography*, trans. Joel Weinsheimer (New Haven: Yale University Press, 2003), 71–91.

16 See my *Gadamer and the Legacy of German Idealism* (Cambridge: Cambridge University Press, 2009).
17 Heidegger's early lectures offer interesting reflections on historical-hermeneutical work. At the heart of these lectures is the intuition that, as Heidegger puts it, "[t]he historical aspect of philosophy is visible only in the very act of philosophizing. It is graspable only as existence." A similar approach, in my view, saturates Gadamer's work. For Heidegger's early philosophy of history (and hermeneutics), see for example the Winter Semester 1921–1922 lectures *Phenomenological Interpretations of Aristotle: Initiation into Phenomenological Research*, trans. Richard Rojcewicz (Bloomington: Indiana University Press, 2001); *Phänomenologische Interpretationen zu Aristoteles. Einführung in die phänomenologische Forschung, Gesamtausgabe*, ed. Friedrich-Wilhelm von Hermann et al. (Frankfurt am Main: Vittorio Klostermann, 1975–), vol. 61 and the Summer Semester 1923 lectures *Ontology: The Hermeneutics of Facticity*, trans. John van Buren (Bloomington: Indiana University Press, 1999); *Ontologie (Hermeneutik der Faktizität), Gesamtausgabe*, vol. 63. The quote is from page 3 of the English translation of the 1921–1922 lectures. See also Benjamin Crowe's discussion in Chapter 9 of the present volume. Gadamer attended Heidegger's seminars from 1923 onwards and later suggests that this was a most formative experience ("Reflections," 9; GW II 485).
18 Robert R. Sullivan importantly emphasizes the influence of the George circle in his *Political Hermeneutics: The Early Thinking of Hans-Georg Gadamer* (State Park: The Pennsylvania State University Press, 1989). He also stresses, again importantly, the influence of the classicist circles at the time.
19 Thus, Gadamer, in the dialogical spirit he himself defends in his early work, will later admit that his presentation of science and of philosophical romanticism were too polemical. See "Reflections," 40 and TM 564; GW II 462. He does not, however, seek to develop more adequate accounts of these disciplines and movements, nor dwell on their relevance for philosophical hermeneutics.
20 Over the past decades, there have been a number of critical studies shedding light on Gadamer's political role in between the wars and during World War II. Two examples are Theresa Orozco, *Platonische Gewalt. Gadamers politische Hermeneutik der NS-Zeit*

(Hamburg: Argument Verlag, 1995) and Richard Wolin, *The Seduction of Unreason: The Intellectual Romance with Fascism from Nietzsche to Postmodernism* (Princeton: Princeton University Press, 2004), 89–129. Though valuable in their own right, these studies are, in my view, too one-sided and it would be a worthwhile challenge to carefully illuminate the broader, intellectual environment in which twentieth-century hermeneutics developed without, for that reason, reducing it to historical and sociological factors alone.

21 On Rudolf Makkreel's reading, Dilthey's hermeneutics expands the Kantian notion of imagination which, in turn, is hermeneutically constituted. Makkreel, though, does not commit (or see Dilthey as committing) to a (proto-)Heideggerian version of this argument. For Makkreel's reading of Kant, see *Imagination and Interpretation in Kant: The Hermeneutical Import of the "Critique of Judgment"* (Chicago: University of Chicago Press, 1990); for his reading of Dilthey, see *Dilthey: Philosopher of the Human Studies* (Princeton: Princeton University Press, 1975). In my view, Kant and his notion of imagination is one important source for Dilthey. However, within Kant's work, we have to be cautious, so as not to overemphasize the notion of imagination and, within the larger scope of eighteenth-century philosophy, we need to stay alert to the multiple sources on which Dilthey draws, not all of whom were Kantian or even Kant-friendly.

22 Two helpful studies that offer more nuanced discussions of school philosophy are Stefanie Buchenau, *The Founding of Aesthetics in the German Enlightenment: The Art of Invention and the Invention of Art* (Cambridge: Cambridge University Press, 2013) and Frederick C. Beiser, *Diotima's Children: German Aesthetic Rationalism from Leibniz to Lessing* (Oxford: Oxford University Press, 2009).

23 I offer an account of this in my *Herder's Hermeneutics: History, Poetry, Enlightenment* (Cambridge: Cambridge University Press, 2017).

24 Dilthey presents Schleiermacher's hermeneutics as a contribution that seeks to combine elements from Herder and Fichte. See Wilhelm Dilthey, *Schleiermacher's Hermeneutical System in Relation to Earlier Protestant Hermeneutics*, trans. Theodore Nordenhaug, in *Hermeneutics and the Study of History, Selected Works*, vol. IV, ed. Rudolf A. Makkreel and Frithjof Rodi (Princeton: Princeton University Press, 1996), 33–229; *Gesammelte Schriften*, 26 vols.

(Göttingen: Vandenhoeck & Ruprecht, 1914–2005), XIV 595–787. See also my "Enlightenment, History, and the Anthropological Turn: The Hermeneutical Challenge of Dilthey's Schleiermacher Studies," in *Anthropologie und Geschichte. Studien zu Wilhelm Dilthey aus Anlass seines 100. Todestages*, ed. Giuseppe D'Anna, Helmut Johach, and Eric S. Nelson (Würzburg: Königshausen & Neumann, 2013), 323–55.

25 Herder, though, is not always balanced in his assessment of indigenous literatures. Some of his more interesting interpretations can be found in the essay on *Ossian*. See for instance *Werke in zehn Bänden*, ed. Martin Bollacher et al. (Frankfurt am Main: Deutscher Klassiker Verlag, 1985–1998), I 465, 478, 488 and his collection of *Volkslieder*, in vol. III 298–9. Further references to Herder's *Werke* will be abbreviated FHA, followed by volume and page number. See also Andreas F. Kelletat, *Herder und die Weltliteratur. Zur Geschichte des Übersetzens im 18. Jahrhundert* (Frankfurt am Main: Peter Lang, 1984).

26 See Michael N. Forster, "Herder and the Birth of Modern Anthropology," in *After Herder: Philosophy of Language in the German Tradition* (Oxford: Oxford University Press, 2010), 199–244.

27 The fact that I focus, in this context, on the Herder, Schleiermacher, Dilthey lineage in hermeneutics does not imply that I rule out the importance and relevance of alternatives within and beyond a Western hermeneutical tradition (see for example Kai Marchal's contribution to the present volume). A focus on these figures, however, has the advantage of being internal to Gadamer's work and can thus also occasion reflection on his hermeneutical practice and the way in which he positions his own alternative as a deliberate step beyond his predecessors in hermeneutics.

28 In their works we find, for example, an emphasis on an informal, holistically oriented and aesthetically conceived (but not, as Gadamer assumes, aestheticizing) *Einfühlung* or *divination*. I discuss this point in more detail in my "Acknowledging the Second Person: Schleiermacher on Imagination, Divination, and the Philosophical Problem of the Other," in *The Imagination in German Idealism and Romanticism*, ed. Gerad Gentry and Konstantin Pollok (Cambridge: Cambridge University Press, forthcoming).

29 Herder notes how cultures "have drunk deep of this pleasant poison, and handed the cup to others," *Outlines of a Philosophy of the History*

of Man, trans. T. Churchill (New York: Bergman Publishers, 1800), 352; FHA VI 513. Herder is also a philosopher who emphasizes the need for genealogy, focusing not only on the historical past, but also on how our narratives about the past often serve to justify the ideologies of the present. His best-known example of such an analysis is the discussion of slavery and colonialism in *This Too A Philosophy of History*, in *Philosophical Writings*, ed. and trans. Michael N. Forster (Cambridge: Cambridge University Press, 2002), 272–361; FHA IV 9–109. These aspects of Herder's philosophy are nicely expounded in Sonia Sikka, *Herder on Humanity and Cultural Difference: Enlightened Relativism* (Cambridge: Cambridge University Press, 2011) and Vicky Spencer, *Herder's Political Thought: A Study of Language, Culture, and Community* (Toronto: University of Toronto Press, 2012).

30 For this dimension of Gadamer's work, see TM 101–34; GW I 107–39. Gadamer is particularly interested in how the structure of the play is independent of the individual subjectivity of the players.

31 Gadamer thus takes Schleiermacher to advocate a version of the hermeneutical circle that seeks to grasp the relation between an individual language-user and the original audience in order to achieve a conclusive unlocking of historical meaning (TM 191; GW I 194). In an early essay, Gadamer compares Schleiermacher and Heidegger's ontological retrieval of understanding, emphasizing Schleiermacher's subjectivizing of this principle. In my view, however, Gadamer's reading is unduly polemical: Schleiermacher's hermeneutics has a subjective component (in that it takes into account the individuality of the speaker), but does not, for that reason, represent a subjectivization of understanding. For Gadamer's essay, see "On the Circle of Understanding," in *Hermeneutics Versus Science?*, ed. and trans. J. M. Connolloy and T. Keutner (Indiana: Notre Dame University Press, 1988), 67–78; "Vom Zirkel des Verstehens," GW II 57–65, see also TM 291–300; GW I 296–305.

32 In spite of this, Gadamer refers to Herder throughout *Truth and Method* (but never discusses his contribution in any detail). He also deals with Herder in a problematic essay written during the war, *Volk und Geschichte im Denken Herders* (Frankfurt am Main: Klostermann, 1942). An edited version of this essay is published as "Herder und die geschichtliche Welt," *Gesammelte Werke*, vol. IV (Tübingen: J. C. B.

Mohr, 1987), 318–35. Heidegger, too, took an interest in Herder and gave lectures on his philosophy of language in 1939: *On the Essence of Language: The Metaphysics of Language and the Essencing of the Word. Concerning Herder's Treatise "On the Origin of Language,"* trans. Wanda Torres Gregory and Yvonne Unna (Albany: SUNY Press, 2004); *Vom Wesen der Sprache. Die Metaphysik der Sprache und die Wesung des Wortes. Zu Herders Abhandlung "Über den Ursprung der Sprache,"* GA 85.

33 This is particularly clear in his discussion of Schleiermacher in the first part of *Truth and Method*. Schleiermacher's method is presented as Kantian and his notion of individuality read in light of a misunderstood version of Kantian genius.

34 Dilthey, by contrast, sees Schleiermacher as affiliated with Herder, and notes that Herder took "his point of departure from Kant, but at the same time [was] in diametrical opposition to him." Dilthey, "Goethe and the Poetic Imagination," trans. Christopher Rodie, in *Poetry and Experience, Selected Works*, vol. V, ed. Rudolf Makkreel and Frithjof Rodi, trans. Lois Agosta, Rudolf Makkreel et al. (Princeton: Princeton University Press, 1985), 285; *Das Erlebnis und die Dichtung* (Göttingen: Vandenhoeck & Ruprecht, 1970), 171.

35 This part of Dilthey's production is not entirely covered by the collected work, but published in *Das Erlebnis und die Dichtung*. I argue for the relevance of this work to our understanding of Dilthey's hermeneutical contribution in "A Task Most Pressing: Dilthey's Philosophy of the Novel," *Interpreting Dilthey*, ed. Eric Nelson (Cambridge: Cambridge University Press, forthcoming).

36 Of particular importance here is Goethe, but also the work of Madame de Staël. De Staël's *De l'Allemagne*, in which she is influenced by, but also gives solid coverage of, Herder's work, was widely translated and read across Europe and the US. For her discussion of Herder, see for example Anne Louise Germaine de Staël, *Germany*, trans. O. W. Wright (Boston: Houghton, Mifflin, and company, 1859), vol. II, 84–9; *De l'Allemagne* (Paris: Firmin-Didot, 1852), 359–62.

37 Hegel's discussion of Humboldt's approach to Indian literature implies important hermeneutical insights. See G. W. F. Hegel, "Über die unter dem Namen Bhagavad-Gita bekannte Episode des Mahabharata. Von Wilhelm von Humboldt (1827)," *Berliner Schriften 1818–1831, Werke*

in 20 Bänden, vol. 11 (Frankfurt am Main: Suhrkamp, 1970), 131–204. For a thorough study of the German (philological) orientation toward Eastern cultures, see Suzanne L. Marchand, *German Orientalism in the Age of Empire: Religion, Race, and Scholarship* (Cambridge: Cambridge University Press, 2009).

38 I do, in other words, not agree with Gadamer's description of Dilthey's philosophy as being situated in the intersection between romanticism and positivism. See Gadamer, "Wilhelm Dilthey nach 150 Jahren (Zwischen Romantik und Positivismus. Ein Diskussionsbeitrag)" (1985), in *Dilthey und die Philosophie der Gegenwart*, ed. Ernst Wolfgang Orth (Freiburg: Karl Alber, 1985), 157–82. Gadamer's point, in turn, is anticipated in Heidegger's discussion of Dilthey and York in *Being and Time*. Here, Dilthey's model is being described as spanned between aestheticism and rationalism (and also mechanism; Heidegger does not at this point distinguish between the two). Heidegger, *Being and Time*; *Sein und Zeit* §77.

39 This is particularly clear in his work on Schleiermacher. See, again, Dilthey, "Schleiermacher's Hermeneutical System"; *Gesammelte Schriften* XIV 595–787.

40 Herder asks ironically: "How can philosophy be reconciled with humanity and politics so that it also really serves the latter?" This, Herder notes, is a "question which [has had] more than one career-philosopher [*graduierten Philosophen*] as answerer, and which least of all needs such a person to decide it." Herder, *Philosophical Writings*, 6; FHA I 108. There is, in his view, a professional tendency to answer this question with reference to mathematics and the theoretical natural sciences ("Where it [philosophy] was victorious, behold, it generally built its throne on the ruins of mathematics," *Philosophical Writings*, 3; FHA I 104). Herder, on his side, advocates for philosophy engaging in an on-going effort to delineate its own boundaries so as to be able to enter into genuinely cooperative interrelations with other disciplines.

41 For an interesting discussion of this point, see Katherina Kinzel, "The History of Philosophy and the Puzzles of Life: Windelband and Dilthey on the Ahistorical Core of Philosophical Thinking," in *The Emergence of Modern Relativism: The German Debates from the 1770s to the 1930s*, ed. Martin Kusch, Katherina Kinzel, Johannes Steizinger, and Niels Wildschut (London: Routledge, forthcoming).

Bibliography

Abu Zayd, Nasr. *Rethinking the Qur'an: Towards a Humanistic Hermeneutics.* Utrecht: Humanistics University Press, 2004.

Alexander, Larry, and Saikrishna Prakash. "'Is That English You're Speaking?' Why Intention Free Interpretation is an Impossibility." *San Diego Law Review* 41 (2004): 967–95.

Alexander, Werner. *Hermeneutica Generalis. Zur Konzeption und Entwicklung der allgemeinen Verstehenslehre im 17. und 18. Jahrhundert.* Stuttgart: M & P Verlag, 1993.

Ankersmit, Frank. *Historical Representation.* Stanford: Stanford University Press, 2001.

Apel, Karl-Otto. *From a Transcendental-Semiotic Point of View.* Edited by Marianna Papastephanou. Manchester: Manchester University Press, 1998.

App, Urs. *The Birth of Orientalism.* Philadelphia: The University of Pennsylvania Press, 2010.

Ashmore, Robert. *The Transport of Reading. Text and Understanding in the World of Tao Qian (365–427).* Cambridge, MA and London: Harvard University Press, 2010.

Assis, Arthur Alfaix. *What is History for? Johann Gustav Droysen and the Functions of Historiography.* New York and Oxford: Berghahn, 2014.

Ast, Friedrich. *Grundlinien der Grammatik, Hermeneutik und Kritik.* Landshut: Jos. Thomann, Buchdrucker und Buchhändler, 1808.

Austin, John L. *Sense and Sensibilia.* Oxford: Oxford University Press, 1962.

Azzouni, Jody. *Semantic Perception: How the Illusion of a Common Language Arises and Persists.* New York: Oxford University Press, 2013.

Baird, William. *History of New Testament Research. Vol. 1: From Deism to Tübingen.* Minneapolis: Fortress Press, 1992.

Bakhtin, M. M. "The Problem of Speech Genres." In *Speech Genres and Other Late Essays.* Edited by C. Emerson and M. Holquist. Austin: University of Texas Press, 1986: 60–102.

Bambach, Charles R. *Heidegger, Dilthey, and the Crisis of Historicism.* Ithaca, NY: Cornell University Press, 1995.

Barnett, Randy E. "Interpretation and Construction." *Harvard Journal of Law & Public Policy* 34 (2011): 65.
Barthes, Roland. *Critique et vérité*. Paris: Seuil, 1966.
― "The Death of the Author." *Aspen Magazine*, Fall 5/6, 1967.
― *Elements of Semiology*. Translated by A. Lavers and C. Smith. New York: Hill & Wang, 1977 [1964].
― *Le plaisir du texte*. Paris: Seuil, 1973.
― *Mythologies*. Translated by R. Howard and A. Lavers. New York: Hill & Wang, 2013 [1957].
― *Œuvres complètes*. Paris: Seuil, 2002.
― *Sollers écrivain*. Paris: Seuil, 1979.
― *S/Z*. Paris: Seuil, 1970.
Barthold, Lauren Swayne. *Gadamer's Dialectical Hermeneutics*. Lanham: Lexington Books, 2010.
Barton, John. *The Cambridge Companion to Biblical Interpretation*. Cambridge: Cambridge University Press, 1998.
Barton, John, and John Muddiman. *The Oxford Bible Commentary*. Oxford: Oxford University Press, 2001.
Bauer, Christoph Johannes. *"Das Geheimnis aller Bewegung ist Zweck" – Geschichtsphilosophie bei Hegel und Droysen*. Hamburg: Meiner, 2001.
Bayer, Oswald. *A Contemporary in Dissent: Johann Georg Hamann as a Radical Enlightener*. Translated by Roy A. Harrisfield and Marc C. Mattes. Grand Rapids: Eerdmans Publishing Company, 2012.
Beck, Hanno. "Kommentar" to *Ideen zu einer Physiognomik der Gewächse* by Alexander von Humboldt. Darmstadt: Wissenschaftliche Buchgesellschaft, 1989.
Beiser, Frederick C. *Diotima's Children: German Aesthetic Rationalism from Leibniz to Lessing*. Oxford: Oxford University Press, 2009.
― *The Fate of Reason: German Philosophy from Kant to Fichte*. Cambridge, MA: Harvard University Press, 1987.
― *The German Historicist Tradition*. Oxford: Oxford University Press, 2011.
Benhabib, Seyla, Wolfgang Bonss, and John McCole, eds. *On Max Horkheimer: New Perspectives*. Cambridge, MA: MIT Press, 1993.
Berlin, Isaiah. *The Magus of the North: J.G. Hamann and the Origins of Modern Irrationalism*. New York: Farrar Straus & Giroux, 1994.
Bernhardi, August Ferdinand. "Review of Herder's Metacritique." In *Metacritique: The Linguistic Assault on German Idealism*. Edited by Jere Paul Surber. Amherst: Humanity Books, 2001: 139–48.
― *Sprachlehre*. Berlin: Heinrich Frölich, 1801.

"Verstand und Erfahrung. Eine Metakritik zur Kritik der reinen Vernunft von J. G. Herder." In *Athenaeum: Eine Zeitschrift von August Wilhelm Schlegel und Friedrich Schlegel*, vol. 3, 1800: 266–81.

Bernstein, Richard J. "What is the Difference That Makes a Difference? Gadamer, Habermas, and Rorty." In *Hermeneutics and Modern Philosophy*. Edited by Brice R. Wachterhauser. Albany: SUNY Press, 1986: 343–76.

Betti, Emilio. "Hermeneutics as the General Methodology of the Geisteswissenschaften." In *Contemporary Hermeneutics: Hermeneutics as Method, Philosophy, and Critique*. Edited by Josef Bleicher. London: Routledge & Kegan Paul, 1980: 51–94.

"Hermeneutics as the General Methodology of the Geisteswissenschaften." In *The Hermeneutic Tradition: From Ast to Ricoeur, Hermeneutics as the General Methodology of the Geisteswissenschaften*. Edited by Gayle L. Ormiston and Alan D. Schrift. Albany: SUNY Press, 1990: 159–97.

Binding, Karl. *Handbuch des Strafrechts – Band I. Systematisches Handbuch der Deutschen Rechtswissenschaft*. Leipzig: Duncker & Humblot, 1885.

Blair, Ann. "The Rise of Note-taking in Early Modern Europe." *Intellectual History Review* 20 (2010): 303–16.

Blanke, Horst Walter, and Dirk Fleischer. *Theoretiker der deutschen Aufklärungshistorie*. 2 vols. Stuttgart, Bad Cannstatt: Frommann-Holzboog, 1990.

Blanke, Horst Walter, and Jörn Rüsen, eds. *Von der Aufklärung zum Historismus: Zum Strukturwandel des historischen Denkens*. Paderborn: Schöningh, 1984.

Bod, Rens, and Julia Kursell, eds. "The History of Humanities and the History of Science." *Isis* 106 (2015): 337–40.

Bödeker, Hans Erich, Georg Iggers, Jonathan Knudsen, and Peter Hanns Reill, eds. *Aufklärung und Geschichte: Studien zur deutschen Geschichtswissenschaft im 18. Jahrhundert*. Göttingen: Vandenhoeck & Ruprecht, 1986.

Boeckh, August. *On Interpretation and Criticism*. Norman: University of Oklahoma Press, 1968.

Bowie, Andrew. *From Romanticism to Critical Theory: The Philosophy of German Literary Theory*. London: Routledge, 1997.

Brandom, Robert B. *Making it Explicit: Reasoning, Representing and Discursive Commitment*. Cambridge, MA: Harvard University Press, 1994.

"Some Pragmatist Themes in Hegel's Idealism." In *Tales of the Mighty Dead: Historical Essays in the Metaphysics of Intentionality*. Cambridge, MA: Harvard University Press, 2002: 210–34.

Brentano, Franz. *Psychology from an Empirical Standpoint*. Translated by Antos Rancurello, D. B. Terrell, and Linda McAlister. Edited by Oskar Kraus and Linda McAlister. London: Routledge, 1973.

Brooks, Cleanth. "Literary Criticism." In *English Institute Essays*. New York: Columbia University Press, 1946: 127–58.

"A Note on the Limits of 'History' and the Limits of 'Criticism.'" *Sewanee Review* 61 (1953): 129–35.

Brooks, Thom. "Philosophy Unbound: The Idea of Global Philosophy." *Metaphilosophy* 44:3 (April 2013): 254–66.

Bruns, Gerald. *Hermeneutics Ancient and Modern*. New Haven: Yale University Press, 1992.

Buchenau, Stefanie. *The Founding of Aesthetics in the German Enlightenment: The Art of Invention and the Invention of Art*. Cambridge: Cambridge University Press, 2013.

Buckle, Henry Thomas. *History of Civilization in England*. London: Parker, 1857.

Buffon, George L. *Histoire naturelle, générale et particulière*, 36 vols. Paris: L'Imprimerie royale, 1749–1778.

Bultmann, Christoph. "Herder's Biblical Studies." In *A Companion to the Works of Johann Gottfried Herder*. Edited by Hans Adler and Wulf Koepke. Rochester: Camden House, 2009: 233–46.

Bultmann, Christoph, and Lutz Danneberg, eds. *Hebraistik–Hermeneutik–Homiletik. Die "Philologia Sacra" im frühneuzeitlichen Bibelstudium*. Berlin: de Gruyter, 2011.

"Historical-Critical Inquiry." In *The Hebrew Bible: A Critical Companion*. Edited by John Barton. Princeton: Princeton University Press, 2016: 431–54.

Buntfuss, Markus et al. "Theologie." In *Herder Handbuch*. Edited by Stefan Greif, Marion Heinz, and Heinrich Clairmont. Paderborn: Wilhelm Fink, 2016: 319–85.

Bush, Douglas. "Marvell's Horatian Ode." *Sewanee Review* 60 (1952): 363–76.

Byrne, Peter. *Kant on God*. Aldershot: Ashgate, 2007.

The Moral Interpretation of Religion. Edinburgh: Edinburgh University Press, 1998.

Natural Religion and the Nature of Religion: The Legacy of Deism. London: Routledge, 1989.

Cassirer, Ernst. *Freiheit und Form. Studien zur deutschen Geistesgeschichte*. Darmstadt: Wissenschaftliche Buchgesellschaft, 1961.

Die Philosophie der Aufklärung. Tübingen: J. C. B. Mohr, 1932.

The Philosophy of the Enlightenment. Translated by Fritz C. A. Koelln and James P. Pettegrove. Princeton: Princeton University Press, 1979.

Chakrabarty, Dipesh. *Provincializing Europe: Postcolonial Thought and Historical Difference*. Princeton: Princeton University Press, 2007 [2000].

Chomsky, Noam. *Cartesian Linguistics*. New York: Harper & Row, 1966.

Cohen, Mordechai Z. and Adele Berlin, eds. *Interpreting Scriptures in Judaism, Christianity, and Islam: Overlapping Inquiries.* Cambridge: Cambridge University Press, 2016.

Condillac, E. B. de. *Essai sur l'origine des connaissances humaines.* Paris: Vrin, 2014 [1746].

Cook, John. "Is Davidson a Gricean?" *Dialogue* 48 (2009): 557.

Corbin, Henry. *Creative Imagination in the Sufism of Ibn Arabi.* Princeton: Princeton University Press, 1969.

Crowe, Benjamin D. *Heidegger's Phenomenology of Religion: Realism and Cultural Criticism.* Bloomington: Indiana University Press, 2007.

Heidegger's Religious Origins: Destruction and Authenticity. Bloomington: Indiana University Press, 2006.

Crowell, Steven G. *Phenomenology and Normativity in Husserl and Heidegger.* Cambridge: Cambridge University Press, 2013.

Dallmayr, Fred. *Being in the World: Dialogue and Cosmopolis.* Lexington: The University Press of Kentucky, 2013.

"Life-World and Critique." In *Between Freiburg and Frankfurt: Toward a Critical Ontology.* Amherst: University of Massachusetts Press, 1991: 13–43.

Damrosch, David. *How to Read World Literature?* Oxford: Wiley-Blackwell, 2017.

Dannhauer, Johann Konrad. *Idea boni interpretis et malitiosi calumniatoris.* Strasbourg: Glaser, 1630.

Dante Aligheri. Il Convivio. https://digitaldante.columbia.edu/library/dantes-works/the-convivio/.

Daston, Lorraine, and Peter Galison. *Objectivity.* New York: Zone, 2007.

Daston, Lorraine, and Glenn W. Most. "History of Science and History of Philologies." *Isis* 106 (2015): 378–90.

Davidson, Donald. "A Nice Derangement of Epitaphs." In *Truth, Language, and History.* Edited by Donald Davidson. Oxford: Clarendon Press, 2009: 89–107.

"Three Varieties of Knowledge." In *Subjective, Intersubjective, Objective.* Edited by Donald Davidson, 205–20. Oxford and New York: Oxford University Press, 2001.

Derrida, Jacques. *Of Grammatology.* Translated by G. Spivak. Baltimore and London: Johns Hopkins University Press, 1974 [1967].

Margins of Philosophy. Translated by A. Bass. Chicago: University of Chicago Press, 1984 [1972].

Writing and Difference. Translated by A. Bass. Chicago: University of Chicago Press, 1978 [1967].

Detmer, David. "Gadamer's Critique of the Enlightenment." In *The Philosophy of Hans-Georg Gadamer*. Edited by Lewis Edwin Hahn. The Library of Living Philosophers XXIV. Chicago and LaSalle: Open Court, 1997: 275–86.

Diderot, Denis. *Pensées sur l'Interprétation de la Nature*. Paris, 1754.

Thoughts on the Interpretation of Nature and Other Philosophical Works. Translated by Lorna Sandler. Manchester: Clinamen Press, 1999.

Dilthey, Wilhelm. "The Construction of the Historical World in the Human Studies." In *Selected Writings*. Edited and translated by H. P. Rickman. Cambridge: Cambridge University Press, 1976: 168–263.

"Das hermeneutische System Schleiermachers in der Auseinandersetzung mit der älteren protestantischen Hermeneutik." In *Gesammelte Schriften*. Vol. 14.2. Stuttgart: Teubner, Vandenhoeck & Ruprecht, 1966: 595–787.

Der Aufbau der geschichtlichen Welt in den Geisteswissenschaften. In *Gesammelte Schriften*. Vol. 7. Göttingen: Vandenhoeck & Ruprecht, 1968.

Das Erlebnis und die Dichtung. Göttingen: Vandenhoeck & Ruprecht, 1970.

Gesammelte Schriften. 26 vols. Göttingen: Vandenhoeck & Ruprecht, 1914–2006.

Hermeneutics and the Study of History. In *Selected Works*. Vol. IV. Edited by Rudolf A. Makkreel and Frithjof Rodi. Translated by Theodore Nordenhaug et al. Princeton: Princeton University Press, 1996.

Poetry and Experience. In *Selected Works*. Vol. V. Edited by Rudolf Makkreel and Frithjof Rodi. Translated by Lois Agosta, Rudolf Makkreel, et al. Princeton: Princeton University Press, 1985.

"The Rise of Hermeneutics." *New Literary History* 3 (1972): 229–44.

Donagan, Alan. *The Later Philosophy of R. G. Collingwood*. Oxford: Clarendon Press, 1962.

Donagan, William. *Laws and Explanation in History*. Oxford: Oxford University Press, 1957.

Dray, William. *Laws and Explanation in History*. Oxford: Oxford University Press, 1957.

Dronke, E. R. *Fabula: Explorations into the Uses of Myth in Medieval Platonism*. Leiden: Brill, 1974.

Droysen, J. G. "Die Erhebung der Geschichte zum Rang einer Wissenschaft." *Historische Zeitschrift* 9 (1863): 1–22. Reprinted in *Outline of the Principles of History* (Boston: Ginn, 1893), 61–89.

Historik. Historical-critical edition by Peter Leyh. 4 vols. Stuttgart/Bad Cannstatt: Frommann-Holzboog, 1977.

Historik, Vorlesungen über Enzyklopädie und Methodologie der Geschichte. Munich: Oldenbourg, 1937.

Historik: Die Vorlesungen über Enzyklopädie und Methodologie der Geschichte. Stuttgart: Bad Cannstatt: Frommann-Holzboog, 1977.

Dryden, John. "The Author's Apology for Heroic Poetry and Poetic Licence." In *Essays of John Dryden*. Edited by W. P. Kerr. Vol. 1. Oxford: Clarendon Press, 1926: 178–90.

Dworkin, Ronald M. "Is There Really No Right Answer in Hard Cases?" In *A Matter of Principle*. Oxford: Clarendon, 1985: 119–45.

Elkins, James. *Chinese Landscape Painting as Western Art History*. Hong Kong: Hong Kong University Press, 2010.

Ekins, Richard. *The Nature of Legislative Intent*. Oxford: Oxford University Press, 2012.

Ermarth, Michael. *Wilhelm Dilthey: The Critique of Historical Reason*. Chicago: University of Chicago Press, 1978.

Ernesti, Johann August. *Elements of Interpretation*. Translated and edited by Moses Stuart. Andover: Flagg and Gould, 1822.

Institutio interpretis Novi Testamenti. Leipzig: Weidmann, 1761.

Principles of Biblical Interpretation. Translated by Charles H. Terrot. Edinburgh: Thomas Clark, 1833.

Esterhammer, Angela. *The Romantic Performative: Language and Action in British and German Romanticism*. Stanford: Stanford University Press, 2002.

Evans, Richard. *In Defence of History*. London: Granta Books, 1997.

Feigl, Herbert. "The Scientific Outlook: Naturalism and Humanism." In *Readings in the Philosophy of Science*. Edited by H. Feigl and M. Brodbeck. New York: Appleton-Century-Crofts, 1953: 11–14.

Felski, Rita. "Critique and the Hermeneutics of Suspicion." *M/C Journal* 15:1 (2012).

Fichte, J. G. *Addresses to the German Nation*. Translated by Isaac Nakhimovsky, Béla Kapossy, and Keith Tribe. Indianapolis: Hackett Publishing Company, 2013.

"Foundations of the Entire Science of Knowledge." In *The Science of Knowledge*. Edited and translated by Peter Heath and John Lachs. Cambridge: Cambridge University Press, 1982.

Foundations of Natural Right. Edited by Frederick Neuhouser. Cambridge: Cambridge University Press, 2000.

Gesamtausgabe der Bayerischen Akademie der Wissenschaften. Edited by Reinhard Lauth and Hans Jacob. Stuttgart–Bad Cannstatt: Frommann, 1962.

"On the Linguistic Capacity and the Origin of Language." In *Language and German Idealism: Fichte's Linguistic Philosophy*. Edited by Jere Paul Surber. New York: Humanity Books, 1996: 117–45.

"Review of Aenesidemus." In *Between Kant and Hegel: Texts in the Development of Post-Kantian Idealism*. Edited by George di Giovanni and H. S. Harris. Albany: SUNY Press, 1985: 105–35.

The Vocation of Man. Edited by R. M. Chisholm. New York: Macmillan, 1985.

Figal, Günter. "*Phronesis* as Understanding: Situating Philosophical Hermeneutics." In *The Specter of Relativism: Truth, Dialogue, and Phronesis in Philosophical Hermeneutics*. Edited by Lawrence K. Schmidt. Evanston: Northwestern University Press, 1995: 236–47.

Findlay, J. N. *Hegel: A Re-examination*. London: Allen & Unwin, 1958.

Fish, Stanley Eugene. "Intention is all there is: A Critical Analysis of Aharon Barak's Purposive Interpretation in Law." *Cardozo Law Review* 29 (2008): 1109–46.

Forrester, John. *Language and the Origins of Psychoanalysis*. New York: Columbia University Press, 1980.

Förster, Eckart. *The Twenty-Five Years of Philosophy: A Systematic Reconstruction*. Translated by Brady Bowman. Cambridge, MA: Harvard University Press, 2012.

Forster, Michael N. *After Herder: Philosophy of Language in the German Tradition*. Oxford: Oxford University Press, 2010.

"Eine Revolution in der Philosophie der Sprache, der Linguistik, der Hermeneutik und der Übersetzungstheorie im späten 18. und frühen 19. Jahrhundert: deutsche und französische Beiträge." In *Friedrich Schleiermacher and the Question of Translation*. Edited by L. Cercel and A. Serban. Berlin and Boston: De Gruyter, 2015: 23–40.

"Gadamer's Hermeneutics: A Critical Appraisal." *Mythos-Magazine* (online), July 2011.

"Genealogy." *American Dialectic* 1:2 (2011): 230–50.

"Genealogy and Morality." *American Dialectic* 1:3 (2011): 346–69.

German Philosophy of Language: From Schlegel to Hegel and Beyond. Oxford: Oxford University Press, 2011.

"Herder's Doctrine of Meaning as Use." In *Linguistic Content: New Essays on the History of Philosophy of Language*. Edited by M. Cameron and R. J. Stainton. Oxford: Oxford University Press, 2015: 201–22.

"Hermeneutics." In *The Oxford Handbook of Continental Philosophy*. Edited by Michael Rosen and Brian Leiter. Oxford: Oxford University Press, 2007: 30–74.

"Ideology." In *The Oxford Handbook of German Philosophy in the Nineteenth Century*. Edited by M. N. Forster and K. Gjesdal. Oxford: Oxford University Press, 2015: 806–28.

"On the Very Idea of Denying the Existence of Radically Different Conceptual Schemes." *Inquiry* 41:2 (1998): 133–85.

Foucault, Michel. *L'archéologie du savoir. The Archaeology of Knowledge*. Translated by Alan Sheridan. New York: Harper & Row, 1972.

"Nietzsche, Genealogy, History." In *The Foucault Reader*. Edited by Paul Rabinow. London: Penguin, 1984: 76–100.

Surveiller et punir. Discipline and Punish. Translated by Alan Sheridan. New York: Pantheon, 1977.

"What is an Author?" In *Language, Counter-Memory, Practice: Selected Essays and Interviews by Michel Foucault*. Edited by D. F. Bouchard. Ithaca, NY: Cornell University Press, 1980: 113–38.

Frank, M. *Das individuelle Allgemeine: Textstrukturierung und -interpretation nach Schleiermacher*. Frankfurt am Main: Suhrkamp, 1985.

Das Sagbare und das Unsagbare. Frankfurt am Main: Suhrkamp, 1990.

Freud, Sigmund. *Standard Edition*. 24 vols. Edited by James Strachey. London: Hogarth Press and Institute of Psycho-Analysis, 1953.

Friedman, Michael. *A Parting of the Ways: Carnap, Cassirer, and Heidegger*. Chicago: Open Court, 2001.

Gadamer, Hans-Georg. "Begriffsgeschichte als Philosophie." In *Gesammelte Werke*. Vol. 2. Tübingen: J. C. B. Mohr (Paul Siebeck), 1986: 77–91.

"The Eminent Text and its Truth." *Bulletin of the Midwest Modern Language Association* 13 (1980): 3–10.

Gadamer on Celan: "Who Am I and Who Are You?" and Other Essays. Translated by Richard Heinemann and Bruce Krajewski. Albany: SUNY Press, 1997.

Gesammelte Werke. 10 vols. Tübingen: J. C. B Mohr (Paul Siebeck), 1985–1995.

Hegel's Dialectics: Five Hermeneutical Studies. Translated by P. Christopher Smith. New Haven: Yale University Press, 1976.

"The Hermeneutics of Suspicion." In *Hermeneutics: Questions and Prospects*. Edited by Gary Shapiro and Alan Sica. Amherst: University of Massachusetts Press, 1984: 54–65.

Hermeneutics Versus Science? Three German Views: Essays. Edited and translated by John M. Connolly and Thomas Keutner. Indiana: Notre Dame University Press, 1988.

Reason in the Age of Science. Translated by Frederick G. Lawrence. Cambridge, MA: MIT Press.

"Reflections on My Philosophical Journey." In *The Philosophy of Hans-Georg Gadamer*. Library of Living Philosophers. Vol. XXIV. Translated by Richard E. Palmer. Edited by Lewis Edwin Hahn. Chicago: Open Court, 1997.

Philosophical Hermeneutics. Translated and edited by David E. Linge. Berkeley: University of California Press, 1977.

Philosophische Lehrjahre. Frankfurt am Main: Vittorio Klostermann, 1977.

Truth and Method (Second, Revised Edition). Translated by Joel Weinsheimer and Donald G. Marshall. New York: Continuum, 2004.

Volk und Geschichte im Denken Herders. Frankfurt am Main: Klostermann, 1942.

Wahrheit und Methode: Gründzuge einer philosophischen Hermeneutik. Tübingen: Mohr Siebeck, 1990.

"Wilhelm Dilthey nach 150 Jahren (Zwischen Romantik und Positivismus. Ein Diskussionsbeitrag)." In *Dilthey und die Philosophie der Gegenwart*. Edited by Ernst Wolfgang Orth. Freiburg: Karl Alber, 1985: 157–82.

Galison, Peter and David Stump, eds. *The Disunity of Science: Boundaries, Contexts, and Power*. Stanford: Stanford University Press, 1996.

Gardiner, Patrick. *The Nature of Historical Explanation*. Oxford: Oxford University Press, 1952.

ed. *Theories of History*. New York: Free Press, 1959.

Gardner, Sebastian. "The Unconscious: Transcendental Origins, Idealist Metaphysics and Psychoanalytic Metapsychology." In *The Impact of Idealism: The Legacy of Post-Kantian German Thought*, Vol. 1: *Philosophy and Natural Sciences*. Edited by Karl Ameriks. Cambridge: Cambridge University Press, 2013: 134–65.

Garfield, Jay. *Empty Words. Buddhist Philosophy and Cross-Cultural Interpretation*. Oxford: Oxford University Press, 2002.

Engaging Buddhism: Why It Matters to Philosophy. Oxford: Oxford University Press, 2015.

Gatterer, Johann. "Vom historischen Plan und dem darauf sich gründenden Zusammenhang der Erzählungen." *Allgemeine historische Bibliothek* I (1767): 80–1.

Gaukroger, Stephen. *The Collapse of Mechanism and the Rise of Sensibility: Science and the Shaping of Modernity 1680–1760*. Oxford: Oxford University Press, 2012.

Gentz, Joachim. *Das Gongyang zhuan: Auslegung und Kanonisierung der Frühlings- und Herbstannalen (Chunqiu)*. Wiesbaden: Harrassowitz, 2001.

Gessinger, Joachim. "August Ferdinand Bernhardi." In *History and Historiography of Linguistics. Vol. 2: 18th–20th Century*. Edited by Hans Josef Niederehe and Konrad Koerner. Amsterdam: John Benjamins, 1990: 561–76.

Girardot, Norman J. *The Victorian Translation of China: James Legge's Oriental Pilgrimage*. Berkeley, Los Angeles, and London: University of California Press, 2002.

Gjesdal, Kristin. "Acknowledging the Second Person: Schleiermacher on Imagination, Divination, and the Philosophical Problem of the Other." In *The Imagination in German Idealism and Romanticism*. Edited by Gerard Gentry and Konstantin Pollok. Cambridge: Cambridge University Press, forthcoming.

"Between Enlightenment and Romanticism: Some Problems and Challenges in Gadamer's Hermeneutics." *Journal of the History of Philosophy* 46 (2008): 285–305.

"Enlightenment, History, and the Anthropological Turn: The Hermeneutical Challenge of Dilthey's Schleiermacher Studies." In *Anthropologie und Geschichte. Studien zu Wilhelm Dilthey aus Anlass seines 100. Todestages*. Edited by Giuseppe D'Anna, Helmut Johach, and Eric S. Nelson. Würzburg: Königshausen & Neumann, 2013: 323–54.

Gadamer and the Legacy of German Idealism. Cambridge: Cambridge University Press, 2009.

Herder's Hermeneutics: History, Poetry, Enlightenment. Cambridge: Cambridge University Press, 2017.

"A Task Most Pressing: Dilthey's Philosophy of the Novel." In *Interpreting Dilthey*. Edited by Eric Nelson. Cambridge: Cambridge University Press, forthcoming.

Glassius, Salomon. *Philologia Sacra*. Leipzig: J. F. Gleditschius, 1743.

Glock, Hans-Johann. "Meaning and Rule Following." In *International Encyclopedia of the Social & Behavioral Sciences* (Second Edition). Edited by James D. Wright. Amsterdam: Elsevier, 2015: 841–9.

"Reasons for Action: Wittgensteinian and Davidsonian Perspectives in Historical and Meta-Philosophical Context." *Nordic Wittgenstein Review* 3 (2014): 7–46.

Godrej, Farah. 2011. *Cosmopolitan Political Thought: Method, Practice, Discipline*. Oxford: Oxford University Press.

Gordon, Peter E. *Continental Divide: Heidegger, Cassirer, Davos*. Cambridge, MA: Harvard University Press, 2010.

Graczyk, Annette. *Das literarische Tableau zwischen Kunst und Wissenschaft*. Munich: Wilhelm Fink, 2004.

Grice, Herbert P. "Meaning." In *Studies in the Way of Words*. Cambridge, MA: Harvard University Press, 1989: 213–23.

Grondin, Jean. *Hans-Georg Gadamer: A Biography*. Translated by Joel Weinsheimer. New Haven: Yale University Press, 2003.

Grotius, Hugo. *The Rights of War and Peace*. Edited by Richard Tuck. Indianapolis: Liberty Fund, 2005.

Grünbaum, Adolf. *The Foundations of Psychoanalysis: A Philosophical Critique*. Berkeley: University of California Press, 1984.

Guignon, Charles. "Authenticity, Moral Values, and Psychotherapy." In *The Cambridge Companion to Heidegger*. Edited by Charles B. Guignon. Cambridge: Cambridge University Press, 1993: 215–39.

Heidegger and the Problem of Knowledge. Indianapolis: Hackett Publishing Company, 1983.

"History and Commitment in the Early Heidegger." In *Heidegger: A Critical Reader.* Edited by Hubert Dreyfus and Harrison Hall. Oxford: Blackwell, 1992: 130–42.

Habermas, Jürgen. "Arbeit und Interaktion. Bemerkungen zu Hegels Jenenser Philosophie des Geistes." In *Natur und Geschichte. Karl Löwith zum 70 Geburtstag.* Edited by H. Braun and M. Riedel. Stuttgart: Kohlhammer, 1967: 132–55.

"The Hermeneutic Claim to Universality." In *Contemporary Hermeneutics: Hermeneutics as Method, Philosophy and Critique.* Edited by Josef Bleicher. London: Routledge and Kegan Paul, 1980: 181–211.

Knowledge and Human Interests. Translated by Jeremy Shapiro. Boston: Beacon, 1971.

"Labor and Interaction: Remarks on Hegel's Jena Philosophy of Mind." In *Theory and Practice.* Translated by John Viertel. Boston: Beacon Press, 1974: 142–69.

On the Logic of the Social Sciences. Translated by Shierry Weber Nicholsen and Jerry A. Stark. Cambridge, MA: MIT Press, 1988.

On the Pragmatics of Communication. Edited by Maeve Cooke. Cambridge, MA: MIT Press, 1998.

"Remarks on the Development of Horkheimer's Work." In *On Max Horkheimer: New Perspectives.* Edited by Seyla Benhabib, Wolfgang Bonß, and John McCole. Cambridge, MA: MIT Press, 1993: 49–66.

Theory of Communicative Action. Vol. 2: *Lifeworld and System.* Translated by Thomas McCarthy. Boston: Beacon, 1987.

Halbfass, Wilhelm. *India and Europe: An Essay in Understanding.* Albany: SUNY Press, 1988.

Hamann, Johann Georg. "Metakritik über den Purismus der reinen Vernunft." In *Schriften zur Sprache.* Edited by Josef Simon. Frankfurt am Main: Klostermann, 1976.

Writings on Philosophy and Language. Edited and translated by Kenneth Haynes. Cambridge: Cambridge University Press, 2007.

Harbsmeier, Christoph. "Chinese Rhetoric." *T'oung Pao*, Second Series, Vol. 85, Fasc. 1/3 (1999): 114–26.

"The Rhetoric of Premodern Prose Style." In *The Columbia History of Chinese Literature.* Edited by Victor H. Mair. New York: Columbia University Press, 2002: 881–908.

Wilhelm von Humboldts Brief an Abel-Rémusat und die philosophische Grammatik des Altchinesischen. Stuttgart-Bad Cannstatt: Friedrich Frommann, 1979.

Hardenberg, Friedrich von (Novalis). *Novalis Schriften*. Edited by P. Kluckhorn and R. Samuel. Stuttgart: Kohlhammer, 1960ff.

Hart, H. L. A. "Discretion." *Harvard Law Review* 127 (2013): 652–65.

"Positivism and the Separation of Law and Morals." *Harvard Law Review* 71:4 (1958): 593–629.

Hayes, John H. "Historical Criticism of the Old Testament Canon." In *Hebrew Bible/Old Testament: The History of its Interpretation. Vol. 2: From the Renaissance to the Enlightenment*. Edited by Magne Sæbø. Göttingen: Vandenhoeck & Ruprecht, 2008: 985–1005.

Hedwig, Klaus. "Brentano's Hermeneutics." *Topoi* 6 (1987): 3–10.

Hegel, G. W. F. *Phenomenology of Spirit*. Translated by A. V. Miller. Oxford: Oxford University Press, 1977.

Science of Logic. Edited and translated by G. di Giovanni. Cambridge: Cambridge University Press, 2010.

Werke in zwanzig Bänden. Edited by Eva Moldenhauer and Karl Markus Michel. Frankfurt am Main: Suhrkamp Verlag, 1970.

"The Writings of Hamann." In *Hegel on Hamann*. Translated by Lisa Marie Anderson. Evanston: Northwestern University Press, 2008: 1–54.

Heidegger, Martin. *Being and Time*. Translated by John Macquarrie and Edward Robinson. New York: Harper & Row, 1962.

Being and Time. Translated by Joan Stambaugh. Albany: SUNY Press, 2010.

On the Essence of Language: The Metaphysics of Language and the Essencing of the World. Translated by Wanda Torres Gregory and Yvonne Unna. Buffalo: SUNY Press, 2004.

Gesamtausgabe. Edited by Friedrich-Wilhelm von Hermann et al. Frankfurt am Main: Vittorio Klostermann, 1975.

Gesamtausgabe. Vol. 2: Sein und Zeit. Frankfurt am Main: Vittorio Klostermann, 1977.

Gesamtausgabe. Vol. 9: Wegmarken. Frankfurt am Main: Vittorio Klostermann, 1976.

Gesamtausgabe. Vol. 17: Einführung in die phänomenologische Forschung. Frankfurt am Main: Vittorio Klostermann, 1994.

Gesamtausgabe. Vol. 40: Einführung in die Metaphysik. Frankfurt am Main: Vittorio Klostermann, 1983.

Gesamtausgabe. Vol. 56/57: Zur Bestimmung der Philosophie. Frankfurt am Main: Vittorio Klostermann, 1987.

Gesamtausgabe. Vol. 58: Grundprobleme der Phänomenologie. Frankfurt am Main: Vittorio Klostermann, 1993.

Gesamtausgabe. Vol. 59: Phänomenologie der Anschauung und des Ausdrucks. Theorie der philosophischen Begriffsbildung. Frankfurt am Main: Vittorio Klostermann, 1993.

Gesamtausgabe. Vol. 60: Phänomenologie des religiösen Lebens. Frankfurt am Main: Vittorio Klostermann, 1995.

Gesamtausgabe. Vol. 61: Phänomenologische Interpretationen zu Aristoteles. Einführung in die phänomenologische Forschung. Frankfurt am Main: Vittorio Klostermann, 1985.

Gesamtausgabe. Vol. 63: Ontologie (Hermeneutik der Faktizität). Frankfurt am Main: Vittorio Klostermann, 1988.

Introduction to Metaphysics. Translated by Gregory Fried and Richard Polt. New Haven: Yale University Press, 2000.

Kant and the Problem of Metaphysics. Translated by Richard Taft. Bloomington: Indiana University Press, 1990.

Kant und das Problem der Metaphysik. Frankfurt am Main: Vittorio Klostermann, 1973.

On the Way to Language. Translated by Peter D. Hertz. New York: Harper San Francisco, 1982 [1971].

Ontology: Hermeneutics of Facticity. Translated by John Van Buren. Bloomington: Indiana University Press, 1999.

Pathmarks. Translated by William McNeill. Cambridge: Cambridge University Press, 1998.

"Phänomenologische Interpretationen zu Aristoteles (Anzeige der hermeneutischen Situation)." *Dilthey Jahrbuch für Philosophie und Geschichte der Geisteswissenschaften* 6 (1989): 228–74.

"Phenomenological Interpretations in Connection with Aristotle: An Indication of the Hermeneutical Situation (1922)." In *Supplements: From the Earliest Essays to Being and Time and Beyond.* Edited and translated by John Van Buren. Albany: SUNY Press, 2002: 111–46.

Phenomenological Interpretations of Aristotle: Initiation into Phenomenological Research. Translated by Richard Rojcewicz. Bloomington: Indiana University Press, 2001.

Sein und Zeit. Tübingen: Max Niemeyer Verlag, 2006.

Supplements: From the Earliest Essays to Being and Time and Beyond. Edited by John Van Buren. Albany: SUNY Press, 2002.

Towards the Definition of Philosophy. Translated by Ted Sadler. London: Athlone Press, 2000.

Vom Wesen der Sprache. Die Metaphysik der Sprache und die Wesung des Wortes. Frankfurt am Main: Vittorio Klostermann, 1999.

Zollikon Seminars [1964–66]. Edited by Medard Boss. Translated by Franz Mayr and Richard Askay. Evanston: Northwestern University Press, 2001.

Helmholtz, Hermann von. "On the Relation of Natural Science to Science in General." In *Science and Culture: Popular and Philosophical Essays.* Edited by David Cahan. Chicago: University of Chicago Press, 1995: 76–95.
Hempel, Carl. "The Function of General Laws in History." *Journal of Philosophy* 39 (1942): 35–48.
Henderson, John B. *Scripture, Canon and Commentary: A Comparison of Confucian and Western Exegesis.* Princeton: Princeton University Press, 1991.
Herder, Johann Gottfried. *Against Pure Reason: Writings on Religion, Language, and History.* Translated and edited by Marcia Bunge. Minneapolis: Fortress Press, 1993.
Ausgewählte Werke in Einzelausgaben: Schriften zur Literatur, 2/1: Kritische Wälder. Edited by Regine Otto. Berlin and Weimar: Aufbau Verlag, 1990: 684–691.
Ideas on the Philosophy of History of Man. Translated by T. Churchill. London: Johnson, 1800.
Outlines of a Philosophy of the History of Man. Translated by T. Churchill. New York: Bergman Publishers, 1800.
Philosophical Writings. Edited and translated by Michael N. Forster. Cambridge: Cambridge University Press, 2002.
Sämtliche Werke. Edited by B. Suphan. Berlin: Weidmann, 1882–1909.
Selected Writings on Aesthetics. Edited and translated by Gregory Moore. Princeton: Princeton University Press, 2006.
"Selections from *A Metacritique of the Critique of Pure Reason.*" In *Metacritique: The Linguistic Assault on German Idealism.* Edited by Jere Paul Surber. Amherst: Humanity Books, 2001: 89–130.
"Shakespeare." In *Eighteenth Century German Criticism.* Edited by Timothy Chamberlain. New York: Continuum, 1992: 143–63.
Shakespeare. Translated by Gregory Moore. Princeton: Princeton University Press, 2008.
Werke in zehn Bänden. Edited by U. Gaier et al. Frankfurt am Main: Deutscher Klassiker Verlag, 1985–1998.
On World History. Edited by Hans Adler and Ernst Menze. Armonk: M. E. Sharpe, 1997.
Herling, Bradley L. *The German Gita: Hermeneutics and Discipline in the Early German Reception of Indian Thought.* New York and London: Routledge, 2006.
Heussi, Karl. *Die Krisis des Historismus.* Tübingen: Mohr, 1932.
Hirsch, Eric D. *Validity in Interpretation.* New Haven: Yale University Press, 1967.

Holborn, Hajo. "Wilhelm Dilthey and the Critique of Historical Reason." *Journal of the History of Ideas* 11 (1953): 93–116.

Honneth, Axel. "On the Destructive Power of the Third: Gadamer and Heidegger's Doctrine of Intersubjectivity." *Philosophy and Social Criticism* 29 (2003): 5–21.

Horkheimer, Max. *Critical Theory*. New York: Herder and Herder, 1972.

——— "The State of Contemporary Social Philosophy and the Tasks of an Institute for Social Research." In *Critical Theory and Society: A Reader*. Edited by Stephen Eric Bronner and Douglas MacKay Kellner. New York: Routledge, 1989: 25–36.

Horkheimer, Max, and Theodore W. Adorno. *Dialectic of Enlightenment*. Edited by Gunzelin Schmid Noerr. Translated by Edmund Jephcott. Stanford: Stanford University Press, 2002.

How, Alan. *The Habermas-Gadamer Debate and the Nature of the Social: Back to Bedrock*. New York: Avebury Series in Philosophy, 1995.

Hoy, David C. *The Critical Circle: Literature, History, and Philosophical Hermeneutics*. Berkeley: University of California Press, 1978.

——— "Interpreting the Law: Hermeneutical and Poststructuralist Perspectives." *Southern California Law Review* 58 (1985): 135–76.

Hoyningen-Huene, Paul. "Context of Discovery and Context of Justification." *Studies in History and Philosophy of Science* 18 (1987): 501–15.

Humboldt, Alexander von and Aimé Bonpland. *Personal Narrative of Travels to the Equinoctial Regions of America, During the Years 1799–1804*. Vol. 1. Translated and edited by Thomasina Ross. London: Bohn, 1852.

Humboldt, Wilhelm. *Gesammelte Schriften*. Edited by Königlich Preussische Akademie der Wissenschaften. Berlin: De Gruyter, 1968.

——— "On the Historian's Task." *History and Theory* 6 (1967): 57–71.

Iggers, Georg. *The German Conception of History: The National Tradition of Historical Thought from Herder to the Present*. Hanover, NH: Wesleyan University Press, 1968.

Iggers, Georg, and James Powell, eds. *Leopold von Ranke and the Shaping of the Historical Discipline*. Syracuse: Syracuse University Press, 1990.

Ingarden, Roman. *The Literary Work of Art: An Investigation on the Borderlines of Ontology, Logic, and Theory of Literature; With an Appendix on the Functions of Language in the Theater*. Translated by George G. Grabowicz. Evanston: Northwestern University Press, 1986.

Ingram, David. "Jürgen Habermas and Hans-Georg Gadamer." In *The Blackwell Guide to Continental Philosophy*. Edited by Robert Solomon and David Sherman. Malden, MA: Blackwell Publishing, 2003: 219–42.

Irmscher, Hans-Dietrich. "Grundfragen der Geschichtsphilosophie Herders bis 1774." In *Bückeburger Gespräche über Johann Gottfried Herder 1983*. Edited by Brigitte Poschman. Rinteln: Bösendahl, 1984: 10–32.

Jackson, Frank, and Philip Pettit. "Functionalism and Broad Content." *Mind* 97 (1988): 381–400.

"Program Explanation: A General Perspective." *Analysis* 50 (1990): 107–17.

"Structural Explanation in Social Theory." In *Reduction, Explanation, and Realism*. Edited by David Charles and Kathleen Lennon. Oxford: Clarendon Press, 1992: 97–131.

Jäger, Friedrich, and Jörn Rüsen, eds. *Geschichte des Historismus: Eine Einführung*. Munich: Beck, 1992.

Jauss, Hans Robert. "De l'Iphigénie de Racine à celle de Goethe." In *Pour une esthétique de la réception*. Paris: Gallimard, 1978: 210–62.

"The Poetic Text within the Change of Horizons of Reading: The Example of Baudelaire's 'Spleen II.'" In *Toward an Aesthetic of Reception*. Translated by Timothy Bahti. Minneapolis: University of Minnesota Press, 1982: 139–88.

Jellinek, Georg. *Verfassungsänderung und Verfassungswandlung: eine staatsrechtlich-politische Abhandlung*. Edited by Walter Pauly. Goldbach: Keip, 1996.

Jenco, Leigh. *Changing Referents: Learning Across Space and Time in China and the West*. Oxford: Oxford University Press, 2015.

Johnson, Samuel. "The Pauses in English Poetry, Adjusted." *Rambler* 90 (January 26, 1751).

Jullien, François. *Detour and Access: Strategies of Meaning in Greece and China*. Translated by Sophie Hawkes. New York: Zone Books, 2004.

Kant, Immanuel. *Critique of Pure Reason*. Edited by Paul Guyer and Allen W. Wood. Cambridge: Cambridge University Press, 1998.

Critique of the Power of Judgment. Edited by Paul Guyer. Translated by Paul Guyer and Eric Matthews. Cambridge: Cambridge University Press, 2000.

Gesammelte Schriften. Berlin: Königlich Preussische Akademie der Wissenschaften, 1900ff.

Political Writings (Second Edition). Edited by Hans Reiss. Translated by H. B. Nisbet. Cambridge: Cambridge University Press, 1991.

Prolegomena to any Future Metaphysics. Edited and translated by Gary Hatfield. Cambridge: Cambridge University Press, 2004.

Religion and Rational Theology. Translated and edited by Allen W. Wood and George di Giovanni. Cambridge: Cambridge University Press, 1996.

Katsafanas, Paul. *Agency and the Foundations of Ethics: Nietzschean Constitutivism*. Oxford: Oxford University Press, 2013.

The Nietzschean Self: Moral Psychology, Agency, and the Unconscious. Oxford: Oxford University Press, 2016.

Keast, W. R. *Seventeenth Century English Poetry: Modern Essays in Criticism*. Oxford: Oxford University Press, 1962.

Keil, Geert. "Beyond Assimilationism and Differentialism: Comment on Glock." In *Welt der Gründe: Vorträge und Kolloquien des XXII. Deutschen Kongresses für Philosophie vom 11. bis 15. September 2011 an der Ludwig-Maximilians-Universität München*. Edited by Julian Nida-Rümelin and Elif Özmen. Hamburg: Felix Meiner Verlag, 2012: 914–22.

"Über die deskriptive Unerschöpflichkeit der Einzeldinge." In *Phänomenologie und Sprachanalyse*. Edited by Geert Keil and Udo Tietz. Paderborn: Mentis, 2006: 83–125.

Kelletat, Andreas F. *Herder und die Weltliteratur. Zur Geschichte des Übersetzens im 18. Jahrhundert*. Frankfurt am Main: Peter Lang, 1984.

Kelsen, Hans. *Pure Theory of Law*. Union: Lawbook Exchange, 2002.

Kinzel, Katherina. "The History of Philosophy and the Puzzles of Life: Windelband and Dilthey on the Ahistorical Core of Philosophical Thinking." In *The Emergence of Modern Relativism: The German Debates from the 1770s to the 1930s*. Edited by Martin Kusch, Katherina Kinzel, Johannes Steizinger, and Niels Wildschut. London: Routledge, forthcoming.

Kisiel, Theodore. *The Genesis of Heidegger's Being and Time*. Berkeley: University of California Press, 1993.

Kitcher, Patricia. *Freud's Dream: A Complete Interdisciplinary Science of Mind*. Cambridge, MA: MIT Press, 1993.

Klass, Gregory M. "Interpretation and Construction Distinction in Contract Law." https://ssrn.com/abstract=2913228.

Knapp, Steven, and Walter Benn Michaels. "Against Theory." *Critical Inquiry* 8 (1982): 723–42.

Kohler, Josef. "Über die Interpretation von Gesetzen." *Zeitschrift für das Privat- und Öffentliche Recht der Gegenwart* 13 (1886): 1–61.

Kohlstrunk, Irene. *Logik und Historie in Droysens Geschichtstheorie: Eine Analyse von Genese und Konstruktionsprinzipien seiner "Historik."* Wiesbaden: Steiner, 1980.

Kripke, Saul A. *Wittgenstein on Rules and Private Language: An Elementary Exposition*. Oxford: Blackwell, 1982.

Kristeva, Julia. "Word, Dialogue, and the Novel." In *Desire in Language: A Semiotic Approach to Literature and Art*. Edited by L. S. Roudiez. New York: Columbia University Press, 1980: 64–91.

Kuhn, Thomas S. *Structure of Scientific Revolutions* (Second Edition). Chicago: University of Chicago Press, 1970 [1962].

Kümmel, Werner Georg. *Das Neue Testament. Geschichte der Erforschung seiner Probleme*. Freiburg: Alber, 1958.

Laband, Paul. *Die Wandlungen der deutschen Reichsverfassung*. Dresden: Jahn & Jaensch, 1895.

Lamberton, Robert. *Homer the Theologian: Neoplatonist Allegorical Reading and the Growth of the Epic Tradition.* Berkeley: University of California Press, 1989.

Lamont, Michèle. *How Professors Think: Inside the Curious World of Academic Judgment.* Cambridge, MA: Harvard University Press, 2009.

Latour, Bruno. *Science in Action.* Cambridge, MA: Harvard University Press, 1987.

Leiter, Brian. "The Hermeneutics of Suspicion: Recovering Marx, Nietzsche, and Freud." In *The Future for Philosophy.* Edited by Brian Leiter. Oxford: Clarendon Press, 2006: 74–105.

Lepore, Ernest, and Matthew Stone. *Imagination and Convention: Distinguishing Grammar and Inference in Language.* Oxford: Oxford University Press, 2015.

Lessing, Gotthold Ephraim. *Philosophical and Theological Writings.* Translated and edited by Hugh Barr Nisbet. Cambridge: Cambridge University Press, 2005.

Lewis, David. "Truth in Fiction." *American Philosophical Quarterly* 15 (1978): 37–46.

Lieber, Francis. "On Political Hermeneutics, or on Political Interpretation and Construction, and Also on Precedents." *American Jurist and Law Magazine* 18 (1837): 37–101.

Lifschitz, Avi. *Language and Enlightenment: The Berlin Debates of the Eighteenth Century.* Oxford: Oxford University Press, 2012.

Lin, Weijie. *Zhu Xi yu jingdian quanshi* [Zhu Xi and the Interpretation of Classics]. Taipei: Taiwan daxue chuban zhongxin, 2008.

Lopez, Donald S., Jr., ed. *Buddhist Hermeneutics.* Delhi: Motilal Banarsidass, 1993.

Lorenzer, Alfred. *Die Wahrheit der psychoanalytischen Erkenntnis. Ein historisch-materialistischer Entwurf.* Frankfurt am Main: Suhrkamp, 1974.

Ma, Lin. *Heidegger on East-West Dialogue: Anticipating the Event.* New York and London: Routledge, 2008.

Ma, Lin, and Jaap van Brakel. *Fundamentals of Comparative and Intercultural Philosophy.* Albany: SUNY Press, 2016.

Makeham, John. *Transmitters and Creators: Chinese Commentators and Commentaries on the Analects.* Cambridge, MA: Harvard University Asia Center and Harvard University Press, 2004.

Makkreel, Rudolf A. *Dilthey: Philosopher of the Human Studies.* Princeton: Princeton University Press, 1975.

———. *Imagination and Interpretation in Kant: The Hermeneutic Import of the Critique of Judgment.* Chicago: University of Chicago Press, 1990.

Malpas, Jeff, and Hans-Helmuth Gander. *The Routledge Companion to Hermeneutics.* London: Routledge, 2015.

Mandelbaum, Maurice. "Historical Explanation: The Problem of 'Covering Laws'." In *The Philosophy of History*. Edited by Patrick Gardiner. Oxford: Oxford University Press, 1974: 51–65.

Mannheim, Karl. "Historismus." *Archiv für Sozialwissenschaft und Sozialpolitik* 52 (1924): 1–60.

Marchand, Suzanne L. *German Orientalism in the Age of Empire: Religion, Race, and Scholarship*. Cambridge: Cambridge University Press, 2009.

Margolis, Joseph. "Reflections on Intentionality." In *The Cambridge Companion to Brentano*. Edited by Dale Jacquette. Cambridge: Cambridge University Press, 2004: 131–48.

Mariña, Jacqueline. *The Cambridge Companion to Friedrich Schleiermacher*. Cambridge: Cambridge University Press, 2005.

Marmor, Andrei A. *Interpretation and Legal Theory*. Oxford: Hart Publishing, 2005.

Marra, Michael F., ed. *Japanese Hermeneutics: Current Debates on Aesthetics and Interpretation*. Honolulu: University of Hawaii Press, 2002.

Martin, Raymond. "Objectivity and Meaning in Historical Studies." *History and Theory* 32 (1993): 25–50.

Martin, Rex. *Historical Explanation*. Ithaca, NY: Cornell University Press, 1977.

Matczak, Marcin. "Does Legal Interpretation Need Paul Grice? Reflections on Lepore and Stone's Imagination and Convention." *Polish Journal of Philosophy* 10 (2016): 67–87. https://ssrn.com/abstract=2716629.

McCarthy, Thomas. "The Idea of a Critical Theory and its Relation to Philosophy." In *On Max Horkheimer: New Perspectives*. Edited by Seyla Benhabib, Wolfgang Bonß, and John McCole. Cambridge, MA: MIT Press, 1993: 127–52.

"Rationality and Relativism: Habermas's 'Overcoming of Hermeneutics.'" In *Habermas: Critical Debates*. Edited by John B. Thompson and David Held. Cambridge MA: MIT Press, 1982: 57–78.

McKim, Donald K. *Dictionary of Major Biblical Interpreters*. Downers Grove: InterVarsity Press, 2007.

Mehta, J. L. *India and the West: The Problem of Understanding*. Atlanta: Scholars Press, 1985.

Meinecke, Friedrich. *Historism: The Rise of a New Historical Outlook*. Translated by J. E. Anderson. London: Routledge & Kegan Paul, 1972 [1936].

Mendelson, Jack. "The Habermas-Gadamer Debate." *New German Critique* 18 (1979): 44–73.

Meyer, Georg Friedrich. *Versuch einer allgemeinen Auslegungskunst*. Edited by Axel Bühler and Luigi Cataldi Madonna. Hamburg: Felix Meiner, 1996.

Minnis, Alistair, and Ian Johnson, eds. *The Cambridge History of Literary Criticism*, vol. 2. Cambridge: Cambridge University Press, 2005.

Minnis, A. J., and A. B. Scott, eds. *Medieval Literary Theory and Criticism: The Commentary Tradition*. Oxford: Oxford University Press, 1988.

Misgeld, Dieter. "Critical Theory and Hermeneutics: The Debate Between Habermas and Gadamer." In *On Critical Theory*. Edited by John O'Neill. New York: Seabury Press, 1976: 164–83.

Mommsen, Katharina. *Goethe und die arabische Welt*. Frankfurt am Main: Insel, 1988.

Moore, Michael S. "Interpreting Interpretation." In *Law and Interpretation: Essays in Legal Philosophy*. Edited by Andrei A. Marmor. Oxford: Clarendon Press, 1995: 1–30.

"Law as a Functional Kind." In *Educating Oneself in Public: Critical Essays in Jurisprudence*. Edited by Michael S. Moore. New York: Oxford University Press, 2000: 188–242.

"Legal Reality: A Naturalist Approach to Legal Ontology." *Law and Philosophy* 21 (2002): 619–705.

"Can Objectivity be Grounded in Semantics." In *Law, Metaphysics, Meaning, and Objectivity*. Edited by Enrique Villanueva. Mexico City: Rodopi, 2007: 235–61.

"Semantics, Metaphysics and Objectivity in Law." In *Vagueness and Law: Philosophical and Legal Perspectives*. Edited by Geert Keil and Ralf Poscher. New York: Oxford University Press, 2016: 127–60.

Moore, Stephen D., and Yvonne Sherwood. *The Invention of the Biblical Scholar: A Critical Manifesto*. Minneapolis: Fortress Press, 2011.

Moravia, Sergio. "The Enlightenment and the Sciences of Man." *History of Science* 18 (1980): 247–68.

Moser, Kata. "La réception arabe de Heidegger." *Bulletin Heideggérien* 5 (2015): 4–16.

Nadler, Steven. "The Bible Hermeneutics of Baruch de Spinoza." In *Hebrew Bible / Old Testament: The History of its Interpretation. Vol. 2: From the Renaissance to the Enlightenment*. Edited by Magne Sæbø. Göttingen: Vandenhoeck & Ruprecht, 2008: 827–36.

Spinoza: A Life. Cambridge: Cambridge University Press, 1999.

Nagel, Ernest. *The Structure of Science*. New York: Harcourt, Brace & World, 1961.

Nassar, Dalia. "Analogy, Natural History, and the Philosophy of Nature: Kant, Herder and the Problem of Empirical Science." *Journal of the Philosophy of History* 9 (2015): 240–57.

"Understanding as Explanation: The Significance of Herder and Goethe's Science of Describing." In *Herder: Philosophy and Anthropology*. Edited by Anik Waldow and Nigel de Souza. Oxford: Oxford University Press, 2017: 106–24.

Nerlich, Brigitte, and David D. Clarke. *Language, Action and Context: The Early History of Pragmatics in Europe and America, 1780–1930.* Amsterdam: John Benjamins, 1996.

Neurath, Otto. "Sociology and Physicalism." In *Logical Positivism.* Edited by A. J. Ayer. New York: Free Press, 1959: 282–317.

Neuwirth, Angelika. *Der Koran als Text der Spätantike. Ein europäischer Zugang.* Berlin: Verlag der Weltreligionen, 2010.

Nietzsche, Friedrich. *Der Antichrist. The Antichrist.* In *The Portable Nietzsche.* Translated by Walter Kaufmann. New York: Viking, 1968.

———. *The Birth of Tragedy and Other Writings.* Edited by Raymond Geuss and Ronald Speirs. Translated by Ronald Speirs. Cambridge: Cambridge University Press, 1999.

———. *Die fröhliche Wissenschaft. The Gay Science.* Translated by Walter Kaufmann. New York: Random House, 1974.

———. *Die Geburt der Tragödie aus dem Geiste der Musik. The Birth of Tragedy.* In *Basic Writings of Nietzsche.* Translated by Walter Kaufmann. New York: Modern Library, 1967.

———. *Zur Genealogie der Moral. On the Genealogy of Morals.* Translated by Walter Kaufmann and R. J. Hollingdale. New York: Random House, 1967.

———. *Götzen-Dämmerung. Twilight of the Idols.* In *The Portable Nietzsche.* Translated by Walter Kaufmann. New York: Viking, 1968.

———. *Jenseits von Gut und Böse. Beyond Good and Evil.* Translated by Walter Kaufmann. New York: Random House, 1967.

———. *Menschliches, Allzumenschliches. Human, All too Human.* Translated by R. J. Hollingdale. Cambridge: Cambridge University Press, 1996.

———. *Morgenröthe. Daybreak.* Translated by R. J. Hollingdale. Cambridge: Cambridge University Press, 1982.

———. *Nietzsche Contra Wagner. Nietzsche Contra Wagner.* In *The Portable Nietzsche.* Translated by Walter Kaufmann. New York: Viking, 1968.

———. *Sämtliche Werke: Kritische Studienausgabe in 15 Bänden.* Edited by Giorgio Colli and Mazzino Montinari. Berlin: Walter de Gruyter, 1967–1977.

Nisbet, Hugh Barr. *Gotthold Ephraim Lessing: His Life, Works, and Thought.* Oxford: Oxford University Press, 2008.

Novick, Peter. *That Noble Dream: The "Objectivity Question" and the American Historical Profession.* Cambridge: Cambridge University Press, 1988.

Obert, Mathias. *Sinndeutung und Zeitlichkeit: Zur Hermeneutik des Huayan-Buddhismus.* Hamburg: Meiner Verlag, 2000.

Oexle, Otto, and Jörn Rüsen, eds. *Historismus in den Kulturwissenschaften.* Cologne: Böhlau, 1996.

Ogilvie, Brian. *The Science of Describing: Natural History in Renaissance Europe.* Chicago: University of Chicago Press, 2006.

Orozco, Theresa. *Platonische Gewalt. Gadamers politische Hermeneutik der NS-Zeit.* Hamburg: Argument Verlag, 1995.

Otto, Rudolf. *Das Heilige* (35th Edition). Munich: Beck, 1963.

Perkins, Franklin. "Virtue, Reason, and Cultural Exchange: Leibniz's Praise of Chinese Morality." *Journal of the History of Ideas* 63:3 (2002): 447–64.

Pettit, Philip. *The Common Mind: An Essay on Psychology, Society, and Politics.* Oxford University Press, 1996.

"Towards Interpretation." *Philosophia* 23 (1994): 157–70.

Pippin, Robert B. *Hegel's Idealism: The Satisfactions of Self-Consciousness.* Cambridge: Cambridge University Press, 1989.

Pitt, David. "Mental Representation." In *The Stanford Encyclopedia of Philosophy.* Edited by Edward N. Zalta.

Plaks, Andrew. "Why the Chinese Gods Don't Suffer." In *Studies in Chinese Language and Culture – Festschrift in Honour of Christoph Harbsmeier on the Occasion of His 60th Birthday.* Edited by Christoph Anderl und Halvor Eifring. Oslo: Hermes Academic Publishing, 2006: 123–34.

Plaul, Constantin. "Johann August Ernesti. Institutio Interpretis Novi Testamenti (1761)." In *Handbuch der Bibelhermeneutiken. Von Origenes bis zur Gegenwart.* Edited by Oda Wischmeyer. Berlin: de Gruyter, 2016: 651–62.

Pollock, Sheldon, Benjamin A. Elman, and Ku-ming Kevin Chang, eds. *World Philology.* Cambridge, MA and London: Harvard University Press, 2015.

Pope, Alexander. *An Essay on Man.* Edited by Maynard Mack. London: Routledge, 2002.

The Major Works. Edited by Pat Rogers. Oxford: Oxford University Press, 2006.

Popper, Karl. *The Poverty of Historicism.* London: Routledge, Kegan & Paul, 1957.

Porphyry. *On the Cave of the Nymphs.* Translated by Robert Lamberton. Barrytown: Station Hill Press, 1983.

Poscher, Ralf. "Interpretation and Rule Following in Law: The Complexity of Easy Cases." In *Problems of Normativity, Rules and Rule-Following.* Edited by Michał Araszkiewicz et al. Heidelberg: Springer, 2015: 281–93.

"The Hermeneutic Character of Legal Construction." In *Law's Hermeneutics: Other Investigations.* Edited by Simone Glanert and Fabien Girard. New York: Routledge, 2017: 207–27.

"The Normative Construction of Legislative Intent." Forthcoming: Droit & Philosophie, Annuaire de l'Institut Michel Villey, 2017. https://ssrn.com/abstract=2861250.

Quine, Willard van Orman. "On Empirically Equivalent Systems of the World." *Erkenntnis* 9 (1975): 313–28.

Quirin, Michael. "Scholarship, Value, Method, and Hermeneutics in Kaozheng: Some Reflections on Cui Shu (1740–1816) and the Confucian Classics." *History and Theory* 35:4 (1996): 34–53.

Ranke, Leopold von. *Sämtliche Werke.* 54 vols. Leipzig: Duncker & Humblot, 1867–1890.

———. *The Theory and Practice of History.* Edited by G. Iggers and K. von Moltke. Indianapolis: Bobbs-Merrill, 1973.

Ransom, John C. *The New Criticism.* Westport: Greenwood Press, 1979.

Rasmussen, David M. "Hermeneutics and Public Deliberation." *Philosophy and Social Criticism* 28 (2002): 505–7.

Redding, Paul. *Hegel's Hermeneutics.* Ithaca, NY: Cornell University Press, 1996.

———. "The Independence and Dependence of Self-Consciousness: The Dialectic of Lord and Bondsman in Hegel's Phenomenology of Spirit." In *The New Cambridge Companion to Hegel and Nineteenth Century Philosophy.* Edited by Frederick C. Beiser. Cambridge: Cambridge University Press, 2008: 94–110.

———. *Thoughts, Deeds, Words, and World: Hegel's Idealist Response to the Linguistic "Metacritical Invasion."* Aurora: Noesis Press, 2016.

Reichenbach, Hans. *Experience and Prediction.* Chicago: University of Chicago Press, 1938.

Reill, Peter Hanns. "Buffon and Historical Thought in Germany and Great Britain." In *Buffon 88.* Edited by Jean Gayon. Paris: Vrin, 1992: 667–79.

———. *The German Enlightenment and the Rise of Historicism.* Berkeley: University of California Press, 1975.

———. "Science and the Construction of the Cultural Sciences in Late Enlightenment Germany: The Case of Wilhelm von Humboldt." *History and Theory* 33 (1994): 345–66.

———. *Vitalizing Nature in the Enlightenment.* Berkeley and Los Angeles: University of California Press, 2005.

Reventlow, Henning Graf. *History of Biblical Interpretation. Vol. 4: From the Enlightenment to the Twentieth Century.* Atlanta: Society of Biblical Literature, 2010.

Reynolds, J. and J. Roffe, eds. *Understanding Derrida.* London: Continuum, 2004.

Ricœur, Paul. *The Conflict of Interpretations: Essays in Hermeneutics.* Edited by D. Ihde. Evanston: Northwestern University Press, 1974.

———. "Ethics and Culture: Habermas and Gadamer in Dialogue." *Philosophy Today* 17 (1973): 153–65.

Freud and Philosophy. Translated by Denis Savage. New Haven: Yale University Press, 1965.

On Psychoanalysis. Cambridge: Polity, 2012.

"Structure et herméneutique." In *Le Conflit des interprétations*. Paris: Seuil, 1969: 31–63.

"The Task of Hermeneutics." *Philosophy Today* 17:2 (1973): 112–28.

From Text to Action. Translated by Kathleen Blamey and John Thompson. Evanston: Northwestern University Press, 1991.

"The Unity of the Voluntary and the Involuntary as a Limit-Idea [1951]." In *Philosophical Anthropology*. Translated by David Pellauer. Cambridge: Polity, 2015: 53–71.

Riskin, Jessica. *Science in the Age of Sensibility: The Sentimental Empiricists of the French Enlightenment*. Chicago: University of Chicago Press, 2002.

Roger, Jacques. *Buffon: A Life in Natural History*. Ithaca, NY: Cornell University Press, 1997.

Ross, Dorothy. "On the Misunderstanding of Ranke and the Origins of the Historical Profession in America." In *Leopold von Ranke and the Shaping of the Historical Discipline*. Edited by Georg Iggers and James Powell. Syracuse: Syracuse University Press, 1990: 154–69.

Rothacker, Erich. "J. G. Droysens Historik." *Historische Zeitschrift* 161 (1940): 84–92.

Rouse, Joseph. *Engaging Science: How to Understand its Practices Philosophically*. Ithaca, NY and London: Cornell University Press, 1996.

How Scientific Practices Matter: Reclaiming Philosophical Naturalism. Chicago and London: University of Chicago Press, 2002.

Rousseau, Jean, and Denis Thouard, eds. *Lettres édifiantes et curieuses sur la langue chinoise. Un débat philosophico-grammatical entre Wilhelm von Humboldt et Jean-Pierre Abel-Rémusat (1821–1831), avec une correspondance inédite de Humboldt (1824–1831)*. Paris: Presses Universitaires du Septentrion, 1999.

Runciman, W. G. *A Critique of Max Weber's Philosophy of Social Science*. Cambridge: Cambridge University Press, 1972.

Rupke, Nicolaas A. *Alexander von Humboldt: A Metabiography*. Chicago: University of Chicago Press, 2008.

Rüsen, Jörn. *Begriffene Geschichte: Genesis und Begründung der Geschichtstheorie J. G. Droysens*. Paderborn: Schöningh, 1969.

"Droysen heute – Plädoyer zum Bedenken verlorener Themen der Historik." In *Droysen-Vorlesungen*. Edited by Lutz Niethammer. Jena: Philosophical Faculty, Historical Institute, University of Jena, 2005: 177–200.

Rush, Fred. *Irony and Idealism*. Oxford: Oxford University Press, 2016.

Saint Augustine. *On Christian Doctrine*. Translated by D. W. Robertson. Indianapolis: Bobbs Merrill, 1980.

Sandys-Wunsch, John. "Early Old Testament Critics on the Continent." In *Hebrew Bible/Old Testament: The History of its Interpretation. Vol. 2: From the Renaissance to the Enlightenment.* Edited by Magne Sæbø. Göttingen: Vandenhoeck & Ruprecht, 2008: 971–84.

Sartre, Jean-Paul. *Being and Nothingness*. Translated by H. E. Barnes. New York: Simon & Schuster, 1956.

The Emotions: Outline of a Theory. Translated by Bernard Frechtman. London: Routledge, 2002.

L'idiot de la famille: Gustave Flaubert de 1821 à 1857. Paris: Gallimard, 1988.

Search for a Method. Translated by H. E. Barnes. New York: Vintage, 1968.

Saussy, Haun. *Great Walls of Discourse and Other Adventures in Cultural China*. Cambridge, MA and London: Harvard University Press, 2001.

Sauter, Eugen. *Herder und Buffon*. Rixheim: F. Sutter & Cie, 1910.

Savigny, Friedrich Carl von. "Methodologie (Vorlesungsnotizen)." In *Vorlesungen über juristische Methodologie 1802–1842*. Edited by Friedrich Carl von Savigny. Frankfurt am Main: Vittorio Klostermann, 1993.

System of the Modern Roman Law. Translated by W. Holloway. Madras: J. Higginbotham, 1867.

Schafer, Roy. "Narration in the Psychoanalytic Dialogue." *Critical Inquiry* 7:1 (1980): 29–53.

Schlegel, Friedrich. *Kritische Friedrich Schlegel Ausgabe*. Edited by E. Behler, J.-J. Anstett, and H. Eichner. Paderborn: Schöningh, 1964ff.

Schleiermacher, Friedrich. *Hermeneutics and Criticism and Other Writings*. Edited by Andrew Bowie. Cambridge: Cambridge University Press, 1998.

Hermeneutik. Edited by Heinz Kimmerle. Heidelberg: C. Winter, 1959.

Hermeneutics: The Handwritten Manuscripts. Edited by Heinz Kimmerle, translated by James Duke and Jack Forstman. Missoula: Scholars Press for the American Academy of Religion, 1977.

Hermeneutik und Kritik. Edited by Manfred Frank. Frankfurt am Main: Suhrkamp Verlag, 1993 [1977].

On Religion: Speeches to its Cultured Despisers. Translated and edited by Richard Crouter. Cambridge: Cambridge University Press, 1998.

Schlink, Bernhard. "Juristische Methodik zwischen Verfassungstheorie und Wissenschaftstheorie." *Rechtstheorie* 7 (1976): 94–102.

Schnur, Harald. *Schleiermachers Hermeneutik und ihre Vorgeschichte im 18. Jahrhundert*. Stuttgart: Metzler, 1994.

Scholz, Oliver R. *Verstehen und Rationalität: Untersuchungen zu den Grundlagen von Hermeneutik und Sprachphilosophie*. Klostermann Rote Reihe. Frankfurt am Main: Vittorio Klostermann, 2016.

Schröter, Marianne. *Aufklärung durch Historisierung. Johann Salomo Semlers Hermeneutik des Christentums*. Berlin: de Gruyter, 2012.

"Johann Salomo Semler. Vorbereitung zur theologischen Hermeneutik (1760)." In *Handbuch der Bibelhermeneutiken. Von Origenes bis zur Gegenwart*. Edited by Oda Wischmeyer. Berlin: de Gruyter, 2016: 729–42.

"Johann Salomo Semler. Neuer Versuch die gemeinnü(t)zige Auslegung und Anwendung des Neuen Testaments zu befördern (1786)." In *Handbuch der Bibelhermeneutiken. Von Origenes bis zur Gegenwart*. Edited by Oda Wischmeyer. Berlin: De Gruyter, 2016: 743–54.

Seebohm, Thomas M. *Hermeneutics: Method and Methodology*. Dodrecht: Kluwer, 2004.

Seifert, Arno. *Cognitio historica: Die Geschichte als Namengeberin der frühneuzeitlichen Empirie*. Berlin: Duncker & Humblot, 1976.

Semler, Johann Salomo. *Abhandlung von freier Untersuchung des Canon*. Halle: C. H. Hemmerde, 1771.

Sheehan, Jonathan. *The Enlightenment Bible: Translation, Scholarship, Culture*. Princeton: Princeton University Press, 2005.

Sherma, Rita, and Arvind Sharma, eds. *Hermeneutics and Hindu Thought: Toward a Fusion of Horizons*. Dordrecht: Springer Netherlands, 2008.

Sikka, Sonia. *Herder on Humanity and Cultural Difference: Enlightened Relativism*. Cambridge: Cambridge University Press, 2011.

Simmel, Georg. *Friedrich Nietzsche – Eine moralphilosophische Silhouette*. In *Aufsätze und Abhandlungen, 1894 bis 1900*. Edited by H. Dahme and D. Frisby. Gesamtausgabe Band 5. Frankfurt am Main: Suhrkamp, 1992: 115–29.

Sloan, Philip. "Buffon, German Biology and the Historical Interpretation of Biological Species." *The British Journal for the History of Science* 12 (1979): 109–53.

"The Buffon-Linnaeus Controversy." *Isis* 67:3 (1976): 356–75.

"The Idea of Racial Degeneracy in Buffon's *Histoire naturelle*." *Studies in Eighteenth-Century Culture* 3 (1973): 293–321.

Slocum, Brian G. *Ordinary Meaning: A Theory of the Most Fundamental Principle of Legal Interpretation*. Chicago: University of Chicago Press, 2015.

Solum, Lawrence B. "The Interpretation-Construction Distinction." *Constitutional Commentary* 27 (2010): 95.

Sontag, Susan. *Against Interpretation*. New York: Dell, 1966.

Sorkin, David. *The Religious Enlightenment: Protestants, Jews, and Catholics from London to Vienna*. Princeton: Princeton University Press, 2008.

Spencer, Vicky. *Herder's Political Thought: A Study of Language, Culture, and Community*. Toronto: University of Toronto Press, 2012.

Spinoza, Baruch (Benedict de). *Theological-Political Treatise*. Edited by Jonathan Israel. Translated by Michael Silverthorne and Jonathan Israel. Cambridge: Cambridge University Press, 2007.

——— *Tractatus Theologico-Politicus* (Latin and German). Edited by Günter Gawlick and Friedrich Niewöhner. Darmstadt: Wissenschaftliche Buchgesellschaft, 1970.

Stadelmann, Rudolf. *Der historische Sinn bei Herder*. Halle: Niemeyer, 1928.

Staël, Anne Louise Germaine de. *De l'Allemagne*. Paris: Firmin-Didot, 1852.

——— *Germany*. Translated by O. W. Wright. Boston: Houghton, Mifflin, and Company, 1859.

Stanley, Jason. "The Crisis of Philosophy." *Inside Higher Ed*. Last modified April 5, 2010. www.insidehighered.com/views/2010/04/05/crisis-philosophy.

Stecker, Robert. *Interpretation and Construction: Art, Speech, and the Law*. Malden: Blackwell, 2003.

Stern, Alexander. *Fallen Language: Benjamin and Wittgenstein on the Aesthetics of Meaning*. Cambridge, MA: Harvard University Press, forthcoming.

Sullivan, Robert R. *Political Hermeneutics: The Early Thinking of Hans-Georg Gadamer*. State Park: The Pennsylvania State University Press, 1989.

Surber, Jere Paul, ed. *Metacritique: The Linguistic Assault on German Idealism*. Amherst: Humanity Books, 2001.

Szondi, Peter. *Introduction to Literary Hermeneutics*. Translated by Martha Woodmansee. Cambridge: Cambridge University Press, 1995.

Tang, Chenxi. *The Geographic Imagination of Modernity: Geography, Literature and Philosophy in German Romanticism*. Stanford: Stanford University Press, 2008.

Thompson, John B., and David Held, eds. *Habermas: Critical Debates*. Cambridge, MA: MIT Press, 1982.

Thomson, Iain D. *Heidegger on Ontotheology: Technology and the Politics of Education*. Cambridge: Cambridge University Press, 2005.

Todorov, T. *Genres in Discourse*. Translated by C. Porter. Cambridge: Cambridge University Press, 1990.

Troeltsch, Ernst. *Der Historismus und seine Probleme*. Tübingen: Mohr, 1922.

Van Zoeren, Steven. *Poetry and Personality: Reading, Exegesis, and Hermeneutics in Traditional China*. Stanford: Stanford University Press, 1991.

Vasilache, Andreas. *Interkulturelles Verstehen nach Gadamer und Foucault*. Frankfurt and New York: Campus Verlag, 2003.

Vessey, David. "Gadamer and the Fusion of Horizons." *International Journal of Philosophical Studies* 17 (2009): 531–42.

Voltaire (F. M. Arouet). "Essai sur la poésie épique." In *Œuvres complètes de Voltaire*. Edited by L. Moland. Paris: Garnier Frères, 1877.

Wach, Adolf. *Handbuch des deutschen Civilprozessrechts, Erster Band*. Leipzig: Duncker & Humblot, 1885.

Wach, Joachim. *Das Verstehen. Grundzüge einer Geschichte der hermeneutischen Theorie im 19. Jahrhundert*. 3 vols. (1926–1933). Reprint: Hildesheim: Olms, 1966.

Walsh, W. H. *Philosophy of History*. New York: Harper & Row, 1960.

Wang, Qingjie. *Jieshixue, Haidege yu Ru Dao jin shi* [Hermeneutics, Heidegger and a New Interpretation of Confucianism and Daoism]. Beijing: Zhongguo renmin daxue chubanshe, 2004.

Warnke, Georgia. *Gadamer: Hermeneutics, Tradition, and Reason*. Stanford: Stanford University Press, 1987.

Watkins, J. W. N. "Ideal Types and Historical Explanation." In *Readings in the Philosophy of Science*. Edited by H. Feigl and M. Brodbeck. New York: Appleton-Century-Crofts, 1953: 723–43.

Weber, Max. "The 'Objectivity' of Knowledge in Social Science and Social Policy." In *Collected Methodological Writings*. Edited by Hans H. Bruun and Sam Whimster. London: Routledge, 2012: 100–38.

"Roscher und Knies und die logischen Probleme der historischen Nationalökonomie." In *Gesammelte Aufsätze zur Wissenschaftslehre*. Tübingen: J. C. B. Mohr, 1973.

The Theory of Social and Economic Organization. Edited by Talcott Parsons. New York: Free Press, 1947.

"Ueber einige Kategorien der verstehenden Soziologie." *Logos* IV (1913): 253–94.

Weimar, Klaus. *Historische Einleitung zur literaturwissenschaftlichen Hermeneutik*. Tübingen: Mohr, 1975.

Whistler, Daniel. *Schelling's Theory of Symbolic Language: Forming the System of Identity*. Oxford: Oxford University Press, 2013.

White, Hayden. "Historik by Johann Gustav Droysen." *History and Theory* 19 (1980): 73–93.

Whitebook, Joel. *Freud: An Intellectual Biography*. Cambridge: Cambridge University Press, 2017.

Whittington, Keith E. *Constitutional Interpretation: Textual Meaning, Original Intent and Judicial Review*. Lawrence: University Press of Kansas, 1999.

Windelband, Wilhelm. "Kritische oder genetische Methode?" (1883). Reprinted in Wilhelm Windelband. *Präludien: Aufsätze und Reden zur Philosophie und ihrer Geschichte*. Vol. 2. Tübingen: Mohr, 1924: 99–135.

Wittgenstein, Ludwig. *Lectures and Conversations on Aesthetics, Psychology, and Religious Belief*. Edited by Cyril Barrett. Oxford: Blackwell, 1966.

Philosophical Grammar. Edited by Rush Rhees. Translated by Anthony Kenny. Oxford: Blackwell, 1974.

Philosophical Investigations. Edited by Gertrude E. M. Anscombe. Oxford: Blackwell, 1953.

Wolin, Richard. *The Seduction of Unreason: The Intellectual Romance with Fascism from Nietzsche to Postmodernism*. Princeton: Princeton University Press, 2004.

Wollheim, Richard. *Freud (2nd Edition)*. London: Fontana, 2008.

"The Mind and the Mind's Image of Itself." In *On Art and the Mind: Essays and Lectures*. Cambridge, MA: Harvard University Press, 1974: 31–53.

Wright, Kathleen. "Hermeneutics and Confucianism." In *The Routledge Companion to Hermeneutics*. Edited by Jeffrey Malpas and Hans-Helmuth Gander. London and New York: Routledge Press, 2014: 674–91.

Wu, Chan-liang. "Historicity, Tradition, Praxis, and Tao: A Comparison of the World Views of Zhang Xuecheng and Modern Philosophical Hermeneutics." In *Interpretation and Intellectual Change: Chinese Hermeneutics in Historical Perspective*. Edited by Ching-i Tu. New Brunswick and London: Transaction Publishers, 2005: 227–44.

Wu, Kuang-ming. *On the "Logic" of Togetherness: A Cultural Hermeneutic*. Leiden, New York, and Köln: Brill, 1998.

Zammito, John. "Are We Being Theoretical Yet?" *Journal of Modern History* 65 (1993): 783–814.

Kant, Herder and the Birth of Anthropology. Chicago: University of Chicago Press, 2002.

A Nice Derangement of Epistemes: Post-Positivism in the Study of Science from Quine to Latour. Chicago: University of Chicago Press, 2004.

"Philosophy of History: The German Tradition from Herder to Marx." In *The Cambridge History of Philosophy in the Nineteenth Century (1790–1870)*. Edited by Allen W. Wood and Songsuk Susan Hahn. Cambridge: Cambridge University Press, 2012: 817–65.

Zhang, Longxi. *The Tao and the Logos: Literary Hermeneutics, East and West*. Durham, NC and London: Duke University Press, 1992.

Zhang, Xianglong. *Haidege'er sixiang yu Zhongguo tiandao* [Heidegger and China's Way of Heaven]. Beijing: Sanlian chubanshe, 1996.

Zilsel, Edgar. "Physics and the Problem of Historico-Sociological Laws." In *Readings in the Philosophy of Science*. Edited by H. Feigl and M. Brodbeck. New York: Appleton-Century-Crofts, 1953: 714–22.

Zuckert, Catherine. "Hermeneutics in Practice: Gadamer on Ancient Philosophy." In *The Cambridge Companion to Gadamer*. Edited by Robert Dostal. Cambridge: Cambridge University Press, 2002: 201–24.

Index

Adorno, Theodor W., 179, 186, 241, 258n16, 277
Aeschylus, 347
aesthetics, 319, 345, 364, 367, 374n10
Akiva, Rabbi, 289
al-Ghazālī, Abū Hāmid Muhammad ibn Muhammad, 286
ambiguity, 184, 194, 336, 350n19
Ankersmit, Frank, 110, 127n1
anthropology, 60n14, 66, 90, 275, 365
antipodal fallacy, 290
anti-universalism, 260–63, 279
Apel, Karl-Otto, 257n2, 257n2, 372n4
application, 140, 152–53, 191, 228, 326, 333–36, 338, 341, 343–45
appropriation, 99, 218, 253
  appropriating, 219, 222
Arabi, Ibn, 296, 302n23
Aristotle, 47–48, 50, 93, 113, 124, 148, 212, 229–30, 232–33, 233n3, 234n6, 235n13, 236n17, 282n36, 286, 288, 297, 301n11, 306–7, 321n4, 373n8
art, 115, 119, 121, 124, 158, 160, 185–86, 212, 214, 224, 226, 229, 231, 233, 255, 267, 274, 283n38, 300n11, 310, 313, 327, 332–33, 335, 339–40, 347, 355, 364–67
  artist, 120
  artistic genius, 117
  artistic interpretation, 51
association, 203, 327, 339–40, 345, 347
Ast, Georg Anton Friedrich, 92
Athenaeum, 72, 95
Augustine, 215, 232, 235n13, 261, 286, 306
Augustine of Dacia, 307, 322n6
Austin, John L., 352n47
author, 33n9, 36n38, 116, 118–19, 134, 264–65, 270–72, 279, 292–93, 308–10, 312, 314, 316–18, 321, 328, 332

authority, 29, 68, 74, 199, 226, 254, 256, 290, 293, 354
Azzouni, Jody, 348n9

background, 78, 91, 116, 179, 195, 247, 265
Badawi, Abdur Rahman, 296
Bakhtin, Mikhail, 278, 285n61, 285n62, 285n64
Barthes, Roland, 271–78, 283n39, 283n41, 283n43, 283n44, 283n44, 283n47, 284n49, 284n53, 284n56, 284n57, 284n59, 285n63, 305, 318, 321n2, 321n3, 324n23, 332
Beck, Hanno, 64n50
Beiser, Frederick, 58n6, 59n7, 113, 120, 129n15, 131n29, 131n34, 132n44, 376n22
Berlin, Isaiah, 88, 104n4, 134
Bernhardi, August Ferdinand, 95–96, 107n28, 107n29, 107n30, 107n33, 107n34, 107n35
Besonnenheit, 81–82, 86n24
Betti, Emilio, 326, 346, 347n3, 353n54
Bi, Wang, 286, 293
Bible, 11, 14, 16–20, 23, 25, 27–30, 32n3, 33n9, 34n12, 281n19, 294
biblical hermeneutics, 11–12, 16, 22–28, 31, 34n12, 229, 307
Boeckh, August, 113, 119, 122, 124, 131n38, 136, 146, 260, 263–65, 274, 277
Bowie, Andrew, 130n27, 322n13, 322n15, 372n6
Brakel, Jaap van, 299n3, 302n21
Brandom, Robert B., 334, 351n28, 372n4
Brentano, Franz, 200–4, 209n39, 209n39, 210n40, 210n44, 210n48
Brooks, Cleanth, 309, 312–16, 323n19, 323n19, 323n21, 323n21
Bruns, Gerald, 323n17
Buckle, Henry Thomas, 121–22, 131n34
Buddhism, 291, 295, 297–98, 299n4
  Zen Buddhism, 276, 292

411

Buffon, George-Louis Leclerc (Comte de), 4, 38–45, 49–51, 58n5, 61n16, 61n17, 61n18, 61n19, 61n21, 61n26, 61n27, 61n28, 62n28, 62n30, 62n30, 62n35, 62n36, 62n37, 62n38, 63n43
Bush, Douglas, 312–16, 323n19, 323n20, 323n21

category, 71, 74, 216
Catholicism, 34n12, 260
causal, 63n48, 93, 123, 144, 149–54, 161, 164, 166, 187, 195, 252, 328, 330, 339
  causality, 124, 152, 188, 200, 208n26
certainty, 42, 62n28, 90, 165, 197, 201, 203
Chakrabarty, Dipesh, 298, 303n28
China, 286–87, 290–91, 293–98, 300n11
Chomsky, Noam, 84
Christianity, 11, 19, 36n37, 269, 306
classicist, 364, 375n18
Collingwood, Robin George, 126, 134, 136, 141–43, 154–55
concept, 167–70, 172, 175, 179, 182n15, 184, 186, 190, 192, 199–200, 205, 214, 217–18, 220–21, 228, 230, 260, 262–63, 269–70, 278, 308, 331
  conceptual, 151, 166–67, 170–71, 182n15, 198, 200, 214, 235n12, 239, 268, 299n3, 340
Conches, William of, 306
Condillac, Étienne Bonnot de, 43, 52, 54, 105n12, 261–64, 280n6
Confucian, 287, 291–93, 296–97, 303n26
Confucius, 291–93
conscious, 199–203, 226, 230, 238
  consciousness, 200–4, 214, 223, 225, 227, 229–31, 246, 251, 297, 319–20
  self-consciousness, 66, 74, 99–100, 122, 184–85, 197, 227, 240
Corbin, Henry, 296
correctness, 187, 192, 225, 231
covering law, 136–41, 144, 146, 150–51, 153–54, 155n3
critical theory, 186, 199, 237–41, 254
criticism, 131n40, 241, 305, 307–8, 311, 314–15, 319
Croce, Benedetto, 154
Crowe, Benjamin, 375n17
Crowell, Steven G., 216
culture, 37, 45–46, 72, 84, 115, 222, 225, 228, 239, 244, 262–65, 277, 286, 288–89, 372n5, 377n29, 380n37
custom, 115, 164, 172, 178, 221, 230, 239

Dannhauer, Johann Konrad, 85n2
Dante, Aligheri, 307
Daodejing, 295
Daoism, 293, 296
Daston, Lorraine, 57n2, 121, 131n32
Davidson, Donald, 299n3, 327, 330–31
death of the author, 271, 278, 284n52
decentering, 271
deconstruction, 270
Derrida, Jacques, 212, 269–71, 277, 281n29, 282n33, 283n38
Descartes, René, 84, 148, 197, 225
destruction, 204, 222, 235n13
determinate, 336
Dew, John, 345
dialogical, 212, 231, 278, 374n13, 375n19
dialogue, 244, 247, 257
Diderot, Denis, 4, 38–39, 41–42, 45, 225
Dilthey, Wilhelm, 37, 66, 79, 98, 112–13, 117–18, 125–26, 129n13, 132n43, 134–36, 142, 144, 146–48, 150, 168, 211, 223, 229, 231, 234n8, 252, 265, 267, 274, 311, 317, 354, 363–70, 376n21, 376n21, 376n21, 376n24, 377n27, 379n34, 379n35, 380n38
discipline construction, 65–66, 77, 110–12, 119, 122, 126, 134, 257, 357, 370
discourse, 19, 110, 112, 114, 145, 194, 196, 198, 216, 249, 267, 273, 275, 278–79
discovery, 67, 140, 218, 340, 347
distorted communication, 246, 249
divination, 79, 119, 377n28
Droysen, Johann Gustav, 112–13, 119–20, 122–24, 131n40, 134–36, 142, 144–50, 156n10, 156n11, 157n15, 225
Dryden, John, 308
dualism, 148, 198, 239, 261

East-West philosophers conference, 296
education, 107n38, 230, 306, 309
Einfühlung, 79, 117, 310, 377n28
Elkins, James, 300n7
embodiment, 92, 100, 148, 205
empathy, 73, 118, 144, 150
empirical, 89, 94, 99–100, 104, 111, 114, 119, 122, 124, 126–27, 144, 152, 188, 193, 199, 237, 239, 248, 264, 329–31, 337, 368–69
empiricism, 77, 110, 365
Engels, Friedrich, 267

Enlightenment, 16, 20, 24–26, 31, 34n12, 35n14, 88, 113, 225, 237, 239–40, 248, 254, 260–61, 309
epic, 264, 277, 285n64, 306
epistemology, 68, 133, 358, 360
Erklären, 311, 318
Ernesti, Johann August, 18–19, 260–61, 263
ethics, 15, 20–21, 31, 179, 229–30
Evans, Richard, 111
event, 48–50, 61n28, 114, 119–21, 123–24, 139–42, 148–49, 190–91, 219, 224, 226, 229, 232, 238, 244–45, 250, 341, 350n19, 353n52, 360
existentialism, 266
experience, 30–31, 66, 69, 71, 82–83, 94, 125, 143–44, 148, 158–60, 165–67, 170, 176, 180, 182n19, 201, 211, 213–14, 219, 230–31, 235n12, 248, 250, 254–57, 266, 276, 297, 320, 341, 348n9, 356–57, 360, 366
explanation, 30, 91, 135–41, 143–44, 149–54, 184, 186, 188–89, 196, 269, 311, 318–19, 329–30
expression, 47, 66, 72, 92, 94, 103, 124–25, 146, 148, 195, 247, 267, 274, 284n52, 308–10, 356, 360, 366

facticity, 211, 215–17, 220, 222, 224, 254
Fazang, 297
feeling, 31, 125, 147, 150, 210n47, 252, 310
Felski, Rita, 319, 323n17
Fichte, Johann Gottlieb, 67, 69, 81–82, 86n26, 88, 91–100, 103, 107n36, 107n37, 107n38, 108n39, 266, 273, 280n14, 280n14, 364, 376n24
fiction, 275
fictive, 328, 332, 338, 340, 344
Findlay, John N., 102
formalism, 360, 363–64, 366
Forster, Michael N., 59n10, 59n10, 59n10, 60n15, 61n15, 62n33, 63n42, 63n42, 85n15, 86n24, 104n3, 105n11, 105n12, 106n19, 109n59, 113, 118–19, 299n1
Foucault, Michel, 179–81, 271, 318
Frankfurt School, 193, 237, 257, 257n2
freedom, 82, 91, 99–101, 198, 266
Freud, Sigmund, 160, 184–206, 206n1, 206n3, 206n7, 207n11, 208n25, 208n25, 209n36, 247, 267–69, 318, 398
Frye, Northrop, 305
fusion of horizons, 212, 230, 236n16, 244, 296, 314

Gadamer, Hans-Georg, 37, 59n7, 59n9, 59n9, 66–67, 77, 85n14, 85n3, 98, 118, 186, 196, 212–13, 215, 218, 223–33, 233n3, 234n3, 234n3, 235n13, 236n15, 236n15, 236n16, 236n17, 236n17, 236n18, 236n18, 236n19, 236n19, 236–37, 241, 243–47, 249–57, 257n2, 257n2, 259n35, 259n44, 259n45, 259n46, 259n47, 259n48, 259n48, 267, 270–71, 274, 282n33, 282n33, 282n34, 286–87, 295–97, 299n2, 302n21, 304, 311, 316–17, 319, 321n1, 323n17, 323n18, 324n28, 326–27, 333, 337–38, 341, 345–47, 353n53, 356–69, 371n2, 371n2, 372n4, 372n5, 372n6, 372n7, 373n8, 374n10, 374n11, 374n13, 374n15, 375n17, 375n19, 375n20, 377n27, 377n28, 378n30, 378n31, 378n31, 378n32, 380n38, 380n38, 382
Galison, Peter, 121, 131n32
Garfield, Jay L., 298, 299n4, 303n27
Gatterer, Johann Christoph, 114, 129n17, 130n17
Gaukroger, Stephen, 60n14
Geisteswissenschaften, 37, 98, 147–48, 209n36, 212, 226, 290
genealogy, 170–71, 173, 175, 180, 268, 352n42, 378n29
generic, 268, 274, 278, 307–8
genre, 76, 262, 264, 276–78, 284n49, 284n56, 285n64, 306–8, 319, 321
geography, 43, 46, 51, 56, 63n49, 64n50
Gjesdal, Kristin, 59n9, 63n44, 85n3, 109n59, 236n19, 259n48, 281n27, 299n1
Glassius, Salomon, 13, 32n4
Goethe, Johann Wolfgang von, 68, 80, 309, 320, 341, 367, 379n36
Graczyk, Annette, 64n50
grammar, 74, 84, 89, 242, 289, 310, 314, 334
grammatical, 57n3, 76, 94, 118, 158, 195, 244, 272, 275, 278, 310, 331, 334
Grice, Herbert P., 327, 331
Grotius, Hugo, 18, 21, 25
Guignon, Charles, 234n8

Habermas, Jürgen, 98, 108n41, 188, 193–99, 208n24, 208n25, 208n26, 208n27, 209n28, 212, 237, 241–49, 252, 254–57, 257n2, 259n48, 372n4, 372n5
Halbfass, Wilhelm, 296
Hamann, Johann Georg, 62n30, 87–92, 95, 97, 102–4, 105n6, 105n8, 261–62, 294
Harbsmeier, Christoph, 292, 301n11

Hart, Herbert L. A., 336, 353n50
Hegel, Georg Wilhelm Friedrich, 67, 88, 92, 97–104, 112–13, 121–24, 133–34, 170–71, 230–31, 250–51, 253, 280n13, 294, 367, 374n10, 379n37
Heidegger, Martin, 66–67, 86n24, 133, 179, 207n11, 207n14, 211–24, 229–33, 233n1, 233n3, 234n3, 234n4, 234n7, 234n8, 234n8, 234n8, 234n8, 235n10, 235n10, 235n11, 235n12, 235n13, 236n13, 249, 253, 259n35, 266–67, 280n13, 287, 295–96, 302n19, 302n19, 302n20, 302n23, 304, 311, 329, 356–57, 359, 361, 368–69, 371n2, 371n3, 373n8, 374n10, 374n10, 374n14, 375n17, 375n17, 378n31, 379n32, 380n38, 380n38
Helmholtz, Hermann von, 168, 182n17
Hempel, Carl, 135, 138–41, 155n2, 155n5, 155n7
Herder, Johann Gottfried, 19–20, 34n13, 34n13, 34n13, 38–39, 42–56, 58n5, 58n5, 59n10, 59n10, 59n10, 60n12, 60n13, 60n15, 61n15, 62n30, 62n30, 62n32, 62n33, 62n38, 62n39, 63n40, 63n41, 63n42, 63n42, 63n44, 63n49, 64n49, 64n50, 64n50, 77, 80–82, 86n16, 86n24, 86n24, 88, 90–93, 95–98, 105n10, 105n12, 106n13, 106n14, 106n15, 106n16, 107n28, 107n29, 112–17, 119, 121, 124, 129n13, 129n17, 130n17, 130n18, 130n19, 130n20, 130n21, 130n22, 130n23, 130n24, 130n25, 134, 186, 198, 209n36, 231, 260–64, 266–68, 274, 276, 281n19, 294, 309, 321, 322n12, 322n14, 364–70, 376n24, 377n25, 377n27, 377n29, 378n29, 378n32, 379n32, 379n34, 379n36, 380n40, 380n40
hermeneutic circle, 245
hermeneutical circle, 124, 146–47, 205, 378n31
hermeneutics of facticity, 211, 217, 220, 222, 224
hermeneutics of suspicion, 160–61, 163, 180, 196, 268–69, 318
heuristic, 144
Heyne, Christian Gottlob, 114
Hillel the Elder, 286
Hirsch, Eric D., 278, 316–17, 324n27, 350n22

historically effected consciousness, 227, 230–31
historicism, 37, 58n6, 117, 126–27, 225–27, 231, 303n26, 318
history, 37, 40–43, 49, 55–56, 65, 74, 91, 110–15, 117, 119–22, 125–27, 227, 229, 232, 244–46, 251, 253, 293–94, 313, 319, 329, 366
History, 121, 226, 254
holism, 75, 79, 84, 125, 145, 166, 180, 293
Homer, 175, 264, 306, 309
Honneth, 250
Honneth, Axel, 237, 249–57
horizon, 160, 219–20, 227–29, 244–45, 247, 297, 310, 314, 319–20, 337, 345
Horkheimer, Max, 179, 186, 237–42, 248–49, 254–55, 277
Hoy, David, 317
human sciences, 58n6, 147, 150, 168, 185–86, 311, 354–56, 359–63, 366, 368, 370
humanism, 12, 88, 124–25, 187, 232, 358, 374n11
humanities, 37, 57n1, 104, 185, 295, 359, 361, 368
Humboldt, Alexander von, 56, 80
Humboldt, Wilhelm von, 68, 80–84, 92, 112–13, 120–22, 124, 134, 294, 365
Hume, David, 225, 261–62, 364
Husserl, Edmund, 194, 211, 231, 369, 371n2

idea, 124, 149, 185, 198, 203, 261, 263, 340
idealism, 77, 85n3, 88, 91–92, 95, 98–99, 104, 107n28, 266
ideal-types, 154
ideology, 208n25, 256, 266–68, 271, 277
Iggers, Georg, 120, 128n8
illocutionary force, 278
imagination, 17, 23, 61n25, 73, 83, 119–20, 126, 147, 345, 376n21
immediacy, 31, 226, 232, 252
indeterminacy, 71, 74, 337, 344–45
individual, 39–40, 44, 46–47, 54, 79, 97, 105n6, 115, 117–18, 120, 123–25, 145, 180, 182n15, 185, 191, 197, 219–20, 232, 238–39, 262–66, 268, 272, 279, 317, 342, 378n30, 378n31, 379n33
inference, 42, 78, 145–46, 148–49, 201, 282n36, 335, 348n9
Ingarden, Roman, 345

intention, 210n41, 272, 275, 292–93, 312, 316–17, 319, 323n15, 327–33, 335–36, 338–39, 341, 345
  intentional fallacy, 316–17
intentionalism, 328, 331, 349n10
intercultural dialogue, 287, 296
interdisciplinary, 239, 354, 368
intersubjective, 95, 124–25, 127, 141, 192, 195, 207n14, 242, 251, 368
intertextuality, 278
intuition, 82–84, 103, 119, 143–44, 147, 150, 214, 217
Irmscher, Hans-Dietrich, 58n5
Ishmael, Rabbi, 289
I-Thou relations, 250–52

Jackson, Frank, 330
Jauss, Hans Robert, 319–20
Jerome, 11
Johnson, Samuel, 308
Jullien, François, 300n9

Kant, Immanuel, 21–23, 25–28, 31, 38, 67–68, 77, 81, 83, 87–96, 99, 102–4, 113, 125, 166–67, 193, 197–98, 239, 294, 333, 338, 356–58, 360, 364–65, 373n8, 376n21
Kantianism, 70, 84, 91–92, 99, 102, 107n28
Keil, Geert, 350n19
Kelsen, Hans, 342
Knapp, Steven, 324n26
Kripke, Saul A., 333
Kristeva, Julia, 278, 285n64
Kuhn, Thomas, 111

Lacan, Jacques, 208n27
Lamberton, Robert, 321n4
Lamont, Michèle, 371n1
language game, 195, 242–44, 246
law, 326–27, 331–33, 335–44, 346–47, 348n9
legal construction, 327, 337–38, 344–46
legal interpretation, 328, 337–38, 343–44, 346
Legge, James, 290
Leibniz, Gottfried Wilhelm, 72, 114, 182n19, 261, 374n11
Leiter, Brian, 161–62
Lepore, Ernest, 348n9
Lessing, Gotthold Ephraim, 17, 28–31, 364

Lieber, Francis, 337
life, 60n11, 97–98, 101, 103, 174, 177, 184–86, 205–6, 211, 213–14, 216–17, 219–21, 232, 237, 299n3
Lifschitz, Avi, 63n46
linguistics, 68, 72, 74, 80–81, 83, 114, 267, 271, 273–74, 277–78, 365
Linnaeus, Carl, 39–40, 43
literary criticism, 304, 306–7, 311, 315–17, 319–21, 321n4, 323n17
literature, 212, 304–11, 315–16, 321n3, 322n13, 377n25
lived experience, 125
Locke, John, 93–94, 261, 263
Lorenzer, Alfred, 208n24, 248
Lowth, Robert, 20, 364
Luther, Martin, 22, 28, 215

Makeham, John, 297, 301n15
Makkreel, Rudolf A., 59n11, 364, 376n21
Mandelbaum, Maurice, 155n3
Mannheim, Karl, 126
Marchal, Kai, 377n27
Martin, Raymond, 110
Martin, Rex, 134, 155
Marvell, Andrew, 312–14
Marx, Karl, 100, 160, 196, 238, 266, 268–69, 318, 366
Marxism, 266, 318
McCarthy, Thomas, 208n26, 237
McDowell, John, 212, 372n4
meaning, 55, 70–76, 78–81, 83–84, 100, 154, 161–62, 166, 168, 170–72, 177–78, 184, 186–93, 195, 198, 202, 205, 211, 213–14, 217–19, 222, 224, 228, 232, 244–48, 261, 266, 268–71, 274, 277, 282n33, 290, 292–93, 304–5, 307, 310, 316–17, 324n26, 327–28, 331–32, 335–36, 339, 345–47, 348n9, 349n11, 356, 358, 363, 369
  pragmatic meaning, 70, 78, 123, 149, 248, 255
  semantic meaning, 331, 338
  sentence, 146
  sentence meaning, 75–76, 101, 118, 145, 305, 331
  speaker's meaning, 243, 249, 305, 331
Mehta, Jaswant Lal, 296
Meinecke, Friedrich, 117, 126
Mengzi, 292

mental, 70, 82–83, 93, 118, 143, 146–48, 184–85, 187–88, 190–92, 194–97, 199–202, 204–5, 209n38, 210n41, 210n43, 328–29, 350n19
metacritique, 87–89, 102–03, 105n6
metaphysics, 68, 88–91, 96–98, 102, 118, 120, 138, 143–44, 147, 188, 373n8
method, 38, 45, 58n6, 66, 78, 112, 114, 116, 118, 120, 122–23, 125, 131n40, 136–44, 146, 148–50, 160, 175, 222, 225, 231, 268, 319–20, 347, 366
    methodology, 42, 55, 76, 114, 119, 122, 137, 140, 160, 168, 179, 187, 225, 229, 232, 255, 260, 287–88, 342, 354, 356–58, 363, 366, 369
Michaels, Walter Benn, 324n26
mind, 40, 43, 90, 93, 148, 153, 185, 188, 192, 197, 205, 210n49, 369
monism, 326, 330
Montaigne, Michel de, 262, 275, 279n4
Montesquieu, 262, 279n4
moral, 20–21, 23–26, 28, 31, 34n12, 68, 158, 161, 171, 173–77, 229–30, 251–52, 262, 306, 341
Moravia, Sergio, 60n14
Most, Glenn W., 57n2
Muhammad, 289

narrative, 23, 25, 27, 122, 124, 195, 245, 273, 321, 363, 378n29
nation, 45, 97, 103, 115, 117, 263–64, 280n4, 288, 308–9
Natorp, Paul, 362
natural law, 21, 25–26, 136
natural religion, 17, 21, 28, 30–31
natural sciences, 37–38, 57n1, 58n6, 66, 98, 119, 125, 138, 141, 143–44, 150, 168, 189, 192, 225, 239, 318, 358–59, 363–64, 368
naturalism, 52, 54, 58n6, 63n46, 186, 190
nature, 38–42, 44–45, 49, 56, 62n38, 99, 102–3, 119, 147, 198, 206, 208n26, 238, 241, 263
neo-Kantianism, 77, 111, 126, 152–53, 214, 222, 224, 229, 235n11, 356, 360–61, 363, 371n2, 374n15
New Criticism, 312, 314, 332
Nietzsche, Friedrich, 158–81, 196, 211, 232, 268–69, 318
non-linguistic, 274–76

non-Western interpretation, 287, 289, 295–96
Norinaga, Motoori, 286
normative, 125, 152, 154–55, 164, 175, 186, 242, 249–52, 332
Novalis, 67–69, 72, 91, 367
novel, 273, 278, 285n64, 324n25
Novick, Peter, 110, 128n8

objectivity, 73, 100–01, 121, 124–25, 127, 132n42, 159, 218, 353n52
ontological, 148, 235n12, 267, 311, 341–42, 361–63, 365, 367, 370, 378n31
ontology, 188, 217, 362, 370, 373n8
original, 97, 185, 192, 204, 206, 207n18, 211, 214, 217, 221, 223, 243, 248, 265, 270, 272, 282n33, 304, 316, 320
originality, 263–64
otherness, 233, 275, 290, 298

performing arts, 335, 345
Pettit, Philip, 330, 350n26
phenomenology, 67, 194, 199, 216, 222, 231, 348n9
Philologia Sacra, 13, 33n9
Philosophiegeschichte, 294
philosophy of history, 45, 58n5, 133–35, 137, 235n11, 375n17
Picasso, Pablo, 332
Pindar, 309
Plaks, Andrew, 290
Plato, 70, 197, 212, 223, 233, 236n17, 272, 278, 295, 306, 338
poetics, 304–7, 320, 321n3
poetry, 20, 74–75, 113, 115, 264, 304, 308, 321
politics, 235n10, 276, 288, 293, 298, 299n5, 337–38, 344, 346, 362, 375n20, 380n40
Pollock, Sheldon, 290, 299n6
Pope, Alexander, 21, 308
Popper, Karl Raimund, 134, 156n7
Porphyry, 306, 322n4
positivism, 111, 125, 138, 156n7, 187–88, 225, 380n38
practices, 37, 59n9, 65, 74, 111, 125, 172, 175, 186, 188, 290, 326, 332, 359
prejudice, 73, 196, 225, 228, 230–31, 243, 246, 256, 293, 314, 366
Protestantism, 65, 260, 267
psychoanalysis, 184–89, 191, 193–200, 208n25, 247–49

INDEX 417

psychological, 78, 118, 124, 149, 172, 186–88, 191–93, 203, 278, 310, 319, 322n15, 330
psychologism, 154, 369
psychology, 78, 152, 186, 192, 196, 201

Quine, Willard van Orman, 111, 127, 282n36
Qur'an, 289, 299n5

Ranke, Leopold von, 111–13, 119, 121–22, 128n7, 134–35, 138, 156n11, 225
rationalism, 85n2, 88, 225, 365, 380n38
rationality, 20, 91–92, 194, 226, 238, 242, 330, 338, 345
realism, 188, 196–97, 201, 203, 205
reason, 17, 20–21, 25–27, 68, 87–91, 93, 95, 105n6, 105n8, 125–26, 137, 151, 186, 226, 237, 239, 241, 249, 254, 256–57, 350n19
reasoning, 105n6, 145–46, 153–54, 200, 202
reconstruction, 84, 113, 119, 153, 222, 225, 248, 319–20, 330, 332, 346, 369
reconstructive sciences, 248–49
Reill, Peter Hanns, 57n5, 58n6, 61n25, 114, 120
Reinhold, Karl Leonhard, 67, 91–92, 95
religion, 15, 17, 19–21, 24–28, 30–31, 36n37, 177, 267, 281n18, 281n19, 294
religious, 11, 13–24, 26, 28–31, 36n38, 65, 267, 281n19, 367
reliving, 126, 136
Renaissance, 37, 57n4, 306, 308
revolution, 68, 111, 220, 222, 260
Rickert, Heinrich, 126, 134–35, 153, 229
Ricœur, Paul, 160–62, 175, 189, 193–94, 196–200, 203, 205
Rilke, Rainer Maria, 212–13, 233
romanticism, 66, 72, 85n3, 92, 107n28, 309, 341, 374n10, 375n19, 380n38
Rorty, Richard, 212
Rothacker, Ernst, 112
Rousseau, Jean-Jacques, 52, 54, 63n46, 271
rule-following, 327, 333, 335–37, 341
Runciman, Walter Garrison, 157n18
Rüsen, Jörn, 112–13, 128n10, 129n12

Salisbury, John of, 307, 322n9
Sanskrit, 74, 81, 289, 294–95
Śāntarakṣita, 288

Sartre, Jean-Paul, 179, 189–90, 192–95, 202, 207n11, 265–66, 280n13
Saussure, Ferdinand de, 270–71, 274
Sauter, Eugen, 62n30, 64n49
Savigny, Friedrich Carl von, 331, 337
Schafer, Roy, 207n20
Schelling, Friedrich Wilhelm Joseph, 67, 92, 98, 206, 374n10
Schlegel, Friedrich, 66–81, 84, 263, 268, 271, 273–74, 294, 309
Schleiermacher, Friedrich D. E., 36n38, 60n15, 67–68, 70, 76–81, 84, 91–92, 96, 112–13, 117–19, 122–25, 136, 146, 260–61, 263, 265, 267–68, 272, 274, 277, 281n19, 286, 294, 310–11, 321, 357–58, 364–65, 369–70, 377n27, 378n31, 379n33, 380n39
Schulze, Gottlob Ernst, 92
science, 37–38, 41, 43, 57n1, 59n9, 60n12, 60n14, 61n25, 110–11, 118–19, 122, 124–27, 137–38, 140, 142, 154, 256, 353n52, 375n19
scientistic, 187, 192, 194, 252
scripture, 18–19, 21–22, 24, 29, 36n38, 289, 307
Seinsgeschichte, 295
semiology, 272, 274–75
Semler, Johann Salomo, 19, 34n11, 34n12
Shakespeare, William, 47–49, 116–17, 264, 272, 309, 365
significance, 213, 217, 221, 345–47
signification, 93–95, 189, 316
Simmel, Georg, 134–35, 179, 182n24
situatedness, 37, 116, 211, 373n9
skepticism, 69, 141, 193, 354
social sciences, 150, 237, 239, 242, 247, 250, 255, 318, 354, 371
Sontag, Susan, 319
source criticism, 112
Spinoza, Baruch (Benedict de), 26–28, 32n2, 114, 261, 273, 374n11
Stadelmann, Rudolf, 117
Staël, Anne Louise Germaine de (Madame de), 280n4, 379n36
Stecker, Robert, 339
Stone, Matthew, 348n9
structuralism, 318
Sturm und Drang, 88, 309
subjective, 73, 77, 127, 145, 187, 192, 341, 358, 378n31

Sullivan, Robert R., 375n18
symbol, 98, 189, 191, 193, 195, 208n27, 243–44, 247, 281n19, 318, 356–57
Szondi, Peter, 314–15, 322n15, 322n7

Tang, Chenxi, 62n38, 63n49
Taylor, Charles, 302n21, 372n4
Tetsurō, Watsuji, 296, 302n22
text, 267–68, 270–73, 278–79
theology, 16, 22–23, 26, 28, 31, 77, 120, 215, 367
Todorov, Tzvetan, 277, 284n60, 285n62
Torah, 286, 289
tradition, 212, 219–23, 225–32, 237–40, 242, 246, 249, 251–56, 358
tragedy, 47–48, 50, 63n42, 176, 264–65, 309
transcendental, 69, 77, 89–90, 94, 99, 104, 214, 224, 236n14, 239, 357, 359–60, 364–65
translation, 243–44
Troeltsch, Ernst, 126, 134
truth, 17, 19–20, 26, 29–30, 39, 41, 61n18, 61n28, 70, 117, 160, 178–79, 187, 212, 227, 257, 330, 354, 358, 365

unconscious, 75, 180, 184–85, 190, 195, 197, 199–202, 255, 267, 269, 313
universalism, 260–62

Verstehen, 117, 123, 126, 138–39, 142, 147, 150, 154, 156n7, 311, 318, 358
Verstehenswissenschaften, 354, 369
Voltaire (F.M. Arouet), 225, 262, 264

Wach, Joachim, 129n13, 156n11
Wagner, Richard, 345
Walsh, William Henry, 134–35, 156n8
Wang, Qingjie, 296, 303n23
Warnke, Georgia, 85n3, 236n15, 372n4
Watteau, Jean-Antoine, 339
Weber, Max, 145, 149, 151–54, 156n9, 157n14, 179
Wimsatt, William Kurtz, 309, 317
Winckelmann, Johann Joachim, 63n42, 114, 364, 367
Windelband, Wilhelm, 125–26, 132n44, 134–35, 153, 229, 369
Wittgenstein, Ludwig, 85n12, 189, 191–95, 242, 244, 252, 282n36, 333–34
Wolff, Christian, 85n2, 113, 261
Wu, Kuang-ming, 296, 302n23

Zammito, John H., 42–43, 58n6, 59n9, 60n14, 62n29, 105n11, 128n3
Zhang, Xianglong, 296
Zhu, Xi, 293, 297

OTHER VOLUMES IN THE SERIES OF CAMBRIDGE COMPANIONS (*continued from page ii*)

FOUCAULT 2nd Edition *Edited by* GARY GUTTING
FREGE *Edited by* TOM RICKETTS *and* MICHAEL POTTER
FREUD *Edited by* JEROME NEU
GADAMER *Edited by* ROBERT J. DOSTAL
GALEN *Edited by* R. J. HANKINSON
GALILEO *Edited by* PETER MACHAMER
GERMAN IDEALISM 2nd Edition *Edited by* KARL AMERIKS
GREEK AND ROMAN PHILOSOPHY *Edited by* DAVID SEDLEY
HABERMAS *Edited by* STEPHEN K. WHITE
HAYEK *Edited by* EDWARD FESER
HEGEL *Edited by* FREDERICK C. BEISER
HEGEL AND NINETEENTH-CENTURY PHILOSOPHY *Edited by* FREDERICK C. BEISER
HEIDEGGER 2nd Edition *Edited by* CHARLES GUIGNON
HIPPOCRATES *Edited by* PETER E. PORMANN
HOBBES *Edited by* TOM SORELL
HOBBES'S 'LEVIATHAN' *Edited by* PATRICIA SPRINGBORG
HUME 2nd Edition *Edited by* DAVID FATE NORTON *and* JACQUELINE TAYLOR
HUME'S 'TREATISE' *Edited by* DONALD C. AINSLIE *and* ANNEMARIE BUTLER
HUSSERL *Edited by* BARRY SMITH *and* DAVID WOODRUFF SMITH
WILLIAM JAMES *Edited by* RUTH ANNA PUTNAM
KANT *Edited by* PAUL GUYER
KANT AND MODERN PHILOSOPHY *Edited by* PAUL GUYER
KANT'S 'CRITIQUE OF PURE REASON' *Edited by* PAUL GUYER
KEYNES *Edited by* ROGER E. BACKHOUSE *and* BRADLEY W. BATEMAN
KIERKEGAARD *Edited by* ALASTAIR HANNAY *and* GORDON DANIEL MARINO
LEIBNIZ *Edited by* NICHOLAS JOLLEY
LEVINAS *Edited by* SIMON CRITCHLEY *and* ROBERT BERNASCONI
LIBERALISM *Edited by* STEVEN WALL
LIFE AND DEATH *Edited by* STEVEN LUPER
LOCKE *Edited by* VERE CHAPPELL
LOCKE'S 'ESSAY CONCERNING HUMAN UNDERSTANDING' *Edited by* LEX NEWMAN
LOGICAL EMPIRICISM *Edited by* ALAN RICHARDSON *and* THOMAS UEBEL
MAIMONIDES *Edited by* KENNETH SEESKIN

MALEBRANCHE *Edited by* STEVEN NADLER
MARX *Edited by* TERRELL CARVER
MEDIEVAL ETHICS *Edited by* THOMAS WILLIAMS
MEDIEVAL JEWISH PHILOSOPHY *Edited by* DANIEL H. FRANK *and* OLIVER LEAMAN
MEDIEVAL LOGIC *Edited by* CATARINA DUTILH NOVAES *and* STEPHEN READ
MEDIEVAL PHILOSOPHY *Edited by* A. S. MCGRADE
MERLEAU-PONTY *Edited by* TAYLOR CARMAN *and* MARK B. N. HANSEN
MILL *Edited by* JOHN SKORUPSKI
MONTAIGNE *Edited by* ULLRICH LANGER
NEWTON 2nd Edition *Edited by* ROB ILIFFE *and* GEORGE E. SMITH
NIETZSCHE *Edited by* BERND MAGNUS *and* KATHLEEN HIGGINS
NOZICK'S 'ANARCHY, STATE AND UTOPIA' *Edited by* RALF BADER *and* JOHN MEADOWCROFT
OAKESHOTT *Edited by* EFRAIM PODOKSIK
OCKHAM *Edited by* PAUL VINCENT SPADE
THE 'ORIGIN OF SPECIES' *Edited by* MICHAEL RUSE *and* ROBERT J. RICHARDS
PASCAL *Edited by* NICHOLAS HAMMOND
PEIRCE *Edited by* CHERYL MISAK
PHILO *Edited by* ADAM KAMESAR
PHILOSOPHICAL METHODOLOGY *Edited by* GIUSEPPINA D'ORO *and* SØREN OVERGAARD
THE PHILOSOPHY OF BIOLOGY *Edited by* DAVID L. HULL *and* MICHAEL RUSE
PIAGET *Edited by* ULRICH MÜLLER, JEREMY I. M. CARPENDALE *and* LESLIE SMITH
PLATO *Edited by* RICHARD KRAUT
PLATO'S 'REPUBLIC' *Edited by* G. R. F. FERRARI
PLOTINUS *Edited by* LLOYD P. GERSON
POPPER *Edited by* JEREMY SHEARMUR *and* GEOFFREY STOKES
PRAGMATISM *Edited by* ALAN MALACHOWSKI
QUINE *Edited by* ROGER F. GIBSON JR.
RAWLS *Edited by* SAMUEL FREEMAN
RENAISSANCE PHILOSOPHY *Edited by* JAMES HANKINS
THOMAS REID *Edited by* TERENCE CUNEO *and* RENÉ VAN WOUDENBERG
ROUSSEAU *Edited by* PATRICK RILEY
BERTRAND RUSSELL *Edited by* NICHOLAS GRIFFIN
SARTRE *Edited by* CHRISTINA HOWELLS
SCHOPENHAUER *Edited by* CHRISTOPHER JANAWAY
THE SCOTTISH ENLIGHTENMENT *Edited by* ALEXANDER BROADIE
ADAM SMITH *Edited by* KNUD HAAKONSSEN

SOCRATES *Edited by* DONALD MORRISON
SPINOZA *Edited by* DON GARRETT
SPINOZA'S 'ETHICS' *Edited by* OLLI KOISTINEN
THE STOICS *Edited by* BRAD INWOOD
LEO STRAUSS *Edited by* STEVEN B. SMITH
TOCQUEVILLE *Edited by* CHERYL B. WELCH
UTILITARIANISM *Edited by* BEN EGGLESTON *and* DALE MILLER
VIRTUE ETHICS *Edited by* DANIEL C. RUSSELL
WITTGENSTEIN 2nd Edition *Edited by* HANS SLUGA *and* DAVID STERN

CPSIA information can be obtained
at www.ICGtesting.com
Printed in the USA
LVHW081908020422
715158LV00010B/219